THE AUSTRALIAN CONSTITUTION AND NATIONAL IDENTITY

THE AUSTRALIAN CONSTITUTION AND NATIONAL IDENTITY

EDITED BY ANNA OLIJNYK
AND ALEXANDER REILLY

Published by ANU Press
The Australian National University
Canberra ACT 2600, Australia
Email: anupress@anu.edu.au

Available to download for free at press.anu.edu.au

ISBN (print): 9781760465636
ISBN (online): 9781760465643

WorldCat (print): 1373643735
WorldCat (online): 1373227481

DOI: 10.22459/ACNI.2023

Cover design and layout by ANU Press

This book is published under the aegis of the Law editorial board of ANU Press.

Contents

Part Three

Acknowledgements

This project had its origins in a workshop at Adelaide Law School in November 2019. We are grateful to all who participated and contributed to the discussions that shaped the ideas in this book. Many papers from that workshop became the chapters in this book.

We thank the research assistants who assisted with the project, especially Tijana Maric and Aeron Leyesa. We also thank Rani Kerin for her editing work and the staff at ANU Press for guiding this project.

1

The Australian Constitution and National Identity

Alexander Reilly and Anna Olijnyk

What does Australia's constitution say about national identity? A conventional answer might be 'not much'. On this view, the Australian Constitution is concerned with structures and institutions of government, and is deliberately silent on values, aspirations and identity.[1] Nor are Australians inclined to rally around their constitution as a focal point of national pride.[2]

And yet …

Reflection on the last few years in Australian constitutional law reveals a wealth of examples of constitutional issues that implicate national identity. Claiming victory in the 2022 election, Anthony Albanese opened his acceptance speech by committing to the Uluru Statement from the Heart's call for a First Nations Voice enshrined in the Constitution. In 2020 the High Court held Aboriginal Australians could not be 'aliens'[3] and in 2022 the High Court heard a case in which the Commonwealth sought to overturn that position.[4] In 2017, many Australians were affronted to

1 See, eg, Jeffrey Goldsworthy, 'Constitutional Cultures, Democracy, and Unwritten Principles' (2012) *University of Illinois Law Review* 683.

2 Justice Patrick Keane, 'In Celebration of the Constitution' (Speech delivered at the Banco Court, Brisbane, 12 June 2008).

3 *Love v Commonwealth* (2020) 270 CLR 152.

4 *Minister for Immigration, Citizenship, Migrant Services and Multicultural Affairs v Montgomery* (High Court of Australia, S192/2021). This case was withdrawn in August 2022.

discover that, in a country in which about half of the population were born overseas or have a parent born overseas,[5] our constitution prohibits dual citizens from sitting in Parliament.[6] A series of cases have examined the limits of Australians' right to protest[7] and communicate about politics.[8] The Australian Republic Movement continues its advocacy for an Australian Head of State.[9] The COVID-19 pandemic brought federalism to the fore, with closed borders and competing priorities pitting State against State, and State against Commonwealth governments.

These constitutional controversies all raise questions about *who we are*. Who are the Australian people? What is the relationship between Indigenous and non-Indigenous Australians? What kind of democracy do we have? Furthermore, does our constitution reflect who we are, or who we want to be? Is it equipped to support our nation in a future with new and emerging challenges?

This book begins to explore the relationship between Australia's national identity and the Australian Constitution. Because this is not purely a legal question, the book draws on historians and political scientists as well as legal scholars to examine the political and social dimensions of the Australian Constitution. The chapters in this book offer a variety of perspectives on how our Constitution might—and does—reflect or shape national identity.

Overall, the book does not take a normative position on whether the Constitution should influence or reflect Australia's national identity. As we discuss later, there is considerable debate about the merits of a strong national identity and about the appropriateness of constitutions as repositories of this identity. However, contributors take various normative positions in their individual chapters.

5 On the dual citizenship crisis, see <www.abc.net.au/news/2017-12-06/fact-file-the-dual-citizenship-scandal/9147418>. On Australian population statistics see, *Australian Bureau of Statistics* <www.abs.gov.au/statistics/people/population/migration-australia/latest-release#:~:text=In%202019%20the%20proportion%20of%20Australia's%20population%20born%20overseas%20was%2030%25>.

6 Australian Constitution s 44(i).

7 *Brown v Tasmania* (2017) 261 CLR 328; *Clubb v Edwards* (2019) 267 CLR 171.

8 Recent cases on this issue include *Comcare v Banerji* (2019) 267 CLR 373 and *Unions NSW (No 2)* (2019) 264 CLR 595; *LibertyWorks Inc v Commonwealth* (2021) 95 ALJR 490.

9 Australian Republic Movement <republic.org.au/>.

This collection is not, of course, exhaustive. Many aspects of national identity are not explored here. Much could be written, for example, on gender as part of constitutional identity,[10] our Constitution's silence on human rights, the implied freedom cases, the voting rights cases and the s 44 cases. The stories of the Uluru Statement and the republic are far from over. We hope this book prompts further reflection on these issues.

I. What is national identity?

Historians and political scientists have developed an extensive scholarship on the concept of national identity.

In his classic work on the nature of nations, Benedict Anderson argues that nations are 'imagined communities'.[11] Nations are *imagined* because they are socially constructed; a nation is not merely a defined territory and population. Ernest Gellner explains that '[n]ationalism is not the awakening of nations to self-consciousness; it *invents* nations where they do not exist'.[12]

In Anderson's terms, national identity might be conceived of as the feat of imagination that binds people into a state-based political community. Similarly, Anthony D Smith describes national identity as the 'bonds of solidarity among members of communities united by shared memories, myths and traditions that … are entirely different from the purely legal and bureaucratic ties of the state'.[13] Smith explains that nations 'provide individuals with "sacred centres", objects of spiritual and historical pilgrimage, that reveal the uniqueness of their nation's "moral geography"'.[14]

Smith uses the concept of 'homeland' to connect national identity to physical geography. He describes 'homeland' as:

> a repository of historic memories and associations, the place where 'our' sages, saints and heroes lived, worked, prayed and fought … Its rivers, coasts, lakes, mountains and cities become 'sacred' places of veneration and exaltation whose inner meanings can be fathomed only by the initiated, that is, the self-aware members of the nation.[15]

10 For an exploration of this topic, see Helen Irving, *Gender and the Constitution: Equity and Agency in Comparative Constitutional Design* (Cambridge University Press, 2008), doi.org/10.1017/CBO9780511619687.
11 Benedict Anderson, *Imagined Communities* (Verso Books, revised ed, 2006).
12 Ernest Gellner, *Thought and Change* (University of Chicago Press, 1964) 169.
13 Anthony D Smith, *National Identity* (Penguin, 1991) 15.
14 Ibid 16.
15 Ibid 9.

Although historical memories provide the foundation for national identity, theorists of history such as Hayden White observe just how shaky this foundation is.[16] The histories of events that form the foundation of national identity are 'cherry-picked' from the past to build an ideologically driven grand narrative. White describes stories as 'emplotted' using a range of literary devices. For example, national identities might draw on 'Romance', which is 'a drama of self-identification symbolized by the hero's transcendence of the world of experience, his victory over it, and his final liberation from it'.[17] The contest over national identity in Australia illustrates well the role of romantic stories. A story of colonial struggle and ultimate success against the elements to create the modern Australian nation has been subject to critical scrutiny by First Nations people and historians particularly in the last 50 years. For many, what was cast as a peaceful settlement was more accurately an invasion. In recent years, this contest of the myth of national origin has coalesced around the appropriateness of the day of first white settlement, 26 January, to commemorate the nation.

The work of Smith, Anderson, White and others provides us with ideas to make sense of national identity, but its formation remains an imprecise and inherently contestable exercise, easier to recognise than define.

Inevitably, views will differ on the value of national identity. There is a close link between a strong sense of national identity and nationalism, with its attendant dangers. But national identity can also be a source of pride and kinship.

II. Does Australia have a national identity?

At the time of federation, by ignoring the existence of Indigenous Australians and non-British immigrants, the Australian nation was declared to share 'one blood or stock or race', a 'glorious heritage (Britain's)' and 'one religion'.[18] The nature of Australian identity has only grown more complex since then. The arc of the historical record is highly contested, as the 'history wars' of the 2000s illustrated. One narrative celebrated Australia's history as manifesting the advance of Western civilisation; another recognised both

16 Hayden White, *Metahistory: The Historical Imagination in Nineteenth-Century Europe* (Johns Hopkins University Press, 1973).

17 Ibid 7.

18 John Hirst, *The Sentimental Nation: The Making of the Australian Constitution* (Oxford University Press, 2000) 16.

the violence of colonisation and the survival of First Nations as unique, sovereign entities. For more recent migrants and their children, neither of these versions resonate.

In light of these unresolved (perhaps unresolvable) debates, we will not attempt to define an Australian identity for the purposes of this book. Instead, we identify and reflect on some focal points around which Australian identity might coalesce and ask questions about the adequacy of these different visions of Australia.

Smith's idea of homeland has a distinctly European feel to it. And yet, it is instructive for Australia. Despite the existence of a pre-existing deep, complex, diverse and ancient connection to the homeland, colonists quickly asserted their own mythological connection to the new country.[19] This was based on the presumption that the land was empty prior to European settlement.[20] With this convenient fiction in place, colonisation occurred through naming the land using the identities and idioms of the coloniser.[21] Like North America, the nation was built on myths of discovery and conquest, and on economic growth.

Today, the non-Indigenous sense of homeland in Australia is, arguably, not strong. It is built on the conquest of the outback, the development of agriculture and mining; yet, for more than a century, most Australians have lived in urban areas. Tellingly, the strongest non-Indigenous national myth occurs outside Australian territory, in Gallipoli.

By way of contrast, the sense of connection to homeland among Indigenous Australians is extremely powerful—based on an ancient connection, with rich stories that are ontological, mythical and historical. There is strength in never having ceded to the coloniser, solace in continuity with that past. Can an Indigenous sense of 'homeland' be the foundation for an Australian national identity?

Multiculturalism has broken down the hegemony of Australian ethnic identity focused around British heritage. Certainly, if there is an Australian national identity, it is much less British-oriented today than in 1901. Running counter to this, there has been a recent focus on common cultural bonds (and hence the expression of new requirements around 'unity'

19 See Bill Gammage, *The Biggest Estate on Earth: How Aborigines Made Australia* (Allen & Unwin, 2011); Sean Ryan, *The Cartographic Eye: How Explorers Saw Australia* (Cambridge University Press, 1997).
20 Ryan (n 19).
21 Paul Carter, *Road to Botany Bay* (Faber and Faber, 1987).

'integration', 'language' and 'Australian values'), but without a clear idea of the character of these bonds. Has multiculturalism been able to provide a sufficiently strong narrative to construct an alternative sense of national identity? Can Australia develop a post-ethnic identity that is nonetheless based on a tangible connection to nation/country/homeland?

Some more recent conceptions of Australia's national identity draw together the strands of Indigenous, British and multicultural influences. Noel Pearson's proposed 'Declaration of Australia and the Australian People' asserts that Australians are united by 'three stories': 'the Ancient Indigenous Heritage which is [Australia's] foundation, the British Institutions built upon it, and the adorning Gift of Multicultural Migration'.[22] Is it possible to construct a coherent modern national identity from these three stories?

A related question is the values that might form part of a coherent national identity. Does Australia's national identity include a commitment to any particular values—perhaps democracy, meritocracy, community,[23] freedom, equality, egalitarianism, prosperity?

III. Constitutions and national identity

The relationship between constitutions and national identity is multidimensional and context specific. There are probably as many variations on this relationship as there are constitutions.

Constitutions can *reflect* an existing national identity. Dylan Lino describes constitutional norms and instruments as 'expressive, cultural artefacts of the polities to which they are attached'.[24] Constitutions can also *shape* national identity by articulating the aspirations of a community and setting the boundaries on government action. Jeff King has argued that constitutions can serve as 'mission statements', expressing 'the political ideas that animate the constitution and polity more broadly'.[25]

22 Cape York Institute, 2 June 2018 <capeyorkpartnership.org.au/constitutional-recognition/in-the-spirit-of-getting-the-ball-rolling-noel-pearson-offers-this-declaration-of-australia-and-the-australian-people/>.

23 These three values are nominated as distinctive Australian values by Benjamin T Jones, *This Time: Australia's Republican Past and Future* (Redback, 2018) 158–9.

24 Dylan Lino, *Constitutional Recognition: First Peoples and the Australian Settler State* (Federation Press, 2018) 102.

25 Jeff King, 'Constitutions as Mission Statements' in Denis J Galligan and Mila Versteeg, *Social and Political Foundations of Constitutions* (Cambridge University Press, 2013) 73, 81, doi.org/10.1017/CBO9781139507509.006.

Manifestations of national identity in constitutions can be either *symbolic*, such as a preamble or statement of recognition, or *operative*, such as the entrenchment of a representative form of government.[26] Of course, many substantive provisions have a symbolic dimension. For example, the choice of a representative form of government may express a community's commitment to democracy and equality.

Constitutional expressions of national identity can be *intentional* and *explicit* in the constitutional text. There are many examples of such provisions.[27] The Constitution of South Africa, for instance, famously opens by acknowledging the injustices of apartheid. But constitutions can also say something *implicit* and perhaps *unintentional* about national identity. Jeremy Webber argues that: 'Even if we wanted to, we could not eradicate symbolism from our Constitution. Language always carries connotations, implications, and points of resonance.'[28] So, for example, Marcia Langton argues that the text and history of the Australian Constitution show that '[c]oncepts of race are fundamental to Australian polity and civic life'.[29] Even omissions from the text can be telling. What does the absence of any mention of First Nations in the Australian Constitution say about the importance of First Nations to Australian political institutions? Arguably this silence echoes the 'great Australian silence'[30] about the place of First Nations in Australia's origin story.

The potential for intersections between constitutions and national identity expands if we take an expanded view of 'constitutions'. Many scholars have conceptualised the domain of constitutional law as extending beyond the constitutional text and its interpretation.[31] On this view, constitutional law embraces convention, usage, shared understandings, common law decisions and '"scattered" fragments of ordinary law'.[32] Australia's 'constitutional canon'[33] might include such pivotal moments in

26 See Jeremy Webber, 'Constitutional Poetry: The Tension Between Symbolic and Functional Aims in Constitutional Reform' (1999) 21 *Sydney Law Review* 260, 268.
27 For a collection of examples, see King (n 25) 83–4.
28 Webber, 'Constitutional Poetry' (n 26) 267.
29 Marcia Langton, 'Why "Race" is a Central Idea in Australia's Construction of the Idea of a Nation' (1999) 18 *Australian Cultural History* 22, 24.
30 WEH Stanner, *The Dreaming and Other Essays* (Black Inc. Agenda, 2009) 176.
31 See, eg, Jeremy Webber, 'Multiculturalism and the Australian Constitution' (2001) 24(3) *University of New South Wales Law Journal* 882, 883; Gabrielle Appleby, *The Role of the Solicitor-General: Negotiating Law, Politics and the Public Interest* (Hart Publishing, 2016) 3–4.
32 Brendan Lim, *Australia's Constitution after Whitlam* (Cambridge University Press, 2017) 19.
33 Ibid 8.

the evolution of our identity as *Mabo v Queensland (No 2)*[34] and the *Statute of Westminster*. Even the way a constitution is understood by its constituents can reflect and build national identity. Bruce Ackerman argues that, for Americans, 'the narrative we tell ourselves about our Constitution's roots is a deeply significant act of collective self-definition; its continual re-telling plays a critical role in the ongoing construction of national identity'.[35]

It is clear, then, that a constitution *can* be a source and a record of shared national values and aspirations, and a key part of a nation's grand historical narrative.

Whether, and to what extent, constitutions *should* play this role is a contested normative question. Jeremy Webber argues that '[w]ritten constitutions are poor instruments for defining a country'.[36] Attempts to capture identity in the constitutional text risk excluding those who do not share the view expressed in the text, falling into tepid platitudes, and becoming anachronisms.[37] Constitutions tend to represent the will of the majority, sometimes ignoring or disadvantaging minorities.[38] A further objection is that a strong sense of national identity is not necessarily a good thing. It can be a short step from pride in national identity to an insular or even aggressive form of patriotism.

In light of these debates, our project is to identify, describe and critique some points of intersection between the Australian Constitution (and, more broadly conceived, Australian constitutional law) and Australian national identity.

IV. The Australian Constitution and national identity

Does the Australian Constitution play the role of articulating and shaping national identity that we observe in some other constitutions? As we indicated at the beginning of this chapter, some would say no: it does not attempt to do so. But, as we have shown, it seems inevitable that a constitution says

34 (1992) 175 CLR 1.
35 Bruce Ackerman, *We the People: Foundations* (Belknap Press, 1991) 36.
36 Webber, 'Multiculturalism' (n 31) 882.
37 Webber, 'Constitutional Poetry' (n 26) 267.
38 Lino (n 24) 104.

something about the nation. A small but growing literature explores this possibility, albeit describing the identity revealed in the Constitution in modest terms: a 'small brown bird'.[39]

At federation, the Constitution arguably provided a sense of identity shared by much of the population. Helen Irving has argued that 'the Australian Constitution was a product of a particularly Australian political culture': 'a local product, typical of a particular culture and region'.[40] In 1901, the Constitution was comfortably familiar, taking on elements of the US Constitution, while entrenching the Westminster system. It was British, Christian and white, reaffirming Australia's place in the Empire. Yet even then, the Constitution was open to the criticism that it ignored large sections of the community, being written by a small, homogeneous group of men with largely similar interests. As we have observed above, it is strongly arguable that Australia's national identity can no longer be understood in these terms. Yet the Constitution remains largely unchanged.

In the past few years an apparent dissonance between Australia's Constitution and its national identity has been increasingly evident. The Constitution's silence on the political status of Aboriginal and Torres Strait Islander peoples, its prohibition on dual citizens running for Parliament, and its continuing links to a British Crown with no legal or political authority and decreasing symbolic significance for Australia have generated concrete proposals for constitutional amendment. The time seems right to ask: how does Australia's constitution relate to Australia's national identity?

V. The structure of this book

The chapters in this book are divided into three sections.

Part One explores the role of the Constitution in forming and reflecting national identity. It introduces the major themes of the book: Australia's national identity; the relationship between constitutions and national identities; and the extent to which Australia's constitution, taken as a whole, reflects or shapes national identity.

39 Elisa Arcioni and Adrienne Stone, 'The Small Brown Bird: Values and Aspirations in the Australian Constitution' (2016) 14(1) *International Journal of Constitutional Law* 60, doi.org/10.1093/icon/mow003, quoting Justice Patrick Keane (n 2).

40 Helen Irving, *To Constitute a Nation: A Cultural History of Australia's Constitution* (Cambridge University Press, 1999) ix.

In Chapter 2, Elisa Arcioni builds on this conceptual foundation. This chapter provides a broad doctrinal overview of the question of national identity as it has developed within the formal context of the Constitution, concluding that the picture of national identity revealed by the Constitution is at best incomplete and evolving. Many of the topics raised in Arcioni's chapter are developed by other authors in later chapters.

In Chapter 3, Anna Olijnyk asks how the interpretation of the Constitution might reflect national identity. Drawing on American scholarship on popular constitutionalism, Olijnyk argues that, despite obvious differences between the American and Australian contexts, the High Court's interpretation of the constitutional text sometimes reflects the evolving values and identity of the Australian people.

Lorne Neudorf adds a comparative perspective in Chapter 4 by looking at the experience of the *Canadian Charter of Rights and Freedoms*.[41] Unlike Australia, Canada self-consciously sought to build national identity through constitutional change. The chapter evaluates 40 years of successes, failures and unexpected outcomes in this ambitious identity-constituting project.

In Chapter 5, Peter D Burdon examines the potential of eco-constitutionalism in Australia. Advocates of eco-constitutionalism are optimistic about the role of constitutions in bringing about environmental protection. Burdon is critical of eco-constitutionalism generally, and in the Australian context. The chapter highlights the gap that can exist between idealist discourse (such as eco-constitutionalism or other identity-based aspirations) and the social forces that operate in a community.

Finally, in Chapter 6, Kim Rubenstein uses the lens of citizenship to reflect on the many changes in Australian society and government since the Constitution came into force. There have been profound changes in Australia's relationship with the United Kingdom and in the cultural make-up of the Australian people. Rubenstein argues for constitutional reform to promote an inclusive national identity that resonates with the lived experience of current Australians and with the rightful place of First Nations.

41 *Canada Act 1982* (UK) c 11, sch B pt I ('*Canadian Charter of Rights and Freedoms*').

Part Two interrogates the legal concepts that have been responsible for the definition and manifestation of national identity within the Australian State. Concepts such as citizen, alien, character, values and allegiance set the boundary between inclusion in, and exclusion from, the nation. These concepts are fundamental in defining the type of national community that is formed under the Constitution.

In Chapter 7, Alexander Reilly examines the notion of membership of, and exclusion from, the nation. Reilly observes that, while the Constitution sets the framework for determining membership, much of the work of drawing distinctions between members and non-members is left to Parliament. The chapter critiques the use of 'character' as a determinant for national membership, contrasting the exclusionary orientation of current migration policy with the inclusive philosophy that characterised Australian identity between the 1970s and 1990s.

Taking up the theme of exclusion, in Chapter 8, Joe McIntyre presents a historical analysis of the alien's power. McIntyre argues that the power was designed to impose domestic disabilities on aliens, rather than to define, through citizenship law, who was a member of the community. The chapter advocates frank acknowledgement of the darker aspects of constitutional history, in order to reframe the Constitution in line with the identity to which we aspire.

Writing from a liberal political theory standpoint, in Chapter 9, Tiziana Torresi asks what role national identity does, and should, play in our conception and practice of citizenship. The chapter contrasts communitarian and cosmopolitan ideas of shared identity, and the ways in which these ideas can be conducive to the rise of right-wing populism. Torresi considers how the institutional framework of constitutions interacts with extra-constitutional social and political factors.

In another piece of political theory analysis, in Chapter 10, Robyn Hollander analyses one of the most prominent features of the Australian Constitution: federalism. Hollander argues that the overlap, duplication and redundancy inherent in the federal system can give voice to minorities. Accordingly, federalism is an important mechanism for reflecting the diverse identities that make up Australia.

Part Three explores some key issues of constitutional reform.

In Chapter 11, Lydia McGrady scrutinises the concept of sovereignty that is foregrounded in the Uluru Statement from the Heart. The chapter questions how 'sovereignty' has been employed to both limit and promote Indigenous peoples. McGrady argues that multiple forms of sovereignty can coexist, and that the notion of Indigenous sovereignty remains crucial to constitutional reform.

In Chapter 12, Benjamin T Jones explores the potential of a new preamble as a source of 'moral power'. The chapter takes a historical perspective, reviewing the failed 1999 referendum and other key moments in the constitutional story. While acknowledging that a preamble may lack legal force, Jones argues that a preamble can be a repository of commonly held ideas about the civic good.

The book concludes in Chapter 13 with Sarah Sorial's insights into the processes that may need to support any movement towards a more identity-based reform of the Constitution. Present levels of constitutional awareness and interest in Australia present a barrier to changing the Constitution by referendum. Sorial introduces the use of citizens' assemblies as a way of improving citizens' democratic literacy and motivating public debate.

Part One

2

The Australian Constitution and Australian National Identity—the Past, the Present and the Possibilities

Elisa Arcioni[1]

The Australian Constitution is a document establishing the federal Commonwealth of Australia. It emerged following a series of debates in the late 1800s regarding the federation of the six British colonies established on the Australian continent from 1788—being a landmass occupied by hundreds of First Nations for millennia. The main reasons for federation were to allow for greater intercolonial cooperation, especially with respect to issues of trade and defence.

National identity was a theme of the federation process, but complicated by the connections between Australia and Britain at the time—in terms of culture and law. During the drafting debates, and even after the enactment of the Constitution, Australia was not a legally and politically independent nation-state. It remained a part of the British Empire and subject to British laws until well after the commencement of the Constitution.[2] This explains

1 With thanks to the participants of the workshop held in November 2019, especially to Alex Reilly and Anna Olijnyk, and with thanks to the anonymous reviewers whose more recent comments have strengthened this work.

2 *Australia Act 1986* (UK); *Australia Act 1986* (Cth). See also Anne Twomey, *The Australia Acts 1986: Australia's Statutes of Independence* (Federation Press, 2010).

why Australians were not given a distinctive *legal* identity as Australian through the Constitution—all Australians were British subjects and part of that broader community. Helen Irving argues that despite Australia not being a nation-*state*, it was nevertheless a 'nation' in which 'Australians had a distinctive, specifically Australian identity' contemporaneous with membership of the larger British community:

> Australia's was both a post-colonial nation and a peculiarly Australian nation, domestically sovereign, culturally distinctive, but still tied in community, language and law to the nation from which it had sprung. At the time, this complex web of affinities seemed very satisfactory to almost everyone, and was nothing like the puzzle it would later appear to be.[3]

This chapter provides an overview[4] of the extent to which Australian constitutional law has contributed to the puzzle of national identity, where any discussion of such identity remains problematic in light of the silence surrounding the colonial origins of the Constitution and consequent lack of recognition of First Nations.

I explore the role of the Constitution in reflecting, determining or indicating Australian national identity. In doing so, I focus on national identity in the sense of who are 'the people' under the Constitution—that is, the identity of the community brought together under the federal Commonwealth established by that document, as seen in constitutional law.

That community is best referred to as 'the people', a phrase seen in the constitutional text and being the umbrella term for the combination of the colonial communities who united in the federal Commonwealth. Historically, those peoples were involved in the drafting and acceptance of the constitutional text in a process that was democratic by the standards of the era. The peoples of the colonies were involved in a formal sense as

3 Helen Irving, *To Constitute a Nation: A Cultural History of Australia's Constitution* (Cambridge University Press, revised ed, 1999) 26. See also Patrick Keane, 'The People and the Constitution' (2016) 42(3) *Monash University Law Review* 529.

4 For detailed doctrinal discussion of each component of the identity of the people as explored in this chapter, refer to the footnoted articles and chapters that chart the case law and historical materials.

electors—of delegates for a majority of the colonies, or of their Parliament who in turn elected delegates to the constitutional conventions.[5] The electors then voted in referenda to adopt the draft constitution.

The franchises in the colonies were more restrictive than those that operate today in Australia. Each colony enfranchised some of their adult (over the age of 21) British subjects. Only South Australia and Western Australia enfranchised women. Queensland and Western Australia had explicit race-based restrictions, while Tasmania imposed an income or property ownership restriction. Despite these limitations, which would not be allowed or accepted today, the Constitution was the product of a popular process whereby 'the people' exercised a significant role in the making of their Constitution. Those historical 'people' became the people of the States and of the Commonwealth.[6]

This chapter assesses the contribution of Australian constitutional law in light of international scholarship regarding constitutional identity. Constitutional identity is a term used in many ways, one of which is to consider how a constitution defines the constitutional subject—the people.[7] This area of legal scholarship looks at patterns and underlying methodologies that have real world effects of legal inclusion in, and exclusion from, a polity.[8] I follow this approach by identifying the various groupings and categories of persons within constitutional law that impact upon membership of 'the people'. Within the international body of literature, 'the people' is often

5 The one exception was the people of Queensland, being from the colony that did not choose delegates and was not represented at the conventions. Nevertheless, the electors in Queensland did vote in the eventual referenda to adopt the draft constitution.

6 Elisa Arcioni, 'Historical Facts and Constitutional Adjudication: The Case of the Australian Constitutional Preamble' (2015) 30 *Journal of Constitutional History* 107.

7 A key contributor to the field is Michel Rosenfeld; see Michel Rosenfeld, *The Identity of the Constitutional Subject: Selfhood, Citizenship, Culture, and Community* (Routledge, 2009) ch 6, doi.org/10.4324/9780203868980; Michel Rosenfeld, 'The Identity of the Constitutional Subject' (1994–1995) 16 *Cardozo Law Review* 1050.

8 Even without reference to the term 'constitutional identity'; see, eg, the work of Shachar, Aleinikoff and Bosniak: Ayelet Shachar, 'Citizenship' in Michel Rosenfeld and Andras Sajo (eds), *The Oxford Handbook of Comparative Constitutional Law* (Oxford University Press, 2012) 1002; Ayelet Shachar, *The Birthright Lottery: Citizenship and Global Inequality* (Harvard University Press, 2009), doi.org/10.4159/9780674054592; T Alexander Aleinikoff, *Semblances of Sovereignty: The Constitution, the State, and American Citizenship* (Harvard University Press, 2002), doi.org/10.4159/9780674020153; T Alexander Aleinikoff, 'Citizens, Aliens, Membership and the Constitution' (1990) 7 *Constitutional Commentary* 9; Linda Bosniak, *The Citizen and the Alien: Dilemmas of Contemporary Membership* (Princeton University Press, 2006), doi.org/10.1515/9781400827510.

constituted by an ethnocultural identity,[9] or defined by their participation in political structures under the constitution in question.[10] As we will see, the Australian example combines both—and more.

Unlike some national constitutions, the Australian one does not explicitly define who 'the people' are. It seems relatively clear that the drafters did have a view as to the nature of 'the people' under the Constitution. This chapter teases out to what extent the historical views of the drafters have been maintained in the ongoing interpretation and application of the Constitution and what has changed over time, to show that the Constitution does give a significant, albeit incomplete, indication as to Australian national identity.

I am not addressing the notion of constitutional identity in the sense of 'the people' themselves using the Constitution as a source or reference for their own identity in a sociological sense.[11] As Helen Irving has argued, the Australian people are not inclined to using constitutional language to define themselves, which is in sharp contrast to the US for example, in relation to which Irving notes:

> Americans ... use ... constitutional words, and the idea of the authority that derives from the Constitution, as a source of identity and of unity. Above and beyond their vast and complicated differences, Americans have a constitutional identity. Pluralism, and cultural diversity are done-deals in the US.[12]

9 See, eg, Michel Rosenfeld, 'Constitutional Identity' in Michel Rosenfeld and Andras Sajo (eds), *The Oxford Handbook of Comparative Constitutional Law* (Oxford University Press, 2012) 756, 763, doi.org/10.1093/law/9780199578610.001.0001.

10 Stephen Tierney, '"We the Peoples": Constituent Power and Constitutionalism in Plurinational States' in Martin Loughlin and Neil Walker (eds), *The Paradox of Constitutionalism: Constituent Power and Constitutional Form* (Oxford University Press, 2008) 229, doi.org/10.1093/acprof:oso/9780199552207.003.0013. Of course there are other iterations of constitutional identity; see, eg, constitutional patriotism (the people defined by a commitment to the constitution itself) developed by the work of Jurgen Habermas: Jurgen Habermas, *The Inclusion of the Other: Studies in Political Theory*, Studies in Contemporary German Social Thought, (The MIT Press, first published Die Einbeziehung des anderen. Studien zue politischen Theorie, 1998); Jurgen Habermas, 'Citizenship and National Identity' in Bart van Steenbergen (ed), *The Condition of Citizenship*, Politics and Culture (SAGE Publications, 1994) 20, doi.org/10.4135/9781446250600.n3.

11 See, eg, the work of Gary Jacobsohn, who relies on an 'ethnographic' approach by considering what a polity holds 'dear' and then considers what occurs during the process of 'legal and political contestation' in order to understand that polity's constitutional identity: Gary Jeffrey Jacobsohn, *Constitutional Identity* (Harvard University Press, 2010) 322, doi.org/10.4159/9780674059399.

12 Helen Irving, 'A Nation Built on Words: The Constitution and National Identity in America and Australia' (2009) 33(2) *Journal of Australian Studies* 211, 219, doi.org/10.1080/14443050902883421.

Australians, by contrast, may 'believe in democracy, and the *Constitution* is democratic. We support the continued existence of states, and the *Constitution* is federal. But we have no sense that these institutions derive from our *Constitution*'.[13]

If we focus instead on what the Australian Constitution says about national identity, we can see a series of intersecting and overlapping groups or categories that together provide the contours of national identity. I address each of those categories below, and conclude that the Constitution inevitably has a role to play in relation to the legal indicators of national identity. If the Constitution were silent as to national identity, that would, of itself, be significant. I illustrate that the Constitution is not silent in this space. Scepticism is sometimes expressed as to the role of the Constitution in doing anything more than simply setting out a series of governmental structures and demarcating public powers between institutions. That is, that the Constitution does not, cannot and should not play a positive, explicit role in relation to national identity. I return to this later in this chapter. I take the position that the Constitution does have a legitimate, but limited, role to play in this space. We can see that the Constitution does play such a role when we look at what the text and its interpretation tell us as to the elements of national identity that are contained in the constitutional law of this country.

I. Constitutional categories and factors affecting the identity of 'the people'

A. Dual identities — national and federal, and the relevance of geography

The Australian Constitution is a document that overlays a national series of governmental structures upon the pre-existing entities now called States, but which were originally the British colonies on the Australian landmass. By creating a federation, the Constitution also created a people who were to be both a national and federal people. That is, the people under the Constitution have dual identities as both peoples of the States and people of the national Commonwealth.[14]

13 Ibid 222.

14 For a detailed analysis of the peoples of the States see Elisa Arcioni, 'The Peoples of the States under the Australian Constitution' (2022) 45(3) *Melbourne University Law Review* 861.

We can see—in the text of the Constitution and in the way the High Court has discussed it—that the peoples of the States are mutually exclusive and distinct groups, defined by territory. The Court developed a notion of the peoples of the States as having a connection with, or membership of, one State and no other, through residence in a State.[15] The people in each State are also distinct entities in the system of representation in the federal Parliament—with senators chosen by the people of a State, and House of Representatives electorates formed within the limits of a State.

The Constitution guarantees representation of each State people in the national Parliament, as well as the people being represented as a national whole.[16] This dual federal and national identity of 'the people' makes sense because the Constitution was a coming together of pre-existing colonial peoples, who—through the Constitution—had a collective national identity overlaid on top of their existing identities. The people's identity seen in the Constitution is, therefore, in part determined by geographic boundaries—where one lives and to which parts of the federation one belongs, while also 'the people' being brought together as one 'indissoluble federal Commonwealth' (the phrase we see in the preamble to the Constitution) to form a nation.

Over time we can see that the stream of High Court case law has downplayed State identities, emphasising instead the national whole, which is consistent with the general thrust of constitutional law centralising power in the Commonwealth and recognising the unified and national reality of Australia.[17]

However, there remain significant distinct State identities in a legal and political sense. A recent example that demonstrates the impact of State identities is the State-based responses to the COVID-19 pandemic. Each State exercised its sovereign power to protect its own people, prevent individuals who were not members of their State people from entering their State, and adopted distinct legal restrictions on a State basis. All challenges against such restrictions failed.[18]

---

15 See cases related to ss 75(iv), 100, 117 of the Constitution, such as *Davies v Western Australia* (1904) 2 CLR 29; *Australasian Temperance and General Mutual Life Assurance Society Ltd v Howe* (1922) 31 CLR 290.

16 See in particular through ss 7, 24 of the Constitution.

17 See, eg, references in *Amalgamated Society of Engineers v Adelaide Steamship Co Ltd* (1920) 28 CLR 129 and later cases such as *DJL v The Central Authority* (2000) 201 CLR 226, in which Kirby J referred in obiter to the growing sense of national independence and identity.

18 See, eg, *Palmer v Western Australia* (2021) 95 ALJR 229.

B. What about Territorians?

In the context of understanding the geographic element of national identity within the Constitution, it is interesting to note that the people in the Territories are somewhat sidelined. Australia has many territories, the most well known being those on the mainland, namely the Northern Territory and the Australian Capital Territory. But there are also offshore territories, which form part of Australia, such as Ashmore and Cartier Reef and Christmas Island. At federation, the Territories were viewed as (and continue to be in law) less secure in their existence and political representation than the States.[19] They were—in a sense—dependencies of the Commonwealth and could be included or excluded, separated from Australia or included within it, at the whim of the Australian government or Parliament. As a consequence, the people of the Territories are not given the same constitutional status as the peoples of the States.

The difference in status feeds into national identity in the sense of Territorians not being as secure in their membership of the national 'people' and being more susceptible to exclusion or differential (including less-beneficial) treatment compared to the protected position of the peoples of the States. Therefore, we have ongoing questions about exactly how the people of the Australian Territories feature within Australian national identity viewed through the lens of the Constitution. We see a trajectory of evolution in the way in which Territorians are now more included in the notion of 'the people' than they were immediately post-federation.

Over the course of case law in the High Court we see two approaches to the notion of the Australian Commonwealth. One is to view the Commonwealth as inclusive of the States *and* Territories. The other is to emphasise federalism, understood as including only the States, and therefore to treat the peoples of the Territories as peripheral to the Commonwealth. The 'integration' line of reasoning is the dominant one, downplaying the disparate position set up by the text of the Constitution itself between people in States and people in Territories. This changing view of the Commonwealth as being inclusive of the Territories leads to the constitutional identity of the Australian people now being more inclusive of the people of the Territories than in the past.

19 Elisa Arcioni, 'Identity at the Edge of the Constitutional Community' in Fiona Jenkins, Mark Nolan and Kim Rubenstein (eds), *Allegiance and Identity in a Globalised World* (Cambridge University Press, 2014) 31, doi.org/10.1017/CBO9781139696654.005. The central constitutional section is s 122.

C. An historical ethnocultural identity

In addition to the geographic elements of national identity seen in the Constitution, we also see an ethnocultural element. The drafters thought Australians were white and British, Australians were not migrants, and they were specifically not Chinese. This historical ethnocultural view of Australians can be seen in the way in which the drafters discussed particular powers that were to be given to the federal Parliament, to achieve what became known as the White Australia policy.[20] The particular powers were those with respect to naturalisation and aliens, races and immigration.[21] Those powers were placed in the Constitution in order to allow the federal Parliament to continue at a national level the racial restrictions that existed prior to (and continued after) federation in some of the colonies that became States.[22]

This ethnocultural identity was not a distinguishing feature between the colonies that became States. Rather, there were a series of racial restrictions that operated in several of them, focused mostly against Chinese immigrants. Rather than incorporate an explicit monocultural national identity at federation, the Constitution simply allowed for any subsisting ethnocultural identities operating in law in the colonies to be allowed to continue to operate and to operate at the national level.

Although that ethnocultural identity seemed strong at federation, it was not made explicit in the text of the Constitution and, over time, the High Court has resisted making it an essential element of the constitutional construct of 'the people'. To the contrary, there are hints that while it was permissible to treat Australian identity in that restrictive way at federation (and indeed it was enshrined in administrative practice for decades), the Court has eschewed it as being *required* by the Constitution. Instead, the Court has moved to a position whereby racial distinctions are treated as constitutionally suspect, although there is no unanimous position on this difficult issue.[23] The Court's lack of clarity with respect to race is related to the evolving position of First Nations peoples under the Constitution.

---

20 Gwenda Tavan, *The Long, Slow Death of White Australia* (Scribe Publications, 2005).

21 See ss 51(xix), (xxvi) and (xxvii), respectively.

22 Elisa Arcioni, 'Tracing the Ethno-Cultural or Racial Identity of the Australian Constitutional People' (2015) 15(2) *Oxford University Commonwealth Law Journal* 173, doi.org/10.1080/14729342.2016.1173350.

23 See discussion of *Love v Commonwealth* (2020) 270 CLR 152 below and the (now abandoned) challenge in *Minister for Immigration, Citizenship, Migrant Services and Multicultural Affairs v Montgomery* Case S192/2021, in which the Commonwealth argued for formal equality eschewing any distinctions to be made on the basis of race or indigeneity.

D. First Nations peoples and the Constitution

Australian national identity, and its constitutional components, has not yet come to terms with the historical and ongoing reality of Aboriginal and Torres Strait Islander peoples as the First Peoples of Australia. The Constitution is silent as to the status of Aboriginal and Torres Strait Islander people. This is explicable because the Constitution was drafted with the assumption that Aboriginal issues were a matter for the States—rather than being 'national' and thus warranting specific mention in the text. As a general statement it is true that, at federation, Aboriginal people had the same legal status as non-Aboriginal people (in terms of being subjects of the Queen and then citizens), but that status did not always include the rights or privileges usually associated with that status (such as being able to vote and exercise liberty of movement). Throughout Australia's history, the position of Aboriginal and Torres Strait Islander people demonstrates a pattern of exclusion or differential (including less-beneficial) treatment—not necessarily due to constitutional text or doctrine, but rather to legislation and administrative actions.[24] In terms of national identity, at federation one could say there was ambivalence as to the place of First Nations peoples.

Today Aboriginal and non-Aboriginal people share the same formal position under law and the High Court is taking initial steps to consider how Aboriginal people feature within the existing constitutional landscape—particularly in its decision in *Love* and subsequent developments that I address later in this chapter.[25] Political developments that include possible constitutional amendment will be part of the ongoing story. For now, I note that the Court does not have a unanimous view as to how the rejection of the historical ethnocultural identity discussed above, including a rejection of distinctions based on race, interacts with issues of indigeneity. The diversity of positions can be seen in the reasoning in *Love*.

The dissentients (being Kiefel CJ, Gageler and Keane JJ) reject any use of race as a basis of distinction in terms of membership, at least to the extent that it would involve the High Court interpreting the Constitution with that distinction in mind. They do not seem to distinguish between questions of race and indigeneity. By contrast, the majority judges either

24 See John McCorquodale, *Aborigines and the Law: A Digest* (Aboriginal Studies Press, 1987); John Chesterman and Brian Galligan, *Citizens Without Rights: Aborigines and Australian Citizenship* (Cambridge University Press, 1997), doi.org/10.1017/CBO9780511518249.

25 See, eg, *Love v Commonwealth* (2020) 270 CLR 152, 210 [133] (Gageler J) ('*Love*').

reasoned in a way that sidelines arguments of race per se,[26] or explicitly distinguished between race and indigeneity. For example, Nettle J stated that, while in general legislative power cannot be constrained on the basis of race,[27] 'different considerations apply … to Aboriginal people'.[28]

As I explore above, the ethnocultural component of Australian national identity under the Constitution has waned over time, but the issue of race continues to be complicated as the law slowly addresses how indigeneity interacts with national identity.

E. A prevailing democratic identity

While some elements of Australian national identity under the Constitution have either waned or are yet to be resolved, there is one defining element that has continued throughout the constitutional law of this country and continues to be key to the constitutional identity of Australians. What has emerged through the High Court's interpretation of the text of the Constitution is that Australians are a democratic people, with political sovereignty through their participation in representative government, and that this is the core component of the constitutional identity of 'the people'.[29] The people are given the power to choose their members of Parliament under ss 7 and 24 of the Constitution. That reference to direct choice by 'the people' has become the cornerstone for the Court's development of law protecting the federal right to vote[30] and an implied freedom of political communication.[31] The Court has itself described this power of the people as a reflection of political sovereignty.[32] Therefore, the constitutional identity of Australians is as a sovereign people, who exercise powers of self-government.

26 See ibid 190 [73] (Bell J).
27 Ibid 245–6 [256].
28 Ibid 248 [263]. See also [370] 282–3 (Gordon J).
29 Elisa Arcioni, 'The Core of the Australian Constitutional People—"The People" as "The Electors"' (2016) 39(1) *University of New South Wales Law Journal* 421 ('The Core of the Australian Constitutional People').
30 *Roach v Electoral Commissioner* (2007) 233 CLR 162 ('*Roach*'); *Rowe v Electoral Commissioner* (2010) 243 CLR 1.
31 *Lange v Australian Broadcasting Corporation* (1997) 189 CLR 520 and the stream of cases following including, eg, *McCloy v New South Wales* (2015) 257 CLR 178 ('*McCloy*'); *Clubb v Edwards* (2019) 267 CLR 171.
32 See, eg, *McCloy* (n 31).

The prevailing democratic identity also applies at the State level, such that 'the people' are a democratic people twice over. The national Parliament and system of government was modelled in general terms on the pre-existing colonial government structures, but with the added federal component. The State and Commonwealth parliaments share the characteristic of being democratic bodies, where the electors choose their members of their parliaments. The High Court has confirmed that the system of representative government operates at both levels of the Commonwealth, even though there remain differences in the details between the various jurisdictions.

F. The missing link — citizenship

What is missing so far in this account of national identity as seen in the Constitution is the very obvious issue of citizenship. Usually when we think of identity in relation to a nation, we think of citizenship—being the formal legal status of membership of a nation-state. The Australian position is complicated in this respect, because the constitutional text is silent as to *Australian* 'citizenship'. As I referred to above, Australia was not an independent nation-state at federation, and the drafters concluded that it made no sense to include a distinct Australian citizenship status. Australians were British subjects within the Empire, and *that* was the relevant legal status of Australians.[33] That is, there was no distinct legal national identity separate from the identity as a component of the British Empire.

The rejection of a distinctive Australian citizenship was due in part to underlying ideas of allegiance to a sovereign. The constitutional text is clear about Australia being a monarchy, with references to the Queen. That Queen was, at federation, the Queen of the UK. Today the relevant Monarch is the Monarch of Australia—different from the Monarch of the UK.[34] That seemingly superficial change of royal title has significant impact in terms of Australian constitutional identity, because it confirms that Australia is no longer a part of the British Empire, but, rather, a distinct nation with a distinct national identity—as Australian. That independence has led to a shift from focusing on the old 'subject' status as determining membership towards the newer status of 'citizenship'. However, that shift requires some

33 Kim Rubenstein, 'Citizenship and the Constitutional Convention Debates: A Mere Legal Inference' (1997) 25(2) *Federal Law Review* 295 ('Citizenship and the Constitutional Convention Debates'), doi.org/10.22145/flr.25.2.5.
34 *Sue v Hill* (1999) 199 CLR 462.

explanation given that I have already noted that Australian citizenship does not appear at all in the Constitution. Here we get to a complicated area of law that is still in a state of flux.

G. Insiders, outsiders and in-between

In the absence of any explicit constitutional mention of citizenship, legislation has stepped into the breach. Since 1949, the Parliament has established the law of citizenship through legislation outlining who is a citizen and how one can become a citizen (as well as how one might lose Australian citizenship).[35] In general terms, the law treats someone who is a citizen as a member of the Australian community, so national identity has some link to the citizenry. However, identity is also revealed by who is excluded. Under the Constitution, we have indicators of exclusion through the categories of immigrants and aliens, and the races power. As noted above, those powers were explicitly included to allow a continuation of racist politics of exclusion, differential treatment and expulsion. How can we understand the interaction between the exclusionary categories under the Constitution—telling us who is not included—and the inclusive status of citizenship under legislation?

For a couple of decades, the High Court case law seemed to suggest that citizenship legislation answered the question of who was included as among 'the people' of the Constitution. That is, Australian national identity was coextensive with the legislated citizenry. If a person was a citizen, they were an insider. If they were not a citizen then they were an alien—an outsider. To make this simple connection between citizenship and alienage is to gloss over complicated details of cases that fell somewhere in-between, discussion of which is beyond the scope of this chapter.[36]

Any simple dichotomy between citizen and alien has been challenged with the decision of *Love* in February 2020. *Love* was about two Aboriginal men who were not Australian citizens. The High Court, by majority, concluded that Aboriginal Australians cannot be aliens (and therefore cannot be deported), regardless of whether or not they hold Australian citizenship. I address below some of the implications of that case. Before doing so, I note one other category of people who fall in-between a simple insider–outsider divide; that is, dual or multiple nationals.

---

35 See Kim Rubenstein with Jacqueline Field, *Australian Citizenship Law* (Thomson Reuters, 2nd ed, 2017) [2.220] [6.190].

36 See Joe McIntyre, Chapter 8, this volume.

In 2017 there was a political crisis regarding the disqualification of members of the federal Parliament. Fifteen members of Parliament were disqualified, many because they held a foreign citizenship.[37] The crucial part of the Constitution was s 44(i), which set as a basis of disqualification the holding of foreign citizenship.[38] Because the rules of eligibility to be a member of Parliament include being an Australian citizen,[39] the interaction between the rules of eligibility and those of disqualification mean that those caught by that subsection of the Constitution include dual (or multiple) nationals. Therefore, the Constitution is ambivalent as to the identity of people with more than only Australian citizenship. While having more than one citizenship is lawful,[40] it also means one is excluded from participation in a central element of the national political system. And if, as I note above, a core component of being part of 'the people' is exercising political sovereignty, then dual nationals straddle insider and outsider status. Dual nationals can be electors but are denied one of the available constitutional elements of political participation—that of being elected as a member of federal Parliament. Further, in 2022, the High Court considered—without having to decide—arguments that foreign citizenship per se is sufficient to make a person an alien and therefore an outsider.[41] At 2000, it was estimated that between 4 and 5 million Australians were dual nationals, or entitled to take out dual nationality.[42] In a report prepared in 2017, it was estimated that, at that date, up to 40 per cent of the Australian population may fall into that category.[43] Far from being a minor issue, foreign citizenship and therefore dual nationality is a common feature of the Australian population. The way in which foreign citizenship interacts with Australian constitutional identity is a significant piece of the national identity puzzle.

37 See, eg, *Re Canavan* (2017) 263 CLR 284 ('*Canavan*').

38 'Any person who: (i) is under any acknowledgment of allegiance, obedience, or adherence to a foreign power, or is a subject or a citizen or entitled to the rights or privileges of a subject or a citizen of a foreign power… shall be incapable of being chosen or of sitting as a senator or a member of the House of Representatives.'

39 *Commonwealth Electoral Act 1918* (Cth) s 93(1) sets out the general eligibility to vote, which is the age of 18 and being an Australian citizen.

40 See the legislative changes over time explained in Rubenstein, *Australian Citizenship Law* (n 35).

41 In addition to *Montgomery* noted above, see also *Alexander v Minister for Home Affairs* (2022) 401 ALR 438.

42 Adrienne Millbank, 'Dual Citizenship in Australia' (Current Issues Brief 5, Parliamentary Library, Parliament of Australia, 28 November 2000) 5–6.

43 John Edward Mangan, Economics & Law Research Institute, *Numbers of Potential Dual-Citizens by Descent in Australia* (Report, 22 September 2017). This report formed part of the Court File in *Canavan* (n 37). Copy on file with author.

H. Overview of past and present constitutional indications of national identity

The overview given so far shows the several ways in which the Constitution gives indications of Australian national identity in the sense of how 'the people' are identified. Those indications include identity based on geography or physical territory, ethnocultural elements and democratic participation, as well as civic indications of inclusion and exclusion through legal status. What we see overall is that some of the historical expectations regarding national identity have been overturned, some have waned in significance and others have been maintained, albeit in new forms.

The element overturned is that of an inherent ethnocultural national identity. Australians are no longer legally defined as white and British non-immigrants. Today the Constitution does not entrench such a conception of 'the people' or the nation. The waning notions of identity are those tied to physical territory. The distinct identities of peoples of a State or Territory still exist—in law and in practice. However, they have become less significant (at least in terms of constitutional law), as noted above.

National identity is stronger than it was at federation—in terms of how the law has developed and cemented a national identity distinct from Australia's historical place within the British Empire. This reflects the trajectory of the development of Australia as a nation from a set of separate British colonies to an independent nation-state. The internal political divisions within the nation are less important today than they were at federation, in that distinct State identities can more easily be overtaken by a national identity as a matter of law. We see this when we consider the expanded power of the Commonwealth and its ability to impose uniform national rules and override differences that exist at the State level. However, as noted above, the fact and law attached to the internal geographic divisions within Australia remain and, as we see in the legal and political responses to the COVID-19 pandemic, State identities can on occasion come to the fore and emphasise the distinct geographically bound communities that exist within the Australian nation.

The maintained (but transformed) elements of identity seen in the Constitution are the democratic ones—where the key components remain the same: that of political participation and self-governance by 'the people'.

The change that has occurred over time, in terms of what the Constitution requires, is that the proportion of the population who get to exercise those roles is now larger than that which applied at federation.

As noted above, at federation the franchise was not as broad as it is today and limitations that applied then on the basis of gender, race and income or property ownership are no longer viewed as justifiable. In particular, the position of women within the nation demonstrates the potential for change over time in terms of how the Constitution interacts with national identity. At federation, despite South Australia's attempts to entrench a universal adult franchise, the Constitution did not guarantee that women would be equal participants in the Australian democratic processes. Shortly after federation, the Parliament extended the vote to women but retained racial grounds of discrimination. Later, the High Court spoke through several cases to the effect that the exclusion of women was contrary to the Constitution—whether related to serving on a jury as a representative of the community[44] or through having a right to vote.[45] Thus, we see the notion of membership and to whom it applies as changing over time—and constitutional law changing to accord with broader social changes.

In summary, the constitutional national identity is that of an inclusive, politically active people, who are a national collective albeit living in a series of sub-national States and Territories. Yet the constitutional contours of national identity have not all been resolved.

II. Unresolved business: Indigeneity and national identity

Now I return to the *Love* case to highlight what that case says about the ongoing development of Australian identity under the Constitution. As I noted at the beginning of this chapter, the Constitution was not written in order to entrench a particular national identity. It assumed British subject status as the relevant legal identifier. That British identity was relevant because the colonies that formed the States were based on an assertion of British sovereignty over the Australian landmass. In theory, that assertion of sovereignty made the Australian landmass British and no other law or

44 Under s 80 of the *Constitution*, see, eg, *Cheatle v The Queen* (1993) 177 CLR 541.
45 *Roach* (n 30).

identity was relevant. The *Love* case challenges that assumption and opens up questions about how the Constitution interacts with national identity and particularly how indigeneity may form part of that picture.

In *Love* the High Court was faced with the circumstances of two Aboriginal Australian men born outside Australia and without Australian citizenship. They both faced deportation and challenged the ability of the government to deport them. They argued they were not 'aliens', so the *Migration Act 1958* (Cth) (under which the deportation would be authorised) did not apply to them. The majority agreed that Aboriginal Australians could not be aliens, and therefore the *Migration Act* would not apply to any such persons.[46]

Each of the seven judges of the High Court wrote a separate judgment and there are great disparities in the reasoning of the judges, even among the majority. What can be said of the case in relation to its effect on how the Constitution determines national identity? For the purpose of this chapter, I note four elements. First, that the case confirms that the Constitution does have a role to play. The arguments in the case all circled around the constitutional term 'alien' and how that determinant of outsider status was to be understood. All the judges agreed that it was for the Court to decide if an outer limit to that concept had been reached—the difference between the majority and minority was that the minority decided Aboriginality was not relevant. Therefore, the Constitution does play a role in marking out the boundaries of who is included and excluded—but we do not have a unanimous view from the High Court as to what those boundaries are.

The second element to highlight is how all the judges agreed with the statement that alienage is affected by the 'ordinary meaning'[47] of that term and then to see what the majority did with that statement. When we see reference to 'ordinary meaning', we need to search for where that meaning comes from. The majority emphasised that the growing social and legal recognition of the unique, deep and spiritual connection to Country at the heart of Aboriginality gives Aboriginal Australians a claim to falling outside the 'ordinary meaning' of aliens. The majority concluded that it is not possible to view someone who has such a connection to Country as 'other' or 'foreign' or lacking connection to Australia such that they could be aliens.

46 *Love* (n 25) 192 [81] (Bell J).
47 *Minister for Immigration & Ethnic Affairs v Pochi* (1980) 31 ALR 666.

This is a new statement of how the identity of who is relevantly Australian takes into account Aboriginal connection to Country—something we have never seen before in the case law of the Court.

This brings me to the third element to note: that membership of the national community is affected by Aboriginality—not just connection to Country, but also Aboriginal self-identification. The High Court has eschewed any reference to subjective feelings of membership as relevant to constitutional status. Self-identification has been irrelevant to the way in which the Constitution interacts with national identity. In *Love* we see something new happening. The Court adopted the tripartite test of Aboriginality, as set out by Brennan J in *Mabo (No 2)*, requiring: descent, self-identification as Aboriginal and Aboriginal community acceptance as such.[48] By including the element of self-identification, the Court is including subjective identity as one part of determining who is relevantly a member of the national community.

The test for Aboriginality also brings me to the last element to note in relation to *Love*; that is, how notions of sovereignty affect national identity. Typically, sovereignty includes the power to govern a people within a defined territory. I have already noted how the Constitution rests on a legal foundation of British sovereignty being asserted over the Australian landmass. That included a rejection of the pre-existing Aboriginal sovereignties of the many Aboriginal societies on that same landmass, which continue to exist in fact. *Love* shows up the challenge of trying to allow some measure of recognition of Aboriginal law that continues to exist in fact, even though the Australian legal system refuses to recognise it as distinct legal systems operating at the same level as the Australian law.

The particular component of Aboriginal law in question here is law as to membership. This is included in the tripartite test to determine who is relevantly Aboriginal. The third component of that test is whether a person is accepted by the relevant Aboriginal community as a member of that community. Such acceptance can be understood as acceptance through the law of membership that applies in that community, thus being a reference to Aboriginal law. What we see is the majority of the Court allowing decisions of a separate legal system to have a measure of constitutional significance.

48 *Mabo v Queensland (No 2)* (1992) 175 CLR 1, 70.

The majority's reasoning, which allowed this aspect of Aboriginal law to play some role in determining membership under the Constitution, was met with fierce resistance by the dissenting judges. The dissenting judges suggested that to give constitutional weight to Aboriginal law in this way attributes to the relevant Aboriginal group a kind of sovereignty,[49] or comes 'perilously close' to such attribution.[50] This is in contrast to the statements of the majority such that membership of the national community necessarily involves a rejection of any separate sovereignty of Aboriginal communities.

We are left with an unresolved tension, derived from the compromise of the *Mabo (No 2)* case itself—of recognising some Aboriginal law for some purposes as relevant to national identity (under the Constitution), but refusing to recognise the underlying sovereignty of those groups whose law is being referred to. The *Love* case, raising many issues—of national identity and the Constitution, as well as others—does not give a complete or satisfactory answer to any of them.[51] Thus, it is illustrative of the broader issue to which I now turn: that of the necessarily limited, partial and iterative nature of the Constitution in working out Australian national identity.

III. The Constitution as a non-exhaustive repository

As discussed above, the Constitution does play a role in reflecting or articulating elements of Australian national identity, in the sense of identifying who 'the people' of Australia are. That role can be seen through its text and how it has been interpreted by the High Court. Yet, what the Constitution reveals is incomplete, through a lack of a comprehensive coverage of identity, and evolutionary in the sense of allowing for change over time.

There is the historically explicable but presently surprising absence of any reference to Australian citizenship. There is no reference to values or commitments to give substance to any notion of national identity. There is text that seems to allow distinctions to be made on the basis of race. Ours is a constitution devoid of clear general indications of national identity, yet

49 *Love* (n 25) 179 [37] (Kiefel J), 226 [197] (Keane J).
50 Ibid 208 [125] (Gageler J).
51 See Elisa Arcioni, 'Competing Visions of the People in Australia: First Nations and the State (2023) 1 *Comparative Constitutional Studies* (forthcoming).

which includes references to the constitutional 'people'. Once we add in the High Court interpretation of the Constitution, we can see many indications of national identity, albeit overlapping and piecemeal.

This partial and iterative character of the way the Constitution interacts with national identity may appear puzzling and concerning, yet it is neither. It is explicable why the Constitution is not exhaustive in terms of providing statements and understandings of national identity. The Constitution has only a modest role. It was not set up to define 'the people', nor has it effectively or significantly driven any particular national identity over time. Though at least part of the reason for this lack of explicit identification in the text may have been that there was a clear sense at federation of who 'the people' were—white, British and not 'foreign' immigrants. Paradoxically, the lack of definition has allowed the notion of 'the people' to be expanded over time.

The Australian Constitution is typically understood as establishing structures of government and dividing power between institutions, rather than commencing a new radical chapter of a people who were claiming independence from another entity (consider the US) or responding to cleavages of the past to begin a new future (consider South Africa). Yet despite the modesty of the Constitution, it has and will continue to play a role in determining or reflecting national identity because elements of identity are contained in the text and the High Court has the role of interpreting that text when cases come before it related to that text.[52] Yet it goes further than this; as we can see from the hints in the *Love* case, the Court on occasion does reach beyond the text to look to deeper questions of identity that exist within the history of the nation and the social and community self-understanding of Australian identity. And it may be that it is the brevity and ambiguity of the text that sometimes demands or at least leaves open to the Court the possibility of looking to those deeper questions.

Another way of expressing the role of the Constitution has been set out by Cheryl Saunders, who argues that constitutional institutions, principles and practices may be the product of national identity: 'a Constitution can help to build national identity, by acknowledging as citizens peoples who ethnically are diverse, by creating the institutions, principles and practices suited to a mixed polity of this kind and by providing an agreed base from

52 Elisa Arcioni and Adrienne Stone, 'The Small Brown Bird: Values and Aspirations in the Australian Constitution' (2016) 14(1) *International Journal of Constitutional Law* 60, doi.org/10.1093/icon/mow003.

which a shared history can grow' and '[t]he evolutionary character of Australia's constitutional arrangements has assisted to conceal the real shifts in its national identity'.[53]

If we are agreed that the Constitution can and does play a role in this space, but that it cannot and will not be the only repository of legal indications of national identity, then how can we complete the picture of national identity? We must look to see how the Constitution interacts with other elements of the legal and political structures of the nation, and also how it interacts with the broader society. We must place the Constitution within its appropriate relationship with the institutions established within it. Most particularly, the relationship between the High Court—and its interpretation of the constitutional text—and the Parliament that is given great leeway in determining the details of the governmental structures. And then to consider how 'the people' themselves play a role.

First, to the inter-institutional interactions. The Constitution sets up structures of government, and also sets up boundaries of power. With respect to questions of identity, the High Court defers a great deal to the Parliament. The text of the Constitution contains very little detail, which leaves the Parliament to be the institution to work out the precise rules of membership and therefore a key actor in determining national identity at law. This is consistent with many parts of the Constitution, where the drafters established a default proviso and then left it for 'Parliament to otherwise provide'. One key provision in this regard is in relation to who are 'the people' who choose the elected members of Parliament.

As Benjamin Saunders and Simon Kennedy have explained:

> The establishment of the architecture of the federal Commonwealth did not require the framers to definitively reach a consensus on who, precisely, 'the people' were. The framers did not attempt to define 'the people', and, subject to ss 7 and 24 of the *Constitution*, left the Commonwealth Parliament to determine the details of the electoral franchise. The framers' approach reflects an understanding that the concepts of 'the people' and their 'will' were themselves contested political concepts whose meaning would evolve over time.[54]

53 Cheryl Saunders, 'Legacies of Luck: Australia's Constitution and National Identity in the 1990s' (1999) 15(3) *South African Journal on Human Rights* 328, doi.org/10.1080/02587203.1999.11835014.
54 Benjamin B Saunders and Simon P Kennedy, 'Popular Sovereignty, "The People", and the Australian Constitution: A Historical Reassessment' (2019) 30(1) *Public Law Review* 36 ('Popular Sovereignty'), ssrn.com/abstract=3394618.

> The concept of 'the people' was thus an ambulatory concept, intended to reflect, and allow for diversity in, prevailing views of political representation among the colonies, as well as further development in political thinking. The prevailing views of 'the people' as at Federation differ from the typical views of today.[55]

The Parliament is also the representative of 'the people', and thus the people themselves have a self-constitutive power to determine their own identity.[56] The people choose the Parliament that influences the constitutional contours of who 'the people' are. So, in the Australian context, we can see that the Constitution interacts with both the Parliament and the people in the way in which it sets up elements of national identity.

We see the High Court deferring to the will of the people—until recently—in the way in which it has approached questions of citizenship. The Court defers to legislative indications of citizenship, reflective of the self-constitutive character of the people and their role in choosing their representative Parliament.

Yet a fundamental element of our constitutional system is that the Parliament is only allowed to legislate within the outer boundaries set by the Constitution, and that the High Court is the institution to work out when those outer boundaries are crossed. That means that the Constitution, through the Court, does have to play a role in relation to national identity by marking out the outer boundaries of the Parliament's power, while leaving the Parliament leeway in its policy decisions within its sphere of power. That is, the Constitution sets baselines and outlines of identity, with the Parliament to determine the fine-grained details and implementation. The Court's approach in *Love* is an instance of the Constitution setting an outer boundary of power, beyond which the Parliament cannot act, while leaving the Parliament to make decisions within that outer boundary.

This is not the place to provide a definitive outline of when it is legitimate for the High Court to articulate a boundary of power on the Parliament and when the Parliament should be given freer rein to make the decisions about membership. However, it should be noted that there are clear dangers in allowing 'the people' to have complete power over identity through their Parliament. While we laud the representative character of our Parliament,

55 Ibid.

56 Arcioni, 'The Core of the Australian Constitutional People' (n 29). See also Saunders and Kennedy, 'Popular Sovereignty' (n 54) 229.

and thus it being a reflection of 'the people', the system in place is majoritarian. It allows for the majority to outvote a minority and thus for a majority alone to determine and restrict membership. This leads to the need for a counter-majoritarian entity (such as a court) to exist to monitor the decisions of the Parliament. Thus, the Court and the Parliament both have legitimate, but distinct, roles in this space.

IV. Conclusion — the Constitution and the future

What of the future? In this chapter I have set out as a descriptive overview the ways in which the Constitution currently interacts with national identity, and stated my position that it is legitimate for the Constitution to exercise that role—albeit in concert with the Parliament and the people. To chart a possible way beyond the existing status quo, I suggest that change is necessary in order to maintain the legitimacy of the Constitution.

I assume that we *should* respond to address some outstanding questions regarding national identity and the Constitution, because the risks attached to the failure to do so are high. Specifically, where there is a serious mismatch between the Constitution and the reality of the community under it, there is a threat to the legitimacy of the Constitution itself. This is so because of the very purpose of the Constitution. The Constitution is, returning to the words of the early High Court, 'intended to apply to the varying conditions which the development of our community must involve'.[57] It is obvious that the Australian community has changed since federation. It is also obvious that there are areas of constitutional law that are in tension with elements of the community and its contemporary identity.

Three areas stand out: first, the constitutional silence regarding Aboriginal and Torres Strait Islanders peoples; second, the ambiguity regarding dual nationals; and third, the issue of whether to become a republic.

It is well known that the Constitution does not explicitly acknowledge or address the legal and extra-legal consequences of the assertion of British sovereignty over the Australian landmass and does not acknowledge the prior sovereignty of Australia's Aboriginal and Torres Strait Islander peoples. While cases like *Mabo (No 2)* and the recent *Love* decision go some way

57 *Jumbunna Coal Mine, NL v Victorian Coal Miners' Association* (1908) 6 CLR 309, 368 (O'Connor J).

to opening up a legal space to address those realities, the High Court's involvement is necessarily limited. It is the text of the Constitution that is silent, and as a consequence the Court is limited in what it can do to articulate and respond to these silences. While the Court has reached what would seem to be an intuitively correct outcome—that Aboriginal Australians cannot be aliens—the reasoning is troubling and the decision does not address the underlying constitutional silence.

A clear avenue for reform in this field comes from the Uluru Statement from the Heart, which sets out how we could move forward without rebuilding the entire system of the Constitution, yet allowing for an iterative process of change to address our historical constitutive flaw.

The second issue is the status of dual nationals. As explained above, dual nationals are prevented from being elected to federal Parliament. This disqualification is significant in that it affects up to 40 per cent of the Australian population. If democratic participation is at the core of the people's identity in a constitutional sense, as I noted above, then this exclusion is untenable.

The third element is whether Australia should remain a constitutional monarchy or transform into a republic. Given the movement away from the British identity that existed at federation—in law and in society—it seems incongruous that Australia remains a monarchy with a Head of State who is also a foreign Head of State, who is not a citizen and who resides on the other side of the world. While the monarch does not exercise in practice political power in Australia or over Australian affairs, the possibility of doing so remains open to them.

Other areas may be candidates for amendment in order for the Constitution to better reflect the diversity and complexity of Australian national identity. The Constitution gives us a partial picture of our national identity. But the whole picture is yet to be painted by all constitutional actors together. That includes the Parliament, the people and, potentially, the Constitution itself through textual change.

The Australian Constitution was not a document established with the specific intent of identifying and crystallising Australian national identity. Nevertheless, the drafters' expectations regarding who 'the people' of the Commonwealth were, the text of the Constitution and the way in which it has been interpreted by the High Court all give indications as to the identity of 'the people'. Those indications are partial, iterative and changing. Some indications have waned, some have continued, some have been transformed, others are as yet unresolved. Thus, the Constitution is an incomplete and evolving reflection of Australian identity. Despite the incomplete nature of the way in which the Constitution reflects Australian national identity, it certainly has a role to play—in combination and sometimes in tension with the role of the Parliament and of 'the people'—in determining the legal elements of identity. The future of Australian constitutional national identity can only be seen through understanding how the combined effect of all those constitutional actors comes together to determine, at any one time, the ever-changing details of Australian national identity.

3

Constitutional Interpretation and the Australian People

Anna Olijnyk

There are several ways to consider the relationship between the Australian Constitution and national identity. One method is to focus on what substantive constitutional principles say about our national identity. For example, other chapters in this volume examine the nature of Australian federalism and the scope of the aliens power. Another method focuses on the words of the constitutional document. Not only are the words the source of substantive legal principles and institutions, but also, as Benjamin T Jones points out in Chapter 12 of this volume, words can carry 'moral power'.

But the words do not always speak for themselves. What, for example, are 'external affairs'? Who is an 'alien'? What does it mean for members of Parliament to be 'chosen by the people'? The task of interpreting these words authoritatively falls to the High Court. In this chapter, I consider whether the High Court's interpretation of the Constitution is another way of shedding light on the relationship between the Constitution and Australian national identity.

Conventional wisdom tells us the High Court uses a method known as 'legalism' to interpret the Constitution. Legalism focuses on the text of the Constitution, read in the context of the document as a whole and the circumstances in which it was written. This method largely avoids recourse to moral values or contemporary opinion.

This chapter complicates this legal orthodoxy by asking whether the High Court's interpretation of the Constitution has the potential to reflect Australia's national identity. Can the Court, by filling out the outlines drawn by the nineteenth-century framers, make the Constitution a living document that embodies the evolving identity and values of Australians?

In the US, a rich body of scholarship (which I refer to as 'popular constitutionalism') explores the relationship between the Supreme Court's interpretation of the US Constitution and the values and identity of the American people.[1] These scholars have observed that the Supreme Court's constitutional decisions generally broadly align with widely held public values of the time. Sometimes the Court's interpretation lags behind the formation of public consensus, and sometimes it leads popular opinion. But seldom has the Court's interpretation been far out of step with popular values. Can this theory apply to Australia?

This chapter begins by outlining the key features of popular constitutionalism as developed in the American literature. Section II speculates about the theory's potential application to Australian constitutional law. While I identify several obvious obstacles to the direct translation of the American theory, I argue these are not as great as they first appear. There is some potential for popular constitutionalism to apply in Australia. Section III makes good this claim by re-examining the 'right to vote' cases, *Roach v Electoral Commissioner* ('*Roach*')[2] and *Rowe v Electoral Commissioner* ('*Rowe*'),[3] from the perspective of popular constitutionalism. I conclude that, while more work is needed to identify the nature, extent and precise functioning of popular constitutionalism in Australia, there are signs that the High Court's interpretation of the Constitution sometimes reflects the evolving values and identity of the Australian people.

1 Major contributions to this scholarship include Alexander M Bickel, *The Least Dangerous Branch* (The Bobbs-Merrill Company, 1962); Neal Devins, *Shaping Constitutional Values: Elected Government, the Supreme Court, and the Abortion Debate* (Johns Hopkins, 1996); Louis Fisher, *Constitutional Dialogues: Interpretation as Political Process* (Princeton University Press, 1988), doi.org/10.1515/9781400859573; Barry Friedman, *The Will of the People* (Farrar, Strauss and Giroux, 2009); Larry D Kramer, *The People Themselves: Popular Constitutionalism and Judicial Review* (Oxford University Press, 2004).

2 (2007) 233 CLR 162 ('*Roach*').

3 (2010) 243 CLR 1 ('*Rowe*').

I. Popular constitutionalism

The American scholarship on popular constitutionalism includes descriptive and normative strands. This article focuses primarily on the descriptive strand, which identifies ways in which the American people express their views on constitutional issues. The descriptive strand of popular constitutionalism argues that these expressions of views may ultimately influence the Supreme Court's interpretation of the US Constitution.

Take, for example, one of the most controversial constitutional questions in the US: whether the Constitution impliedly guarantees a right to abortion—and, if so, in what circumstances.[4]

Since the Supreme Court's 1973 decision in *Roe v Wade*,[5] American people have expressed their views on both sides of this question. People have joined pro-life or pro-choice groups to engage in organised protests and advocacy, sometimes with an explicit constitutional dimension. For example, the annual March for Life commemorates the anniversary of *Roe v Wade* with a march from the Washington Monument to the Supreme Court.[6] People with views on the issue have voted for political candidates (at State and federal level) whose view on this issue reflects their own. Those candidates have made laws and implemented policies that push at the edge of known constitutional boundaries. This in turn has led to constitutional litigation, sometimes supported by civil society organisations with their own constitutional agenda.[7] Repeated litigation has kept abortion on the Supreme Court's agenda and has forced the Court to refine its jurisprudence, affirming the precedent of *Roe v Wade* while backing away from its application in some circumstances and ultimately overruling the decision in 2022.[8]

But the influence of the American people on the interpretation of the US Constitution does not end there. The process of appointing US Supreme Court judges is avowedly political. People can vote for a presidential

4 Abortion is the topic of an extended study from the perspective of popular constitutionalism: see Fisher (n 1).

5 410 US 113 (1973).

6 'National March for Life', *March for Life* (Web Page) <marchforlife.org/national-march-for-life/>.

7 The American Civil Liberties Union is perhaps the most well-known example of an organisation that seeks to further its objectives through constitutional litigation: see 'ACLU History' *American Civil Liberties Union* <www.aclu.org/about/aclu-history>.

8 *Dobbs v Jackson Women's Health Organization* 597 US (2022).

candidate knowing that candidate will appoint judges who lean a certain way on contentious issues. In the Senate confirmation hearings, the people's elected representatives grill the Supreme Court nominees on their approach to constitutional interpretation and even their views on specific constitutional issues. For example, since *Roe v Wade*, the nominee's position on abortion 'has played a critical part in nearly every Supreme Court appointment'.[9]

In popular constitutional theory, the American people hold levers that can shift the Supreme Court's constitutional interpretation. The quality and extent of the people's influence varies. The people's contributions can be direct and targeted (for example, a civil society organisation commencing constitutional litigation). They can be indirect and diffuse (for example, voting for a candidate who shares your constitutional view), individual or collective. Importantly, contributions to popular constitutionalism may be more or less self-conscious. The constituent who votes for a representative with pro-life views may not see themselves as engaging with constitutional issues. Yet, in combination with thousands of other like-minded voters, this constituent can push a contested constitutional position to the forefront of the political agenda and into the Supreme Court. Popular constitutional theory would describe this constituent as one of thousands contributing to the 'shared elaboration of constitutional meaning'.[10]

What is the result of these 'tugs and pulls between elected government and the Court' that 'permeate constitutional decision-making'?[11] Popular constitutionalists such as Barry Friedman argue that 'constitutional interpretation is an elaborate discussion between judges and the body politic'.[12] The Supreme Court's role in this discussion is 'highly interactive':[13] 'Courts act as go-betweens in the dialogue, synthesizing the views of society and then offering the synthesis to society for further discussion'.[14] The key descriptive insight of popular constitutionalism is 'that judicial interpretations of the [US] Constitution reflect popular will over time'.[15]

---

9 Devins (n 1) 104.

10 Christine Bateup, 'The Dialogic Promise: Assessing the Normative Potential of Theories of Constitutional Dialogue' (2006) 71 *Brooklyn Law Review* 1109, 1118.

11 Devins (n 1) 55.

12 Barry Friedman, 'Dialogue and Judicial Review' (1993) 91(4) *Michigan Law Review* 577, 654, doi.org/10.2307/1289700.

13 Ibid 668.

14 Ibid 669.

15 Barry Friedman, 'Mediated Popular Constitutionalism' (2003) 101 *Michigan Law Review* 2596, 2599.

This leads us to the normative claims of popular constitutionalism. Popular constitutional scholars claim the continuous dialogue between the people and the Supreme Court results in 'more vibrant and durable constitutional interpretation'[16] that is neither crudely populist nor frozen in time.[17] The normative value of popular constitutionalism lies in its potential to create an 'equilibrium' between different conceptions of the public interest, which may change over time.[18] Popular constitutionalism can strike a balance 'between dynamism and finality'.[19] When popular constitutionalism works well, the contributions of each actor serve to inform the others of alternative views, shape and sharpen constitutional debates, test the limits and practicality of new constitutional principles, and accommodate different interests and views. Neal Devins argues that popular constitutional dialogue is particularly useful in relation to complex, emotionally charged and divisive social issues. Such issues 'are best resolved through political compromises that yield middle-ground solutions, rather than through an absolutist and often rigid judicial pronouncement'.[20]

Evaluation of the normative claims of popular constitutionalism is beyond the scope of this chapter.[21] However, these normative claims hint at the tantalising potential for popular constitutionalism to cut through some of the most intractable problems of constitutional interpretation. Originalist or textualist approaches risk committing polities to interpretations that no longer serve their needs. Yet more progressive interpretive theories can blur the line between constitutional principles, transient popular views and subjective preferences of those in power. Popular constitutionalism emphasises that constitutional development is both dynamic and incremental, offering a principled democratic justification for incremental change. This normative potential is another reason why it is worthwhile exploring the applicability of popular constitutional theory to Australia.

16 Devins (n 1) 162.

17 See Miguel Schor, 'Constitutional Dialogue and Judicial Supremacy' (Research Paper No 10-66, Suffolk University Law School, December 2010) 8–12, doi.org/10.2139/ssrn.1730202.

18 William N Eskridge, Jr and Philip P Frickey, 'The Supreme Court 1993 Term; Foreword: Law as Equilibrium' (1994) 108 *Harvard Law Review* 26, doi.org/10.2307/1341990.

19 Friedman (n 12) 652.

20 Devins (n 1) ch 3.

21 For some relevant critiques, see Robert Post and Reva Siegel, 'Roe Rage: Democratic Constitutionalism and Backlash' (2007) 42 *Harvard Civil Rights-Civil Liberties Law Review* 373 ('Roe Rage'); Bateup (n 10).

II. Popular constitutionalism in Australia?

Can the insights of popular constitutionalism apply in Australia? This question has been considered by only a few Australian scholars, in relation to specific problems rather than at a general level.[22]

For anyone familiar with Australian constitutional law, there are several reasons to doubt the relevance of popular constitutionalism for Australia. In this section, I identify the most obvious objections and argue these objections are not as great as they first appear.

A. Ignorance and apathy

The most obvious obstacle to popular constitutionalism applying in Australia is the widespread ignorance of the Australian Constitution. As Sarah Sorial explains in Chapter 13 of this volume, Australians have limited understanding or even awareness of the Constitution and the role of the High Court. It seems fanciful to expect Australian people to make a meaningful contribution to the development of constitutional law when they do not understand what the Constitution does.

But popular constitutionalism offers a way of contesting the claim that people who do not know about the technicalities of the Constitution cannot contribute to its interpretation. Popular constitutional theory shows that a person can contribute to constitutional interpretation without necessarily identifying their opinions as *constitutional* opinions. People do express opinions about the proper role of governments, even when they do not frame their opinions in that way. A person who votes for a candidate promising tough law-and-order policies expresses their opinion about the appropriate balance between liberty and security. If thousands of people vote for candidates with such policies over a period of decades, it may be possible to draw a conclusion that a large section of the Australian people holds a similar opinion about the proper extent of government interference in liberties.

22 Brendan Lim, *Australia's Constitution after Whitlam* (Cambridge University Press, 2017); Lael K Weis, 'Constitutional Amendment Rules and Interpretive Fidelity to Democracy' (2014) 38(1) *Melbourne University Law Review* 240; Bateup (n 10).

There is also an argument that the very apathy of Australian people reflects an acceptance of the constitutional status quo. History and experience show that if people are deeply dissatisfied with the structure of government in their country, they tend to take action. This action may range from self-education about the content of the constitution and methods of changing it, to outright revolution. The lack of interest in Australia's constitution may be a sign that, for most Australians, the constitutional arrangements work tolerably well most of the time.

This is not to deny that sections of the Australian community are systemically disadvantaged by existing constitutional arrangements. Nor is it to diminish the intense efforts of some groups within the community to bring about constitutional change. This book highlights two movements towards change: the reforms proposed in the Uluru Statement from the Heart, and the long-running republican movement. But, as we will see, even the most carefully developed cases for change have struggled to secure the community support needed for a successful referendum. While there have been outspoken critics of these reforms, the real enemy has been ignorance and apathy. For many Australians, it seems, constitutional change is not a high priority.

B. Legalism

A second reason for doubting the applicability of popular constitutional theory to Australia is the dominance of the legalist method of constitutional interpretation. Sir Owen Dixon's famous endorsement of 'strict and complete legalism'[23] continues to be cited with approval by the High Court.[24] Legalism emphasises the text of the Constitution, together with the circumstances in which the text was written and the common law and statutory history preceding writing the text.[25] Strict legalism would seem to limit the possibility of the High Court considering contemporary public opinion and values.[26]

23 Sir Owen Dixon, Speech upon Appointment as Chief Justice, reported at (1952) 85 CLR xiv.

24 For examples of approving citation by more recent courts, see Tanya Josev, *The Campaign against the Courts: A History of the Judicial Activism Debate* (Federation Press, 2017) 113 n 95.

25 The most well-known statement of this method appears in *Amalgamated Society of Engineers v Adelaide Steamship Co Ltd* (1920) 28 CLR 129, 152 (Knox CJ, Isaacs, Rich and Starke JJ) ('*Engineers Case*').

26 Elisa Arcioni and Adrienne Stone, 'The Small Brown Bird: Values and Aspirations in the Australian Constitution' (2016) 14(1) *International Journal of Constitutional Law* 60, 76, doi.org/10.1093/icon/mow003.

But this objection may be overstated. Legalism does not *completely* foreclose all consideration of values that are not explicit in the constitutional text. In practice (as opposed to in an abstract, caricatured form), legalism can accommodate elements of creativity and values-based reasoning. Leslie Zines pointed out, with reference to the work of the Dixon Court:

> whatever 'strict and complete legalism' referred to, it was not inconsistent with the finding of some large implications in the Constitution, with attributing broad social and economic purposes to particular provisions, or with the application of external theories and concepts in constitutional interpretation.[27]

Even if legalism does limit the influence of values and public opinion on constitutional interpretation, legalism is not the only method of constitutional interpretation used by the High Court. Legalism may be the orthodoxy, but the history of the High Court is peppered with examples of progressive, realist and functional reasoning as well as countless judgments that do not fit neatly into any single interpretive category. The truth, as Callinan J pointed out, is that 'no judge can claim to stride the high ground of exclusive interpretative orthodoxy'.[28] In short, legalism may present an impediment to applying popular constitutional theory, but not an absolute bar.

Perhaps it is unsurprising that legalism has been unable to answer all questions when applied to a constitution with so few words to work with. The language of Australia's constitution is spare and sometimes ambiguous. Such language is typical of constitutions that are designed to endure for decades and centuries.[29] The very 'spaciousness' of constitutional language invites interpretation, value judgments and change over time.[30]

Australia's legal culture poses another obstacle to popular constitutionalism. While legalist *method* makes it hard for the High Court to incorporate values and public opinion in their judgments, legalist *style* makes it difficult for everyday Australians to understand the High Court's constitutional decisions. Even when the substance of a judgment is not an example of strict and complete legalism, the form and language of the judgment will be pitched to a legal audience. Constitutional judgments are typically dry, technical and

27 Leslie Zines, 'Legalism, Realism and Judicial Rhetoric in Constitutional Law: 2002 Sir Maurice Byers Lecture' (2002) *Bar News* 13, 14.

28 *New South Wales v Commonwealth* (2006) 229 CLR 1, 301–4.

29 See Aharon Barak, *Purposive Interpretation in Law*, tr Sara Bashi (Princeton University Press, 2005) 372.

30 See Friedman (n 12) 649.

dispassionate in tone.[31] Appeals to emotion or popular sentiment are rare. The High Court's practice, since 2006, of publishing one-page, plain English, judgment summaries goes some way towards ameliorating this situation, but these summaries usually focus on the facts and outcome of each case, offering limited insight into the constitutional reasoning. Nor are these summaries necessarily pitched at a non-legal audience.

C. Judicial appointments

A further possible check on the application of constitutional theory is the relatively apolitical process of appointing judges in Australia. US Supreme Court judges are nominated by the US president and subject to Senate approval.[32] These processes create opportunities for dialogue on constitutional values between elected representatives and (future) members of the Court, and between the president and the Senate. This has made the appointments process one of the most direct drivers of popular constitutionalism in the US.[33] As Neal Devins observes, 'the [P]resident and the Senate both recognize that the best way to shape outputs (Court rulings) is to control inputs (ie, to control who sits on the Court)'.[34]

Judicial appointments in Australia are far less politicised. High Court judges are formally appointed by the Governor-General on the advice of the Executive Council.[35] In practice, the selection is made by the Attorney-General and approved by Cabinet. Beyond an obligation to 'consult' with the attorneys-general of the States,[36] there are no legislative requirements governing the process. In sharp contrast to the US, the legislature is not involved. George Williams has observed that the appointment process 'gives an unfettered power to the executive' with 'no transparency and little accountability'.[37] There is no public scrutiny of candidates before appointment. There is virtually no input from the general public.

31 Though not always. Exceptions include Brennan J in *Mabo v Queensland (No 2)* (1992) 175 CLR 1 and Heydon J in *Monis v The Queen* (2013) 249 CLR 92.

32 *United States Constitution* art II § 2(2).

33 Devins (n 1) 104; Michael J Gerhardt, 'The Federal Appointments Process as Constitutional Interpretation' in Neal Devins and Keith E Whittington (eds), *Congress and the Constitution* (Duke University Press, 2005) 110, doi.org/10.2307/j.ctv11smpx5.9.

34 Devins (n 1) 28.

35 *Australian Constitution* s 72(i).

36 *High Court of Australia Act 1979* (Cth) s 6.

37 George Williams, 'High Court Appointments: The Need for Reform' (2008) 30 *Sydney Law Review* 163. More recent calls for reform have followed the findings that Dyson Heydon sexually harassed staff members at the High Court. See Letter from Gabrielle Appleby (signed by more than 500 women in the legal profession) to Christian Porter (Attorney-General), 6 July 2020.

Despite this, appointments to Australia's High Court have, at least for the past 40 years, generally been politically uncontroversial. For the most part, judges are not seen as political actors. Few High Court judges are household names outside the legal profession. High Court judges are most commonly drawn from the ranks of serving judges and leading barristers. Even when a judge has publicly known political leanings, this is not usually seen as affecting their ability to decide cases according to law. For example, Chief Justice Robert French stood as a candidate for the Liberal Party in the 1969 federal election; yet he was appointed to the High Court by a Labor government in 2008, with no suggestion that his politics would affect his role on the Court. David Solomon has identified resistance, in Australia's 'political and legal culture', to governments appointing judges 'sympathetic to their own philosophies'.[38]

Yet the overall picture is more complex. It would be inaccurate to say that judicial appointments in Australia are completely apolitical. In the first 75 years of federation, it was reasonably common for members of the government of the day to be appointed to the High Court.[39] The last and, with hindsight, the most controversial of these was federal Attorney-General Lionel Murphy, appointed to the Court in 1975.[40] Since then, governments have eschewed appointments that may be seen as party-political. But throughout the history of federation, Australian governments have used High Court appointments:

> to affirm the direction of the Court's jurisprudence as within the bounds of majority or community opinion, by appointing a judge with a similar legal or political philosophy; or else to seek to redirect the course of the Court's decisions, by appointing a judge who is known to favour a distinctive approach to interpretation.[41]

38 David Solomon, *The Political High Court* (Allen & Unwin, 1999) 220.

39 For a description of this history and an analysis of its decline, see Douglas McDonald, 'Worlds Apart: The Appointment of Former Politicians as Judges' (2016) 41(1) *Alternative Law Journal* 17, doi.org/10.1177/1037969X1604100105.

40 For an account of the controversy, see Tony Blackshield, 'Murphy Affair' in Michael Coper, Tony Blackshield and George Williams (eds), *The Oxford Companion to the High Court of Australia* (Oxford Reference, Online, 2007).

41 Rosalind Dixon and George Williams, 'Introduction' in Rosalind Dixon and George Williams (eds), *The High Court, the Constitution and Australian Politics* (Cambridge University Press, 2015) 1, 11, doi.org/10.1017/CBO9781107445253.

Similarly, political scientist Paul Donegan contends 'that Australian governments have at times appointed candidates with judicial approaches and outlooks similar to their own and that this is to some extent inevitable'.[42]

There are two prominent examples of High Court appointments being used to influence the course of constitutional interpretation in Australia: Callinan and Heydon JJ. The so-called 'Mason Court' of the early to mid-1990s made a string of innovative decisions in constitutional and common law cases, employing a more progressive, less realist approach to constitutional interpretation. The Howard government, in power between 1996 and 2007, made a practice of appointing 'black letter' judges to push the Court back towards the legalist orthodoxy.[43] In 1997, Deputy Prime Minister Tim Fischer said the next High Court appointment would be a 'capital C conservative'.[44] Justice Callinan, appointed in 1998, was that person, having been publicly critical of 'judicial activism' and the Mason Court's departure from orthodox judicial method.[45] Justice Heydon, appointed in 2003, was renowned as a black letter lawyer; his speech at a *Quadrant* magazine function, provocatively entitled 'Judicial Activism and the Death of the Rule of Law',[46] is regarded as his 'job interview' for the High Court.

More recently, the Court's controversial decision in *Love v Commonwealth* ('*Love*')[47] prompted an unusual degree of scrutiny into the link between Court appointments and constitutional interpretation. Journalist Chris Merritt pointed out that three of the four majority judges were Coalition appointees. Merritt and others[48] argued the government should use its upcoming appointments to steer the Court in a more conservative, less 'activist' direction.[49]

42 Paul Donegan, 'The Role of the Commonwealth Attorney-General in Appointing Judges to the High Court of Australia' (2003) 29 *Melbourne Journal of Politics* 40, 43.
43 See ibid; Benjamin Jellis, 'The High Court Under Howard' (Samuel Griffith Society).
44 Nikki Savva, 'Fischer Seeks a More Conservative Court', *The Age* (Melbourne), 5 March 1997, 1–2.
45 See Josev (n 24) 168–9.
46 Dyson Heydon, 'Judicial Activism and the Death of the Rule of Law' (2003) 47(1) *Quadrant* 9.
47 (2020) 270 CLR 152 ('*Love*').
48 See, eg, Morgan Begg, 'Activist Judges Misrepresent Mabo to Create Privileged Class', *The Australian* (online, 12 February 2020) <www.theaustralian.com.au/commentary/activist-judges-misrepresent-mabo-to-create-privileged-class/news-story/6c9d0372378f803a16ef6c68067bc2b1>.
49 Chris Merritt, 'Judging the High Court's Justices', *The Australian* (online, 19 February 2020) <www.theaustralian.com.au/inquirer/judging-the-high-courts-justices/news-story/6c819b096c60180d761d0ca9ab38b2eb>.

To sum up, the nature of the appointment process in Australia may mean the 'political calculus'[50] that informs appointment decisions is often opaque. This avenue of communication between the Australian people and the element of the dialogue process is, therefore, more subtle and less visible in Australia than in the US; yet it is still present. Ultimately, High Court appointments may have a comparable effect on constitutional interpretation to the US, but, as explained in the next section, with a more limited range of issues on which to express different constitutional views.

D. Bill of rights

Now we come to a major difference between the US and Australian constitutions: the absence, in the Australian Constitution, of a bill of rights.

The US Bill of Rights is a major site of public debate, and the Supreme Court's interpretation of these provisions inevitably engages with the values of the community. It is easy for laypeople to hold and express opinions about the meaning of constitutional expressions such as 'due process' and 'freedom of speech'. Laypeople can, therefore, engage with and critique Supreme Court decisions interpreting those words. Robert Post and Reva Siegel point out that the Bill of Rights contains contestable, 'open-ended' provisions that express 'national ideals' about matters such as freedom and equality.[51] Judicial interpretation of these provisions, therefore, can 'provoke popular resistance because they are topics about which Americans disagree and care passionately'.[52] The Supreme Court's decisions are not just for lawyers and litigants; they reach 'a much wider audience outside the Court and beyond the particular parties to litigation'.[53]

By contrast, Australia's constitution is devoted to structural matters that seem dry and technical even to those who are interested in law and politics. The totemic cases in Australian constitutional law are about the extent of Commonwealth legislative power and the separation of judicial power—hardly matters to set the layperson's pulse racing. Even the cases about the implied freedom of political communication and the implied right to vote tend to be couched in technical, legal language, virtually impenetrable to the non-lawyer.

50 Ibid.

51 Post and Siegel, 'Roe Rage' (n 21) 378.

52 Ibid 378–9.

53 Andrew Lynch, 'Introduction—What Makes a Dissent "Great"?' in Andrew Lynch (ed), *Great Australian Dissents* (Cambridge University Press, 2016) 1, 17, doi.org/10.1017/CBO9781316665824.

But, once again, this factor should not be exaggerated. When a High Court case receives media attention, it is presented in terms that the general public can understand. And some High Court decisions *do* provoke a public reaction, especially those decisions that implicate national identity or contestable moral values. The Court's decisions on native title in *Mabo v Queensland (No 2)* ('*Mabo (No 2)*')[54] and *Wik Peoples v Queensland* ('*Wik*')[55] made a significant impression on the national psyche, with *Mabo (No 2)* earning a reference in that iconic distillation of Australian identity, *The Castle*.[56] More recently, *Love*,[57] in which the Court held Aboriginal people could not be aliens in Australia, received extensive attention in the general media. Some reporting was positive, seeing the decision as an affirmation of the connection of First Nations to Australia.[58] Others saw the decision as protecting foreign criminals and creating unwelcome race-based distinctions.[59] Another recent example is *Re Canavan* ('*Citizenship 7 Case*')[60] in which the High Court held five members of Parliament were disqualified from sitting by virtue of s 44(1) of the Constitution. The s 44 controversy sparked many discussions (beyond the legal community) about the appropriateness, in a modern multicultural society, of disqualifying dual citizens from Parliament, and the need for constitutional reform.[61]

54 (1992) 175 CLR 1 ('*Mabo (No 2)*').

55 *Wik Peoples v Queensland* (1996) 187 CLR 1 ('*Wik*').

56 Although *Mabo (No 2)* and *Wik* were not concerned with the text of the Constitution, these cases may be considered 'small c' constitutional, in that they concern the fundamental legal framework of the Australian government.

57 *Love* (n 47).

58 See, eg, Aiesha Saunders, 'High Court Rules Indigenous Australians Cannot Be Deported', *The Sydney Morning Herald* (online, 11 February 2020) <www.smh.com.au/politics/federal/high-court-rules-indigenous-australians-cannot-be-deported-20200211-p53znd.html>; Stan Grant, 'The High Court Has Widened the Horizon on What It Is to Be Indigenous and Belong to Australia', *ABC News* (online, 15 February 2020) <www.abc.net.au/news/2020-02-15/unresolved-question-of-indigenous-sovereignty-haunts-australia/11962834>.

59 See, eg, Jennifer Oriel, 'High Court's Racist Ruling is a Low Blow to Equality and Democracy', *The Australian* (online, 6 February 2020) <www.theaustralian.com.au/commentary/high-courts-racist-ruling-is-a-low-blow-to-equality-and-democracy/news-story/2d67f520cf615f57564a14343d01577d>; John Roskam, 'Why the Aboriginal Citizenship Ruling is Alien to All Ideas of Law', *Australian Financial Review* (online, 20 February 2020) <www.afr.com/politics/federal/why-the-aboriginal-citizenship-ruling-is-alien-to-all-ideas-of-law-20200220-p542o6>.

60 (2017) 263 CLR 284 ('*Citizenship 7 Case*').

61 See, eg, Michelle Grattan, 'View from The Hill: Section 44 Remains a Constitutional Trip Wire that Should be Addressed', *The Conversation* (online, 14 April 2019) <theconversation.com/view-from-the-hill-section-44-remains-a-constitutional-trip-wire-that-should-be-addressed-115435>; Robert Angyal, 'Section 44 of the Constitution Means NOBODY is Eligible to be Elected to Parliament', *Huffington Post* (online, 16 August 2017) <www.huffingtonpost.com.au/robert-angyal/section-44-of-the-constitution-means-nobody-is-eligible-to-be-el_a_23078667/>.

The attention generated by cases such as these suggests that, despite the lack of a bill of rights, the Australian Constitution does throw up issues that touch a chord in the Australian people. For the most part, morally contestable issues of great interest to the Australian people are debated in the forum of normal, rather than constitutional, politics. When these issues have a constitutional dimension, the Australian people are quite capable of forming and expressing opinions about the desirable content of the law. As argued above, the people's silence on most constitutional issues may be evidence of widespread satisfaction with the structural aspects of the Constitution.

III. An example: Implied right to vote cases

The analysis so far suggests that there is, at least, a possibility that popular constitutionalism could be an analytical tool with some relevance to Australia. To show how this might work, I will consider how popular constitutionalism might give us some insights into the 'implied right to vote' cases: *Roach*[62] and *Rowe*.[63]

In *Roach* and *Rowe*, the High Court struck down amendments to Commonwealth electoral laws on the basis that the laws infringed a constitutional guarantee of universal adult franchise. This guarantee was derived from the words of ss 7 and 24 of the Constitution, which provide that members of the federal Parliament are to be 'chosen by the people'. In *Roach*, the law excluded from voting any person serving a sentence of imprisonment. In *Rowe*, the law abridged the 'grace period', following the issue of writs for an election, during which a person could enrol to vote or change their details on the roll.

These cases raised a classic dilemma of constitutional interpretation. At federation, universal adult franchise (as we would understand that concept today) was clearly not the norm in Australia. The voting age was 21. Women had the right to vote in South Australia and Western Australia, but not in other States. Different colonies excluded people from voting for reasons including race, receipt of charitable funds, commission of particular

62 *Roach* (n 2).

63 *Rowe* (n 3).

categories of offence, and membership of the police or armed forces.[64] The 'grace period' at issue in *Rowe* was not mentioned in the Constitution, and was not a statutory requirement until as late as 1983.[65] Therefore, the High Court's decisions in *Roach* and *Rowe* held that certain features of the electoral system were now constitutionally mandated, even though they had not been constitutional requirements when the Constitution was drafted. These decisions clearly depended on an interpretation of ss 7 and 24 that took into account social and legislative developments since 1901.

In *Roach*, a majority of the High Court[66] held invalid a 2006 amendment to the *Commonwealth Electoral Act 1918* (Cth) disqualifying all prisoners serving a sentence from voting. The Court unanimously held that the legislative provisions in place *before* the 2006 amendments—disqualifying any prisoner serving a sentence of three years or more—were valid.

The majority judgments accepted that the content of constitutional principles could change over time. Gummow, Kirby and Crennan JJ referred to the 'evolutionary' and 'dynamic rather than purely static' nature of the institutions of representative government created by the Constitution.[67] Gleeson CJ stated that 'the words of ss 7 and 24, because of changed historical circumstances including legislative history, have come to be a constitutional protection of the right to vote'.[68] The majority concluded the words 'chosen by the people' had come to mandate universal adult franchise, subject to exceptions justified by a proportionality test.

These judgments might be seen as an example of popular constitutionalism in Australia. The Court's interpretation of the words 'chosen by the people' relied on broadly held values that had evolved since federation. While it may once have been acceptable to exclude large swathes of the population from the franchise, this was no longer the case. How did the Court ascertain these values? As Hayne J (in dissent) pointed out, if constitutional meaning was to depend on 'generally accepted Australian standards', 'there is the obvious difficulty of determining what those standards are, and to what extent they

64 See Anne Twomey, 'The Federal Constitutional Right to Vote in Australia' (2000) 28(1) *Federal Law Review* 125, 144–5, doi.org/10.22145/flr.28.1.6; *Roach* (n 2) 213–5 (Hayne J).

65 *Commonwealth Electoral Legislation Amendment Act 1983* (Cth). Until that point, the 'grace period' had been created informally by an executive practice of announcing the election several days prior to issuing the writs: see *Rowe* (n 3) 30–2 [57–61] (French CJ).

66 Gleeson CJ, Gummow, Kirby and Crennan JJ, Hayne and Heydon JJ dissenting.

67 *Roach* (n 2) 186–7 [45] (Gummow, Kirby and Crennan JJ).

68 174 [7].

are "generally accepted"'.[69] The mechanisms by which 'the people' had expressed these values were not defined with precision, but at least included the legislative developments to which Gleeson CJ referred.[70] Lael K Weis has argued that the use of legislation in this case to set a 'constitutional baseline'[71] is defensible as a relatively objective proxy for community views on moral questions.[72] Similarly, popular constitutional theory would characterise this reliance on legislation as the Court incorporating widely held community views, as expressed in legislation passed by elected representatives.

Hayne J's dissent in *Roach* is illuminating for its resistance to the elements of the majority judgments that might be described as examples of popular constitutionalism. Hayne J rejected the proposition that the Commonwealth Parliament's power to legislate for voter qualifications 'is constrained by what may, from time to time, be identified as politically accepted or acceptable limits'.[73] His Honour continued:

> Political acceptance and political acceptability find no footing in accepted doctrines of constitutional construction. The meaning of constitutional standards does not vary with the level of popular acceptance that particular applications of the power might enjoy.[74]

This passage encapsulates the resistance we might expect popular constitutional theory to encounter in Australia. It is difficult to fit a version of constitutional interpretation that incorporates the popular will within a text-based, legalist model of interpretation in which the judiciary enjoys unquestioned supremacy. But equally significantly, this was a minority view. For the majority, the constitutional concept of choice by 'the people' could, and did, change over time.

The majority judgments in *Roach* met some sharp academic criticism.[75] Critics saw the judgments as ahistorical and contrary to legalist principle. Nicholas Aroney described the majority judgments as relying, to a significant

69 Ibid 219 [158].
70 This included legislation extending the franchise to women and Indigenous people. See ibid 173 [5].
71 That is, a standard against which State action may be evaluated for compliance with constitutional requirements: Lael K Weis, *Legislative Constitutional Baselines* (2019) 41(4) *Sydney Law Review* 481, 482.
72 Ibid 510–2.
73 *Roach* (n 2) 219 [159].
74 Ibid.
75 James Allan, 'The Three "Rs" of Recent Australian Judicial Activism: Roach, Rowe and (No)'Riginalism' (2012) 36(2) *Melbourne University Law Review* 743; Nicholas Aroney, 'Towards the "Best Explanation" of the Constitution: Text, Structure, History and Principle in *Roach v Electoral Commissioner*' (2011) 30(1) *University of Queensland Law Journal* 145.

extent, on 'freestanding ethical and prudential judgments' with only 'minimal' and selective attention to the reasoning's 'fit' with 'authoritative sources of law (text, structure, and doctrine, illuminated by history)'.[76] James Allan went further, criticising both *Roach* and its successor, *Rowe*, as 'prime examples of judicial activism'[77] resting on 'the most implausible and far-fetched understanding of the meaning of the *Australian Constitution*'.[78] Allan was critical of Gleeson CJ's reliance on legislation to inform the interpretation of the Constitution, considering it 'odd' that 'past legislation can alter the Constitution's meaning'.[79]

Three years later, the High Court revisited these issues in *Rowe*. French CJ's explanation of the relationship between legislation and constitutional interpretation provides an even clearer example of how popular constitutional theory might operate in Australia. His Honour reaffirmed that the concept of 'chosen by the people' could evolve over time, and that the content of that concept depended on 'the common understanding of the time'.[80] His Honour expanded on this theme:

> The term 'common understanding', as an indication of constitutional meaning in this context, is not to be equated to judicial understanding. Durable legislative development of the franchise is a more reliable touchstone. It reflects a persistent view by the elected representatives of the people of what the term 'chosen by the people' requires.[81]

This passage eschews the criticism that, when purporting to interpret the Constitution in line with changing values, judges are really drawing on their own subjective views. In French CJ's view, legislation offers an objective way of ascertaining community values. But it is only *durable* legislative developments that can be taken into account in constitutional interpretation.

French CJ's approach in *Rowe* has been criticised for 'attribut[ing] power to the Parliament to change the meaning of the Constitution'.[82] Certainly, this approach is difficult to square with strict legalism. But popular constitutional

---

76 Aroney (n 75) 149.
77 Allan (n 75) 744.
78 Ibid 745.
79 Ibid 768.
80 *Rowe* (n 3) 18 [18], quoting *Attorney-General (Cth); Ex rel McKinlay v The Commonwealth* (1975) 135 CLR 1, 36 (McTiernan and Jacobs JJ) ('*McKinlay*').
81 *Rowe* (n 3) 18 [19].
82 Anne Twomey, '*Rowe v Electoral Commissioner*—Evolution or Creationism?' (2012) 31 *University of Queensland Law Journal* 181, 190.

theory provides a different way of understanding the judgment (and, indeed, the approach of Gleeson CJ in *Roach*). When Parliament enacts legislation, that legislation can be seen as expressing the community's current values. For French CJ, this expression only gains constitutional significance once it has endured for some (admittedly imprecise) time, with the community's continued acquiescence indicating that the values expressed in the legislation have remained acceptable, or at least not objectionable, to the community over time.

The manner in which *Rowe* came before the Court also has significance from the point of view of popular constitutional theory. The plaintiffs, two students affected by the removal of the 'grace period',[83] might in ordinary circumstances have lacked the resources to pursue a High Court challenge. The litigation was, in effect, initiated and run by an online-based political action group, GetUp!, which 'crowdfunded' the action through donations, as part of a broader campaign to encourage enrolment.[84] This shows the potential for individuals and organisations to contribute to constitutional interpretation by bringing a case before the Court. The people who donated their money may not have thought of themselves as expressing a constitutional viewpoint. But they may well have disagreed with the version of representative government embodied in the impugned legislation and had their own preference for a more inclusive franchise. A sufficiently large group of people felt strongly enough to donate their money so the High Court could rule on these competing constitutional visions.

From this brief analysis, we can see that the 'right to vote' cases might fit within a broader context of High Court jurisprudence articulating a distinctly Australian version of democracy. How might popular constitutionalism help us to understand cases on the implied freedom of political communication,[85] equality of voting franchise[86] and disqualification of members of Parliament under s 44 of the Constitution?[87] What would this tell us about the way the High Court has collaborated with the Australian people to mould a modern, independent Australian democracy?

83 One of the plaintiffs was an 18-year-old who had not enrolled to vote by the time the rolls closed; the other had moved to a different electorate since enrolling to vote and had not updated his details on the roll.
84 GetUp!'s role in the 2010 election campaign generally, and *Rowe* specifically, is analysed in Ariadne Vromen and William Coleman, 'Online Movement Mobilisation and Electoral Politics: The Case of Getup!' (2011) 44 *Communication, Politics and Culture* 76.
85 See, eg, *Lange v Australian Broadcasting Corporation* (1997) 189 CLR 520.
86 *McKinlay* (n 80); *McGinty v Western Australia* (1996) 186 CLR 140.
87 See, eg, *Sue v Hill* (1999) 199 CLR 462; *Re Canavan* (2017) 263 CLR 284.

IV. Conclusion

Despite some unpromising first impressions, I believe Australian constitutional law demonstrates some traces of an Australian version of popular constitutionalism. Popular constitutionalism will not look the same in Australia as in the US. But it may nonetheless offer new insights into Australian constitutional law. From the (admittedly selective) example of the right to vote cases, we can see how popular constitutional theory might give us a new way of reading Australian constitutional cases. Popular constitutional theory gives us an alternative to seeing these cases as either a poor example of legalism or as manifestations of judges' personal political views.

Finally, we should remember that Andrew Inglis Clark, writing in 1901, said the language of the Constitution:

> must be read and construed, not as containing a declaration of the will and intentions of men long since dead, and who cannot have anticipated the problems that would arise for solution by future generations, but as declaring the will and intentions of the present inheritors of sovereign power … who are in the immediate presence of the problems to be solved. It is they who enforce the provisions of the Constitution and make a living force of that which would otherwise be a silent and lifeless document.[88]

Regardless of your view of the normative force of this position, the potential for the Australian people to drive an interpretation of the Constitution that serves the needs and meets the standards of the present day has been present since the creation of the document.

88 Andrew Inglis Clark, *Studies in Australian Constitutional Law* (Legal Books, 1997) 21.

4

Building National Identity through the Constitution: The Canadian *Charter* Experience

Lorne Neudorf[1]

> Writers and poets have always searched for the Canadian identity ... But what is Canada itself? With the charter in place, we can now say that Canada is a society where all people are equal and where they share some fundamental values based upon freedom. The search for this Canadian identity ... has led me to insist on the charter.
>
> — Pierre Elliot Trudeau, *Memoirs*

This book brings together leading scholars to consider a series of important questions on the relationship between constitutions and national identity. In their chapters, contributors discuss the possibility of future amendments to the Australian Constitution, what those amendments might look like and the effect they could have in shaping national identity. This is a creative, forward-looking conversation that grapples with fundamental questions of how Australia sees itself and what it aspires to become, both at home and in the world. This chapter adds a comparative dimension to this discussion by looking at the experience of the *Canadian Charter of Rights and Freedoms* (the '*Charter*').[2] It seeks to aid the deliberation by providing an example

1 The author thanks Olga Pandos for her research assistance. The standard disclaimer applies.
2 *Canada Act 1982* (UK) c 11, sch B pt I.

of a country that embarked on a journey to build national identity through a radical change to its Constitution. With the perspective gained from nearly 40 years since the *Charter* came into force, there are valuable lessons to be learnt from its successes, failures and unexpected outcomes.[3] This chapter will also consider whether the *Charter* has succeeded in achieving its nation-building goals and transforming Canada into the just society envisioned by its framers.

There is little doubt that the *Charter* has become strongly connected to Canadian national identity. It is recognised by Canadians as the most important symbol of their country, ranking above the flag, the national anthem and ice hockey.[4] The *Charter*'s perceived importance is hardly surprising in light of the seismic legal and political changes that it unleashed. The *Charter* reshaped the institutional balance of powers and produced many (sometimes divisive) changes to Canadian law, a process that continues to the present. It also sparked a paradigm shift in terms of thinking about law: at least half the content of the constitutional law courses taught at Canadian law schools focus on the *Charter*, while *Charter* issues make up about 50 per cent of the Supreme Court of Canada's case load.[5] Speaking from experience, it is challenging for Canadian law students to imagine that a legal issue might *not* involve the *Charter*! After almost four decades, politicians, jurists and academics continue to debate the role and meaning of the *Charter* and its rights and freedoms.

The Canadian *Charter* provides a useful comparator in considering potential changes to the Australian Constitution given a number of similarities between the two countries. Australia and Canada share a heritage of English common law, the Westminster parliamentary system, a partly written and partly unwritten constitution, and federalism. Both countries have been influenced by English and American legal traditions. Both have similar demographic profiles and advanced resource-based economies. And both countries face persistent challenges on the long road to reconciliation with

3 While the *Charter* came into force in 1982, the commencement of s 15, its equality guarantee, was delayed until 1985.

4 'Canadian Identity, 2013', *Statistics Canada* (Web Page) <www150.statcan.gc.ca/n1/pub/89-652-x/89-652-x2015005-eng.htm>. But for a competing perspective see Nik Nanos, 'Charter Values Don't Equal Canadian Values: Strong Support for Same-Sex and Property Rights' (February 2007) *Policy Options* 50, 55: 'Canadians generally support the Charter, but don't see it as essential to their Canadian values or identity' at 55.

5 Because of the *Charter*'s strong legal rights protections, many *Charter* cases arise in the context of criminal proceedings: see 'Decisions and Resources', *Supreme Court of Canada* (Web Page) <scc-csc.lexum.com/scc-csc/en/nav.do>.

their First Nations peoples. Despite these similarities, there are also some key differences between Australia and Canada. The *Charter* experience must therefore be appropriately contextualised. Accordingly, this chapter does not argue in favour of Australia adopting the *Charter* model of rights or any particular *Charter* provision.[6] Through a *Charter* case study, it instead seeks to provide a better understanding of the *process* that is involved in using constitutional change to build national identity, highlight some of the potential outcomes of that process and offer an evidence-based jumping off point for discussions about Australia's constitutional future. It also makes two interrelated claims. First, constitutions *can* contribute to building a new sense of national identity over time. Second, the way in which constitutions ultimately shape national identity *cannot* be entirely controlled or even accurately predicted from the outset.

I. Trudeau's constitutional vision: A just society

Ever since the pivotal English victory over the French on the Plains of Abraham in 1759, the question of Quebec's position in British North America, and later Canada, has loomed large in politics and law. The strained relationship between Anglophone and Francophone communities, the 'two solitudes', has presented an ongoing challenge to the development of a Canadian identity. Pierre Elliott Trudeau, a charismatic Quebec lawyer and professor, faced a severe crisis that threatened to break up the country after becoming prime minister in 1968.[7] Starting in the early 1960s, the Front de libération du Québec, a separatist paramilitary group, had carried out hundreds of attacks and bombings, mainly in the English-speaking suburbs of Montreal and at federal offices. The violence culminated with the October 1970 kidnapping of a British diplomat and the killing of the Quebec deputy premier. The wisdom of Trudeau's use of martial law, which suspended the civil liberties of millions of Canadians to give police greater powers

6 Although some scholars have held up the *Charter* as an innovative constitutional model that can serve as a template for others: see, eg, Lorraine Weinrib, 'Canada's Constitutional Revolution: From Legislative to Constitutional State' (1999) 33(1) *Israel Law Review* 13, doi.org/10.1017/S0021223700015880.

7 Pierre Trudeau served as Canada's prime minister from 1968 to 1979 and again from 1980 to 1984.

to stamp out the separatist violence, continues to be debated by scholars.[8] The October Crisis played a role in the formation of the Parti Québécois to advance Quebec sovereignty peacefully through the political process. In 1976, the Parti Québécois won a majority government in Quebec, and, in 1980, it held a referendum asking Quebecers whether they would support secession from Canada. The proposal was rejected by 59.6 per cent of voters.

During the referendum campaign, Trudeau became the chief spokesman for the 'no' side, promising that he would patriate the Canadian Constitution from the United Kingdom and enact a bill of rights if sovereignty was defeated.[9] Several prime ministers had previously attempted to bring home the Constitution but failed because of intractable federalism disputes with the provinces. Trudeau was not dissuaded. He saw the potential of constitutional patriation to move Canada beyond a society that was still largely a relic of British colonial history and that remained divided along English/French and European/Aboriginal lines:

> The Canadian nation is composed of citizens who belong to minorities of many kinds: linguistic, ethnic, racial, religious, regional and so on … Canadian history has consisted of a difficult advance toward a national unity that is still fragile and is often threatened by intolerance—the intolerance of the English speaking majority toward francophones, the intolerance of whites toward the indigenous populations and non-white immigrants, intolerance toward political and religious dissidents such as Communists and Jehovah's Witnesses.[10]

In Trudeau's view, a new constitutional arrangement could help build a more unified, modern and progressive country. According to Jean Chrétien, Trudeau's Minister of Justice and a key player in the design of the *Charter*, '[it] was time for people to take a stand'.[11] Bringing home the Constitution was intended to make Canadians masters of their own destiny and help develop

8 See, eg, William Tetley, *October Crisis 1970: An Insider's View* (McGill-Queen's University Press, 2007); Dominique Clément, 'The October Crisis of 1970: Human Rights Abuses under the *War Measures Act*' (2016) 42(2) *Journal of Canadian Studies* 160, doi.org/10.3138/jcs.42.2.160.

9 Pierre Trudeau made the promise during the referendum campaign: Jean Chrétien, 'Bringing the Constitution Home' in Thomas S Axworthy and Pierre Elliott Trudeau (eds), *Towards a Just Society: The Trudeau Years* (Viking Penguin, 1990) 282, 290. Trudeau had previously attempted but failed to patriate the Constitution with the Victoria Charter. Earlier prime ministers had made attempts since 1927, but could not obtain agreement from the provinces for a domestic constitutional amendment process, at 282–6.

10 Pierre Elliott Trudeau, 'The Values of a Just Society' in Thomas S Axworthy and Pierre Elliott Trudeau (eds), *Towards a Just Society: The Trudeau Years* (Viking Penguin, 1990) 357, 365–6 ('Just Society').

11 Chrétien (n 9) 285.

a new sense of national pride. It would also present an opportunity to move past historical divisions by writing down the shared values of Canadians.[12] Trudeau identified these values as including democracy, equality, diversity, mutual respect for difference and the multicultural heritage of Canadians.[13]

The first chapter of Canada's Constitution—the *British North America Act, 1867*[14]—had already been written. It was a foundational but sterile document establishing the mechanics of State institutions and allocating powers classed by subject matter to the federal and provincial legislatures. Trudeau referred to it as a deficient and 'inadequate' Constitution, holding 'little educative value ... [and] little that inspires patriotism'.[15] By contrast, the *Charter* was designed to be both inspirational and aspirational by guaranteeing fundamental rights to Canadians in the pursuit of a more egalitarian society.[16] The *Charter* would reflect 'the very nature of Canada',[17] and would 'lead to a new national spirit among Canadians to work for the creation of a richer life together'.[18]

Although Parliament enacted the *Canadian Bill of Rights*[19] in 1960 (which remains in force), the legislation was limited in its transformative effect. Its guarantees were construed narrowly by the courts and no individual remedies were available. Instead, the statute directed courts to interpret and apply federal laws in a manner that would be consistent with the enumerated rights.[20] Trudeau's vision for the *Charter* went far beyond this model. As part of the Constitution, the *Charter* would be enforceable by the courts as Canada's supreme law over inconsistent federal or provincial law. Its constitutional entrenchment would also guarantee a lasting legacy,

12 Pierre Elliott Trudeau, *Memoirs* (McClelland & Stewart, 1993) 322, 366 ('*Memoirs*').

13 See generally, Pierre Elliott Trudeau, *A Time for Action: Toward the Renewal of the Canadian Federation* (Government of Canada, 1978) ('*A Time for Action*').

14 *British North America Act, 1867* (UK), c 3 (30 & 31 Vict), renamed the *Constitution Act, 1867* by the Schedule to the *Constitution Act, 1982* (n 2).

15 Trudeau, *A Time for Action* (n 13) 8.

16 The *Charter* includes some rights that apply exclusively to Canadians, such as voting and mobility rights, along with others that apply to everyone such as the protection against unreasonable search or seizure. At the *Charter*'s proclamation ceremony on 17 April 1982, Pierre Trudeau stated that the *Charter* 'defines the kind of country in which we wish to live': Pierre Elliott Trudeau, 'Remarks at the Proclamation Ceremony', *Library and Archives Canada* (Web Page, 17 April 1982) <www.canadahistory.com/sections/documents/leaders/Pierre_Trudeau/Patriation.html>.

17 Chrétien (n 9) 285.

18 Trudeau, *A Time for Action* (n 13) 13.

19 *Canadian Bill of Rights*, SC 1960, c 44.

20 Ibid s 2.

as it would become difficult to change under a series of new amendment formulae. In short, the *Charter* was designed to set in motion a legal, political and social transformation for the decades ahead.[21]

Underlying the *Charter* was Trudeau's vision of a just society. According to Trudeau, a just society was one that was based on individual freedom, in which each person enjoyed an equality of opportunity.[22] In order to provide and protect this freedom, individuals would hold 'basic rights that cannot be taken away by any government'.[23] The *Charter's* purpose was therefore to 'strengthen Canadian unity through the pursuit of ... freedom and equality'.[24] Trudeau's political philosophy had formed decades earlier in Montreal when he helped found *Cité Libre*, a magazine that published young intellectuals critical of Quebec politics.[25] Trudeau and the editors promoted federalism and liberal values through the magazine. By focusing on these values, the *Charter* was intended to unite Canadians and reverse a trend towards regionalism. Commenting on the state of the nation before the *Charter*, Trudeau wrote that:

> Canada, along with Switzerland, was already one of the two most decentralized countries on earth with respect to jurisdictions and public finances. However, the two countries being very different in size, Canada needed stronger bonds to hold the parts together. Furthermore, although the Swiss comprised four distinct nationalities, they had developed a common sense of belonging over many centuries and would speak without hesitation of the 'Swiss nation'. Canada, in contrast, had grown territorially as late as 1949, and its writers and politicians were still seeking a national identity. Edward Blake and Heni Bourassa, two of Canada's most brilliant parliamentarians, had both—forty years apart—deplored the absence of a pan-Canadian national feeling. Seventy years later, the provincial premiers would reject a draft preamble to the constitution because they considered the terms 'Canadian people' and 'Canadian nation' unacceptable![26]

21 See, eg, Michael Ignatieff, *The Rights Revolution* (Anasi Press, 2007).

22 Trudeau, 'Just Society' (n 10) 357–8. For a further description of the just society see Pierre Elliott Trudeau, *The Essential Trudeau* (McClelland & Stewart, 1998) 16–20.

23 Trudeau, *Memoirs* (n 12) 322.

24 Trudeau, 'Just Society' (n 10) 368.

25 Ibid 357.

26 Ibid 376.

Constitutional patriation would be harnessed by Trudeau in an attempt to pull the country together and build a new sense of national identity. The *Charter* would set out 'a system of values such as liberty, equality, and the rights of association that Canadians from coast to coast could share'.[27] It would seek to achieve a common standard of living, wealth redistribution, English and French as the official languages for federal services, equality and the protection of minorities and opportunity for all persons to prosper anywhere in the country.[28]

II. Transforming vision into legal text

It is rarely a straightforward matter to translate a constitutional vision into formal legal text. After encountering provincial opposition to constitutional change that would enlarge the role of the federal government, Trudeau bifurcated his vision to focus on a 'people's package' of patriation and the *Charter*.[29] A 'politician's package' to revisit federalism and the balance of power between the federal and provincial governments would have to wait.[30] The drafting of the *Charter* was assisted by an all-party joint committee, which heard from a broad range of individuals and groups over a period of three months.[31] In receiving submissions from more than 900 individuals and nearly 300 groups, and broadcasting its hearings on television, the committee generated substantial interest in the *Charter* and imbued its work with a sense of legitimacy.[32] It has been suggested that the entire project might have failed without this public support.[33] The committee made several changes to the proposed *Charter* text, including adding new protections for women and disabled persons. In light of a surprise 1981 Supreme Court of Canada ruling,[34] which recognised a constitutional

27 Trudeau, *Memoirs* (n 12) 322.
28 Adapted from Chrétien (n 9) 285.
29 Trudeau, *Memoirs* (n 12) 309.
30 Ibid.
31 For an overview of the proceedings, see Peter W Hogg and Annika Wang, 'The Special Joint Committee on the Constitution of Canada, 1980–81' (2017) 81 *Supreme Court Law Review* (2d) 3; Adam Dodek (ed), *The Charter Debates: The Special Joint Committee on the Constitution, 1980–81, and the Making of the Canadian Charter of Rights and Freedoms* (University of Toronto Press, 2018), doi.org/10.3138/9781442623934.
32 Hogg and Wang (n 31) 7.
33 Ibid 23, citing Deputy Minister of Justice Roger Tassé. Pierre Trudeau wrote that through the committee process, '[a] national constituency had been created in favour of the charter': Trudeau, *Memoirs* (n 12) 322.
34 *Reference Re Resolution to amend the Constitution* [1981] 1 SCR 753.

convention obliging the federal government to obtain a substantial degree of consent from the provinces for constitutional change, Trudeau met with provincial leaders, which resulted in further changes to the *Charter*.[35] The major change was the insertion of s 33, the 'notwithstanding clause', which permitted a legislature to exempt its laws from certain *Charter* rights for a period of up to five years, renewable indefinitely.[36] This 'kitchen accord' compromise, negotiated between Chrétien and two premiers, brought all of the provinces—except Quebec's formidable René Lévesque—on board. The final text of the *Charter* was then sent to the United Kingdom by a joint address of the Parliament of Canada to the Queen. While it was debated in Westminster,[37] the *Charter* was duly enacted without amendment as Schedule B of the *Canada Act 1982*,[38] which also terminated the United Kingdom's power to make further changes to the Canadian Constitution. In its place, Part V of the *Constitution Act, 1982* included new amendment formulae, which established procedural and political hurdles for making future constitutional changes, all of which would now take place in Canada.[39]

The Quebec government immediately rejected the *Constitution Act, 1982* and the *Charter*, denouncing the revised constitutional settlement as illegitimate given its lack of consent. For several years after the *Constitution Act, 1982* came into force, Quebec's legislature invoked s 33 to proclaim that all of its laws operated notwithstanding the *Charter*.[40] While Quebec's political rejection of the Constitution itself had no legal effect on its

35 The case was brought by several provincial governments on the basis of Pierre Trudeau's announcement that he would be willing to proceed with constitutional amendment unilaterally. While the majority of the Supreme Court of Canada held that there existed a convention of substantial provincial support for constitutional change, it was not legally enforceable: ibid 774–5.

36 While Pierre Trudeau opposed the notwithstanding clause, he was persuaded to accept it 'rather than give up the idea of a charter altogether': Trudeau, 'Just Society' (n 10) 372.

37 For example, during parliamentary debate Lord Carrington observed that the *Charter* 'is still contested by Quebec and by some of the indigenous peoples of Canada': United Kingdom, *Parliamentary Debates*, House of Lords, 18 March 1982, vol 428 col 758. Members of the House of Commons encouraged their colleagues 'not to nit-pick' the legislation as it was 'the concern of the Canadian people': United Kingdom, *Parliamentary Debates*, House of Commons, 17 February 1982, vol 18, col 327 (Kevin McNamara). The *Charter* was also held up as a 'magnificent modern statement of the human rights and freedoms which the common law countries of the world seek to maintain [and a] magnificent contribution to the jurisprudence of human rights': United Kingdom, *Parliamentary Debates*, House of Lords, 18 March 1982, vol 428, col 794 (Lord Scarman).

38 *Canada Act 1982* (n 2).

39 Ibid s 52(3) provides that amendments to the Constitution of Canada must be made exclusively in accordance with the amendment formulae prescribed therein.

40 Notably, Quebec had already put in place its own bill of rights that had been in force since 1976: *Quebec Charter of Human Rights and Freedoms*, CQLR, c C-12.

application in the province,[41] the situation was far from ideal in terms of developing a new sense of Canadian national identity. For the next decade, the federal government sought to obtain Quebec's support for the *Charter* through a series of new constitutional amendments to deal with outstanding federalism issues: the politician's package. Fresh rounds of talks led to two major proposals, both of which failed. First, the 1987 Meech Lake Accord would have increased provincial powers and further protected Quebec's linguistic and cultural heritage as a 'distinct society'. The Accord failed to gain the legislative consent required by the *Constitution Act, 1982* within the prescribed time limit, despite the support of Prime Minister Brian Mulroney and all provincial premiers.[42] The process by which the Accord had been created—namely, closed door meetings between the prime minister and the provincial leaders at a wilderness resort—was viewed as secretive and undemocratic. Speaking from retirement, Trudeau stated that he opposed the Accord on the basis that it would make Canada 'totally impotent' by divesting power from the federal government and handing it to the provinces.[43] Aboriginal groups felt excluded by both the process and the substance of the proposal. Elijah Harper, a First Nations lawmaker in Manitoba, played a decisive role in the defeat of the Accord by blocking its progression in that province.[44]

41 Quebec also claimed that it could veto the *Constitution Act, 1982*, but this argument was rejected by the unanimous Supreme Court of Canada in *Re: Objection by Quebec to a Resolution to amend the Constitution* [1982] 2 SCR 793.

42 For an overview of the Meech Lake Accord, including its political dynamics, see, eg, Patrick J Monahan, *Meech Lake: The Inside Story* (University of Toronto Press, 1991), doi.org/10.3138/9781487576691; Katherine E Swinton (ed), *Competing Constitutional Visions: The Meech Lake Accord* (Carswell, 1988); Pierre Fournier, *A Meech Lake Post-Mortem: Is Quebec Sovereignty Inevitable?* (McGill-Queen's University Press, 1991); Richard Simeon, 'Meech Lake and Shifting Conceptions of Canadian Federalism' (1988) 14(S) *Canadian Public Policy / Analyse de Politiques* 7, doi.org/10.2307/3551215; Katherine Swinton, 'Amending the Canadian Constitution: Lessons from Meech Lake' (1992) 42(2) *The University of Toronto Law Journal* 139, doi.org/10.2307/825875; Roderick A Macdonald, 'Meech Lake to the Contrary Notwithstanding (Part I)', (1991) 29 *Osgoode Hall Law Journal* 253; Louis Bruyere, 'Aboriginal Peoples and the Meech Lake Accord' (1988) 49 *Canadian Human Rights Yearbook* 49.

43 'Pierre Trudeau Comes Back to Tackle Meech Lake', *CBC Digital Archives* (Web Page) <www.cbc.ca/archives/entry/back-to-tackle-meech-lake> (site discontinued).

44 S 39(2) of the *Constitution Act, 1982* (n 2) imposes a three-year time limit for the requisite legislatures to adopt the amending resolution for the amendment to succeed. The period commenced when the National Assembly of Quebec adopted the resolution in 1987. In order for the resolution to come to the floor of the Manitoba Legislative Assembly nearly three years later, it required the unanimous consent of the members. This consent was not obtained because of the refusal of Elijah Harper. Notably, there remains some uncertainty about whether this timeline was actually applicable for an amendment package that included amendment proposals subject to different formulae: see, eg, FL Morton, 'How Not to Amend the Constitution' (1989) 12(4) *Canadian Parliamentary Review* 9.

The 1992 Charlottetown Accord was a second attempt by the federal government to secure Quebec's support for the *Constitution Act, 1982* and the *Charter*. While the Charlottetown Accord included constitutional reforms similar to Meech Lake, it also proposed to enhance the recognition of Aboriginal peoples and their right to self-government. In relation to national identity, it included a new provision that would have required the Constitution to be interpreted according to a list of Canadian values that included parliamentary democracy, federalism, Aboriginal peoples and self-government, Quebec's distinct society and culture including the *Code civil du Québec*,[45] linguistic minorities, racial and ethnic equality, diversity and multiculturalism, individual and collective rights and freedoms, and provincial equality with respect for different regional characteristics.[46] While not constitutionally required, Mulroney introduced legislation to facilitate a popular referendum on the Accord. The Accord was supported by the leaders of all major federal and provincial parties, but was again opposed by Trudeau.[47] In the end, the Accord was rejected by 55 per cent of Canadians.

The failure of the accords created a new sense of betrayal in Quebec, where political leaders reasserted the self-determination of the Quebec nation. It also increased support for Quebec independence with the Parti Québécois winning majorities in the provincial elections of 1994 and 1998 and the separatist Bloc Québécois forming the Official Opposition in Parliament after the 1993 federal election. The sovereignty movement reached its peak in a second cliffhanger Quebec referendum in 1995, in which 50.6 per cent of voters rejected the proposed separation arrangement.[48]

Transforming Trudeau's vision of a just society into legal text involved twists and turns along the way, not all of which could have been predicted from the outset. The political dynamics, including Trudeau's leadership style and his willingness to proceed unilaterally, along with the individual personalities of the provincial premiers and their interests, impacted the

45 *Code civil du Québec*, c CCQ-1991.

46 'Charlottetown Accord: Document', *The Canadian Encyclopedia* (Web Page, 2006) Part I <www.thecanadianencyclopedia.ca/en/article/charlottetown-accord-document>.

47 Trudeau, *Memoirs* (n 12) 364.

48 For a popular account of the referendum, see Chantal Hébert and Jean Lapierre Source, *The Morning After: The 1995 Referendum and the Day That Almost Was* (Knopf, 2015). The referendum was followed by a groundbreaking unanimous Supreme Court of Canada reference case ruling on the legality of Quebec secession from Canada in *Reference re Secession of Quebec* [1998] 2 SCR 217. The principles from the judgment were later enacted as a federal statute: *Clarity Act*, SC 2000, c 26.

process and ultimately the outcome.[49] Parliamentarians on the joint committee helped shape the *Charter* text, as did the submissions received from hundreds of individuals and groups. The Supreme Court of Canada's ruling that discovered a constitutional convention of substantial provincial support for constitutional change gave the provinces a greater say in the *Charter* design part-way through the process, leading to the insertion of the notwithstanding clause. While the *Charter* succeeded in the sense that it was enacted as part of the *Constitution Act, 1982*, questions of national identity raised by the process were far from resolved. Trudeau's inability to obtain Quebec's support created a fresh national crisis with Quebec rethinking its place in Canada. The loss of this constituency nearly resulted in the breakup of Canada. Questions about Quebec's relationship with Canada dominated politics over the next decade and its reverberations are still felt.[50] The *Charter*'s birth therefore created an urgent imperative for the federal government to save the country all over again. A major new roadblock in responding to the crisis, however, was that any further constitutional change would now need to clear the *Constitution Act, 1982*'s amendment hurdles, a considerably more difficult way of getting things done as compared to simply asking Westminster. While the Constitution could now be said to truly belong to Canadians, its terms created new challenges for effecting change and were used by a single lawmaker in a province with less than 4 per cent of the country's population to block the Meech Lake Accord. Mulroney's decision to put the Charlottetown Accord to Canadians through a referendum carried its own risks, which ultimately materialised in its defeat.

III. Lessons from the Canadian *Charter* experience

The Canadian *Charter* experience provides several important lessons for creating constitutional change that is intended to reflect core values and build national identity. First, the process of proposing a constitutional amendment must be seen as legitimate. Opposition or resentment from key constituencies can limit or even prevent a successful outcome. The failure

49 Trudeau, *Memoirs* (n 12) 272. See also Trudeau, *Memoirs* (n 12) 300–2, 306, 310; Chrétien (n 9) 298–9.

50 For instance, in 2006, Parliament passed a motion recognising the Québécois as a nation within a united Canada: 'House Passes Motion Recognizing Quebecois as Nation', *CBC News* (Web Page, 27 November 2006) <www.cbc.ca/news/canada/house-passes-motion-recognizing-quebecois-as-nation-1.574359>.

to secure Quebec's support for the *Charter* is instructive of the risk and the challenging consequences that can follow. Legitimacy is enhanced, although not assured, by maintaining a high standard of transparency and consultation. The formulation of constitutional amendments should be carried out openly, such as the televised proceedings of the joint parliamentary committee that helped draft the *Charter* text.[51] This lesson was ignored by Mulroney in putting together the Meech Lake Accord behind closed doors, leading to its defeat. Because questions of national identity lie at the core of how individuals see themselves vis-a-vis the State, a legitimate consultation must include stakeholders and diverse communities to canvass a range of views. To build support, the process will need to demonstrate genuine engagement and responsiveness to different perspectives.[52] In addition, opening a constitutional dialogue on questions of national identity is bound to awaken dormant grievances. Skilful leadership will be needed to address the various challenges that arise. It should be remembered that the constitutional amendment process can be a useful opportunity to identify and remedy past injustices, while maintaining a forward-looking orientation.

Second, the drafting process must be taken seriously as a 'constitutional moment' and given the care and attention that it deserves. As Chrétien observed in his reflections:

> [C]onstitutional reform is very difficult to achieve and takes a long time. It requires compromise, negotiating ability, enormous political will and tenacity, and most of all, a substantial national consensus, which can come only after much debate and discussion.[53]

While it is sensible to first obtain a consensus for a high-level vision to guide the process, the detail resides in the text, and the proposal can be threatened by what may initially seem like a minor question of textual formulation. Translating constitutional vision into legal text is likely to be contentious. Draft text should be proposed and discussed early in the process to identify areas of disagreement and where there is already common ground. Legal text is always important, but especially so when it is constitutionally entrenched, as it will take priority over all other sources of law. Words and phrases must

51 Sarah Sorial, Chapter 13, this volume, discusses the Irish experience of citizen's assemblies.

52 Adapted from Jeremy Waldron, 'Principles of Legislation' in Richard W Bauman and Tsvi Kahana (eds), *The Least Examined Branch: The Role of Legislatures in the Constitutional State* (Cambridge University Press, 2006) 15, 27, doi.org/10.1017/CBO9780511511035.003.

53 Chrétien (n 9) 308.

be carefully considered to ensure that the framers' intentions are expressed as clearly as possible and with the intended level of precision to create the appropriate degree of discretion for judicial interpretation.[54] The drafting process must also be sufficiently flexible for the proposal to evolve based on information that comes out of consultation. Patience will be needed. Even a small change to the text sought by one group may generate new demands for changes from the others. The goal is to make continual progress towards a consensus by revealing the interests of stakeholders, finding common ground and proposing compromises, all while staying true to the original vision.

Third, the decision-making process for moving the proposal forward will need to balance different interests and ultimately pick winners and losers. It will not be possible to accommodate all interests, as many will compete directly. Not all individuals or groups will support every part of the proposal, no matter how long it is discussed. Effective leadership will be necessary to encourage a broad consensus about the constitutional package as a whole on the understanding that nobody will get exactly what they want. The conversation should be pragmatic, reiterating to stakeholders the importance of the broader national interest and what progress can be achieved with an imperfect—but significantly improved—constitutional settlement. Yet, before moving the proposal forward, it is worth pausing to consider whether there are any final changes that should be made. Once closed, the window for constitutional change may not open again for some time. Problems that can be solved should not be avoided simply because there is agreement on a preliminary draft and a desire to move things along. Chrétien writes that:

> [T]he difficulty of obtaining constitutional change means that when made, it should be right or as right as possible. Changes—even improvements—cannot be easily made and flaws cannot be easily corrected. Flaws that are recognized while discussions are still going on should be corrected before they become entrenched in the Constitution as part of the basic law of the land, when they can be changed only by amendments to the Constitution.[55]

54 For example, the constitutional amendment procedure should be drafted with a high degree of precision to avoid any doubt over the applicable requirements to make future changes, whereas it may be desirable for a provision guaranteeing equal treatment to be drafted more simply and abstractly to allow flexibility in its application in future cases.

55 Chrétien (n 9) 308.

Such final changes will, however, require careful management to ensure that they do not risk derailing the entire proposal.

Fourth, the final text of the proposal must be shepherded through the formal constitutional amendment process. As discovered with the Meech Lake and Charlottetown Accords after the coming into force of the *Constitution Act, 1982*, the requirements of the process can themselves become a major obstacle to overcome. If a national referendum is part of the process, as it is in Australia,[56] a campaign strategy must be developed to promote the proposal and secure public support. Questions to be asked include: Who will be the public face of the campaign? Which individuals and groups are likely to support and oppose the proposal? How will the broad vision and the detail of the proposal be communicated? What are the issues that are likely to resonate with the public? How will misinformation and inaccuracies about the proposal be countered?

Fifth, thought must be given to what happens the day *after* the proposal succeeds. Again, a number of questions need to be considered: How will the transition process be managed? How are institutions likely to take up their new roles and adjust to a new balance of powers? What additional resources might they need? Will courts require new procedures for dealing with constitutional litigation? Which existing statutes and practices should be reviewed and possibly changed in light of the amendment?

It is clear from the *Charter* experience that there are many challenges to be overcome in the process of transforming constitutional vision into legal reality. The final proposal is unlikely to perfectly reflect the original vision. What emerges from the drafting process will instead be a different, and possibly more limited, version of the original. While constitutional amendment is difficult, it is only the beginning of a much longer process of transformation: changing the Constitution will set in motion a series of further changes. By way of example, an entrenched bill of rights like the *Charter* will create a new balance of powers and change institutional roles, the implications of which will only become clear over time. Litigants will begin contesting the meaning of the new constitutional provisions and seek to enforce their rights, sparking the creation of constitutional jurisprudence and its gradual accumulation into a new body of law. Through its power of interpretation, the Canadian judiciary became a part architect of the *Charter* and influenced the development of a new national identity.

56 *Constitution of the Commonwealth of Australia* s 128.

IV. A new balance of powers and institutional roles

The *Charter* recast the roles of Canadian legal and political institutions and shifted significant power over questions of public policy from the legislative branch to the judiciary. While some institutional changes were immediately obvious from the *Charter* text, others became clear only over time, resulting from a gradual institutional realignment in light of a new constitutional landscape. This process, which involved institutions working out a new balance of powers by testing their boundaries, did not always go smoothly. Institutional clashes brought contested roles and competing *Charter* interpretations into sharp relief and at times threatened to weaken democratic institutions.[57] The Supreme Court of Canada played a determinative role in resolving these contestations as the final arbiter of the new constitutional text, much of which had been framed broadly, inviting judicial interpretation. The Supreme Court, in turn, was influenced by the views of scholars, especially in relation to a newly minted dialogue theory of institutions.[58]

In terms of its content, the *Charter* proclaims that it guarantees various rights and freedoms, including those relating to conscience and religion; thought, belief and expression; peaceful assembly; association; democratic participation; mobility; life, liberty and security of the person; unreasonable search or seizure; equality; and the use of English and French.[59] The *Charter* protects individuals against arbitrary detention or imprisonment and requires reasons to be provided when a person is detained or arrested by an

57 For recent examples, see Benjamin Perrin, 'The Supreme Court *vs.* Parliament', *Macdonald-Laurier Institute* (Web Document, 2016) <www.macdonaldlaurier.ca/files/pdf/MLI_SupCourtYrReview_2016_Fweb.pdf>. In 2014, a clash between the federal government and the Supreme Court of Canada resulted in an unprecedented condemnation of the Canadian government by the International Commission of Jurists for infringing the integrity and independence of the judiciary: Mark Kennedy, 'International Panel Slams Stephen Harper for Treatment of Supreme Court Justice', *Ottawa Citizen* (Web Page, 25 July 2014) <ottawacitizen.com/news/national/international-jurists-slam-stephen-harper-for-his-treatment-of-supreme-court-justice>. For an overview of the events, see Aaron Wherry, 'Stephen Harper, Beverly McLachlin and an Historic Mess', *Macleans* (Web Page, 6 May 2014) <www.macleans.ca/politics/stephen-harper-beverley-mclachlin-and-historic-mess>; Jamie Cameron, 'Law, Politics, and Legacy Building at the McLachlin Court in 2014' (2015) 71 *Supreme Court Law Review* (2d) 1.

58 Peter McCormick, 'The Judges and the Journals: Citation of Periodical Literature by the Supreme Court of Canada, 1985–2004' (2004) 83(3) *The Canadian Bar Review* 633 (statistical overview); *Vriend v Alberta* [1998] 1 SCR 493, [137]-[139] (Iacobucci J) (endorsement of dialogue theory).

59 *Charter* (n 2) ss 2, 3, 6, 7, 8, 15, 16–22.

agent of the State.[60] When detained, an individual has the right to promptly retain and instruct counsel and to have the validity of their detention judicially reviewed.[61] In the context of criminal proceedings, the *Charter* provides a suite of protections for the benefit of the accused.[62] Notably, protections for private property rights are not included in the *Charter* text.[63]

While the *Charter* forms part of the supreme law of Canada,[64] its rights and freedoms are subject to a key overarching limitation: *Charter* guarantees can be constrained by 'reasonable limits prescribed by law as can be demonstrably justified in a free and democratic society'.[65] In other words, *Charter* rights are limited in their application if the State seeks to justify a law that infringes a right and when a court is persuaded that the justification is reasonable. The Supreme Court of Canada has developed a body of law on what is necessary to justify a limitation of *Charter* rights in this way.[66] The balance struck between the individual and the public interest (as represented by the State) is therefore an essential part of cases where a *prima facie* infringement of the *Charter* is made out.

In terms of the scope of its application, the *Charter* extends to the federal and provincial governments, and while it does not directly bind private parties, it can extend to statutory authorities and other quasi-public bodies where there is a sufficient degree of government control.[67] To enforce *Charter* rights, a person may apply to a court for a determination and remedy.[68] As many *Charter* rights apply to both individuals and corporate entities, claims can be brought by corporations to protect their business interests from interference by legal regulation or State action—a fact that has not escaped academic attention.[69] Important *Charter* jurisprudence has

60 Ibid s 9, sub-s 10(a).
61 Ibid sub-ss 10(b)-(c).
62 Ibid ss 11–14.
63 Alexander Alvaro, 'Why Property Rights Were Excluded from the Canadian Charter of Rights and Freedoms' (1991) 24(2) *Canadian Journal of Political Science / Revue Canadienne de Science Politique* 309, doi.org/10.1017/S0008423900005102.
64 *Constitution Act, 1982* (n 2) sub-ss 52(1)-(2).
65 *Charter* (n 2) s 1.
66 *R v Oakes* [1986] 1 SCR 103 is the leading case.
67 *Douglas/Kwantlen Faculty Assn v Douglas College* [1990] 3 SCR 570; *McKinney v University of Guelph* [1990] 3 SCR 229; *Lavigne v Ontario Public Service Employees Union* [1991] 2 SCR 211. Note that Canadian common law is shaped by *Charter* values and, in this way, it has a horizontal effect on private parties: see, eg, *R v Salituro* [1991] 3 SCR 654.
68 *Charter* (n 2) sub-ss 24(1)-(2); *Constitution Act, 1982* (n 2) sub-s 52(1).
69 See, eg, Joel Bakan, *Just Words: Constitutional Rights and Social Wrongs* (University of Toronto Press, 1997), doi.org/10.3138/9781442676466; Andrew Petter, *The Politics of the Charter: The Illusive Promise of Constitutional Rights* (University of Toronto Press, 2010), doi.org/10.3138/9781442698864.

therefore been forged in the context of a corporate claimant, including an early *Charter* ruling by the Supreme Court of Canada on the question of religious freedom and discrimination.[70]

Where a court has determined that a *Charter* claim has been successfully made out, broad remedial discretion is provided by the *Constitution Act, 1982*, giving courts the principal role in determining the legal effect of a *Charter* infringement.[71] *Charter* remedial jurisprudence continues to evolve: for example, monetary damages have in recent years been accepted for breaches of *Charter* rights by the police, such as in the case of an unreasonable search.[72] Courts have also crafted entirely unique remedies, including suspending a declaration of unconstitutionality for laws that infringe the *Charter*. Originally devised in a case where many Manitoba laws were unconstitutional for not being enacted in both English and French,[73] the remedy seeks to ameliorate the harsh consequences that can follow a finding of legal invalidity. It suspends the court's judgment for a certain period to give the legislature time to amend the law and cure the constitutional defect.[74] While the Manitoba case did not itself involve *Charter* rights, the remedy has since caught on and is now used in *Charter* cases. It has, however, attracted criticism on the basis that it portrays the court as initiating a 'dialogue' with the legislature, when in fact the legislature has little choice but to follow judicial directions to change the law to become *Charter* compliant within the time limit specified by the court.[75] Broad remedial discretion, including the use of a suspended declaration of invalidity, has therefore altered the pre-*Charter* institutional balance by placing courts in the position of 'suggesting' legislative amendment to Parliament in many different areas of law that implicate a *Charter* right.

Despite the significant expansion of judicial power under the *Charter*, the legislature holds a trump card in the form of a derogation. Section 33 allows federal and provincial legislatures to opt out of the application of certain *Charter* protections, ensuring legislation will have legal effect notwithstanding rights infringements. A justification or explanation is not

70 *R v Big M Drug Mart* [1985] 1 SCR 295.

71 *Charter* (n 2) sub-ss 24(1)-(2); *Constitution Act, 1982* (n 2) sub-s 52(1).

72 *Vancouver (City) v Ward* [2010] 2 SCR 28 (relating to police detention and search); *Henry v British Columbia (Attorney General)* [2015] 2 SCR 214 (relating to prosecution).

73 *Re Manitoba Language Rights* [1985] 1 SCR 721.

74 An extension of the time period was later granted.

75 Depending on the remedial specificity, there may be legislative discretion for how the law is changed to cure the defect. The amended law, however, may be challenged in court again.

required. To be effective, legislative declarations must only be passed by a legislative majority. Declarations automatically expire after five years, unless renewed. Certain core *Charter* guarantees are not subject to the exemption, including those related to citizen mobility and democratic rights.[76] As discussed earlier, this notwithstanding clause was inserted into the *Charter* as a last-minute compromise to secure provincial support. The provision has been seen by some scholars to establish a 'weak form' of constitutional review.[77] Yet it is likely that the provision increased judicial power as courts were emboldened in adjudicating *Charter* claims, secure in the knowledge that the legislature could opt out of their rulings. In reality, the provision is rarely invoked and remains controversial. Former Prime Minister Paul Martin promised to repeal the notwithstanding clause if re-elected, but was subsequently defeated in a general election.[78] Restricting *Charter* rights is likely to be politically unpopular. Recently, however, Quebec invoked the notwithstanding clause to shield a law that prohibits public employees from wearing prominent religious symbols from a *Charter* challenge.[79] The law has high levels of public support in Quebec and the government's use of the notwithstanding clause was likely seen as politically beneficial.[80] New Brunswick also introduced legislation to invoke the notwithstanding clause. The Bill required evidence of immunisation for children in public schools or a medical exemption. It was defeated on its third reading.[81]

Before the *Charter*, Canadian courts adopted a much more limited constitutional role that focused on questions relating to the division of powers between the federal and provincial legislatures.[82] While the *Canadian Bill of Rights* was enacted in 1960, it was limited in its application and remedies as earlier discussed. The *Charter* transformed the court into a powerful forum for enforcing rights by tasking judges with scrutinising legislation and State action for *Charter* compliance and invalidating what was found to be inconsistent with its rights and freedoms. In a break with the past, courts embraced this new role. Chief Justice Brian Dickson, writing in an early *Charter* case, held that judges should take a 'broad, purposive' approach

76 *Charter* (n 2) sub-s 33(1). In addition, other provisions of the *Constitution Act, 1982* (n 2), outside the *Charter*, are not subject to the notwithstanding clause.

77 See, eg, Mark Tushnet, 'The Rise of Weak-Form Judicial Review' in Tom Ginsburg and Rosalind Dixon (eds), *Comparative Constitutional Law* (Edward Elgar, 2011) 321, 325.

78 Thomas S Axworthy, 'The Notwithstanding Clause: Sword of Damocles or Paper Tiger?' (March 2007) *Policy Options* 58.

79 *Act Respecting the Laicity of the State*, L-0.3 (Q) s 34.

80 See <www.legnb.ca/en/legislation/bills/59/3/11/an-act-respecting-proof-of-immunization>.

81 *Bill 11, An Act Respecting Proof of Immunization* (NB).

82 *Constitution Act, 1867* (n 14) ss 91, 92.

in interpreting the *Charter* and see it as a living tree that could grow over time.[83] While providing flexibility, the approach adopted by the Supreme Court of Canada has not always produced interpretations of rights that would have been expected by the *Charter*'s framers.[84] This is not considered by Canadian judges to be problematic: they do not feel constrained by an originalist approach to interpreting the *Charter* and openly acknowledge constitutional evolution over time.[85] The questions are when, in what direction and to what extent the *Charter* should grow—questions that can bring judicial preferences and ideology into the mix.

In its *Charter* judgments, the Supreme Court of Canada has established jurisprudence to guide courts in the process of adjudicating *Charter* rights. The process typically involves a multi-step, structured legal test to explicitly take account of relevant interests.[86] While balancing interests through a multifactorial analysis pays attention to *Charter* values, and provides a measure of consistency and fairness across different cases and courts, there remains scope for judicial discretion.[87] Canadian judges have openly acknowledged the shift from legalism—the view that the correct answer to a legal dispute can be worked out simply by the proper application of

83 *Hunter v Southam Inc* [1984] 2 SCR 145, 155–6, quoting Viscount Sankey in *Edwards v Attorney-General for Canada* [1930] AC 124, 136 (PC).

84 For example, the Supreme Court of Canada rejected that the *Charter* guarantee to freedom of association included a right to associate for the purpose of collective bargaining for 25 years. Only in *Health Services and Support—Facilities Subsector Bargaining Assn v British Columbia* [2007] 2 SCR 391 did it finally overrule its previous holding, observing that the 'framers of the *Charter* intended to include [collective bargaining] in the protection of freedom of association', at [40]. For other examples, see James B Kelly and Christopher P Manfredi (eds), *Contested Constitutionalism: Reflections on the Canadian Charter of Rights and Freedoms* (UBC Press, 2009); Jeremy Webber, 'Tales of the Unexpected: Intended and Unintended Consequences of the Canadian Charter of Rights and Freedoms' (1993) 5 *Canterbury Law Review* 207.

85 For example, Chief Justice Brian Dickson observed in *Hunter v Southam Inc* (n 83) at 155 that the *Charter* 'must … be capable of growth and development over time to meet new social, political and historical realities often unimagined by its framers'.

86 US rights jurisprudence is frequently considered by the Supreme Court of Canada in developing these tests: see, eg, Christopher P Manfredi, 'The Use of United States Decisions by the Supreme Court of Canada under the Charter of Rights and Freedoms' (1990) 23(3) *Canadian Journal of Political Science / Revue Canadienne de Science Politique* 499, doi.org/10.1017/S0008423900012737.

87 The emphasis or weighting placed on different components of a legal test can be a matter of discretion, leading to a divided bench. In 2019, only 40 per cent of the Supreme Court of Canada's judgments were unanimous: Cristin Schmitz, 'Supreme Court of Canada Hits Record Low 40% Unanimity Rate in 2019; Many Appeals Came from Quebec', *The Lawyer's Daily* (Web Page, 20 January 2020) <www.thelawyersdaily.ca/articles/17529/supreme-court-of-canada-hits-record-low-40-unanimity-rate-in-2019-many-appeals-came-from-quebec>. For a study of judicial preferences at the Supreme Court of Canada, see CL Ostberg and Matthew E Wetstein, *Attitudinal Decision Making in the Supreme Court of Canada* (UBC Press, 2008); Benjamin Alarie and Andrew Green, 'Policy Preference Change and Appointments to the Supreme Court of Canada' (2009) 47(1) *Osgoode Hall Law Journal* 1.

precedent and the canons of construction—to judicial discretion.[88] Chief Justice Beverley McLachlin, who led the Supreme Court for nearly two decades, was particularly influential in this regard.[89] Through her speeches and published articles, McLachlin also increased the public profile of the Chief Justice as the spokesperson for the judiciary, with the goal of helping Canadians better understand the role of the courts under the *Charter*.[90]

Over time, the judicial consideration of complex social problems in *Charter* cases led to further institutional changes to the court. The transformation of courts into a forum to adjudicate *Charter* rights attracted new kinds of litigants who hired lawyers to dress their claims in the clothes of *Charter* rights. Many of these litigants were groups or individuals who had been unsuccessful (or who expected to be unsuccessful) in achieving their goals through direct government action or legislative reform. The resulting 'court party' has been criticised by both conservative and liberal scholars for privileging those with resources to pursue litigation and for creating opportunities for social engineering by judges who altered compromises among competing interests that had been struck by elected representatives.[91] In evaluating *Charter* claims, the Supreme Court of Canada began taking in more social science evidence and embracing individuals and groups as intervenors, to better inform itself of the relevant economic and social contexts.[92] In addition, greater public awareness of the Court's *Charter* judgments engaging with potent political issues such as criminal sentencing,

88 See, eg, Chief Justice Beverley McLachlin, 'Judging in a Democratic State', *Supreme Court of Canada* (Web Page, 3 June 2004) <www.scc-csc.ca/judges-juges/spe-dis/bm-2004-06-03-eng.aspx>. The downside of this flexibility is lack of legal certainty and perhaps less rigorous *legal* analysis.

89 Ibid.

90 'Speeches', *Supreme Court of Canada* (Web Page) <www.scc-csc.ca/judges-juges/spe-dis/index-eng.aspx>.

91 See, eg, FL Morton and Rainer Knopff, *The Charter Revolution and the Court Party* (University of Toronto Press, 2000) for a conservative critique. On the left, scholars tended to see judges as reflecting conservative values, thereby protecting private interests over the community and those who were disadvantaged: Petter (n 69). Notably, the federal government funds some *Charter* litigation (against itself) through the Court Challenges Program, cancelled during Stephen Harper's tenure as prime minister and reinstated by current Prime Minister Justin Trudeau: 'Court Challenges Program', *Government of Canada* (Web Page) <www.canada.ca/en/canadian-heritage/services/funding/court-challenges-program.html>.

92 Geoffrey D Callaghan, 'Intervenors at the Supreme Court of Canada' (2020) 43(1) *Dalhousie Law Journal* 1; Benjamin RD Alarie and Andrew J Green, 'Interventions at the Supreme Court of Canada: Accuracy, Affiliation, and Acceptance' (2010) 48(3) *Osgoode Hall Law Journal* 381; Ian Brodie, *Friends of the Court: The Privileging of Interest Group Litigation* (State University of New York Press, 2002). See also Lorne Neudorf, 'Intervention at the UK Supreme Court' (2013) 2(1) *Cambridge Journal of International and Comparative Law* 16, for a comparative perspective. The judiciary's embrace of intervenors may also assuage concerns about the limited policy experience of judges as compared to legislators, the court as an unsuitable forum for policy debates and even the lack of the judiciary's democratic credentials through a broad group of participants.

abortion, public health care, same-sex marriage, gun regulation, language rights, campaign finance and the corporal punishment of children led the Court to be seen more like a political institution.[93]

To counter perceptions of political interference, and to enhance its legitimacy in carrying out its *Charter* work, the Supreme Court of Canada sought to strengthen its impartiality and independence. While it acknowledged judicial discretion under the *Charter*, the Supreme Court made clear in the *Provincial Judges Reference* case[94] that it decided cases independent of government preferences, a major fairness concern as the State appeared in the Court as a litigant in *Charter* cases. Any suggestion of improper influence from the other branches, or even the *potential* for such influence, would be taken seriously. While judges are rightly concerned about their independence to preserve their status as a third party to a legal dispute, the Supreme Court arguably went beyond what was necessary to promote judicial legitimacy. In 1997, for example, it 'discovered' an unwritten constitutional principle of judicial independence that applied to all judges, not just the superior courts.[95] The majority found that the principle was grounded in the preamble to the *Constitution Act, 1867*.[96] The case was brought by provincial judges who challenged an across-the-board reduction of their salaries as part of public sector cost-cutting measures by provincial governments facing budget crises. The Supreme Court held that the reductions in judicial compensation were inconsistent with judicial independence and that governments would be required to establish independent compensation commissions to recommend judicial salaries to avoid direct negotiations between the judiciary and the executive.[97] Since 1997, litigation has continued in relation to this unwritten principle, including efforts by judicial officers to use it to challenge the renaming of a court building, overturn a decision to disallow a travel claim for a Swiss conference and to demand that the State pay legal fees to defend against allegations of misconduct.[98] In addition, the doctrine has been used by senior judges to rebuff civil litigation reforms to modernise

93 See, eg, FL Morton, 'The Political Impact of the Canadian Charter of Rights and Freedoms' (1987) 20(1) *Canadian Journal of Political Science* 31, doi.org/10.1017/S0008423900048939; Donald A Songer, *The Transformation of the Supreme Court of Canada: An Empirical Examination* (University of Toronto Press, 2008), doi.org/10.3138/9781442689473.

94 *Ref re Remuneration of Judges of the Prov Court of PEI; Ref re Independence and Impartiality of Judges of the Prov Court of PEI* [1997] 3 SCR 3 ('*Provincial Judges Reference*').

95 Ibid.

96 Originally referred to as the *British North America Act, 1867* (n 14).

97 *Provincial Judges Reference* (n 94) [113].

98 For an overview, see Lorne Neudorf, 'Judicial Independence: The Judge as a Third Party to the Dispute' (2015) *Oxford University Comparative Law Forum* 2, 5.2.3.

the litigation process.[99] One of the major challenges of this doctrine is that it involves judges deciding how far their own independence extends to shield them from what they see as improper interference—a context that strains perceptions of judicial impartiality. Unfortunately, these developments can have the effect of trivialising judicial independence as they are premised on an unrealistic view of Canadian judges as being willing to compromise their integrity in the absence of such protections.[100]

Growing judicial power and independence under the *Charter* also prompted closer judicial scrutiny: Who were the unelected judges interpreting and applying these new constitutional rights over other sources of law? What are their policy preferences and ideological commitments? Legal scholarship flourished to try to answer these questions. Researchers designed entirely new qualitative and quantitative studies on judicial appointments and preferences, influenced by the well-developed scholarship in this area in the US.[101] While less intense than the Senate confirmation process in the US, the appointment process for the Supreme Court of Canada has been reformed in recent years to partly depoliticise judicial selection and provide more transparency. The process now involves open applications, a shortlist of candidates compiled by a non-partisan committee and the prime minister's selection of the appointee from the shortlist.[102] A public parliamentary committee scrutiny process for potential appointees was initiated by former Prime Minister Stephen Harper and later abandoned.[103]

In the years following the enactment of the *Charter*, Canadian courts have emerged as a forum for drawing attention to important social challenges and the plight of minorities and disadvantaged persons. While *Charter*

99 Ibid.

100 Peter W Hogg, 'The Bad Idea of Unwritten Constitutional Principles: Protecting Judicial Salaries' in Adam Dodek and Lorne Sossin (eds), *Judicial Independence in Context* (Irwin Law, 2010) 25; Jamie Cameron, 'The Written Word and the Constitution's Vital Unstated Assumptions' in Pierre Thibault, Benoit Pelletier and Louis Perret (eds), *Essays in Honour of Gerald A Beaudoin* (Les Editions Yvon Blais, 2002) 89.

101 See, eg, Emmett Macfarlane, *Governing from the Bench: The Supreme Court of Canada and the Judicial Role* (UBC Press, 2013) (qualitative); Benjamin Alarie and Andrew Green, 'Should They All Just Get Along? Judicial Ideology, Collegiality, and Appointments to the Supreme Court of Canada' (2008) 58 *University of New Brunswick Law Journal* 73, doi.org/10.2139/ssrn.1091479 (quantitative). For a review of socio-legal scholarship noting US influence, see Harry W Arthurs and Annie Bunting, 'Socio-Legal Scholarship in Canada: A Review of the Field' (2014) 41(4) *Journal of Law and Society* 487, doi.org/10.1111/j.1467-6478.2014.00682.x.

102 'Supreme Court of Canada Appointment Process 2019, Appointment of the Honourable Nicholas Kasirer', *Government of Canada* (Web Page) <www.fja-cmf.gc.ca/scc-csc/2019/index-eng.html>.

103 See Lorne Neudorf, 'Independence and the Public Process: Evolution or Erosion?' (2007) 70(1) *Saskatchewan Law Review* 53.

rulings have at times been controversial, courts have also led public opinion and the Supreme Court of Canada has become an internationally respected institution.[104] But this growth in judicial power came largely at the expense of the legislature's role in formulating public policy.[105] By contrast, the executive branch has consolidated power in recent decades through the government's effective control of the legislature, often with majority governments elected through a first-past-the-post system of voluntary voting (although, as of writing, there is presently a minority federal government). The Senate remains an appointed chamber and, as such, it does not usually block government Bills. All provincial legislatures are unicameral, allowing majority governments to quickly pass any legislation they wish. In addition, tremendous lawmaking power has been delegated by legislatures to the executive branch, a trend that appears to be accelerating.[106] Pinpointing the *Charter*'s precise role in relation to this increase of executive power is elusive, but the *Charter*'s weakening effect on the legislature as a forum for formulating public policy has undoubtedly left it vulnerable to greater executive control and influence.

V. Did the *Charter* create a just society?

Nearly four decades after the *Charter* came into force, it is worth considering whether it has been able to deliver on its promise of creating a just society. The *Charter* has certainly contributed to the development of Canada as a modern and progressive country. Canada enjoys a reputation as an international leader in human rights, a status that is partly attributable to the *Charter*'s equality rights, which prompted important advances in Canadian law. In 2003, for instance, the Court of Appeal for Ontario held that the *Charter* required officials to grant marriage licenses to same-sex couples.[107] In light of this ruling, and subsequent rulings of other appeal

104 See, eg, Aharon Barak, 'A Judge on Judging: The Role of a Supreme Court in a Democracy' (2002) 116(1) *Harvard Law Review* 16, doi.org/10.2307/1342624, writing that the jurisprudence of the Supreme Court of Canada 'serves as a source of inspiration for many countries around the world', at 114.

105 See, eg, Lorne Neudorf, 'The Supreme Court and Parliament: Evolving Roles and Relationships' (2017) 78 *Supreme Court Law Review* (2d) 3, doi.org/10.2139/ssrn.3416995.

106 For my work on this topic, see Lorne Neudorf, 'Strengthening the Parliamentary Scrutiny of Delegated Legislation: Lessons from Australia' (2019) 42(4) *Canadian Parliamentary Review* 25; Lorne Neudorf, 'Reassessing the Constitutional Foundation of Delegated Legislation in Canada' (2018) 41(2) *Dalhousie Law Journal* 519; Lorne Neudorf, 'Rule by Regulation: Revitalizing Parliament's Supervisory Role in the Making of Subordinate Legislation' (2016) 39(1) *Canadian Parliamentary Review* 29, doi.org/10.2139/ssrn.3417001.

107 *Halpern v Canada (Attorney General)* (2003) 65 OR (3d) 161 (CA).

courts,[108] Parliament enacted the *Civil Marriage Act*,[109] extending same-sex marriage nationwide, one of the first countries in the world to do so. The *Charter* has expanded individual freedoms, including over one's body, such as when the Supreme Court of Canada struck down legislation restricting access to abortion services.[110] *Charter* protections have caused courts to invalidate or read down restrictions on religion and expression.[111] Individual freedom has also been enhanced by the *Charter*'s legal protections. For example, courts have excluded evidence in cases where it was obtained in an unreasonable search.[112] Police officers are trained to take into account *Charter* rights and their investigative techniques have adapted to better protect rights, thereby having a potentially powerful preventative effect on rights infringements.[113] Opportunities for citizen mobility have increased as courts have struck down interprovincial barriers, including those relating to the practice of a profession.[114] In terms of the use of English and French, the *Charter* facilitated important changes to the federal government that allow Canadians to communicate with and access services in the official language of their choice.[115] The *Charter*'s promotion of multiculturalism resulted in the enactment of the *Canadian Multiculturalism Act*,[116] establishing policies and authorising programs to support cultural diversity. While it is not officially part of the *Charter*,[117] s 35 of the *Constitution Act, 1982* protects existing Aboriginal rights. This section has led to the judicial recognition

108 A number of provincial and territorial courts followed the lead of the Court of Appeal for Ontario and declared same-sex marriage to be a requirement of the *Charter*'s equality guarantee. In addition, the Supreme Court of Canada decided a reference case clearing the way for Parliament to legislate to change the existing common law definition of marriage, while avoiding a ruling directly on the *Charter* requirement in light of the pending legislation: *Reference re Same-Sex Marriage* [2004] 3 SCR 698.

109 *Civil Marriage Act*, SC 2005, c 33.

110 *R v Morgentaler* [1988] 1 SCR 30.

111 See, eg, *Loyola High School v Quebec (Attorney General)* [2015] 1 SCR 613 (religion); *Ford v Quebec (Attorney General)* [1988] 2 SCR 712 (expression).

112 See, eg, *R v Collins* [1987] 1 SCR 265.

113 Kathryn Moore, 'Police Implementation of Supreme Court of Canada Charter Decisions: An Empirical Study' (1992) 30(3) *Osgoode Hall Law Journal* 547.

114 See, eg, *Black v Law Society of Alberta* [1989] 1 SCR 591.

115 Guaranteed by the *Charter* (n 2) s 20. For an overview of bilingualism in Canada, see Linda Cardinal, 'The Limits of Bilingualism in Canada' (2010) 10(1) *Nationalism and Ethnic Politics* 79.

116 *Canadian Multiculturalism Act*, RSC 1985, c 24 (4th Supp).

117 The *Charter* comprises Part I, ss 1-34, of the *Constitution Act, 1982* (n 2). Aboriginal rights are guaranteed in s 35. Among other things, its placement means that it is not subject to the *Charter* limitations of ss 1, 33.

of constitutionally protected native title claims.[118] Finally, the *Charter* has become a powerful symbol that has helped create a sense of national identity around its rights and freedoms.[119]

The transformative potential of the *Charter* has, however, been limited in other ways. Litigated *Charter* claims do not always succeed. Racism and discrimination remain serious problems in Canadian society.[120] While the risk of Quebec separating has diminished in recent years, regionalism continues.[121] The *Charter* has also had a significant 'judicialising effect' on rights and freedoms. Governments see the *Charter* as an obstacle to avoid in making law and policy: its enforcement is the purview of judges. The judicialising of legal rights has encouraged governments to restrict freedoms up to the point of barely avoiding a *Charter* infringement, as opposed to taking *Charter* values to heart and championing them. The *Charter*'s guarantee against unreasonable search provides a compelling illustration of the phenomenon.[122] Despite the greater potential for citizen mobility, Canada is not economically egalitarian: income inequality is growing.[123] While bilingualism has moderately increased, less than one in five Canadians can have a conversation in both English and French.[124] Major problems continue to affect Canada's Aboriginal communities, including disgraceful conditions in reserves that suffer from a lack of adequate housing and clean

118 See, eg, *Tsilhqot'in Nation v British Columbia* [2014] 2 SCR 257.
119 'Canadian Identity, 2013' (n 4).
120 See 'Building a Foundation for Change: Canada's Anti-Racism Strategy 2019–2022', *Government of Canada* (Web Page) <www.canada.ca/en/canadian-heritage/campaigns/anti-racism-engagement/anti-racism-strategy.html>.
121 The 2019 federal election laid bare an East–West division, with the governing Liberal Party failing to win a single seat in Alberta or Saskatchewan. The election prompted a minority of Western Canadians to advocate for separation from Canada: see 'Wexit Making Waves? Hundreds Rally for Western Separation in Edmonton', *CBC News* (Web Page, 2 November 2019) <www.cbc.ca/news/canada/edmonton/wexit-western-separation-rally-edmonton-1.5346025>. The separatist Bloc Québécois also won the most seats in over a decade.
122 Despite former Chief Justice Brian Dickson's warning that the *Charter* was 'not in itself an authorization for governmental action': *Hunter v Southam Inc* (n 83) 156. In the context of unreasonable search jurisprudence, the State tends to push against lines drawn by the court by adapting investigative techniques or technologies, inviting further *Charter* challenges. See Lorne Neudorf, 'Home Invasion by Regulation: Truckers and Reasonable Expectations of Privacy under Section 8 of the Charter' (2012) 45(2) *UBC Law Review* 551.
123 'Changes in Wealth across the Income Distribution, 1999 to 2012', *Statistics Canada* (Web Page) <www150.statcan.gc.ca/n1/pub/75-006-x/2015001/article/14194-eng.htm>.
124 Although it recently reached a new high of 17.9 per cent: 'English-French Bilingualism Reaches New Heights', *Statistics Canada* (Web Page, 2 August 2017) <www12.statcan.gc.ca/census-recensement/2016/as-sa/98-200-x/2016009/98-200-x2016009-eng.cfm>.

water.[125] Aboriginal peoples make up a disproportionate number of the criminally accused and prison population.[126] Canada has also been strongly criticised by the United Nations for its failings in relation to missing and murdered Aboriginal women.[127] While the Canadian government supports immigration and refugees, Canadians themselves have mixed views: two-thirds of Canadians believe that multiculturalism allows individuals to practice customs that are incompatible with mainstream values.[128]

Where does all of this leave us? It would be unfair to expect a document like the *Charter* to transform a society entirely on its own. The answer to the question of whether the *Charter* has created the just society envisioned by Trudeau is nuanced: there have been some successes, failures and unexpected outcomes. It is clear that the *Charter* has raised important issues and pulled the country towards Trudeau's articulation of liberal values. While Trudeau's vision of a just society may not be fully realised, the *Charter* cannot be characterised as a failure. The overall trend is progress towards the vision of its framers, which is perhaps the best that a legal document can do.

VI. Conclusion

The *Charter* has played an important role in building a sense of Canadian national identity. As the most significant constitutional development since the country's founding in 1867, the *Charter* ushered in radical changes to the legal order. It reshaped the institutional landscape, altering the balance of powers and enlarging the role of the judiciary. It created a constitutional yardstick for federal and provincial legislation and State action, measuring

125 'The Housing Conditions of Aboriginal People in Canada', *Statistics Canada* (Web Page, 25 October 2017) <www12.statcan.gc.ca/census-recensement/2016/as-sa/98-200-x/2016021/98-200-x2016021-eng.cfm>; Amanda Coletta, '"Third World Conditions": Many of Canada's Indigenous People Can't Drink the Water at Home', *Washington Post* (Web Page, 15 October 2018) <www.washingtonpost.com/world/the_americas/third-world-conditions-many-of-canadas-indigenous-people-cant-drink-the-water-at-home/2018/10/14/c4f429b4-bc53-11e8-8243-f3ae9c99658a_story.html>.

126 'Aboriginal Issues', *Office of the Correctional Investigator* (Web Page) <www.oci-bec.gc.ca/cnt/priorities-priorites/aboriginals-autochtones-eng.aspx>.

127 'Canada's Failure to Effectively Address Murder and Disappearance of Aboriginal Women a "Grave Rights Violation"—UN Experts', *United Nations Human Rights, Office of the High Commissioner* (Web Page, 6 March 2015) <www.ohchr.org/EN/NewsEvents/Pages/DisplayNews.aspx?NewsID=15656>.

128 Douglas Todd, 'Multiculturalism "Incompatible" with Canadian Norms, Say Two of Three', *Vancouver Sun* (Web Page, 31 January 2017) <vancouversun.com/news/staff-blogs/multiculturalism-incompatible-with-canadian-norms-say-two-of-three>.

them against its rights and freedoms. The *Charter* facilitated progress towards the just society that was envisioned by its founders, despite this progress remaining incomplete or even stalled in some respects.

The *Charter* experience demonstrates that constitutions *can* contribute to building national identity. They do so by planting the seeds of a country's future direction and creating a common framework for the exercise of public power. Constitutions can encourage transformational change, but they are not likely to succeed on their own. Trudeau rightly observed that '[a] country is something that is built every day out of certain basic shared values'.[129] Constitutional text might describe fundamental rights, freedoms and values, but it requires institutions and individuals to give it meaning and life. Constitutions also set in motion a series of changes that are difficult to predict. They change political and power dynamics, create new winners and losers and are shaped by individual personalities as they become sewn into the legal, political and social fabric. Institutions may clash and their roles will enlarge or diminish as a result of these contests. An entrenched bill of rights will become a public forum in which ideas are contested and adjudicated. As the constitutional text is never complete, important details will be filled in by the courts in deciding individual cases. This continuing process to give the Constitution meaning and make it relevant in light of new contexts risks altering the course from the original vision. Other foundational unwritten principles and norms like judicial independence, the separation of powers and democratic accountability will also shape the constitutional landscape as they mesh with the amended constitutional text.

The project of building national identity through a constitution is always an experiment. Creating national identity in a multicultural, pluralist society presents a particular challenge. How can a constitution ask individuals to think beyond their own identities to something bigger like a nation and what that nation should become? What core values are shared in a heterogeneous population? While the *Charter* illustrates that there can be answers to these questions, and that constitutions can make progress towards their national identity–building goals, constitutional change will create new problems to be solved. The picture that ultimately emerges will be influenced by factors that can be difficult to accurately predict. It will also continue to change over time. Through comparative study, the experience of other jurisdictions like Canada can provide important insights to help identify and manage these risks and improve the prospect of the Constitution delivering on its promise.

129 Trudeau, *Memoirs* (n 12) 366.

5

Eco-Constitutionalism

Peter D Burdon

Considering the central role that law plays in shaping human societies, a growing chorus of scholars have begun to advocate for constitutionalism playing a greater role in the regulatory arsenal that is being deployed to confront the current environmental crisis. For this paper, the environmental crisis is conceptualised as a human-induced phenomenon, and extends beyond climate change and biodiversity loss. The paper employs the concept of the Anthropocene to describe a geological epoch in which human beings have the power to impact the Earth system as a whole.[1] In this period, human beings have become weather-makers.

While there is a burgeoning literature that celebrates our new-found power,[2] advocates of eco-constitutionalism have focused their attention on methods to place accountability and the precautionary principle at the centre of decision-making. The central contention is that, as the highest authority in national law, constitutions have a role to play in environmental protection. Louis Kotzé, for example, has argued: 'A constitutionalised global environmental law and governance order would arguably be better able to respond to the Anthropocene's unprecedented exigencies than a non-constitutionalised one.'[3] Evidence suggests that many lawmaking bodies around the world agree. Reflecting a growth in environmental consciousness, three-quarters of countries now have ecological protections

1 Clive Hamilton, *Defiant Earth: The Fate of Humans in the Anthropocene* (Allen & Unwin, 2017).
2 See 'An Ecomodernist Manifesto' (Web Page) <www.ecomodernism.org>.
3 Louis J Kotzé, *Global Environmental Constitutionalism in the Anthropocene* (Hart, 2016).

of some kind incorporated into their national constitution.[4] Tim Hayward even suggests that there is virtually unanimous agreement 'about the importance of making some form of provision for environmental protection at the constitutional level, even if in the form of a state duty or objective rather than necessarily as a fundamental individual right'.[5]

I am not so confident and my intention in this chapter is to subject eco-constitutionalism to critique. To present this critique, I first introduce the idea of eco-constitutionalism and give examples from around the world of countries that have incorporated strong ecological principles. This discussion is broken into three types of recognition: human rights to a healthy environment, individual responsibilities to protect the environment and obligations on the State to protect the environment.

Following this, I unpack the idea of critique that is motivating my intervention. As I make clear, by critique I do not mean criticism or trashing the idea that constitutions can play a role in environmental protection. Rather, I understand critique to be a method whereby a reader can get beneath the surface of an argument and bring to light the presumptions and presuppositions that underpin it. With this in mind, I argue that eco-constitutionalism is an idealist discourse and promotes abstract representations of the relationship between human beings and the environment. This is the key reason I argue that eco-constitutions are unable to fulfil their commitment to environmental protection despite holding out that commitment. Exacerbating this problem, in the Australian context, is the fact that there is currently no committed social force that is pushing for this kind of reform. Finally, while eco-constitutionalism aims to be politically neutral, I argue that its posture reinforces the status quo and leaves untouched the powers that course through civil society and law, leading to the exploitation of the environment.

I. Eco-constitutionalism

The *Australian Constitution* is silent on matters of environmental significance. In this sense, it reflects its time and the notion that history is something that human beings make over or against the physical environment.[6] If one was

4 David Boyd, *The Environmental Rights Revolution: A Global Study of Constitutions, Human Rights, and the Environment* (UBC Press, 2012) 47.

5 Tim Hayward, *Constitutional Environmental Rights* (Oxford University Press, 2005) 4, doi.org/10.1093/0199278687.001.0001.

6 Jacob Burckhardt, *Reflections on History* (Liberty Fund, 1979) 31.

seeking to use the text of our Constitution to extrapolate notions of our national character, those remarks might be limited to viewing nature in connection to navigation or as a resource for irrigation. However, we can go further and note that the Constitution has been interpreted to empower the Australian government to pass laws that give effect to our international obligations to protect world heritage areas.[7] This reading of the external affairs power suggests a character that elevates matters of national and international concern to the central government. More recently, the High Court has recognised that the implied freedom of political communication encompasses non-violent protest and freedom of assembly.[8] Here, the High Court also recognised that the 'physical space in which a protest occurs is inextricably tied up with that protest's communicative function'.[9] For example, a protest outside a forestry building or on a clearing site has the potential to communicate a much more powerful political message than a similar action that is forced to the side of a road or away from the places protestors seek to utilise.[10]

These examples reflect a very gradual broadening of the role and function of the Australian Constitution in relation to the Australian environment. However, they are also fundamentally human-centred and focused on our powers and (implied) rights. By contrast, the phrase eco-constitutionalism tries to situate human action within a broader living system and to limit freedom for the good of the whole. Broadly speaking, the term eco-constitutionalism brings together two substantive areas of research: (1) the worldwide 'greening' of national constitutions that has occurred since the 1980s and (2) the growing interest in 'global constitutionalism' that seeks to identify and justify constitutionalist principles in international law. The most public example of the latter is the United Nations–backed initiative to adopt a Global Pact for the Environment.[11]

---

7 *Commonwealth v Tasmania* (1983) 158 CLR 1 ('Tasmanian Dams Case'). See also Afshin Akhtar Khavari, 'Logging and Acquiring World Heritage: Can Something Go Wrong with What the Tasmanian Dams Case Achieved?' in Nicole Rogers and Michelle Maloney (eds), *Law as if Earth Really Mattered: The Wild Law Judgement Project* (Routledge, 2017).

8 *Brown v Tasmania* (2017) 261 CLR 328. See also Peter Burdon and Mary Heath, 'Protest and Political Communication after Brown v Tasmania' 40(1) *Bulletin: Law Society of South Australia* 10, 10–11.

9 John Eldridge and Tim Matthews, 'The Right to Protest after Brown v Tasmania' *AusPubLaw* (Blog Post, 2 November 2017) <auspublaw.org/2017/11/the-right-to-protest-after-brown-v-tasmania/>.

10 Ibid.

11 'Global Pact for the Environment', *International Union for Conservation of Nature* (Web Page) <www.iucn.org/our-union/commissions/world-commission-environmental-law/our-work/history/foundational-documents-2>.

The origins of eco-constitutionalism can be traced to the German constitutional debates held between 1985 and 1990. Klaus Bosselmann has done the most work to bring the substance of these debates to an English-speaking audience.[12] He notes that, during the 1980s, the environmental movement had such a strong social base that it was able to instigate a public debate about the merits of a new State objective (*Staatsziele*).[13] State objectives have a more formal standing than a policy position; Bosselmann describes them as '[a] binding constitutional law requiring government to seek to fulfil [a] certain task'.[14] The constitutional debates were an exemplary form of public discourse and involved sophisticated discussions about whether or not the environment should be recognised as having intrinsic value, or value because of the services it provided to human beings. In the end, a compromise was reached and art 20a was incorporated into the basic law.[15] It read:

> The State, also in its responsibility for future generations, protects the natural foundations of life in the framework of the constitutional order, by legislation, and, according to law and justice, through the executive and the courts.[16]

Following further advocacy and civil society discussion, an additional amendment was made in 2002 to include reference to non-human animals.[17]

---

12 Klaus Bosselmann, *The Principle of Sustainability: Transforming Law and Governance* (Routledge, 2016) 154–7, doi.org/10.4324/9781315553962. See also Klaus Bosselmann, *Ökologische Grundrechte* (Baden-Baden, 1998).

13 Bosselmann (n 12) 154.

14 Ibid.

15 In 1993, the Joint Constitutional Commission released a Final Report that stated:

> Environmental protection cannot be subject of protection in its own right, especially cannot claim unilateral priority. Rather it needs to be seen in the context of multifaceted situations of tension, for example, with economic growth, industrial development, creation of jobs, housing, energy supply or transport services.

Klaus Bosselmann, 'Eco-Constitutionalism: A New Area of Legal Research and Advocacy' (Conference Paper, Australian Earth Law Alliance Conference, 11 November 2011) 13 <www.earthlaws.org.au/wp-content/uploads/presentations/Bosselmann,-K.-Eco-Constitutionalism-A-new-area-of-legal-research-and-advocacy.pdf>.

16 Bosselmann (n 12) 154. The German Constitution also recognises that human property comes with inherent obligations: see, eg, art 14, which notes: 'Ownership creates obligations. Its use shall at the same time serve the common good.' Scholars have read this to include the good of the ecological community: see, eg, Murray Raff, *Private Property and Environmental Responsibility, a Comparative Study of German Real Property Law* (Kluwer Law International, 2003).

17 The section now reads: 'Mindful also of its responsibility towards future generations, the state shall protect the natural foundations of life and animals by legislation and, in accordance with law and justice, by executive and judicial action, all within the framework of the constitutional order'. *Grundgesetz für die Bundesrepublik Deutschland* [Basic Law for the Federal Republic of Germany] art 20a <fra.europa.eu/en/law-reference/basic-law-federal-republic-germany-33>.

While Germany was undergoing these changes, a similar push from civil society resulted in even stronger amendments to the Swedish Constitution. For example, in 1992, art 120 of the Federal Constitution was inserted to recognise the *Würde der Kreatur*. This is a difficult term to translate, but the Swedish government has offered an official translation: 'the dignity of creation'.[18] The context of these words is an article related to gene technology and, as Peter Saladin has argued, the provision suggests that creation has an essential core or essence that must not be altered by human technology.[19]

While Germany and Switzerland have led the 'greening' of national constitutions, they should also be located within a broader global trend in that direction. In fact, there are hundreds of examples that cannot be reproduced here. To help order this material I have split examples into three main groups: human rights, individual responsibility and obligations that are placed on the State. For contrast and inclusivity, I have also selected examples from jurisdictions around the world and from majority/minority countries.[20]

A. Group 1

Constitutions that recognise a human right to a healthy environment include:

- Angola—art 39(1): 'Everyone has the right to live in a healthy and unpolluted environment and the duty to defend and preserve it.'
- Benin—title II, art 27: 'Every person has the right to a healthy, satisfying and lasting environment, and has the duty to defend it.'
- Cape Verde—pt II, title III, art 72(1): 'Everyone shall have the right to a healthy, ecological balanced environment, and the duty to defend and conserve it.'
- Portugal—pt I, s 3, ch 2, art 66(i): 'Everyone has the right to a healthy and ecologically balanced human environment and the duty to defend it.'

18 Bosselmann (n 12) 155.

19 Ibid. The whole article reads:

1. Persons and their environment shall be protected against abuse of gene technology.
2. The Confederation shall legislate on the use of the reproductive and genetic material of animals, plants, and other organisms. In doing so, it shall take into account the dignity of creation and the security of man, animal and environment, and shall protect the genetic multiplicity of animal and vegetal species.

'Federal Constitution of the Swiss Confederation', *Fedlex: The Publication Platform for Federal Law* (Web Page) <www.fedlex.admin.ch/eli/cc/1999/404/en>.

20 These translations are all from James May and Erin Daly, *Global Environmental Constitutionalism* (Cambridge University Press, 2014) 281–324, doi.org/10.1017/CBO9781139135559.

B. Group 2

Constitutions that place the onus of responsibility on the individual to protect the environment include:

- Czech Republic—Charter of Fundamental Rights and Freedoms, art 35(3): 'In exercising his or her rights nobody may endanger or cause damage to the environment, natural resources, the wealth of natural species, and cultural monuments beyond limits set by law.'
- Finland—ch 2, s 20: 'Nature and its biodiversity, the environment and the national heritage are the responsibility of everyone.'
- France—Charter of the Environment, art 2: 'Everyone is obliged to take part in the preservation and improvement of the environment'; art 3: 'Everyone shall, subject to the conditions defined by the law, avoid any disturbance which he or she is likely to cause to the environment or, if that is not possible, limit its consequences'; art 4: 'Everyone shall contribute to the reparation of the damages which he or she caused to the environment, subject to the conditions defined by the law.'

C. Group 3

Constitutions that place obligations on the State to protect the environment include:

- Columbia—art 7, 8, 67 and 79 impose obligations on the State to protect the diversity and integrity of the environment, to conserve the areas of special ecological importance, and to foster the education for the achievement. The State must also cooperate with other nations in the protection of the ecosystems in border areas.
- Sudan—ch 11(1): 'The State and the citizens have the duty to preserve and promote the country's biodiversity.'
- Yemen—art 35: 'Environmental protection is the collective responsibility of the state and the community at large. Each individual shall have a religious and national duty to protect the environment.'

This is just a very brief overview and, of course, many countries combine these approaches or place legal duties on citizens to protect the environment. For example, ch 2, s 6, art 86 of the Constitution of Poland holds: 'Everyone is obliged to care for the quality of the environment and shall be held responsible for causing its degradation.' In a similar way, ch 2, art 58 of the Constitution of the Russian Federation holds: 'Everyone is obliged to preserve nature and the environment and care for natural wealth.' Article 71 of the Constitution of Ecuador is even more eco-centric, recognising that nature itself has the right to 'integral respect for its existence and for the maintenance and regeneration of its life cycles, structure, functions and evolutionary processes'.[21] Linked to these rights is a broad-standing provision that empowers all 'persons, communities, peoples and nations' to 'call upon public authorities to enforce the rights of nature'.[22] Finally, art 72 places obligations on the Ecuadorian State to restore despoiled nature, including in circumstances where the damage was caused by the 'exploitation of non-renewable natural resources'.[23]

In fact, the greening of national constitutions has occurred concomitantly with a burgeoning academic literature, the overwhelming thrust of which is that constitutional law can and should play a key role in environmental protection. Here are two examples from the leading theorists on eco-constitutionalism. First, Klaus Bosselmann argues: 'the proposed grounding of the rule of law in nature by implementing an environmental grundnorm appears to be an appropriate way forward'.[24] While more hedged in his advocacy, Louis Kotzé presents a similar argument:

> [C]onstitutionalism should also be a vital component of the global regulatory arsenal that is currently being shaped as a social-institutional response to the Anthropocene's socio-ecological crisis ... a constitutionalised global environmental law and governance order would arguably be better able to respond to the Anthropocene's unprecedented exigencies than a non-constitutionalised one.[25]

I do not share this perspective; in the space remaining, I offer some critical observations in the spirit of 'critical loyalty'[26] to the broader objectives that we share. My critical approach is grounded in several diverse sources,

21 For the full text, see 'Constitution of the Republic of Ecuador', *Political Database of the Americas* (Web Page) <pdba.georgetown.edu/Constitutions/Ecuador/english08.html>.

22 Ibid.

23 Ibid. For a critical engagement with these provisions, see Peter Burdon and Claire Williams, 'Rights of Nature: A Constructive Analysis, in Douglas Fisher (ed), *Research Handbook on Fundamental Concepts of Environmental Law* (Edward Elgar Publishing, 2016).

24 Bosselmann (n 12) 231.

25 Kotzé (n 3) 11. See also Boyd (n 4) 3: 'While no nation has yet achieved the holy grail of ecological sustainability ... evidence ... indicates that constitutional protection of the environment can be a powerful and potentially transformative step toward that elusive goal.'

26 J. Ronald Engel, 'Summons to a New Axial Age: The Promise, Limits, and Future of the Earth Charter' in Laura Westra and Mirian Vilela (eds), *The Earth Charter, Ecological Integrit, and Social Movements* (Earthscan, 2014) xv.

including radical and liberal philosophy. First, I refuse to equate critique with criticism[27] or the Critical Legal Studies practice of trashing.[28] As bell hooks has argued: '[T]here is a useful distinction to be made between critique that seeks to expand consciousness and harsh criticism that attacks or trashes.'[29] Critique derives from the Greek word *krisis*, which, as Wendy Brown reminds us, refers to a practice of 'sifting, sorting, judging and repairing' the social world.[30] Seen in this light, critique has a generative or restorative role in public discourse. Moreover, in this chapter, I also adopt Karl Marx's approach to critique, which aims to shed light on the presumptions and presuppositions that underpin an argument but are not necessarily available on the surface.[31]

Further to these ideas, my approach to critique is also influenced by John Rawls who, in teaching moral and political philosophy, would issue the following instruction to his students:

> I always took for granted that the writers we were studying were much smarter than I was. If they were not, why was I wasting my time and the students' time by studying them? If I saw a mistake in their arguments, I supposed those writers saw it too and must have dealt with it. But where? I looked for their way out, not mine. Sometimes their way out was historical: in their day the question need not be raised, or wouldn't arise and so couldn't then be fruitfully discussed. Or there was a part of the text I had overlooked, or had not read. I assumed there were never plain mistakes, not ones that mattered anyway.[32]

This is easy to say but hard to do. What impresses me the most about Rawl's injunction is that it invites generous reading and a philosophical engagement that is constructive, mutual and directed towards a shared undertaking. It regards scholarship as a collective striving for knowledge and eschews individualism, competition or point scoring. With this noted, I turn now to present a critique of eco-constitutionalism.

27 Mary Heath, 'On Critical Thinking' [2012] (4) *The International Journal of Narrative Theory and Community Work* 11, 14.
28 Mark Kelman, 'Trashing' (1984) 36(1/2) *Stanford Law Review* 293.
29 Ibid. See also bell hooks, *Teaching Critical Thinking: Practical Wisdom* (Routledge, 2010) 137.
30 Wendy Brown, 'Introduction' in Talal Asad et al (eds), *Is Critique Secular? Blasphemy, Injury and Free Speech* (Fordham University Press, 2009) 9, doi.org/10.2307/j.ctt1c5cjtk.4.
31 Karl Marx, 'On the Jewish Question' in Robert C Tucker (ed), *The Marx-Engels Reader* (Norton, 1978) 26; Karl Marx, 'For a Ruthless Criticism of Everything Existing' in Robert C Tucker (ed), *The Marx-Engels Reader* (Norton, 1978) 13: '[W]e do not attempt to dogmatically … prefigure the future but want to find the new world only through a criticism of the old.'
32 John Rawls, *Lectures on the History of Moral Philosophy* (Harvard University Press, 2000) xvii.

II. Eco-constitutionalism and idealism

The foundation of my critique of eco-constitutionalism rests on the distinction between two philosophical schools—idealism and materialism. A neat line cannot be drawn between them and so I regard them more as propensities, leanings or postures. An idealist, for example, will emphasise the role of ideas in determining material reality and driving historic change. When faced with a problem, such as the environmental crisis, an idealist might emphasise the importance of adopting an alternative worldview (such as ecocentrism)[33] or focus on strategies grounded in argument and education. An idealist is also likely to focus their attention on law reform that either constrains choice or promotes certain kinds of behaviour.

Materialism, by contrast, is an alternative philosophy that holds that what moves history is the organisation of material life or how human societies subsist and reproduce themselves. The most reduced way we might speak about this today is political economy of the economic order of human existence.[34] Because materialism is not the dominant position today, its perspective is less intuitive for most readers. The easiest way to understand this is to reflect on how changes in the material order—from feudalism to capitalism, for example—impacted the way we think, the dominant family form, our social organisations and social relations.[35] More recently, we might also reflect on the reappearance of 'family values' under the neoliberal economic order.[36] Thus, from a materialist perspective, the environment crisis is not the result of anthropocentrism or other dominant ideas. It is the result of how we organise the means of production in a capitalist economy.

As noted above, these two positions intersect and so a materialist would also hold that the economic order gives rise to dominant ideas, and an idealist might conclude that law reform projects aimed at transforming the means of production is the best way to address a justice issue. What I am trying to focus on is where each philosophical approach places its emphasis. Idealism

33 This has been the central premise of environmental philosophy since its inception and is most overt in schools such as deep ecology. For a recent statement in law, see Fritjof Capra and Ugo Mattei, *The Ecology of Law: Toward a Legal System in Tune with Nature and Community* (Berrett-Koehler, 2018).

34 For a thorough account, see Karl Marx, 'The German Ideology' in Robert C Tucker (ed), *The Marx-Engels Reader* (Norton, 1978).

35 See Immanuel Wallerstein, *The Modern World-System III: The Second Era of Great Expansion of the Capitalist World-Economy, 1730s–1840s* (University of California Press, 2011), doi.org/10.1525/9780520948594.

36 For an exhaustive survey, see Melinda Cooper, *Family Values: Between Neoliberalism and the New Social Conservatism* (Zone Books, 2019).

is primarily focused on the role of ideas in shaping society and history, while materialism focuses on the ways human beings organise and arrange their mode of subsistence.

With this background in place, I can articulate the first strand of my critique of eco-constitutionalism: it reflects and perpetuates idealism. Following my understanding of critique, I do not present this as a bad thing in itself. However, the idealist nature of eco-constitutionalism is a presupposition that is not obvious or part of the everyday self-description provided by advocates of eco-constitutionalism. Karl Marx was the first person to explicitly draw out this line of critique and think about the limits of an idealist approach to history. His 1848 essay, 'On the Jewish Question'[37] (OJQ), remains the best analysis of the dilemmas of the modern nation-state[38] and circles around the question of what it is about constitutional democracies that limit their capacity to fully deliver on enshrined promises (that is, equality for all). Central to Marx's critique is his contention that constitutional democracies emerge from the nature of capitalist production. This is nothing more than an application of materialism and is distinct from arguments that liberal democracies emerged because of the power of that idea.[39] With the emergence of constitutional democracy, Marx argues that citizens concentrated on how things are described in law rather than focusing on how they are experienced in material life. There is, he argues, a growing split between these two things.

Constitutional States improved the legal status and material condition for many people.[40] However, as our focus turned to the conditions of formal equality (what Marx called political emancipation) and how individuals were described in law, the gap between our political and material life grew. Think, for example, of laws that hold out the promise that all citizens are free and equal. While undeniably an improvement on overtly discriminatory laws, statements like this do not necessarily challenge the powers that course through civil society and limit certain kinds of access based on race, class, gender, sexuality, etc. Thus, there is a gap between how a person is conceived

37 Marx, 'On the Jewish Question' (n 31).

38 For a fuller analysis, see Peter Burdon, 'On the Limits of Political Emancipation and Legal Rights' (2019) 34(2) *International Journal for the Semiotics of Law* 319, doi.org/10.1007/s11196-019-09634-3.

39 Francis Fukuyama took this idea to its extreme in his 'End of History' thesis: see Francis Fukuyama, *End of History and the Last Man* (Free Press, 2006).

40 Marx, 'On the Jewish Question' (n 31) 35. Marx is very clear that constitutional States are an improvement on feudalism. For example, he argues that political emancipation is 'the final form of emancipation within the framework of the prevailing social order'. In other words, it is the best outcome under a liberal constitutional State.

in law (as a legal person) and their daily life. A guarantee of equality does not make it so and for those still labouring under discrimination it would be experienced as an abstraction. This was true for the Jewish community that Marx was describing in OJQ and it remains true for people today who march under the banner #BlackLivesMatter and #metoo. So, the key question becomes: How do you convert an abstract idea like equality into a reality? And can you do so by placing constitutional provisions at the vanguard of change?

Marx did not think so. His contention in OJQ is that the split between abstract representations of us and the reality of our material difference is commensurate with an emphasis on idealism[41] as a dominant form of political rationality. That is why, he argues, constitutional States are ultimately unable to deliver on their promise to guarantee equality or emancipation for all citizens. Change that is grounded in idealism might emancipate us politically but not at the deeper level of our material lives.[42] Radical or deep change requires not only substantive legal reform *but* also an alteration to the ways we produce and reproduce our daily existence. To be more concrete, full human emancipation may require an equitable distribution of wealth or an economic system that does not so radically segregate workers from owners.[43]

This same logic can be applied to eco-constitutionalism. While it might be an improvement for the Australian Constitution to contain a substantive statement about human rights to a healthy environment or impose obligations on the federal government to guarantee clean air or water for citizens, we should also be attentive to how this kind of reform widens the gap between our political and material lives. Forms of injustice are less eliminated than depoliticised through abstract legal statements.[44] And it is

41 In this essay, Marx is focusing on German idealism. But I contend that the same is true for all approaches to idealism, including legalism and liberalism.

42 At this early point in his career Marx has not really figured out a strong position on emancipation and only offers some brief thoughts that will be developed in subsequent work. For example, he argues:

> Human emancipation will only be complete when the real, individual man has absorbed into himself the abstract citizen; when as an individual man, in his everyday life, in his work, and in his relationships, he has become a species-being; and when he has recognized and organized his own powers (*forces propres*) as social powers so that he no longer separates this social power from himself as political power.

Marx, 'On the Jewish Question' (n 31) 46.

43 There is a substantive literature in historical materialism on the relationship between racism and capitalism. For an introduction, see Peter Hudis, 'Racism and the Logic of Capitalism', *Historical Materialism* (Web Page) <www.historicalmaterialism.org/articles/racism-and-logic-capitalism>.

44 Marx, 'On the Jewish Question' (n 31) 45.

equally possible that eco-constitutional reform in Australia will lead to no substantive change in environmental stewardship. This has been the case in countries like Ecuador that, after recognising the rights of nature in their constitution, have maintained an extractive economy that continues to threaten areas such as the Galapagos Islands.[45] Moreover, all the countries listed above with constitutional provisions related to the environment continue to despoil their environment and very few are taking steps to live within Earth's carrying capacity.[46] There are complex reasons for this and nobody is holding out eco-constitutionalism as the panacea for the environmental crisis. But if I was going to recommend eco-constitutionalism as a strategy for environmental protection, it would be useful to see some evidence of its effectiveness.

III. Inception and neutrality

In the preceding section, I illustrated how critique can proceed by bringing to light the presumptions and presuppositions that underpin a proposal like eco-constitutionalism. In this section, I wish to go deeper into Marx's critical method and focus on his injunction that to ask a question properly is to begin to resolve it.[47] Another way to approach critique is to ask a series of parallel questions such as: What was it about this historical moment that has led to the *x* being presented in the way that it has? What are the contradictions in the existing political and social and economic life that keep us from being able to resolve *x*? To reframe for our discussion: What is it about this historical moment that has given rise to advocacy for eco-constitutionalism?

In overseas jurisdictions, eco-constitutionalism has been driven by the emergence of an ecological sensibility (as discussed above in Germany[48]) or as part of attempts to modernise outdated governance instruments. The same motivating forces are not yet present in Australia. To the extent

45 Andrew Chappelle, 'Ecuador Struggles to Contain Oil Spill in Galapagos Port', *Aljazeera News* (online, 24 December 2019) <www.aljazeera.com/news/2019/12/ecuador-struggles-oil-spill-galapagos-port-191224132308019.html>.

46 There are various ways of measuring this. See, eg, Amanda Erickson, 'Few Countries are Meeting the Paris Climate Goals. Here Are the Ones That Are', *The Washington Post* (online, 12 October 2018) <www.washingtonpost.com/world/2018/10/11/few-countries-are-meeting-paris-climate-goals-here-are-ones-that-are/>.

47 Marx, 'On the Jewish Question' (n 31) 26.

48 Bosselmann (n 12) 154–7.

that there is an active conversation on eco-constitutionalism, it is limited to scholars of comparative international law.[49] Moreover, while the Australian public have an increased awareness of environmental issues and most of the population would like more action from government,[50] nobody has proposed that our Constitution is the best venue for a statement of ecological principle.[51] At most, eco-constitutionalism is constructed as a political project aimed at leveraging the Constitution for our protection. We are only talking about it because other avenues and strategies for environmental protection have not worked (or are not working). To paraphrase Robert Macfarlane, I regard eco-constitutionalism as part of our Anthropocene moment: 'At once hopeful and desperate, it is a late-hour attempt to prevent a slow-motion ecocide.'[52]

In noting this, I am not trying to suggest that emancipatory projects cannot emerge out of a crisis,[53] only that we should be honest about the rationale for eco-constitutionalism and think about how its potential is marked by the circumstances of its inception. We might think, for example, about whether there are any risks associated with leveraging a governance document at a moment of political emergency and whether emergency is fertile soil for progressive demands. Historically, emergency politics has led to the suspension of politics, debate and civil liberties.[54] For example, declarations of wartime emergency allowed governments to 'ban strikes, implement censorship, prosecute pacifists and do whatever else they deemed necessary to win the war'.[55] More recently, the Northern Territory Intervention was

49 See, in particular, ibid; Kotzé (n 3).

50 For example, numerous polls indicated that Australians would like the federal government to do more on climate change: see Annika Blau, 'What Australians Really Think about Climate Action', *ABC News* (online, 5 February 2020) <www.abc.net.au/news/2020-02-05/australia-attitudes-climate-change-action-morrison-government/11878510?nw=0>.

51 As noted above, advocacy hinges on the view that we are better placed to respond to the environmental crisis with these reforms in place than without.

52 Robert Macfarlane, 'Should This Tree Have the Same Rights as You?', *The Guardian* (online, 2 November 2019) <www.theguardian.com/books/2019/nov/02/trees-have-rights-too-robert-macfarlane-on-the-new-laws-of-nature>.

53 Although the historical record suggests that crisis is more often an opportunity for even more predatory forms of capitalism and exploitation. See Naomi Klein, *The Shock Doctrine* (Picador, 2008); David McNally, Eddie Yuen and James Davis, *Catastrophism: The Apocalyptic Politics of Collapse and Rebirth*, ed Sasha Lilley (PM Press, 2012); Antony Loewenstein, *Disaster Capitalism: Making a Killing Out of Catastrophe* (Verso, 2017).

54 Jeff Sparrow, '"Climate Emergency" Endangers Democracy', *Eureka Street* (online, 21 June 2019) <www.eurekastreet.com.au/article/-climate-emergency--endangers-democracy>. See also Giorgio Agamben, *State of Exception* (University of Chicago Press, 2004), doi.org/10.7208/chicago/9780226009261.001.0001.

55 Ibid.

used to justify the militarisation of First Nations communities.[56] And in response to the environmental emergency, I contend that the most robust response from the Australian government has been to attack environmental organisations[57] and expand policing of environmental activists.[58] This was picked up by Paul Krugman who wrote shortly after the 2019–20 Australian Bushfires: 'The sick irony of the current situation is that anti-environmentalism is getting more extreme precisely at the moment when the prospects for decisive action should be better than ever.'[59]

Increasing this risk is the fact that there is no network of people advocating for eco-constitutionalism in Australia. If such a change was proposed right now it would mean that citizens have not done the vital work of internalising the ideas, thinking about their meaning and (most importantly) understanding how their application would require radical change at the level of civil society and the economy. The reform would be handed down by the political class, like Athena emerging fully formed from the head of Zeus. Constitutional reforms with a high chance of changing the material lives of citizens look more like the campaign for a First Nations Voice to Parliament. This reform has an organised social base and largely reflects the views of First Nations people.[60] As this experience shows, emancipatory proposals are something we collectively define and construct. They are like a piece of music that 'unfolds over time' and 'gets its sense of stability from the ongoing creation and resolution of various forms of tension'.[61] To be clear, I would still regard this change as idealistic (in a philosophical sense). But a robust participatory process has a much greater chance of reducing the gap between the ideas promoted in the reform and the concomitant material change.

56 Stan Grant, 'A Decade on from the NT Intervention, the "Torment of Powerlessness" Lives On', *ABC News* (online, 21 June 2017) <www.abc.net.au/news/2017-06-21/stan-grant-a-decade-on-from-the-nt-intervention/8638628>.

57 Peter Burdon, 'Government Inquiry Takes Aim at Green Charities that "Get Political"', *The Conversation* (online, 16 April 2015) <theconversation.com/government-inquiry-takes-aim-at-green-charities-that-get-political-40166>.

58 Peter Burdon, 'The Targeting of Environmentalists with State-Corporate Intelligence Networks' in Kirsten Anker et al (eds), *From Environmental to Ecological Law* (Routledge, 2020), doi.org/10.4324/9781003001256-5.

59 Paul Krugman, 'Apocalypse Becomes the New Normal', *The New York Times* (online, 2 January 2020) <www.nytimes.com/2020/01/02/opinion/climate-change-australia.html>.

60 See, eg, Pat Anderson AO and Mark Leibler AC, *Final Report of the Referendum Council* (Final Report, 30 June 2017); Megan Davis, 'Constitutional Recognition: Two Decades On', *Indigenous Constitutional Law* (Blog Post, 1 March 2021) <www.indigconlaw.org/home/constitutional-recognition-two-decades-on>.

61 Joseph William Singer, *Entitlement: The Paradoxes of Property* (Yale University Press, 2000) 13.

From a materialist perspective, the constitutional statements that I highlighted above do not directly confront the core reasons for the environmental crisis or the powers in civil society that foreclose certain kinds of demands from being heard.[62] For example, eco-constitutionalism is not necessary to implement immediate legal changes that would improve environmental outcomes and governance. An incomplete list includes tightening rules for political donations to stamp out the influence of the fossil fuel industry on governance, legislating binding targets to reduce emissions in line with the Paris Climate Agreement, or placing a moratorium on new coal mines or fossil fuel extraction. A materialist perspective would also concentrate on the inconsistency between capitalism and environmental protection[63] and advocate measures to transition the economy towards steady-state or retraction. There is, of course, a lot missing from this view,[64] but its intention is to focus on the conditions of our material reality and not abstract representations of ourselves.

A natural reply to this analysis would be to suggest that we do not need to choose between idealist reforms and material changes to the way our society reproduces itself. A variation of this reasoning suggests that reform at the level of the Constitution can be the thing that drives substantive change at the level of economy and society. It is not my intention here to foreclose these possibilities or to suggest that there is only one right way to address the substantial environmental difficulties we face. We need people working at all levels and a healthy scepticism towards anybody that suggests they have all the answers. However, it is my contention in this chapter that eco-constitutionalism only rises to the level of political emancipation and risks staying at that level without addressing the more systemic reasons for environmental destruction. Moreover, because we are operating on a limited time scale, it is also important to be strategic about where we place our emphasis.

---

62 See John Bellamy Foster, *Marx's Ecology: Materialism and Nature* (Monthly Review Press, 2000); Kohei Saito, *Karl Marx's Ecosocialism: Capital, Nature, and the Unfinished Critique of Political Economy* (Monthly Review Press, 2017), doi.org/10.2307/j.ctt1gk099m.

63 See Christopher Wright and Daniel Nyberg, *Climate Change, Capitalism, and Corporations: Processes of Creative Self-Destruction* (Cambridge University Press, 2015), doi.org/10.1017/CBO9781139939676; Jason W Moore, *Capitalism in the Web of Life* (Verso, 2015).

64 Most important, I think, is that materialism is largely blind to the way that a dominant logic in society influences the subjectivity of citizens. For example, how neoliberal rationality had rendered economic growth natural and environmental protection virtually unthinkable. This is captured in Fredrick Jameson's haunting line: 'it is easier to imagine an end to the world than an end to capitalism'. Wendy Brown, *Undoing the Demos: Neoliberalism's Stealth Revolution* (Zone Books, 2015), doi.org/10.2307/j.ctt17kk9p8.

One key way that materialist and idealistic approaches to environmental protection differ is in the extent to which they name and expressly engage the powers that are giving rise to a problem. The constitutional provisions listed earlier in this chapter are phrased in neutral language and are largely apolitical.[65] This approach is useful if one is seeking to build a broad coalition of support and avoid conflict by naming a material structure such as capitalism. However, to be indifferent to the powers that organise society is ultimately not a neutral position—it is to side with the status quo. For example, if extractive capitalism is a site of social power and something that frames our political demands (that is, protect the Great Barrier Reef because that is good for tourism) then for a constitution to feign neutrality or talk in general terms about environmental human rights is to side with existing privilege and foreclose certain kinds of arguments from gaining traction.

IV. Conclusion

In this chapter, I have undertaken to present a critique of eco-constitutionalism. By framing it as an idealistic approach to politics, I sought to bring to the surface the ways it abstracts from the reality of human–Earth relations and leaves unchallenged the material causes of environmental exploitation. While my analysis has focused on eco-constitutionalism, a similar kind of critique could be made of other approaches to political change that focus on the constitution or ground their theory of change in abstract representations of the human condition. Thus, while campaigns for human rights and equality are unquestionably an advance on an overtly discriminatory legal system, they also create a gap between how individuals are represented politically and the conditions of their daily life. From a materialist perspective, this gap can only be addressed by engaging the material causes of an injustice and challenging the status quo at the level of political economy. Silence about these factors is not neutrality—it maintains the status quo.

While there is a growing environmental awareness in Australia, it has not given rise to a movement for eco-constitutionalism. There is also no suggestion that such a reform would greatly change or influence the development of our national character. Where similar reforms have occurred overseas,

65 Even the language of human rights seeks to be politically neutral and appeal to universal ideals: see Samuel Moyn, *The Last Utopia: Human Rights in History* (Harvard University Press, 2010), doi.org/10.2307/j.ctvjk2vkf.

they have either been driven from below and, thus, captured a prevailing sensibility, or responded to calls for modernisation. However, there is no evidence that eco-constitutionalism has led to greater environmental stewardship in those countries.[66] This is consistent with the theoretical argument advanced in this chapter—namely, that eco-constitutionalism can only be an idealist demand if it is applied in the context of growth economics or extractive capitalism.

To be fair to those advocating eco-constitutionalism, many of them agree with this position. That is why both Bosselmann and Kotzé pair their advocacy with other reforms that they contend are necessary for true sustainability. Where we differ, I think, is that I place my emphasis on strategies that have a firm social base, have immediate impact and challenge the underling material causes of the environmental crisis. Without this emphasis, I fear that we are focusing on reforms that look significant but really provide window dressing for business as usual. In this scenario, the only thing eco-constitutionalism will liberate is more coal.[67]

66 This can be measured in a number of ways. For example, none of the countries discussed in the second part of this chapter have put forward Nationally Determined Contributions that are compatible with limiting global warming to two degrees: 'Countries', *Climate Action Tracker* (Web Page) <climateactiontracker.org/countries/>. Expressed another way, those same countries continue to contribute to rapid biodiversity decline: see Anthony Waldron et al, 'Reductions in Global Biodiversity Loss Predicted from Conservation Spending', *Nature* (Web Page, 25 October 2017) <www.nature.com/articles/nature24295>. See also the latest IPBES report: 'Global Assessment Report on Biodiversity and Ecosystem Services', *Intergovernmental Science-Policy Platform on Biodiversity and Ecosystem Services* (Web Page) <ipbes.net/global-assessment>.

67 Mckenzie Wark, *Molecular Red: Theory for the Anthropocene* (Verso, 2016) xiv.

6

Activating Australian Citizenship through Constitutional Change: Towards an Inclusive Australian National Identity

Kim Rubenstein[1]

At the time of federation in 1901, the 'people of the Commonwealth' for whom the Constitution was formed were not Australian citizens.[2] Members of part of a broader 'common-wealth',[3] the framers[4] who marked out their new constitutional territory were British subjects, and positively determined to remain so, owing their allegiance to Her Majesty, the Queen

1 Parts of this piece draw from my earlier scholarship, including Kim Rubenstein, 'Power, Control and Citizenship: The Uluru Statement from the Heart as Active Citizenship' (2018) 30(1) *Bond Law Review* 19, doi.org/10.53300/001c.5659.

2 Kim Rubenstein, 'From Supranational to Dual to Alien Citizen: Australia's Ambivalent Journey' in Simon Bronitt and Kim Rubenstein (eds), *Citizenship in a Post-National World: Australia and Europe Compared* (Federation Press, 2008) 1–15.

3 Helen Irving explains, in her term as the Harvard Chair in Australian Studies, that the term Commonwealth is derived from James Bryce's three-volume work, published in 1888, *The American Commonwealth*. Irving states that it was from this source 'that in 1891 the very fitting name "Commonwealth" was chosen for the new federal nation under construction': Helen Irving, 'A Nation Built on Words: The Constitution and National Identity in America and Australia' (2009) 33(2) *Journal of Australian Studies* 211, 214, doi.org/10.1080/14443050902883421.

4 The framers of the Constitution were white men.

of England.[5] Over time, Her Majesty became the Queen of Australia, and the status of Australian citizenship was independently formed.[6] Since federation there have been many significant changes to Australian society, beyond the changed relationship with the Queen and the start of Australian citizenship. The 2021 Census identified nearly half (48 per cent) of the Australian community had a parent born overseas (first-generation Australian).[7] Immigration, which was the focus of *restriction* as a motivating force for federation, has become a defining feature of modern Australia. At federation, Australia's Indigenous population, while formally British subjects, were treated like 'aliens' in every other sense of the word.[8] Each of these aspects of membership and identity in Australia—its changed relationship with the Queen, its changed multicultural make-up and its changing relationship with Indigenous Australians—is fundamental to an Australian constitutional coming of age. This chapter argues that it is time to activate Australian citizenship through constitutional change. There is no question that the nation of Australia of the 2020s is 'very different from that imagined by the bearded men of federation'.[9] It is time to promote an inclusive national identity that represents the 'lived experience' of the current members, rather than being constitutionally locked into the norms and identities of the framers from the 1890s.[10]

The starting point for this argument is that modern constitutions are foundational legal frames for promoting and affirming national identity and contributing to a socially cohesive society. Whether one thinks of a constitution as being 'affirmative', as in 'confirming, in the present, the political and legal rules and values that already exist', as the Australian

---

5 Kim Rubenstein, 'Citizenship and the Constitutional Convention Debates: A Mere Legal Inference?' (1997) 25(2) *Federal Law Review* 295, doi.org/10.22145/flr.25.2.5.

6 Although concurrently held with British subject status until 1987, Australian citizenship is now the statutory term representing membership of the Australian community. Note the decision of *Love v Commonwealth* (2020) 270 CLR 152 that also identifies non-alien constitutional status for Indigenous Australians.

7 '2021 Census: Nearly Half of Australians Have a Parent Born Overseas, *Australian Bureau of Statistics* (Media Release, 28 June 2022) <www.abs.gov.au/media-centre/media-releases/2021-census-nearly-half-australians-have-parent-born-overseas>.

8 Peter Prince, 'Aliens in Their Own Land. "Aliens" and the Rule of Law in Colonial and Post-Federation Australia' (PhD Thesis, The Australian National University, 2015), doi/org/10.25911/5d78d624005bb.

9 See Tamson Pietsch and Frances Flanagan, 'Here We Stand: Temporal Thinking in Urgent Times' (2020) 17(2) *History Australia* 252, 264, doi.org/10.1080/14490854.2020.1758577.

10 Indeed, I have written elsewhere of the gendered nature of the framing of the Constitution, including Deborah Cass and Kim Rubenstein, 'Representation/s of Women in the Australian Constitutional System' (1995) 17(1) *Adelaide Law Review* 3.

Constitution has been categorised,[11] or 'transformative', as in serving to change or to break with the past or to overcome the defects or injustices of the past, as was the case in the United States of America,[12] modern constitutionalism has affirmed *the people* as sovereign and the people's consent as essential to a legitimate government. In liberal democratic societies like Australia, bound by the rule of law, where those with institutional power, such as the Parliament, the executive and the courts are subject to the law, it is fundamental that the *foundations* to those rules, as set out in the Constitution, are connected to and mirror the experience of those bound by them.

The Constitution, as it currently stands, does *not* reflect those fundamental changes to Australia's relationship with the Queen, or with multicultural Australia, and has never represented its connection with Indigenous Australians. The values of the 1890s that formed the legal and political rules of the 1901 Constitution have clearly evolved and transformed so that there is a lack of harmony between Australia's constitution and its 'people'.[13] This has affected the quality of Australian citizenship and Australia's national identity. Constitutional change or transformation is therefore necessary to shore up Australia's constitution to ensure the current political values and societal membership of Australia are affirmed. This change would represent the legal transformation of the Constitution to be a framework for promoting a more inclusive and activated citizenship. This is possible in Australia given that the Constitution mandates in s 128 that constitutional change *requires* the direct involvement of the people, by requiring a majority of voters throughout Australia, as well as a majority of States, to vote in favour of any proposal for constitutional change.

I. My own Australian citizenship

I am developing this argument not only as a scholar of Australian constitutional and citizenship law but also as a sixth-generation Jewish Australian. One of my ancestors, Henry Cohen, was indicted in London at the Old Bailey on 20 March 1833 for having received stolen 'promissory

11 Irving (n 3) 215.
12 Ibid.
13 Elisa Arcioni and Kim Rubenstein, '*R v Pearson; Ex parte Sipka*: Feminism and the Franchise' in Heather Douglas et al (eds), *Australian Feminist Judgments* 55 (Hart Publishing, 2014).

notes',[14] 'each, the property of our sovereign Lord the King'. His indictment is electronically accessible on the Old Bailey website[15] and I read each of the statements of witnesses called by the Crown to make the case against him, including that he had been found to have been in possession of stolen promissory notes in the past.[16] The 'prisoner' provided his defence, in writing. 'Gentlemen, I have taken these notes in my business, and I am entirely innocent of any guilty knowledge.' Indeed, he asked:

> [I]f I had I would not have gone to Messrs. Masterman and Co. (the bank) where I must have been well known, having paid at that house monies at different times to a large amount, for bills of exchange accepted by me.

Moreover, practically, he explained if:

> I refuse to take (promissory) notes, I may as well shut up my shop, as some weeks I take 60l. or 70l. in notes; and am in the habit continually of taking country notes, living near the Paddington-canal, where boats come from all parts of the country, and coaches also.

Protesting his innocence, he asked to be restored 'to my wife and ten helpless children'. That restoration was not to occur in England: he was found guilty and, at the age of 43, was transported (for 14 years), arriving in Sydney, Australia, on 18 December 1833.

Thanks to the excellent work of Rabbi Dr John S Levi AC,[17] we know Henry's wife and 10 children (and two of their servants) travelled to Australia on a separate ship, arriving three days after the convict transport that carried Henry.[18] Henry was sent to Port Macquarie where he was 'assigned' in January 1834 to Major Archibald Clunes Innes in whose 'service' he remained for six years. In June 1839, Cohen requested a pardon, which was supported by Clunes Innes and by February the following year he was given a 'leave ticket' but had to remain in the District of Port Macquarie.

14 A promissory note is a legal instrument (more particularly, a financial instrument and a debt instrument), in which one party (the *maker* or *issuer*) promises in writing to pay a determinate sum of money to the other (the *payee*), either at a fixed or determinable future time or on demand of the payee, under specific terms. I think of this like a modern-day 'cheque', although they are no longer so 'modern'.

15 'Henry Cohen, Theft: Receiving, 16th May 1833', *The Proceedings of the Old Bailey* (Web Page) <www.oldbaileyonline.org>.

16 In the hearing, it alleges that this had happened four times before but Henry said, 'No, Sir, it is only the third': Ibid.

17 John S Levi, *These are the Names: Jewish Lives in Australia, 1788–1850* (Miegunyah Press, 2nd ed, 2013). Rabbi Levi's Companion of the Order of Australia (AC) was awarded on 26 January 2021.

18 Ibid 141–2.

His service did not prevent him having two more children, born in Port Macquarie in 1834 and 1837, and his wife Elizabeth kept a clothing store in Horton Street in the centre of town. Henry eventually received a conditional pardon and, by 1845, *The Sydney Morning Herald* reported him thanking the 'settlers for their support' and resigning the management of the store to his sons. His full pardon is said to have materialised in 1847 with Henry returning to Sydney.

Henry affirmed his Jewish identity with his participation as a 'collector' for 'The Jerusalem Fund' for the maintenance of the poor in the Holy Land and his election as president of the York Street Synagogue in Sydney in 1859.[19] It is through his second son, Samuel Cohen, that I then descend as the sixth generation, remarkably still living as an identifying Jewish Australian. As John Levi explains of Henry's early colonial Australia, '[a]part from the indigenous Australians, the Jews constituted the only non-Christian minority' and they were a 'small urban class of outsiders'. They formed 1 per cent of the convict population and their descendants today would number in the hundreds of thousands, although those who identify as Jewish Australians, estimated to number 120,000 people in 2021, constitute just 0.5 per cent of the national population.[20] In other words, assimilation impacted on that Jewish convict lineage. Knowing that I am in a small group of descendants who are still living Jewish lives has been part of my own sense of identity, and is relevant to my interest in legal and social questions about membership and citizenship. Indeed, even though not part of my direct family heritage, the Holocaust has nevertheless been significant to my own thinking.[21] If I had been born in Europe, it would have been me, and that realisation profoundly shapes my commitment to the role of law as a means to protecting human rights and promoting social inclusion.

So, with my own experience of 'Australian citizenship' transparent, it is helpful to reflect that one of the Jewish framers of the Australian Constitution, Sir Isaac Isaacs, directly proposed that there would be *no* clear reference to Australian citizenship in the Australian Constitution. In Isaac Isaacs's view,

19 'Australian Jewish Community and Culture: York Street Synagogue, Sydney', *State Library of New South Wales* (Web Page) <www.sl.nsw.gov.au/stories/australian-jewish-community-and-culture/york-street-synagogue-sydney>.

20 'Australia's Jewish Population at an All-Time High', *J-Wire*, 28 June 2022 (Web Page) <www.jwire.com.au/australias-jewish-population-at-an-all-time-high/>.

21 My father's ancestors fled Poland at the end of the nineteenth century and headed to England and then out to Australia at the turn of the century, seeking a new life well before the European tragedy of the Holocaust.

such a federal power to regulate a contested concept of citizenship 'will land us in innumerable difficulties'.[22] I have argued elsewhere[23] that this decision has had a continuing impact on the quality of membership in Australia.

II. Citizenship in Australia

In the late 1890s, when propertied, white, male Australians—those bestowed with formal, active, voting rights—came together to write the Constitution, there was a democratic element to its formation. The participants were elected directly to the 1897 and 1898 constitutional conventions established to draft Australia's constitution, rather than drawing from the existing representative colonial parliaments. For that reason, those conventions were known as the '[p]eople's convention[s]'.[24] That women and Indigenous Australians were not part of the people underlines an imbalance of power from the nation's inception.[25]

This is not to discount the voice of the women who were campaigning for the vote and who, as active citizens, ensured that s 41 of the Constitution guaranteed those who already had the right to vote in the colonies would be able to vote in federal elections of the new Commonwealth of Australia.[26] This included Indigenous and white women in South Australia who had the vote at that time and, by the time of federation, white women in Western Australia, too. Indigenous South Australian women who were not already on the electoral roll in that State would later lose a right to vote when the *Commonwealth Electoral Act 1902* (Cth), which introduced the franchise for women in federal elections, specifically excluded Indigenous people.[27]

22 Rubenstein (n 5).
23 Ibid. See also Kim Rubenstein 'Citizenship, Sovereignty and Migration: Australia's Exclusive Approach to Membership of the Community' (2002) 13 *Public Law Review* 102; Kim Rubenstein 'Looking for the "Heart" of the National Political Community: Regulating Membership in Australia' (2007) 9 *UTS Law Review* 84.
24 The full records of these conventions have now been scanned and are available online, see Records of the Australasian Federal Conventions of the 1890s, *Parliament of Australia* (Web Page) <www.aph.gov.au/About_Parliament/Senate/Powers_practice_n_procedures/Records_of_the_Australasian_Federal_Conventions_of_the_1890s>.
25 See Cass and Rubenstein (n 10).
26 Section 41 states: 'No adult person who has or acquires a right to vote at elections for the more numerous House of the Parliament of a State shall, while the right continues, be prevented by any law of the Commonwealth from voting at elections for either House of the Parliament of the Commonwealth.'
27 For an explanation of s 41 and the role of South Australian women in its evolution, see Arcioni and Rubenstein (n 13) 55.

Beliefs around people's equality (or lack of it) influenced the balance of power within society at that time. Indeed, it was not until 1962 that Indigenous Australians' right to vote was passed into the *Commonwealth Electoral Act* (Cth).[28] Formal citizenship status, which Indigenous Australians had by their birth in Australia,[29] as did women, did not mean they had substantive citizenship rights.[30] It meant that, for the first 48 years, full membership status in Australia was solely as a British subject, and the newly minted 'Australian citizen' only came into being on 26 January 1949 with the introduction of the *Nationality and Citizenship Act 1948* (Cth), which later became the *Australian Citizenship Act 1948* (Cth), before being repealed and replaced by a new *Australian Citizenship Act* (Cth) in 2007. Australians were *both* British subjects *and* Australian citizens until the term British subject was repealed and Australians became solely Australian citizens in 1987.[31] This change had consequences for British subjects who were resident in Australia and who were not Australian citizens, but its impact was felt more widely than this.[32]

The passing of the *Australia Act* (Cth) in 1986—which has a long title reflecting its purpose 'to bring constitutional arrangements affecting the Commonwealth and the States … into conformity with the status of the Commonwealth of Australia as a sovereign, independent and federal nation'—reflected a change to Australian conceptions of sovereignty. It was also a time when the Australian executive acknowledged that, no matter which country a person came from, they had equal access to applying for Australian citizenship.[33] Each of these changes is relevant to the argument that the people of Australia today have a different understanding of and connection to Australia than did the framers of the Constitution and those resident in Australia in 1901.

Finally, Isaacs's statement regarding the 'innumerable difficulties' he foresaw around placing citizenship within a federal power in that period of drafting is also relevant to the importance of returning to the Constitution to activate a form of citizenship that reflects Australian society's make-up today, as a

28 See Kim Rubenstein with Jacqueline Field, *Australian Citizenship Law* (Thomson Reuters, 2nd ed, 2017) [2.220] [6.190].

29 See discussion about citizenship by birth: Ibid 11 n 67, [3.50], [4.50], [4.70], [4.200], [4.250], [7.8].

30 Ibid 9–10 [1.20].

31 See the discussions about British subject status: Ibid [3.120], [4.140], [4.170], [4.180], [4.190].

32 This included British subjects being able to be deported under the *Migration Act 1958* (Cth). See also Kim Rubenstein and Niamh Lenagh Maguire, 'Citizenship Law' in Hugh Selby and Ian Freckleton (eds), *Appealing to the Future: Michael Kirby and His Legacy* (Thomson Reuters, 2009) 105–130.

33 See Rubenstein with Field (n 28) [4.190].

constitutional affirmation of that reality. Indeed, Indigenous Australians have recently led the way regarding returning to the Constitution as a form of active citizenship to which this piece now turns.

III. Uluru Statement as active citizenship

Indigenous Australians' experience of citizenship and membership provides a particularly illuminating reminder of the disjuncture between formal legal status and substantive membership. Formal citizenship status, which Indigenous Australians had by their birth in Australia, first as British subjects at federation, and then also as Australian citizens when the term was created on the 26 January 1949, did not mean they had substantive citizenship rights.[34] As discussed above, Indigenous Australians were not given the federal vote until 1962,[35] and much government regulation affecting Indigenous Australians occurred through the State parliaments. For example, to escape discrimination under other Western Australian (WA) laws, including restrictions on freedom of movement, Indigenous Australians living in WA had to apply for 'citizenship' under the *Natives (Citizenship Rights) Act 1944* (WA). The statute purported to grant 'citizenship' to Indigenous applicants who 'adopted the manner and habits of civilised life'. A successful applicant was 'deemed to be no longer a native or aborigine'. When seeking advice around the constitutionality of the legislation, Commonwealth Attorney-General Sir Garfield Barwick, Solicitor-General Kenneth Bailey and senior Commonwealth lawyers found no contravention of the Australian Constitution. Barwick said WA 'citizenship' was 'really no more than a certificate of exemption' from the operation of State laws, especially the *Native Welfare Act 1904* (WA). That law prevented the sale of liquor to any 'native'. Indeed, many laws around the country in different States discriminated against Indigenous Australians who were British subjects and then Australian citizens.[36] The inconsistency of their treatment is made clear by pointing out that all Indigenous Australians became Australian citizens on 26 January 1949, when the term came into being, yet, different States continued to legislate to discriminate against them. This example illustrates

34 See John Chesterman and Brian Galligan, *Citizens without Rights: Aborigines and Australian Citizenship* (Cambridge University Press, 1997), doi.org/10.1017/CBO9780511518249. For a fuller account of the disjuncture between formal citizenship status and the rights that flow from that citizenship, see broadly, Rubenstein with Field (n 28), including a discussion on women and Indigenous Australians.

35 Rubenstein with Field (n 28) [2.220] [6.190].

36 Chesterman and Galligan (n 34).

the fractured and fragmented experience of membership of the nation for Indigenous Australians. Despite being British subjects, and then Australian citizens, they experienced legal regimes that stripped them of the most basic rights associated with citizenship.

And, while the 1967 referendum did make changes to the Constitution to represent the start of a journey of recognising Australia's Indigenous people to be counted (as the Uluru Statement identifies), and in relation to the Commonwealth's power to make laws for them, it did not correct the imbalance between formal citizenship, which Indigenous Australians already held, and their unequal substantive membership. Indigenous activism around an Indigenous voice in our democratic system and the enabling of an active citizenship to ensure a road to substantive membership is not new. It follows a long line of Indigenous claims for a more engaged membership[37] that is now central to public policy for all Australians interested in an inclusive national identity.

The Uluru Statement from the Heart is the outcome of the 12 First Nations Regional Dialogues culminating in the National Constitutional Convention at Uluru in May 2017. The convention represented the First Peoples from across the country forming a consensus position on the form constitutional recognition should take. This direct involvement of Australia's First Peoples around the country was the first of its kind in Australia's history and was a significant response to the historical exclusion of First Peoples from the original process that led to the adoption of the Australian Constitution.[38] In those deliberations, Referendum Council member Galarrwuy Yunupingu, in his essay 'Rom Watangu', stated:

> What Aboriginal people ask is that the modern world now makes the sacrifices necessary to give us a real future. To relax its grip on us. To let us breathe, to let us be free of the determined control exerted on us to make us like you. And you should take that a step further and recognise us for who we are, and not who you want us to be. Let us be who we are—Aboriginal people in a modern world—and be proud of us. Acknowledge that we have survived the worst that the past had thrown at us, and we are here with our songs,

37 See John Maynard, 'The Voice to Parliament Isn't a New Idea: Indigenous Activists Called for it Nearly a Century Ago', *The Conversation* (online, 3 January 2020) <theconversation.com/the-voice-to-parliament-isnt-a-new-idea-indigenous-activists-called-for-it-nearly-a-century-ago-122272>.

38 See Pat Anderson AO and Mark Leibler AC, *Final Report of the Referendum Council* (Final Report, 30 June 2017) <www.referendumcouncil.org.au/sites/default/files/report_attachments/Referendum_Council_Final_Report.pdf> iii–iv.

> our ceremonies, our land, our language and our people—our full identity. What a gift this is that we can give you if you choose to accept us in a meaningful way.[39]

This is a rousing call to *all Australians* to rethink Australian citizenship and the ways in which engaging with the foundational aspects of our constitutional arrangements and how they impact on the nature of membership in Australia today is central to an activated Australian citizenship.

Looking closely at the Uluru Statement, it begins by recognising that: 'Our Aboriginal and Torres Strait Islander tribes were the first sovereign Nations of the Australian continent and its adjacent islands, and possessed it under our own laws and customs.' This recalibrates the story and acknowledges the foundational imbalance of power at the time of federation: the failure to recognise the existing sovereignty, or power, that the Indigenous community held over itself. This is an honest, transparent statement providing a foundation for moving forward. It also reaffirms Indigenous Australians' continuing identity linked to the land. It then affirms: 'It has never been ceded or extinguished, and co-exists with the sovereignty of the Crown.' How fitting that a nation that saw Australian citizenship status sitting happily with British subject status (rights sitting side-by-side), is now also able to affirm the co-existing sovereignty with Indigenous citizenship.

The Uluru Statement continues: 'With substantive constitutional change and structural reform, we believe this ancient sovereignty can shine through as a fuller expression of Australia's nationhood.' This speaks to an inclusive understanding of all aspects of citizenship, in its structural framing, to provide a meaningful expression of First Nations' formal *legal status* through a 'First Nations Voice enshrined in the Constitution', as well as empowering them to exercise their *rights* and to *participate* with a positive affirmation of their *identity*—'walk[ing] in two worlds' with 'their culture' as 'a gift to their country'. The active contribution of citizenship as *political participation* is specifically identified with this powerful ending: 'In 1967 we were counted, in 2017 we seek to be heard.' This strong statement should be affirmed by all Australians; it is Indigenous Australia's call to move from formal Australian citizen status to substantive Australian citizenship—that is, to be active citizens and to claim a true acceptance of Indigenous Australians' rightful place in the Australian nation.

39 Ibid.

That recognition of a special and distinctive starting point was also affirmed with the 2020 High Court decision in *Love v Commonwealth*.[40] The majority of the Court determined that Indigenous Australians can be non-citizens and non-aliens, recognising a special and unique status under the Australian Constitution. That status now needs to be further affirmed. Steps need to be taken towards implementing the Uluru Statement in Australia's constitution and securing that continuing recognition in an active sense, with First Nations' participation in decisions directly affecting them assured through a referendum process involving the whole Australian electorate.[41]

IV. Section 44 and multicultural Australia

Section 44(i) is also of paramount importance when thinking about questions around membership in light of Australia's migration history. If we recognise Indigenous Australia as Australia's starting point, as discussed above, we also need to recognise the journey since, including the growing population that has expanded beyond the set of white-bearded people who met during the constitutional conventions to frame the Constitution. Section 44(i) disqualifies from Parliament any person who 'is under any acknowledgement of allegiance, obedience, or adherence to a foreign power, or is a subject or a citizen or entitled to the rights or privileges of a subject or a citizen of a foreign power'.[42] Notice the words used: 'foreign power', 'allegiance', 'a subject or citizen … of a foreign power'. This is the only use of the word 'citizen' in the Constitution. It reflects on the distinction between 'subjects' of other Commonwealth countries who were not 'foreign powers', and those who were subjects of other Kingdoms or citizens of other non-monarchical or republican States, and is not used in relation to Australians who fell within the 'subject' category. Citizens were 'others' when they were connected to 'foreign powers'.

During the Constitutional Convention debates, there was agreement around s 44(i), which was intended to safeguard against treason by 'prevent[ing] persons with foreign loyalties or obligations from becoming members of the

40 (2020) 270 CLR 152.

41 In March 2023, the Albanese Labor government introduced a Bill to the Parliament with question to be put to the Australian People at a referendum on whether to add an Aboriginal and Torres Strait Islander Voice to the Constitution. The referendum is expected to be held before the end of the year.

42 Australian Constitution s 44(i).

Australian Parliament'.[43] The delegates were content to disqualify people whose allegiance was to a foreign power because '[p]ersons who have taken the oath of allegiance to a foreign power are not to be classed in the same category as citizens of the country for the purpose of joining in legislation'.[44] This led to an interjection—'And not to be trusted!'[45] The framers' presumption that dual nationality was undesirable and incompatible with individual loyalties reflected the international norms of the eighteenth and nineteenth centuries, 'characterised by aggressive nationalism and territorial competition',[46] and the unresolved question of whether sole allegiance is central to Australian citizenship.[47] It did not engage with the fact that they, themselves, were subjects of the Commonwealth, which involved connections to other countries beyond the territory of Australia. This supranational concept of membership sat 'comfortably' with their national identity and there was no sense of tension or irony at the time.[48] But the concept of citizenship has changed since, with the advent of dual citizenship in an increasingly interdependent world.[49]

Dual citizenship involves two aspects. First, there are questions of dual citizenship for those persons seeking Australian citizenship by grant. What are the consequences for those persons for their existing citizenship? This is not necessarily a question of Australian law, but rather a question of law for the country of origin. There is nothing in the provisions of the Act for the grant of Australian citizenship requiring a person to renounce their former citizenship. Second, there is the issue of dual citizenship for existing Australian citizens who take up citizenship of another country in addition to their Australian citizenship. Up until 4 April 2002, Australian citizens lost their citizenship when taking up a new citizenship.

---

43 *Sykes v Cleary* (1992) 176 CLR 77, 127 ('*Sykes*'). See also HK Colebatch, 'How the Australian Constitution, and Its Custodians, Ended Up So Wrong on Dual Citizenship', *The Conversation* (online, 6 February 2018) <theconversation.com/how-the-australian-constitution-and-its-custodians-ended-up-so-wrong-on-dual-citizenship-91148>.

44 Rubenstein (n 5) 302.

45 Ibid.

46 Ibid. See also Peter Spiro, 'Dual Nationality and the Meaning of Citizenship' (1997) 46(4) *Emory Law Journal* 1411.

47 Ibid. See also Rubenstein (n 5).

48 See further Kim Rubenstein, 'From Supranational to Dual to Alien Citizen: Australia's Ambivalent Journey' in Simon Bronitt and Kim Rubenstein (eds), *Citizenship in a Post-National World: Australia and Europe Compared* (Federation Press, 2008) iii–73.

49 See Kim Rubenstein, 'Citizenship in a Borderless World' in Antony Anghie and Gary Sturgess (eds), *Legal Visions of the 21st Century: Essays in Honour of Judge Christopher Weeramantry* (Kluwer Law International, 1998).

In the first case, where citizens of another country become Australian citizens, the approach in practice, not law, has varied. The pledge taken upon becoming an Australian citizen has changed over the years. Between 1966 and 1986, the words included 'renouncing all other allegiance'.[50] However, this wording had no legal consequence for their status as citizens of the other country. The High Court of Australia confirmed this in *Sykes v Cleary (No 2)*,[51] where two of the persons who ran for Parliament, and whose positions were challenged, were citizens of other countries.[52] It was alleged that they were ineligible for election due to s 44(i) of the Constitution, which disqualifies people who owe an allegiance to another country.[53] While both persons had taken an oath of allegiance to Australia, with words indicating they were renouncing their former citizenship,[54] it was not sufficient in law to shed them of their former citizenship. The Court held that the foreign citizen must comply with the laws of the foreign country regarding renunciation of citizenship in order to be divested of that citizenship and this

50 Introduced by Act No 11 of 1966, s 11 (commenced 6 May 1966) and repealed by Act No 70 of 1986, s 11 (commenced 28 August 1986).

51 (1992) 176 CLR 77.

52 As a matter of international law, it is for the country of citizenship to determine when a citizen loses his or her citizenship. In this case, neither Greece nor Switzerland mandated the loss of citizenship upon the adoption of a new citizenship.

53 Section 44(i) states:

> Any person who is under any acknowledgment of allegiance, obedience, or adherence to a foreign power, or is a subject or a citizen or entitled to the rights or privileges of a subject or a citizen of a foreign power; shall be incapable of being chosen or of sitting as a senator or a member of the House of Representatives.

54 The second respondent, Mr Delacretaz, was born in Switzerland and, in 1960, was naturalised as an Australian citizen pursuant to the *Nationality and Citizenship Act 1948* (Cth). The oath or affirmation of allegiance required by the 1948 Act, as it stood in 1960, did not involve the renunciation of prior allegiance. Despite this, Mr Delacretaz, in fact, formally renounced all other allegiance as a preliminary to taking the oath. It appears from the Second Reading Speech for the *Nationality and Citizenship Act 1967* (Cth) (which introduced the form of oath and affirmation involving renunciation of all other allegiance) that, for some time past, there had been a 'practice of requiring applicants … to renounce allegiance to their former countries' in 'a prominent and separate part of the naturalisation ceremony'. It was clear from Mr Delacretaz's naturalisation certificate that that is what happened in his case: see *Sykes* (n 43) 138–9 (Gaudron J). The third respondent, Mr Kardamitsis, was born in Greece and became an Australian citizen in 1975 pursuant to the *Australian Citizenship Act* 1948 (Cth) and, in so doing, renounced all other allegiances and swore the oath of allegiance in a form similar, but not identical, to that sworn by the second respondent. The form of oath and affirmation required by the *Citizenship Act*, as it stood in 1975, was introduced in 1966 when s 11 of the *Nationality and Citizenship Act 1966* (Cth) amended the Sch 2 to the 1948 Act 'by inserting after the letters "AB" … the words "renouncing all allegiance"'. At the same time, s 12 of the 1966 Act introduced Sch 3, which contained the form of oath and affirmation required in the case of women wishing to be registered as British subjects without citizenship. This also involved the renunciation of all other allegiance: see *Sykes* (n 43) 133 (Gaudron J).

has since been re-examined in the cases of *Re Canavan*[55] and *Re Gallagher*[56] where multiple members of Parliament were disqualified from membership of the Parliament. Many countries allow their citizens to take up a new citizenship without losing their original or existing citizenship[57] and others bestow citizenship upon descendants not born in their country with or without application. This means that there were many people in Australia who were lawfully dual citizens before s 17 of the *Australian Citizenship Act 1948* (Cth) was amended in 2002. In the second case, from the inception of the *Australian Citizenship Act 1948* (Cth) until 4 April 2002, there had been a provision mandating loss of Australian citizenship for a person who acquired a new citizenship.[58] Although the provision has been repealed, it has enduring relevance, due to the implications of dual citizenship for parliamentary membership under s 44(i).

Section 44(i) regulates who can and cannot be elected to Parliament and significantly impacts upon the nature of popular sovereignty and representative government. While not every Australian will necessarily aspire to be a Member of Parliament, the capacity to run for public office can be understood as one of the 'highest' reflections of citizenship through representing fellow Australians in Parliament and, consequently, a reflection of a person's fullest form of membership within the Australian community. By articulating clear prerequisites to sitting in Parliament, s 44(i) sets a threshold requirement for nomination to be considered for election and represents current restrictions on active citizenship in Australia—limiting dual citizens to voting as the fullest form of civic participation and restricting full membership in Australia from anyone who has access to another citizenship, which may reflect other aspects of their identity but does not necessarily impact on their commitment to represent their fellow citizens in Parliament.

55 (2017) 263 CLR 284.

56 (2018) 263 CLR 460. See also Noa Bloch and Kim Rubenstein, 'Reading Down Section 44(i) of the Australian Constitution as a Method of Affirming Australian Citizenship in the 21st Century' (2018) 30 (2) *The Denning Law Journal* (online) <www.ubplj.org/index.php/dlj/article/view/1699>.

57 See Joint Standing Committee on Migration, Parliament of Australia, *Australians All: Enhancing Australian Citizenship* (Parliamentary Paper No 46, 1994): Table 6.1 lists countries that allowed dual citizenship at the time of taking evidence. See also James Morgan, 'Dual Citizenship and Australian Parliamentary Eligibility: A Time for Reflection of Referendum?' (2018) 39(2) *Adelaide Law Review* 439, which lists those countries who do not expect dual citizens to renounce a citizenship in becoming a Member of Parliament.

58 In fact, the prevention of dual nationality began before the legal concept of Australian citizenship existed. Section 21 of the *Nationality Act 1920* (Cth) provided that a person would lose their British nationality when, through a 'voluntary and formal' act, they became naturalised in a foreign state.

The impact of the disqualification of a series of members of Parliament led the prime minister to refer matters relating to s 44 to the Joint Standing Committee of the Australian Parliament on Electoral Matters in November 2017. In its May 2018 report, titled *Excluded: The Impact of Section 44 on Australian Democracy*,[59] the chair, Senator Linda Reynolds, highlighted how the Constitution sets out both qualifications and disqualifications for nomination for election, yet while the qualifications in s 34 of the Constitution include a short list of criteria, significantly, the section allows the Parliament to update qualifications over time to meet contemporary community expectations, which it has done. In contrast, the disqualifications, including the prevention of dual citizens from sitting in Parliament, do not include that parliamentary amendment power, which has left the section less responsive to the needs of contemporary Australia and diminished democratic representation in Australia. The committee recommended a referendum be initiated to ensure the matter went back to the people on two levels: (1) to add 'Until Parliament otherwise provides' to s 44, mirroring its counterpart in s 34; (2) to enable Parliament to continue, from now and into the future, to represent the current people's view on whether dual citizenship should prevent people from the highest form of active citizenship.

V. The republic

To complete this constitutional renewal, it is also fundamental to bring all the *Australian* Constitution's elements back to the Australian people by enabling an Australian citizen, rather than a British citizen, to fulfil hierarchically the highest role of the executive, as Australia's Head of State. Some have argued that, as an Australian fulfils the role of representative of the Queen, as Governor-General, the practical reality is that this is already the case. Interestingly, it was Sir Isaac Isaacs, one of Australia's framers, earlier referred to in this chapter, and a Jewish Australian who was the first Australian-born Governor-General.

59 See Joint Standing Committee on Electoral Matters, Parliament of Australia, *Excluded: The Impact of Section 44 on Australian Democracy* (Report, May 2018) <parlinfo.aph.gov.au/parlInfo/download/committees/reportjnt/024156/toc_pdf/Excluded.pdf;fileType=application%2Fpdf>. See also Morgan (n 57) 339–451.

As the late Sir Zelman Cowan writes in the *Australian Dictionary of Biography*,[60] according to Garran, in February or March 1930, Cabinet decided to recommend Isaacs to replace the then Governor-General Lord Stonehaven and so informed the UK Prime Minister Ramsay MacDonald.

> By April the rumoured appointment had produced violent opposition, based largely on party-political grounds, to preferment of an Australian. It was argued that a local man would inevitably have personal involvements and that a distinguished citizen of the United Kingdom would better secure the bonds of Empire.[61]

Another factor that made it complicated (now settled through the passing of the *Australia Act 1988* (Cth)) was that the constitutional position was uncertain in that it was not clear where the constitutional advice for the appointment of a Governor-General should originate. Cowan writes that, 'while the Imperial Conference of 1926 had precluded the tendering of advice by the United Kingdom government, it did not then state that the source of advice for appointment was the prime minister of the relevant Dominion'.[62] Ultimately, the Imperial Conference confirmed early in November 1930, that a Governor-General should be appointed on the advice of the dominion government concerned, though only after informal consultation. Late in November 1930, in audience with the King, Australia's Prime Minister James Scullin stood firm, and Cowan writes that the King reluctantly approved his choice, and the announcement of Isaacs's appointment was made with a clear implication of the King's displeasure.

While that displeasure did not prevent the norm, since 1931, of an Australian fulfilling the role of Governor-General, the continuing impact of the Queen of England also holding the role of Head of State as the Queen of Australia impacts on legal issues in Australia.[63] But beyond the legal implications, this is also the other piece of the puzzle needing reform to fully activate Australian citizenship. This is the other referendum needed to alter the Constitution to ensure an Australian citizen, rather than the Queen of Australia, fulfils the role of the Head of State. This will not remove Australia from the Commonwealth, nor deny that aspect of Australia's history, but rather show Australia is ready to move, as have other Commonwealth

60 Zelman Cowen, 'Isaacs, Sir Isaac Alfred (1855–1948)', *Australian Dictionary of Biography* (Web Page) <adb.anu.edu.au/biography/isaacs-sir-isaac-alfred-6805>.

61 Ibid.

62 Ibid.

63 See *Hocking v Director-General of the National Archives of Australia* (2020) 379 ALR 395.

countries, to being independent and sure in its own citizenship. It would signify the completion of the change in 1987 of removing Australians' status as British subjects, completing the fulfilment of Australians' identity as Australian citizens.

The question and mechanics of a republic are discussed elsewhere in this collection and so, in this chapter, and in thinking through active citizenship in one other dimension, around gender and substantive active citizenship, I include one further proposal for constitutional change within the move to a republic to take a further step towards an inclusive activated Australian citizenship.

A central aspect of the position of the Head of State is that person's ability to best reflect the identity and collective experience of the people. If men are always, or mostly occupying that position, given only one woman, Dame Quentin Bryce has held the role of Governor-General, then women's identity and collective experience will not be properly reflected. In a society where women make up 52 per cent of the population, any new system of appointing or electing a Head of State should properly address the equal representation of women in such a position.

The most conclusive way of ensuring that women are properly included in the selection of Head of State is to mandate the alternating gender of the position.[64] For instance, the Constitution could guarantee that the gender of the first person appointed as Head of State would then be the basis upon which gender would alternate for the position. Therefore, if a woman was appointed or elected as the first Head of State in a move to a republic, then the Constitution would mandate that the next person for the position would be a man.

The advantages of this system include that, no matter what process of selection is chosen (election by the people or appointment by the Parliament),[65] equality in outcome would be guaranteed. This process would set clearly in our constitutional document the fundamental importance of

64 I acknowledge that another aspect of this proposal is to consider the position of non-binary individuals. I would be interested in feedback on ways to ensure that the historic exclusion of women be addressed, also taking into account this aspect of human experience. One option that I would propose is for the category of 'Women and Non-Binary', and 'Men and Non-Binary' for each alternation. So that if it turned out that two non-binary individuals were elected to Head of State in succession, that would be a positive recognition of moves towards an inclusive community.

65 Or a combination of both parliamentary nominees and a vote as suggested by the Australian Republican Movement. See the Australian Choice Model (online) <republic.org.au/policy>.

the equal opportunity for men and women to the most senior position in our constitutional structure. It would establish that all Australians, regardless of gender, could realistically consider that they have the opportunity of being considered for the position of Head of State.

The idea of placing such a condition on the position of Head of State is not without precedent. For instance, one can look at the US presidency as an example in which conditions are attached to who is entitled to be elected as Head of State. A person who has occupied the position for two terms cannot be re-elected as president. This condition reflects the principle that no person should accumulate power for more than a particular length of time. The parallel principle exists on a broader level with this proposal—that no one gender should accumulate power over the other (which has been the experience with public positions in Australia). Both examples reflect the belief that the institution of president has built in principles that need to be reflected in the appointment process.

Another related example is the federal principle that can influence the choice of appointments to the High Court. In choosing a new High Court justice, the system currently favours 'representation' of the States. That is, if a South Australian judge is not on the Court, this should be one factor influencing the new appointment.[66] Or, more specifically, our current democratic institutions skew a pure democratic system to take into account the representation of States in both our Senate and House of Representatives. These are examples illustrating that positions of public power often incorporate other values that are important to us in best representing the community and its interests.

Some will argue that this consideration of gender should not be put above 'merit' for the position. This argument suggests that the 'best' person for the position may miss out because of the mandate of gender for the position. Underlying this argument are several assumptions that need unpacking. First is the notion that there will only ever be one 'best' person for the position of Head of State. This is not a fair or realistic reflection of the pool of people available to take up the position at any one time. Another issue is that 'merit' is in itself a complicated issue. What do we mean by merit when we look at the position of Head of State? Some of the characteristics we would put next to the position of Head of State are as follows: integrity,

66 Disappointingly, there has never been a High Court justice from South Australia in Australia's federal history.

wisdom, intellect, judgment, objectivity in exercising any constitutional powers. These are all matters for which gender is irrelevant. However, because men have traditionally exercised public positions of power, there is a subtle implication that men best reflect these characteristics, and implicit bias shows that men and women often unthinkingly prefer a man for the position due to the historical preference for men for those positions.

Other matters important to the role of Head of State (as opposed to a regular company chief executive or school principal) include reflection of the community, responsiveness to the community's needs and life experiences reflecting those of the community. We need to ensure the diversity of our community is reflected in the position of Head of State. This is one of the meritorious matters needing consideration in the appointment of the person. Some argue that this would, in fact, be an unnecessary exercise of affirmative action. Once again, there are some assumptions about the current process in need of questioning. It could be argued that we currently have a position of affirmative action favouring men. This reality can be seen in situations in which men are appointed for positions that women could easily occupy. This system, which is not transparent, is arguably more insidious in its impact on society than one that openly proclaims the importance of men and women equally holding the position of Head of State.

The argument that the position of women would be devalued due to the mandatory nature of women holding the position also needs to be unravelled. This has never been a problem for men who have benefited from a system working in their favour. Moreover, this system would also have the benefit of showing the range of women who are available, competent, meritorious and worthy of the position of Head of State. It is not that there will only ever be one woman who is available; rather, there is a pool of women, from the 52 per cent of women in society, who should properly be regarded for the position of Head of State.

This will also better emphasise the diversity of women's experience in society—women are not one monolithic group. The more women who occupy the position of Head of State, the more likely this will be better understood and reflected in our public institutions. This final aspect of gender equality in the position of Head of State would be a further activation of an inclusive Australian citizenship, reinforced structurally in our foundational document, constraining and fashioning the exercise of power throughout the country.

VI. Conclusion

It is time to reactivate Australian citizenship—that is, to make the foundational legal document of Australia resonate with the people who it governs—and the best way to do that is to engage the people in ensuring that process occurs. Given that s 128 of the Australian Constitution requires this, politicians from all parties should adopt a multi-partisan, non-adversarial approach, acknowledging the significance of these incontrovertible three major changes in Australia since federation to set the amendment process in place.

The practical requirement of s 128—that is, of the people's involvement—is often the reason given by politicians to claim that constitutional change is *not possible*. However, an aspect of the argument of this chapter is that constitutional change will *ensure* the involvement of the entire citizenry, including all those whose lived experience is clearly different to that of those living in Australia in 1901. If all leaders can elevate themselves to a multi-partisanship spirit around this engagement, to positively encourage Australians to become engaged in the process of constitutional change, so that the Constitution acknowledges Australian identity as it exists today, then the laws binding all people in Australia will reflect a coming of age—an activated Australian citizenship.

Changing the Constitution to reflect this will be a constitutional coming of age—one in which activated Australian citizens can positively see themselves reflected in their own constitutional base, enabling a healthier framework for Australia's institutional evolution, impacting on the day-to-day lives of those living on Australian land.

Anthony D Smith describes national identity as the 'bonds of solidarity among members of communities united by shared memories, myths and traditions that … are entirely different from the purely legal and bureaucratic ties of the state'.[67] Smith explains that nations 'provide individuals with "sacred centres", objects of spiritual and historical pilgrimage, that reveal the uniqueness of their nation's "moral geography"'.[68] This moral geography now needs reckoning with from the perspectives of Indigenous Australia, multicultural Australia and an Australia confident in its independent future that proclaims from its very underpinning a truly inclusive base—to truly enable equality of opportunity for all.

67 Anthony D Smith, *National Identity* (Penguin, 1991) 15.
68 Ibid 16.

Part Two

7

Character and Exclusion from the Nation

Alexander Reilly

When Australia was established as a penal colony, sentences of deportation reflected that persons with the traits of convicts were undesirable and were to be excluded from civilised society in the United Kingdom. And yet there was no question of excluding convicts from UK society altogether. The penal colonies remained part of the Empire. Although there was a question of the status of a convict once they had completed their sentence and had been 'emancipated', they remained subjects of the Crown at liberty to return to the UK. This stands in contrast to the deportation of non-citizens for failing the character test under s 501 of the *Migration Act 1958* (Cth) ('*Migration Act*').[1] Like convicts of the eighteenth and nineteenth centuries, the banishment of these people may follow conviction for the commission of both serious and minor crimes. However, the formal status of long-term Australian residents as non-citizens means their banishment is absolute. Their formal connection to other places, no matter how tenuous in practice, facilitates the cutting of their ties with Australia. Long-term Australian residents who are deported for failing the character test under s 501 face the prospect of being forcibly placed into societies in which they may have no physical, cultural or language connections. They face the prospect of never being able to return to Australia to their immediate families, and to the places they have always called home. And this banishment is based on a

1 *Migration Act 1958* (Cth) ('*Migration Act*').

statutory assessment that the commission of a crime, for which they receive a punishment of 12 months or more, so reflects on their 'character' that they forfeit the entitlement to membership in the Australian polity.

'Member' necessarily has a constitutional status. A constitution constitutes a nation and a nation has people. Griffith CJ observed that:

> [A]n elementary part of the concept of human society [is] the division of human beings into communities. From this it follows that every person becomes at birth a member of the community into which he is born, and is entitled to remain in it until excluded by some competent authority. It follows that every human being (unless outlawed) is a member of some community, and is entitled to regard the part of the earth occupied by that community as a place to which he may resort when he thinks fit.[2]

If a constitution does not identify who is a 'member of the community', then it relies on national laws to draw distinctions between members and non-members. But those laws can only ever operate within the limits of the constitution and therefore can only ever exclude those who are not intrinsically members. The focus in Australia has been on the constitutional concepts of aliens and immigrants. The High Court has consistently maintained that there are constitutional members beyond the reach of the law (non-aliens and non-immigrants).[3] But the Court has remained non-committal as to what precisely constitutes membership, deferring as much as possible to Parliament to define these terms.[4]

With constitutional membership left vague, the law has created criteria to make distinctions between members and non-members. One such criteria is 'character'. This chapter focuses on the concept of character and its role as a ground for removal from the political community in the character test in s 501 of the *Migration Act*. It interrogates the notion of character and its function as a determinant of membership to understand what it signifies as a basis for exclusion from the community, and what it therefore reflects about Australia's national identity. It draws on philosophical and social scientific conceptions of character to understand the meaning of character. It reveals that character is far from a stable concept. The concept of character expressed in s 501 of the *Migration Act* is one of many ways of measuring character and contains

2 *Potter v Minihan* (1908) 7 CLR 277, 289.
3 See, eg, *O'Keefe v Calwell* (1949) 77 CLR 261; *Shaw v Minister for Immigration and Multicultural Affairs* [2005] FCAFC 106 ('*Shaw*'); *Singh v Commonwealth* (2004) 222 CLR 322 ('*Singh*').
4 *Singh* (n 3) 329 (Glesson CJ), 395–8 (Gummow, Hayne and Heydon JJ).

within it a number of fundamental assumptions about the nature of character and its relevance to national identity that are open to challenge. This chapter identifies a core debate in the literature over whether character is dispositional or situational, and what these understandings of character suggest about its function as a determinant of national membership.

This chapter then questions the role of character as a determinant of membership at all. Concentrating on character individualises the criteria for membership, focuses on worthiness, and contains inherent class and ethnic biases consistent with the over-representation of the poor and non-white populations among criminal offenders. The chapter draws on a number of theoretical perspectives to make the argument for alternative criteria for the membership of permanent residents from a personal, societal and global viewpoint.

I. Membership and constitutions

Connection to a territory and its people is a substantive notion, the product of emplacement, sociality, cultural familiarity and co-dependence. These are reflected in the primary forms of recognition in citizenship regimes around the world—birth, ancestry and residence. When connection is sufficiently intrinsic, we accept a person as a member regardless of their contribution to society and their personal characteristics. This commitment to people who are intrinsically one of us is partly administrative[5]—membership is a way of organising people on a global scale—and partly reflects that connection between people in a political community.

Those from elsewhere who have entered the political community and lived within it develop attachments over time. There is a difficult substantive question of when, if at all, those attachments convert into membership. The position of people who live in a community without legal acknowledgement of their membership is inherently precarious.

The terms upon which a migrant joins a new community are at the behest of existing members. As Michael Walzer puts it, the foremost entitlement of a political community is the power to determine its membership.[6] There are a range of views on how this entitlement should be exercised. For example,

5 Christian Joppke, *Citizenship and Immigration* (Polity, 2010) ch 1.
6 Michael Walzer, *Spheres of Justice: A Defense of Pluralism and Equality* (Basic Books, 1983) ch 2.

cosmopolitan and liberal theorists favour limited barriers to entry, and a correspondingly narrow range of entitlements attached to membership.[7] Republicans and communitarians, on the other hand, believe the decision to permit entry into the community is a decision of grave consequence, as once a person is admitted, they ought to be treated as an equal member.[8]

Modern citizenship regimes sit between these extremes. States exercise tight control over entry, as communitarians require, but do not offer full membership upon entry. Instead, a range of membership statuses are offered, all of which are subject to removal on specified grounds. In this sense, membership is treated as a contractual arrangement. There is a clear logic to the exchange. Membership is a scarce and valuable commodity. Different levels of membership are offered depending on what migrants have to offer the State. The character test fits within this logic. What migrants have to offer is diminished by conduct unacceptable to the host community.

What is required of existing members and potential members is asymmetrical. Those who are members automatically have to be encouraged to be good citizens—through education, the creation of social norms and expectations—whereas those who seek to join the community must demonstrate they have skills (such as employment experience in certain valued occupations), traits (youth and physical health) and values (belief in democracy and tolerance of different beliefs) that will make them good citizens.

There is a point at which outsiders become insiders. Formally, this is the process of naturalisation. Informally, a person develops ever strengthening ties in a new nation, being closely connected to its people, including the person's own relatives who may themselves be members, and identifying with its culture and idioms. The longer a person remains in a new State, and the stronger their ties become, the greater the disconnect between their official status as a non-citizen and their identity as a member of the national community.

This disconnect raises the question of whether there is a point at which non-members, through the passage of time, become members, and can no longer be considered outsiders, or 'aliens'. In Australia, the High Court has said there is no such point. An alien is always an alien, until they are formally naturalised. In Australian law as it stands there is but one exception to this rule: those who identify as Aboriginal, can trace their ancestry to before

7 Joseph Carens, *The Ethics of Immigration* (Oxford University Press, 2013).

8 Walzer (n 6).

white settlement and are accepted as members of an established Aboriginal community. A person so identifying, and identified, is a non-alien in Australia, regardless of their formal citizenship status.[9] Only two judges have briefly contemplated circumstances in which non-citizens might be non-aliens. In *Re Minister for Immigration and Multicultural Affairs; Ex Parte Meng Kok Te*, Kirby J gave the example of 'a ninety-year-old non-citizen ... [who] had lived peacefully in Australia virtually all her life'.[10]

In the gap between the formal and substantive criteria for membership in Australia, the legal criterion for removing a person whose substantial ties are mainly or exclusively to Australia becomes a key indicator of membership, and of significance in the formation of national identity. In the *Migration Act*, in relation to the membership status of permanent residents who have not become formal citizens, the character test plays this role.

II. The changing role of 'character' in deportation decisions in Australia

'Character' plays a dual role in relation to the membership rights of permanent residents. First, it acts as a barrier to full membership. For those wishing to become citizens, being of good character is a requirement in addition to length of residence and knowledge of Australia, its institutions and its core societal values (as assessed by the citizenship test).[11] Second, character acts as a threshold requirement for maintaining the entitlement to residence. The threshold for long-term permanent residents was altered significantly in 1998 when the character test was introduced in s 501.[12] Up until that time, ss 200 and 201 limited the power to deport a permanent resident to those who had lived in Australia for less than 10 years. Section 501 has been held to override this distinction, rendering long-term residents vulnerable to deportation if they do not pass the character test.[13]

9 *Love v Commonwealth Love v Commonwealth* (2020) 270 CLR 152 ('*Love*').

10 (2002) 212 CLR 162, 217.

11 *Australian Citizenship Act 2007* (Cth) s 21 ('*Citizenship Act*').

12 *Migration Legislation Amendment (Strengthening of Provisions Relating to Character and Conduct) Act 1998* (Cth).

13 In a report on s 501 in 2006, the Commonwealth Ombudsman expressed the opinion that the relationship between ss 200 and 201 and s 501 should be reviewed, and that there should be the requirement for the government to provide a 'clear indication of the circumstances' that warranted the application of s 501 to long-term permanent residents: Commonwealth and Immigration Ombudsman, *Administration of s 501 of the Migration Act 1958 as it Applies to Long-term Residents* (Report No 1, February 2006) 35–6 <www.ombudsman.gov.au/__data/assets/pdf_file/0023/26267/investigation_2006_01.pdf>.

The role of 'character' begs the question of what it is. According to s 501(6), the key criteria in determining whether someone passes the 'character test' is whether their conduct suggests they are not of good character. Being involved in criminal conduct, or being associated with others involved in criminal conduct, is a key indicator of bad character.[14] However, non-criminal conduct may also reflect on character, particularly if it indicates a person may be a risk to others in the community or is likely to lead to future criminal conduct.[15]

In the assessment of character, there is no weighing up of good traits to counter the bad. There is no consideration of what a person might have contributed to the community, or is likely to contribute to the community, to counter the assessment that they have done some harm to the community through their past and possible future behaviour.

The threshold for passing the character test has been trending upward in line with changes to the understanding of citizenship. In the last 20 years, citizenship law has developed a new focus on Australian values and identity. A simplified *Australian Citizenship Act 2007* (Cth)[16] was introduced in 2007. It introduced a 'citizenship test' as a criterion for naturalisation in response to recommendations in a 2006 taskforce report, *Australian Citizenship: Much More than a Ceremony*.[17] To pass the test, applicants are required to have a basic knowledge of Australian history, icons, values and system of government.

In 2014, the government introduced the Australian Citizenship and Other Legislation Amendment Bill, which proposed to increase the discretion of the Minister for Immigration to make unreviewable decisions revoking citizenship on character and security grounds.[18] It also proposed limiting the automatic acquisition of citizenship of people born in Australia to children whose parents had maintained lawful residence in Australia throughout the

14 *Migration Act* (n 1) ss 501(6)(a)–(b).
15 Ibid (c)–(d).
16 *Citizenship Act* (n 11).
17 Citizenship Taskforce, 'Australian Citizenship: Much More than a Ceremony' (Discussion Paper, Department of Immigration and Multicultural and Indigenous Affairs, 2006) <catalogue.nla.gov.au/Record/3791091>.
18 Australian Citizenship and Other Legislation Amendment Bill 2014 (Cth).

first 10 years of their life.[19] This Bill passed the House of Representatives on 24 November 2014, but lapsed on the prorogation of the Senate on 17 April 2016.[20]

In 2015, the Abbott government commissioned a national consultation on citizenship. The covering letter to the report, *Australian Citizenship: Your Right, Your Responsibility*, stated: 'Australians are concerned … that citizenship is undervalued by some in our community. This concern is most acute in the cases of Australians who by their conduct have chosen to break with the values inherent in being an Australian citizen.'[21]

The report described citizenship as 'a unifying symbol in our multicultural society'[22] and 'the "glue" that helps bind our nation together'.[23] According to the report, this glue (of citizenship) was being tested by 'the threat of terrorism'.[24] Echoing the Australian Citizenship Council's report of 2000, it recommended that a strong civics education program be implemented for all citizens, through schools and settlement services.[25]

The *Australian Citizenship Amendment (Allegiance to Australia) Act 2015* (Cth)[26] introduced a range of new activities that could lead to the revocation of citizenship. The activities were all related to participating in 'terrorist' activity.[27] The activities ranged from participation in activities outside Australia that were considered to support terrorist causes, such as providing material support or training to organisations deemed to be terrorist organisations, to the commission of offences in Australia that were deemed to be terrorist in nature, ranging from violent acts against persons to destruction of property. The rationale for the revocation of citizenship was that engaging in terrorism, like fighting for the enemy, indicated a lack of allegiance to Australia.[28]

19 Commonwealth, Parliamentary Debates, House of Representatives, 23 October 2014, 11744 (Paul Fletcher, Parliamentary Secretary to the Minister for Communications) <parlinfo.aph.gov.au/parlInfo/search/display/display.w3p;query=Id%3A%22chamber%2Fhansardr%2F4916447f-6ab8-4251-9d7e-93017c2ba328%2F0008%22>.

20 'Australian Citizenship and Other Legislation Amendment Bill', Parliament of Australia (Web Page) <www.aph.gov.au/Parliamentary_Business/Bills_LEGislation/Bills_Search_Results/Result?bId=r5181>.

21 Department of Immigration and Border Protection, *Australian Citizenship: Your Right, Your Responsibility* (Final Report, 2014) 3 <www.homeaffairs.gov.au/reports-and-pubs/files/australian-citizenship-report.pdf>.

22 Ibid 9.

23 Ibid 10.

24 Ibid.

25 Ibid 12.

26 *Australian Citizenship Amendment (Allegiance to Australia) Act 2015* (Cth).

27 Ibid.

28 Commonwealth, *Parliamentary Debates*, House of Representatives, 24 June 2015, 7369 (Peter Dutton, Minister for Immigration and Border Protection).

The reframing of citizenship as an 'extraordinary privilege'[29] has occurred alongside the lowering of thresholds of tolerance of wrongdoing among those who are not citizens. In 2014, the government introduced *mandatory* cancellation of the visas of permanent residents who failed the character test for serving a term of imprisonment of one year or more. In 2019, the government introduced a Bill to Parliament with a new category of offence for which conviction alone was a ground for visa cancellation on character grounds.[30] 'Designated offences' involve violence, non-consensual conduct of a sexual nature, breaching court orders for personal protection or use of a weapon, and include very serious offences, such as murder, and a wide range of potentially minor offences, such as throwing an object at a train, for which the maximum penalty can be as low as two years.

Conviction for a designated offence in itself is sufficient to make a person liable to cancellation of their permanent resident visa at the discretion of the minister regardless of the sentence imposed for the offence. There is a subtle shift in the rationale underpinning a designated offence. The current character test focuses on a person's actual behaviour, reflected in the length of the sentence imposed for the commission of an offence, whereas a designated offence relies on the generic conduct identified in the offence as indicating a lack of character in the individual. The Bill was defeated in the Senate in October 2021. It was introduced again in November 2021, and passed in the House of Representatives in February 2022. The Bill was not introduced to the Senate before the federal election on 21 May 2022.

A. The character assessment under s 501(6)

Direction 90 under s 499 of the *Migration Act* guides decisions-makers on how they should weigh character considerations (as expressed through criminal behaviour) in decisions to refuse or cancel a visa under ss 501 and 501CA.[31] Considerations are divided into primary and other considerations.

29 Commonwealth, *Parliamentary Debates*, House of Representatives, 15 June 2017, 6610 (Peter Dutton, Minister for Immigration and Border Protection).
30 Migration Amendment (Strengthening the Character Test) Bill 2019 (Cth).
31 Minister for Immigration and Border Protection (Cth), *Direction No 90: Visa Refusal and Cancellation under s501 and Revocation of a Mandatory Cancellation of a Visa under s501CA* (8 March 2021).

Under cl 8 of the practice direction, there are four primary considerations:

1. protection of the Australian community from criminal or other serious conduct;
2. whether the conduct engaged in constituted family violence;
3. the best interests of minor children in Australia;
4. expectations of the Australian community.

According to the direction, community expectations are that people with a substantial criminal record should be deported. Only the third primary consideration, the welfare of children, relates to the visa holder's substantive connection to people and place in Australia. It makes the judgment that the relationship with children is more significant from a membership perspective than other relationships. A decision might be made not to deport on the basis of a person's relationship with a child, despite concerns over their character.

Under cl 9 of the practice direction, 'other considerations' include:

a. international non-refoulement obligations;
b. impediments to removal;
c. impact on victims;
d. links to the Australian community, including:
    i. Strength, nature and duration of ties to Australia;
    ii. Impact on Australian business interests.

It is noteworthy that 'the strength, nature and duration of ties to Australia' comes near the end of the list of other considerations. And yet, it is these ties that provide a person's sense of personal and national identity.

The role of the character test in the determination of visa cancellation of long-term Australian residents has been subject to criticism. In a report on s 501 in 2006, the Commonwealth Ombudsman expressed the opinion that the relationship between s 501, and ss 200 and 201, which limit deportation on character grounds to people who have been permanent residents for less than 10 years, should be reviewed. The report recommended that there should be a requirement for the government to provide a 'clear indication of the circumstances' that warranted the application of s 501 to long-term permanent residents.[32] Others have critiqued the law for its narrow focus on the formal criteria for citizenship without accounting for the deep substantive connections of long-term, permanent residents to Australia.[33]

III. Understanding character

There are many ways of thinking about character. Character has been understood as a set of inherent personal dispositions that some people possess and others do not, or as a learnt set of personal dispositions. There is also a body of literature that suggests people do not have personal dispositions that reflect a particular character, either inherent or learnt. Instead, this literature suggests that people have quite predictable reactions that are characteristic of humans as a species when placed in conditions of stress or social suggestion.

A. Character as inherent ('virtue ethics')

The idea of character as 'dispositional' has its origins in the writing of Aristotle.[34] *The Nichomachean Ethics* establishes a moral code based on a person's positive attributes and behaviours.[35] Aristotle describes 11 virtues: courage, self-mastery (or temperance), liberality (or generosity), magnificence, magnanimity, right ambition, gentleness, friendliness, truthfulness, liveliness (or jocularity) and justice.[36] These are the mid-points between negative extremes or 'vices' that involve possessing too much or too little of the virtue. For example, courage sits between rashness and cowardice,[37] and liveliness sits between buffoonery and clownishness.[38]

The virtues establish a moral or 'ethical'[39] code of behaviour that is inherent to the individual and towards which individuals should strive. A virtuous person displays *all* the virtues. Importantly, for Aristotle, the virtues are developed for most people through habit rather than instruction.

32 Commonwealth and Immigration Ombudsman (n 13).

33 See, eg, Michelle Foster, '"An 'Alien' by the Barest of Threads": The Legality of the Deportation of Long-Term Residents from Australia' (2009) 33(2) *Melbourne University Law Review* 483.

34 Aristotle, *The Nichomachean Ethics*, tr DP Chase (Walter Scott Publishing, 1890) pt II ch V, 46.

35 Ibid pt I.

36 Ibid pt II ch V.

37 Ibid pt II ch V, 52.

38 Ibid 54–5.

39 Ethics means character in Greek.

Nonetheless, virtues are not 'emotions' or 'faculties' over which we have no control.[40] As long as we make a choice of action voluntarily, we can be held responsible for its consequences.[41] For example, a person who displays impatience is exhibiting a vice that reflects badly upon him or her.[42]

In ancient Greece, only those who were sufficiently worthy or virtuous were eligible for citizenship, and these champions of the State could be relied upon to rule wisely and set an example for all.[43] The virtues in Aristotle's *Ethics* are not only an individual code of ethical conduct but also have an important role to play in shaping society. As Alasdair MacIntyre explains: 'Courage is important, not simply as a quality of individuals, but as the quality necessary to sustain a household and a community'.[44] It is the expression of the virtues through action that links them to communal existence. To judge a person, therefore, 'is to judge [their] actions'.[45] MacIntyre adds a further important dimension that shapes the individual and their identity. A person is not an isolated being but is born into and lives in a community. This placement of a person in a society forms who they are:

> What I am, therefore, is in key part what I inherit, a specific past that is present to some degree in my present ... And thus, insofar as the virtues sustain relationships required for practices, they have to sustain relationships to the past—and to the future—as well as in the present.[46]

B. Character as learnt

A second understanding of character is that it is a product of environment, shaped by upbringing, opportunity and the situation one finds oneself in, and it is something that can be shaped through exposure to new experiences and education. Immanuel Kant argued that it is through education that we can transform our initial 'animal nature into human nature'.[47] Education is the pathway to 'moral perfection', which is the 'final destiny of the human

40 Aristotle (n 34) pt I, 24–5.
41 Ibid bk III.
42 Ibid ch 5–6.
43 Derek Heater, *Citizenship: The Civic Ideal in World History, Politics and Education* (Manchester University Press, 3rd ed, 2004) 3–16.
44 Alasdair MacIntyre, *After Virtue: A Study in Moral Theory* (Duckworth, 3rd ed, 2007) 122.
45 Ibid.
46 Ibid 221.
47 Immanuel Kant, 'Lectures on Pedagogy' in Gunter Zoller and Robert Louden (eds), *Anthropology, History, and Education* (Cambridge University Press, 2007) 441.

race'.[48] This sociological alternative to virtue ethics accepts that it is possible to establish a set of values necessary for a functioning society, and then teach them to prospective citizens. The potential to teach values raises the possibility of the State playing a role in moulding the values of a society and influencing the behaviour of members. It also suggests that a member who has been taught the values of the society can rightly be held responsible for failing to later comply with those values in his or her daily living.

Civics education programs in State education systems conform to this understanding of character. Civics education focuses on creating active and loyal citizens by teaching them about their system of government, and the core values, such as freedom, equality and community,[49] that are required for that system to function effectively.[50] Hannah Arendt captured this role of education in her poetic description of education as:

> [the point] where we decide whether we love our children enough not to expel them from our world and leave them to their own devices, nor to strike from their hands their chance of undertaking something new, something unforeseen by us, but to prepare them in advance for the task of renewing a common world.[51]

The hope and promise of civics education is that, when people understand the system and its core values, they will inhabit those values and practice them. This idea is captured in a speech that followed a series of riots in the UK in 2011. David Cameron stated: '[E]ducation doesn't just give people the tools to make a good living—it gives them the character to live a good life, to be good citizens'.[52]

Educationalists make a number of assumptions in their advocacy for civics education. First, they believe that a strong grounding in morality is important for successful participation in civil society. Second, they believe that young people lack a sufficient understanding of morality from their

48 Klas Roth and Paul Formosa, 'Kant on Education and Evil—Perfecting Human Beings with an Innate Propensity to Radical Evil' (2019) 51(13) *Educational Philosophy and Theory* 1304, doi.org/10.1080/00131857.2019.1520357.

49 Gabrielle Appleby, Alexander Reilly and Laura Grenfell, *Australian Public Law* (Oxford University Press, 3rd ed, 2019) 30–4.

50 James Arthur and Tom Harrison 'Exploring Good Character and Citizenship in England' (2012) 32(4) *Asia Pacific Journal of Education* 489, doi.org/10.1080/02188791.2012.741097.

51 Hannah Arendt, 'The Crisis in Education', *Humanities Institute: University of California Santa Cruz* (Web Page, 1954) 13 <thi.ucsc.edu/wp-content/uploads/2016/09/Arendt-Crisis_In_Education-1954.pdf>.

52 Arthur and Harrison (n 50).

traditions and family upbringing. Third, they believe that it is possible to inculcate the required values for participation in communal life through learning a moral code of behaviour and how to practice it.[53] Arthur and Harrison state:

> [P]eople now are more dependent on values and virtues in their lives, yet appear less in touch with their moral compass. This alienation from the source of moral values is most pronounced in young people where a weak moral education has left many of them without some of the resources to build strong characters. The task of supplying young people with these resources should fall primarily to parents, but also to education in schools, which should provide a moral education and not simply the means with which to pass exams.[54]

There is a lack of agreement in modern society on what constitutes the fundamental principles of morality underpinning the virtues. There have been many philosophical variations on the foundations of morality, but no agreement on what these are and how they can be translated into rules of justice.[55] MacIntyre uses the incompatibility of the theories of justice of John Rawls (based on an underlying principle of equality) and Robert Nozick (based on an underlying principle of entitlement) to illustrate the problem of gaining agreement on a set of justice principles for modern society.[56] Ultimately, MacIntyre argues that the moral and social commitments expressed in the Aristotelian tradition can be restated in an intelligible and rational way for modern societies,[57] forming the basis for a civics education.

Under both a dispositional and learnt understanding of morality and the virtues, a person retains the capacity to choose whether to act virtuously or not. The existence of individual free will means that society can judge the choices a person makes. Defining behaviours as criminal is society's way of judging individual choices of action. In responses to crime, the focus is not only on the harm done, but also on the motivation of the actor. Was the act intentional? Was it malicious? Was it motivated by personal gain at the expense of others? And, in defending against crime, accused persons may call on witnesses to testify to their good character to limit the punishment

53 See, eg, ibid; Kevin Ryan and Karen E Bohlin, *Building Character in Schools: Practical Ways to Bring Moral Instruction to Life* (Josey-Bass,1999); Judy Dunn and Richard Layard, *A Good Childhood: Searching for Values in a Competitive Age* (Allen Lane, 2009) 491.
54 Arthur and Harrison (n 50) 491.
55 MacIntyre (n 44) 244.
56 Ibid 246–51.
57 Ibid 259.

for their crimes.[58] Criminal defences focus on reasons for harmful conduct that do not reflect on a person's character. Self-defence and duress provide reasons for errant behaviour that is consistent with a person retaining good character. The partial defence of provocation suggests that displaying negative character traits in the heat of the moment (that is, intentionally killing someone when provoked to sudden anger) is less blameworthy than displaying negative character traits while calm and considered.

Under a virtue ethics framework, for those who believe character is dispositional, imprisonment and banishment are logical responses to crime as a punishment, as a deterrent and as a means of protecting society from people of bad character. Conversely, there is a limited role for rehabilitation.

C. There is no such thing as character

The discussion of ethics above is largely in the realm of philosophy and sociology. Beginning from first principles, a theory can be developed about the nature of character, what is contained in a good character and how it manifests in a person or in communities. Psychologists bring a very different perspective, looking for empirical validation of theories of character.[59]

In reviewing the psychological literature, John Doris concludes that people generally lack character. He critically reviews the assumption that character is consistent and stable, and that one trait is predictive of other traits within an individual. For example, a person might be honest but lack courage.[60] They may have a character trait of conviction but have beliefs that are lacking in virtue.[61]

Psychology suggests the most significant predictor of our behaviour is the context or situation in which we find ourselves. There are many experiments that suggest most people faced with a scenario that is against their values and beliefs will nonetheless follow the social and psychological cues that lead them to behave contrary to those beliefs. As Doris states, 'behavioural outcomes are inevitably a function of a complex interaction between organism and environment'.[62] There are experiments that show that a

58 Arthur and Harrison (n 50) 491.
59 John M Doris, *Lack of Character: Personality and Moral Behaviour* (Cambridge University Press, 2005) 6.
60 Ibid 23–4.
61 Ibid 17–18.
62 Ibid 26.

society that is characterised by positive feelings, emotions and behaviours will have pro-social members.[63] This highlights the responsibility of the State to create an environment for people to behave positively.

IV. What understanding of character is reflected in s 501 of the *Migration Act*?

The character test in s 501 is used as a mechanism to remove people who are considered a burden to the community through their participation in crime. From the perspective of virtue ethics, criminal behaviour might be considered to be a proxy for character to the extent that it is the result of performing one or more vices.

It can be noted immediately that the character test places full responsibility on the individual for demonstrating a want of character. The State itself takes no responsibility either for the bad behaviour or for any response to the behaviour through rehabilitation. According to Iris Young, for the State to focus so narrowly on an individual's responsibility for the commission of a bad act is to fail to account for the structural causes of injustice.[64] Young theorises a 'social connection model' that attributes responsibility for justice to 'all those who contribute by their actions to structural processes'.[65] Hence, a poor person should not be blamed for their homelessness, for example. Young does not deny personal liability but instead focuses on other factors that may have contributed to a person's action. She also argues that those who share responsibility for injustice have an obligation to participate in the structural reform required to make unjust acts, such as crimes, less likely in the future.[66]

Young's theory is a response to retributive systems of criminal justice. However, it is even more pertinent in relation to State responses to wrongdoing by permanent residents. Permanent residents have already borne responsibility for their crimes through the criminal justice system. Liability has, therefore, been accounted for, and the only question is responsibility for future action. In relation to future action, the State is necessarily implicated as the creator of structures that facilitate the crime, and for falling short in

63 Ibid 30.
64 Iris Marion Young, *Responsibility for Justice* (Oxford University Press, 2011) 95.
65 Ibid 96.
66 Ibid.

the task of rehabilitation and education. 'Our responsibility derives from belonging together with others in a system of interdependent processes of cooperation and competition through which we seek benefits and aim to realize projects.'[67]

Young's analysis of responsibility suggests that, in determining the worthiness of another for membership in the political community, those making the determination need to consider their own actions and level of responsibility for creating the society that led to the commission of the crime in the first place, and also their responsibility to aid permanent residents to thrive in the community.

In determining a person's character under s 501 of the *Migration Act*, no consideration is given to the role of the State in producing the conditions that lead to the criminal behaviour. However, the courts have noted that this broader sense of responsibility is a relevant consideration in determining whether someone has failed the character test. In *Shaw v Minister for Immigration and Multicultural and Indigenous Affairs*,[68] Justice Spender stated:

> Jason Shaw came to Australia with his parents, aged eighteen months. He has been here ever since. He has a lengthy criminal history, and it is not in doubt that he fails the character test in s 501(6) of the Act. While he is a criminal, he is an 'Australian' criminal. He is now thirty-two years of age. I note that it seems thoroughly unfair to the United Kingdom to send Mr Shaw there for no good reason other than that he is now a person of poor character who happens to have spent the first eighteen months of his life there.

There are several factors to note in the focus on criminality in the character test. First, criminal behaviour reflects on a number of Aristotle's vices, including lack of temperance or dishonesty. A person might engage in crime and yet be courageous, generous, magnanimous, patient and friendly.

Second, the focus on protecting the Australian community from 'criminal or other conduct' suggests that what is at issue is *the risk to the community* of a person's *conduct* rather than a lack of character. The greater the focus on community risk, the less important the reflection on character. This is evident in the proposed introduction of designated offences. Prior to the

67 Ibid 105.
68 *Shaw* (n 3) [18].

concept of designated offences, a sentence of imprisonment was proxy both for a person's degree of wrongdoing and for the level of danger they posed to the community. Designated offences lower the bar for culpability—a conviction is enough—while suggesting that the imperative of protecting the community remains.

Third, the concept of character in s 501 reflects an understanding of character that is dispositional. There is no opportunity for a person to learn from their mistake and no concern over whether imprisonment rehabilitates the person. There is also no investigation of whether a person continues to represent a threat to the community (if they ever did) in pursuing the stated goal of protecting the Australian community. In short, the character assessment is blunt, one-dimensional and not holistic. Poor character is used as a trigger for removal without there being any genuine assessment.

V. Why substantive connections should be of primary concern in deportation decisions

As discussed above, the personal connections of permanent residents to people and places in Australia are only a secondary consideration in the determination of whether to deport a person who does not meet the character test under s 501 of the *Migration Act*. Of the primary considerations under Ministerial Direction 90, only one, 'the best interests of minor children', considers a person's substantial connections. The fact that relationships with children are singled out in this way suggests that the rationale for this consideration is focused on compliance with Australia's obligations under the *Convention on the Rights of the Child*.[69] To the extent that it is concerned with substantive relations, the concern is exclusively on the interests of the child, and not the interests of the person subject to deportation.

'The strength and duration of a visa holder's ties to Australia' is a secondary consideration, to be considered only after the primary considerations of community protection, the interests of minor children and community expectations.[70] The marginalisation of a person's substantive connections in deportation decisions diminishes the significance of membership for

69 *Convention on the Rights of the Child*, opened for signature 20 November 1989, 1577 UNTS 3 (entered into force 2 September 1990).

70 Minister for Immigration and Border Protection (Cth) (n 31).

everyone. It means that the intrinsic connection to the political community that makes people members of a society is not linked in a substantial sense to the fact of living, contributing and relating in a particular place.

This links directly to a second concern about the centrality of character as the criteria for determining the membership rights of non-citizens. If a permanent resident can be removed from Australia for minor infractions that are deemed to reflect on their character, they and their families will necessarily feel less secure, less welcome and less committed to contributing to the Australian community. For example, with the threat of visa cancellation and deportation hanging over them for minor offences, permanent residents who are innocent victims of violence may be reluctant to approach the police for fear that they will be accused of initiating the confrontation. They may also be reluctant to help others who are the victims of violence for fear they will be dragged into a confrontation. With the stakes so high, permanent residents may second-guess their natural community-minded instincts. Fear of the consequences of assisting authorities as a result of insecure membership status was starkly displayed in the case of a migrant worker in Adelaide who was not completely open about his connection to a pizza bar in response to questions from contact tracers.[71]

In a report into migration settlement outcomes, the Joint Standing Committee on Migration received a number of submissions expressing concern over the impact of visa cancellation on a person's wellbeing in the community.[72] One submission outlined a number of negative consequences, both for permanent residents and the community as a whole, including an increase in alienation in the broader migrant community, the reinforcement of societal divisions, the possibility that migrants may perceive that they cannot overcome racial or religious stigma and be turned away from contributing to Australian society, and the increased risk of extremism.[73]

71 Royce Krumelovs, 'South Australia Makes Pizza Worker Scapegoat for COVID-19 Failures', *The Guardian* (online, 23 November 2020) <www.theguardian.com/world/2020/nov/21/south-australia-makes-young-pizza-worker-scapegoat-for-covid-19-failures>.

72 Joint Standing Committee on Migration, Parliament of Australia, *No One Teaches You to Become an Australian: Report of the Inquiry into Migrant Settlement Outcomes* (Report, December 2017) 155–9.

73 Harris Wake Pty Ltd, *Submission No 23 to the Joint Standing Committee on Migration, No One Teaches You to Become an Australian: Report of the Inquiry into Migrant Settlement Outcome* (30 January 2017) 2.

A low threshold for removal such as the character test in s 501 may affect the sense of loyalty and commitment that permanent residents feel for Australia. In *Political Emotion*,[74] Martha Nussbaum describes the centrality of emotion in developing a sense of connection to place and developing patriotism.[75] She suggests that promoting love and compassion over more negative emotions such as fear, envy and shame are positive strategies for developing a strong sense of connection to the political community.[76]

In *Spheres of Justice*,[77] Walzer highlights the importance of full membership in political communities for achieving justice for individuals in the community. Walzer accepts that political communities have absolute discretion over whether to admit someone. However, once a person has been admitted, the State must fully commit to the person and relinquish the power to remove them. For this reason, Walzer is highly critical of guest worker schemes, describing guest workers as 'live-in servants'.[78] Walzer's requirement to grant full membership to all people living in the political community applies to permanent residents. A reduction in security of residence and diminution in rights of access to family reunion or other services creates divisions in membership status that are harmful, both to the individuals involved and the broader community.

Finally, membership needs to be considered from a global perspective. Membership is a status that is allocated across the world. An important principle in international relations is that everyone ought to have a nationality. The *Convention Relating to the Status of Stateless Persons*[79] and the *Convention on the Reduction of Statelessness*[80] ('*Conventions on Statelessness*') aim to ensure that the human rights of stateless people are protected, and to eliminate statelessness over time. Australia is a signatory to both conventions and complies with its obligation not to deport stateless people.

The *Conventions on Statelessness* have implications for formal citizenship law. They prevent nations from denaturalising citizens and rendering them stateless. The rationale for reducing statelessness is the same as that

74 Martha Nussbaum, *Political Emotions: Why Love Matters for Justice* (Belknap Press, 2013).
75 Ibid ch 8.
76 Ibid 202.
77 Walzer (n 6).
78 Ibid.
79 *Convention Relating to the Status of Stateless Persons*, opened for signature 28 September 1954, 360 UNTS 117 (entered into force 6 June 1960).
80 *Convention on the Reduction of Statelessness*, opened for signature 30 August 1961, 989 UNTS 175 (entered into force 13 December 1975).

for ensuring that all members of a political community, regardless of their formal citizenship status, are secure in their membership. Many permanent residents who have their visas cancelled are cast into a foreign country where they have no understanding of the culture, no family or friends, and where they do not speak the native language.[81] Under such circumstances, despite having formal citizenship, they face the same risks associated with statelessness: isolation, homelessness, destitution and a serious risk to physical and mental health.[82]

Most long-term permanent residents who fail the character test because they have committed crimes come from a background of poverty and are inherently vulnerable. Deportation thrusts them into countries that may have no substantive connection to them, and no desire to provide them with the support they require. Such practices are not welcomed by the receiving countries. For example, the dramatic increase in the deportation of Australian permanent residents to New Zealand since 2014 has been criticised by successive New Zealand prime ministers, namely John Key and Jacinda Ardern, and has caused tension between the two countries.[83]

VI. A different criteria for membership of permanent residents: 'Belonging'

In the *Fate of Place*,[84] Edward Casey argues that place locates us, providing us with a sense of origin and knowledge of where we are going.[85] Place secures us against perpetual movement, and allows us to make sense of our journey:

> To be at all—to exist in any way—is to be somewhere, and to be somewhere is to be in some kind of place. Place is as requisite as the air we breathe, the ground on which we stand, the bodies

81 For a discussion of some of these cases, see Foster (n 33) 483.

82 UN Deputy Secretary-General, 'Statelessness Not Complex, Intractable, "It Is a Problem We Can Solve", Deputy Secretary-General Tells Treaty Accession Ceremony', United Nations (Press Release, 7 October 2019) <www.un.org/press/en/2019/dsgsm1356.doc.htm>.

83 See, eg, Eleanor Ainge Roy and Amy Remeikis, 'Jacinda Ardern Tells Scott Morrison Australia's Deportation Policy "Corrosive"', *The Guardian* (online, 22 February 2019) <www.theguardian.com/australia-news/2019/feb/22/jacinda-ardern-tells-scott-morrison-australias-deportation-policy-corrosive>; Shelailah Medhora, 'John Key to Question Malcolm Turnbull over Departing New Zealanders', *The Guardian* (online, 16 October 2015) <www.theguardian.com/australia-news/2015/oct/16/john-key-to-question-malcolm-turnbull-over-deporting-new-zealanders>.

84 Edward Casey, *Fate of Place: a Philosophical History* (University of California Press, 1997).

85 Ibid xi.

> we have. We are surrounded by places. We walk over and through them. We live in places, relate to others in them, die in them. Nothing we do is unplaced. How could it be otherwise? How could we fail to recognize this primal fact?[86]

In short, where we live is a proxy for where we belong.

In *Love v Commonwealth*,[87] the majority of the High Court held that the concept of 'alien' could not be extended to Aboriginal people in Australia who had been born elsewhere but retained a unique connection to the land and waters in Australia through their Aboriginal heritage. *Love* represents an important innovation on the interpretation of the concept of 'alien' under the Constitution. The majority judges' explanation for why Aboriginal people cannot be aliens under the Constitution is highly significant. All four majority judges discussed the importance of the unique connection that Aboriginal people have to Country in Australia as the foundation of their non-alien status. For Justice Edelman, this unique relationship to Country meant that Aboriginal people were 'belongers' to Australia, a relationship that was beyond Parliament's power to remove.[88] The tie of a belonger such as Aboriginal people, or children born in Australia to Australian parents, is metaphysical in nature. It creates such a deep bond that they cannot legally be denied the status of one who belongs.

Long-term residents, no matter how strong their connection to Australia, and no matter how remote their connection to any other place, have been held by the Court not to have the status of one whose relationship to country is so strong and intrinsic that it is constitutionally protected from laws of removal.[89] Nonetheless, the fact that there is a constitutional status of a 'belonger' based on such a deep relationship to Australia that it cannot be denied is instructive when determining a basis for the removal of long-term residents in the law.

The status of a non-alien, or 'belonger', in the Constitution is in no way related to 'character'. A belonger may be a person of poor character, no matter how the concept is defined. The point of belonging is not that a person contributes positively to the community, it is that factors such as birth and descent, or Aboriginality, 'evince fundamental norms of

86 Ibid 1.

87 *Love* (n 9).

88 Ibid 288–9 [394]–[396].

89 *Minister for Immigration and Multicultural and Indigenous Affairs v Nystrom* (2006) 228 CLR 566.

attachment to country'.[90] Australia is the place in the world that they belong. The designation of a person as a statutory citizen is another way the law marks them as one who belongs. Citizenship is conferred on those who have a strong connection to Australia based on their residence and demonstration of values. The designation of the legal status in itself might be said to 'shape' a person's connection to Australia.[91]

The concept of belonging provides a more meaningful and positive determinant of the political community. In many ways, the relationship between permanent residents and the Australian State is already focused on belonging. The vast majority of the Joint Standing Committee on Migration Report into Migrant Settlement Outcomes, *No One Teaches You to Become an Australian*, is focused on ways to assist permanent residents to integrate into the Australian community, recognising that the transition to life in the new society can be particularly difficult for some.[92] The report looks at the current provision of settlement services and how they can be improved.[93] It focuses on the importance of education and employment to assist new migrants with integration.[94] It acknowledges that new, and particularly young, permanent residents may get into trouble and need help to get back on a path to social wellbeing, and to contribute to the Australian community.

The report thus understands that permanent residents are already part of the Australian community; that having accepted people into the community, we have a responsibility to assist them to integrate successfully. It also recognises that permanent residents need to feel secure in Australia to integrate effectively, and not to fear deportation if they break the law.

The primary values of safety, cohesion and tolerance in the Australian community will be much better served through supporting permanent residents who commit offences rather than through finding ways to exclude them from the community.

90 *Love* (n 9) 311 [445].
91 Ibid 308 [437].
92 Joint Standing Committee on Migration (n 72).
93 Ibid ch 2.
94 Ibid ch 3, 4.

VII. Conclusion

There is a clear choice to be made in relation to our national attitude to belonging, and thus to our identity as a community. We can have an exclusionary or an inclusionary orientation. In a world with food and water scarcity, rising numbers of forced migrants and (most likely) increased conflict, there is a natural tendency towards exclusion, with advocacy for strong borders, anti-immigration policies and a focus on the national interest in preference to the global interest. An exclusionary orientation frames membership as a privilege. It creates a tiered society of members, denizens and guests.[95] It signals that full membership, in the form of statutory citizenship, is a highly prized status. It is hard to obtain for those born outside the political community, and those who have not yet obtained it remain insecure while they attempt to acquire it, no matter how long they have been a resident and participant in the body politic. The character test is simply a mechanism for exclusion in this context, not being concerned with true measures of character, if indeed character is a meaningful concept at all. The exclusionary orientation fails to recognise that migrants' connection to people and place increases through living and participating in the community, such that the attitude to behaviour reflecting on character must also change.

The alternative is to return to the philosophy of full inclusion that characterised Australian national identity between the 1970s and the 1990s, and in which permanent residents were encouraged to take up citizenship. It requires taking responsibility for those for whom Australia is their place of belonging, regardless of their past, present and likely future behaviour. It is a reorientation from individual to State responsibility, from punishment and exclusion to rehabilitation and acceptance, and from a liberal to a republican conception of the State.

95 See, eg, Linda Bosniak, *The Citizen, and the Alien: Dilemmas of Contemporary Membership* (Princeton University Press, 2006) , doi.org/10.1515/9781400827510; Saskia Sassen, *Guests and Aliens* (New Press, 1999).

8

Alienage and Identity in Australia's Constitutional Legal History

Joe McIntyre

> And if a stranger sojourn with thee in your land, ye shall not vex him. But the stranger that dwelleth with you shall be unto you as one born among you, and thou shall love him as thyself; for ye were strangers in the land of Egypt.[1]

The identity of a body politic is inevitably intertwined with that of the excluded other: the deeply tribalistic duality of 'us' and 'them'. For Australia, questions of national identity have—since the earliest days to federation—been inexorably intertwined with concepts of inclusion and exclusion. This obsession has shaped not only how we talk about membership of the Australian polity, but also (and to our national shame) how we have limited and restricted the rights of those lacking an 'adequate' degree of belongingness.

These two interwoven concepts—how we define 'belonging' and the consequences of not belonging—are core to our shared national identity. However, and despite the relationship between them, the two concepts are distinct.

1 This quote was used as the opening quotation in HSQ Henriques, *The Law of Aliens and Naturalisation: Including the Text of the Aliens Act* (Butterworth & Co, 1906).

To properly understand the role of the Constitution in shaping and reflecting our Australian national identity, it is as important that we understand the distinctions, as well as the interactions, between such concepts. Unfortunately, when it comes to the core constitutional structures of belonging—exclusions and their consequences—the distinctiveness of the underlying concepts have become deeply blurred. Australian nationality was never a driving force for federation. This has not only left our derivative constitutional identity upon an insecure footing, but also, too often, it has blinded us to the difference between definition and consequences.

This matters because it has obscured the repugnant uses for which the constitutional provision regarding consequences were designed, and facilitated a repurposing of those provisions for more palatable purposes. In turn, this has distracted us from both the urgent need to provide a secure footing for constitutional concepts of belonging, and to have open and frank discussions about what Australian identity means and how it should be properly supported and reflected in our constitution.

This chapter examines these themes by reference to the 'naturalisation and aliens' power in s 51(xix) of the Australian Constitution. I argue that this power has transformed from one directed to the *consequences* of exclusion to one that supports the *definition* of belonging. Further, I argue that this transformation is not only historically inappropriate, but also diminishes us in the national identity it supports.

I. The alien power of the Commonwealth and the national identity

From the very earliest days of the common law, the quintessential political 'other' has been the 'alien', with the 'subject' being the included 'us'. It is natural to draw on this contrast between alien and subject, and to think that this is a division of 'nationality'—that the non-alien subject was simply a proto-citizen. In such a conception, the regulation of aliens becomes a means of regulating nationality—both concepts are concerned with definition, not consequences. In this way, the express constitutional power to regulate 'naturalisation and aliens' in s 51(xix) has come to be seen as the hook upon which to hang the Commonwealth's power to regulate Australian nationality and citizenship.[2]

2 See *Hwang v Commonwealth* (2005) 222 ALR 83 ('*Hwang*').

Given that the Australian colonies were obsessed with exclusions—the rollout of the White Australia policy being one of the first legislative priorities of the Commonwealth—this connection between alienage, immigration and nationality (and, thus, eventually citizenship) appears inevitable.

However, this chapter argues that this conception is historically wrong. I argue that the scope and purpose of the 'aliens power' has been miscast, and that, as a matter of history, its true analogue was the race power, not immigration. The power was designed to regulate the domestic *disabilities* of aliens (and the removal of those disabilities through naturalisation). That is, this power was directed to *consequences*, not *definition*. This is reflected in the fact that the meaning of 'alien' at federation was clear and unambiguous. Subsequent jurisprudence that suggests otherwise conflates the definition–consequences boundary.

This chapter begins by taking a dip into the historical record to demonstrate that, under the common law, the regulation of aliens has been concerned with the consequences of 'others' and not definitional issues. Where Parliament sought to legislate for aliens, it was not to alter definitions, but to alter rights and liabilities. Alienage was not seen as a proxy for (non-) nationality, but as a burden or disability, the weight of which would wax or wane over time depending upon the will of Parliament. The alien was accepted as the 'other', the individual who does not owe allegiance to the domestic sovereign. It is by reference to allegiance that the 'alien' has always been defined. In this context, naturalisation is seen as an act of inclusion by which the alien becomes a subject through the creation of an obligation of allegiance.

In the second part of this chapter, I argue that this was how the regulation of aliens was understood at federation. I examine the drafting process and debates to show that the power to regulate aliens was never intended to be a de facto power to regulate nationality and citizenship. Rather, that power was intended to allow the federal Parliament to regulate the consequences of alienage. Its true analogue was the race power, not the immigration power (much less a de facto nationality or citizenship power).

In the final part of the chapter, I briefly outline how this power has come to be used for a constitutional purpose entirely removed from its foundation. I show that this power has come to be seen as providing a foundation for a modern citizenship regime.[3] Modern discussion of the limits of 'naturalisation and aliens' power, and the meaning of 'alien', have focused on these tests of nationality, with the fluidity between these doctrines of nationality seen as evidence of the lack of clear meaning for that constitutional term. I argue that this is a historical misconception.

While constitutional purposes and meaning can, of course, shift over time, much of the disagreement in the contemporary debate has evolved from a failure to appreciate the historical foundation and purpose of this power—a power directed to consequences, not definition. I argue that the creation of a national identity was never an object of federation. The fathers of the Constitution sought to exclude, to impose disabilities and burdens, but not to create. The 'aliens' power of the Commonwealth was not intended to be a de facto nationality or citizenship power, and its closest analogue was the race power (allowing the imposition of disabilities on certain classes of persons) rather than the immigration power (regulating which persons could physically enter the territory of Australia). The rights, identity or immunities that are granted to 'citizens' (or 'nationals') is conceptually distinct.

An alien should not be seen as the opposite of a citizen. At federation, it was clear that an alien was one who did not owe allegiance. By consequence of that status, the alien was liable to suffer a range of domestic disabilities, including restrictions on capacity to maintain legal actions, to own property and resist its seizure, to travel and to congregate freely. In contrast, a subject was immune to such disabilities by consequence of their bond of allegiance.

A citizen is something more. A citizen acquires a broad set of rights, including rights to participate in the governance of the nation, rights of abode and rights of protection. A citizen is more than simply immune to certain liabilities. A citizen is part of the polity—one who belongs and has special rights as a consequence of that belonging. Their identity and that of the nation are entwined.

It is, therefore, a mistake to extrapolate out from the regulation of aliens to the regulation of citizens. Both may be related to notions of identity and nationality, but that relationship is not a direct inversion.

3 See ibid; *Singh v Commonwealth* (2004) 222 CLR 322 ('*Singh*'); *Love v Commonwealth* (2020) 270 CLR 152 ('*Love*').

II. The history of alienage and the imposition of domestic disabilities

At the time of the Constitution's framing, an individual member of the British Empire (including Australia) was not a 'citizen' but a 'subject'.[4] This division was undoubtedly related to the international law concept of nationality that governs the 'status of an individual … in relation to a particular … state'.[5] This 'national' status is either natural from birth or acquired,[6] and it is now accepted that each State should have the right to choose the criteria by which it determines who are nationals.[7]

In practice, there are two main principles in this determination.[8] The first, the *jus soli* or territorial principle, grants nationality following birth on the State's territory, regardless of parentage.[9] The second, the *jus sanguinis* or principle of descent, confers nationality by descent from a parent who is already a national.[10]

While no State relies exclusively on one of these principles,[11] all tend to emphasise one more than the other,[12] so that the United States emphasise the *jus soli*[13] while Belgium prefers the *jus sanguinis*.[14] This division largely follows legal systems, with the common law accepting nationality by place of birth,[15] while the *jus sanguinis* is identified with civil law.[16]

Underlying the status of the subject is the concept of allegiance. In the British Empire, the status of the subject was governed by *jus soli,* so that, in general, someone born on British soil owed allegiance to the British Crown and was, therefore, a British subject. An alien was one lacking that tie of allegiance. This *definition* was clear at federation in Australia and reflected

4 John W Salmond, 'Citizenship and Allegiance' (1902) 18 *Law Quarterly Review* 49.

5 Sir Alexander James Edmund Cockburn, *Nationality: Or the Law Relating to Subjects and Aliens, Considered with a View to Future Legislation* (William Ridgway, 1869) 6.

6 Ibid.

7 Ann Dummett and Andrew Nicol, *Subjects, Citizens, Aliens and Others: Nationality and Immigration Law* (Weidenfeld & Nicolson, 1990) 7.

8 Ibid 7. See also Cockburn (n 5) 6.

9 Dummett and Nicol (n 7) 7.

10 Ibid.

11 Polly J Price, 'Natural Law and Birthright Citizenship in Calvin's Case (1608)' (1997) 9(1) *Yale Journal of Law & the Humanities* 73, 77.

12 Dummett and Nicol (n 7) 7.

13 *United States Constitution* amend XXIV § 1.

14 Dummett and Nicol (n 7) 7.

15 Kim Rubenstein, *Australian Citizenship Law in Context* (Lawbook, 2002) 49.

16 Price (n 11) 77.

a stable concept through 700 years of common law history. In contrast, the *consequence* of that status was variable and deliberately contingent upon the choices of the legislature.

A. Definition of alien: 'One who does not know allegiance'

The term 'alien'[17] is derived from the Latin word '*alienus*',[18] with the etymology signifying one 'borne in a strange country, under the obedience of a strange prince',[19] and bears a 'sense of foreignness ... of belonging to another'.[20] Alienage has always been linked with the concept of belonging, with English law defining the status of 'alien' in the negative, an outsider in opposition to the 'subject' who belongs. This was, to Blackstone, the 'first and most obvious division of the people',[21] with every man 'either *aliengena*, an alien born, or *subditus*, a subject born'.[22]

From the Roman Empire of Gaius to the late twelfth-century English law of Ganvill, Bracton and Britton, personal legal relationships revolved around 'the *varying amount* of privileges ... a person was allowed to enjoy',[23] so that the primary division of personal status was between the 'free or unfree (*serui*)'.[24] Feudalism began to develop a new order of ideas, 'essentially territorial and personal'[25] in nature, so eventually the new question became: 'Are you in or are you out?'[26] An alien was one who was out.

However, despite this 'very ancient law' regarding strangers as enemies,[27] the legal distinction between aliens and subjects did not begin to crystallise until the thirteenth century,[28] when the concept of allegiance emerged as the unifying bond for the body politic.

17 Or, according to Coke, '*alienigena*': Edward Coke, *The First Part of the Institutes of the Laws of England*, ed Charles Butler (Professional Books, 19th ed, 1985) 129a.
18 Ibid. See also George Hansard, *A Treatise on the Law Relating to Aliens; and Denization and Naturalisation* (A & R Stevens and GS Norton, 1844) 92.
19 Coke (n 17).
20 Dummett and Nicol (n 7) 24.
21 William Blackstone, *Commentaries on the Laws of England* (Clarendon Press, 8th ed, 1778) 366.
22 *Calvin's Case* (1608) 7 Co Rep 1a, 17a; 77 ER 377 ('*Calvin's Case*').
23 Keechang Kim, *Aliens in Medieval Law: The Origins of Modern Citizenship* (Cambridge University Press, 2000) 3–4.
24 Henry de Bracton, *On the Laws and Customs of England*, tr Samuel E Thorne, ed George E Woodbine (Belknap Press, 1968) vol 1, 29.
25 Sir William Holdsworth, *A History of English Law* (Methuen & Co, 1938) vol ix, 73.
26 Keechang (n 23) 7–8.
27 Frederick Pollock and Frederick William Maitland, *The History of English Law Before the Time of Edward I* (Cambridge University Press, 2nd ed, 1911) vol 1, 460.
28 Dummett and Nicol (n 7) 26.

1. The early common law

The rule of birthplace, where birth in the King's '*ligeance*' made one a subject,[29] can be traced to at least 1290,[30] when it was laid down that 'all persons born on English soil, no matter what their parentage, owed allegiance to, and were therefore subjects of the King'.[31] Parliament and the courts confirmed that persons born in any territory, outside England, though belonging to the King, were subjects.[32] The courts further recognised that an alien's son, born in England, 'is English, and not an alien',[33] for the child 'is a liege-man', despite alien parents.[34] Alternatively, birth out of the allegiance of the King would make one an alien, irrespective of the nationality of the parents.[35]

By Sir Thomas Littleton's time, the demarcation of aliens and subjects was clear,[36] with aliens those 'born out of the ligeance of our soveraigne lord the king'.[37] English law was recognising this demarcation in practice long before it explained it in theory.[38]

2. *Calvin's Case* and the theory of allegiance

It was not until Sir Edward Coke's influential opinion in *Calvin's Case*[39] that a 'theory of allegiance and subjectship was fully articulated'.[40] This case, regarded as the 'pure milk of the common-law doctrine of allegiance',[41] is the most important event in the history of English nationality law.[42]

29 Ibid 24.

30 *Elyas de Rababyn* (1290) II *Rotuli Parliamentorum* 139.

31 Holdsworth (n 25) 75, citing *Elyas de Rababyn* (1290) II *Rotuli Parliamentorum* 139 (17 Ed III, n 19). See also Clive Parry, *Nationality and Citizenship Laws of the Commonwealth and of The Republic of Ireland* (Stevens & Sons, 1957) vol 1, 30–1; Pollock and Maitland (n 27) 463.

32 Holdsworth (n 25) 76.

33 *Anon* (1544) Bro NC 57; 73 ER 872.

34 *Anon* (1563) 2 Dyer 225a; 73 ER 496, 224a–b [496].

35 *Valentine Hyde v Hill* (1572) Cro Eliz 4; 78 ER 270.

36 James H Kettner, *The Development of American Citizenship, 1608–1870* (University of North Carolina Press, 1978) 5.

37 Littleton s 198 in Coke (n 17) 129a.

38 Kettner (n 36) 13.

39 *Calvin's Case* (n 22). See also Thomas Bayly Howell and William Cobbett, *Cobbett's Complete Collection of State Trials and Proceedings for High Treason and Other Crimes and Misdemeanors from the Earliest Period to the Present Time* (Palala Press, 2018) 559.

40 Kettner (n 36) 7.

41 Mervyn Jones, *British Nationality Law and Practice* (Clarendon Press, 2nd ed, 1956) 51.

42 Parry (n 31) 41.

Calvin's Case summed up and adapted the existing nationality law to the conditions of the modern territorial State,[43] and articulated the nature of the bond between monarch and subject.[44] Despite citing few precedents,[45] the decision closely followed existing practice[46] and is now accepted as a case 'of the highest and undoubted authority'.[47]

Following the accession of James VI of Scotland to the throne of England in 1603, debate arose as to the status of his Scottish subjects in England, particularly the *post-nati*, or those born after his accession. Parliament was unwilling to pass an Act clarifying the position.[48] *Calvin's Case* was contrived as a vehicle for resolving this issue of whether the *post-nati* of Scotland were aliens in England.[49] The case arose after a young Robert Calvin, a Scottish *post-nati* born in 1606, came by land in England. Actions were brought by his guardians to protect his interests, with the defence arguing Calvin was incapable of holding land or bringing real actions in England.[50] The fundamental issue of the case was whether Calvin was, despite Scottish birth, a subject in England.

While the decision of Lord Ellesmere is recorded,[51] it is the decision of Coke that is remembered and has 'emerged as the definitive statement of the law'.[52] Coke based his division of subject and alien upon the doctrine of allegiance, so that those born under the obedience or *ligeance* of the King 'are natural subjects, and not aliens'.[53] This allegiance is:

> A true and faithful obedience of the subject due to his Sovereign. [It] … is an incident inseparable to every subject: for as soon as he is born, he oweth by birth-right ligeance and obedience to his Sovereign.[54]

43 Holdsworth (n 25) 72.
44 Genevieve Louise Ebbeck, 'Australian Citizenship' (PhD Thesis, University of Adelaide, 1996) 37.
45 Jones (n 41) 55.
46 Keechang Kim, '*Calvin's Case* (1608) and the Law of Alien Status' (1996) 17(2) *Journal of Legal History* 155, 163, doi.org/10.1080/01440369608531154.
47 *Re Stepney Election Petition; Isaacson v Durant* (1886) 17 QB 54, 59.
48 *Le Case Del Union, Del Realm, D'Escose, Ove Angleterre* (1606) Moore (KB) 790; 145 ER 908.
49 Gavin Loughton, 'Calvin's Case and the Origins of the Rule Governing "Conquest" in English Law' (2004) 8 *Australian Journal of Legal History* 143, 163.
50 See Edward Coke, *The Selected Writings of Sir Edward Coke*, ed Steve Sheppard (Liberty Fund, 2003) vol 1, 166; Price (n 11) 80–2.
51 *Calvin's Case* (n 22) [70] (Lord Ellesmere).
52 Kettner (n 36) 17.
53 *Calvin's Case* (n 22) 5b.
54 Ibid 4b.

A subject is, therefore, defined by this bond of allegiance due from the subject to the natural person of the King.[55] While Coke identifies four kinds of allegiance—natural, acquired, local and legal[56]—it is the natural allegiance of birth that defines the natural-born subject.

Coke identifies an 'alien' as one 'born out of the ligeance of the King',[57] who owes only a temporary local allegiance when in the King's dominions.[58] Alternatively, a subject, who owes a perpetual natural allegiance 'that cannot be altered',[59] is identified by the following incidents:

> 1. That the parents be under the actual obedience of the King;
> 2. That the place of his birth be within the King's dominion; and
> 3. The time of his birth is chiefly to be considered.[60]

A subject's allegiance is assessed at birth,[61] and it is birth within *allegiance*, rather than within territory, that makes one a subject.[62] As Calvin was born 'within the King's power or protection',[63] he owed a natural allegiance to the King and 'cannot be an alien born'.[64]

Coke's decision founded the basis of the common law test for allegiance laying out a 'general rule for the acquisition of the status of a natural-born subject'[65] that depended on the personal tie of allegiance to the Crown.[66] It secondly laid down rules to the acquisition of the status of a subject[67] and, thirdly, confirmed[68] that the status of a subject was indelible.[69]

55 Ibid 10a.
56 Ibid 5b.
57 Ibid 16a.
58 Ibid 6a.
59 Ibid 25a.
60 Ibid 18b.
61 Ibid 18b.
62 Ibid 6a, 18a–b.
63 Ibid 24b.
64 Ibid 14a–b.
65 Holdsworth (n 25) 83.
66 Ibid.
67 Ibid.
68 Following decisions such as *Storie's Case* (1571) 3 Dyer 300b; 73 ER 675.
69 Holdsworth (n 25) 84.

3. The common law since *Calvin's Case*

The cases that followed *Calvin's Case* adopted Coke's principles, for example, clarifying and examining the 'essential character of naturalisation'[70] whereby one acquired allegiance and became 'to all intents and purposes a British subject'.[71] However, at no stage was the validity of *Calvin's Case*, or the fundamental principles of *jus soli* and indelibility that it articulated, challenged.

The common law continued to recognise that the word 'alien' is a legal term that implies 'being born out of the ligeance of the King'.[72] As the character of alien and natural-born subject could not be united in the one person,[73] the test remained that an alien is one 'who has not been born within the allegiance of the Crown of this kingdom'.[74] It was confirmed that allegiance is owed to the King,[75] and that such allegiance is 'to be determined by the laws of this country'.[76]

Second, the common law maintained that, as allegiance was indelible, a subject 'could not divest him/herself of allegiance'.[77] Despite accusations that it was a 'slavish principle',[78] the law remained that a subject could not 'shake off his allegiance'—either by action[79] or the passage of time.[80]

At common law, the fundamental test of allegiance and alienage were unaltered with Coke's authoritative interpretation remaining 'embedded in the law; where it continued to exert a profound influence'.[81] This conclusion is supported by analysis of the last 400 years of legal scholarship. Unsurprisingly, Coke's *Institutes* recognise *ligeance*, that 'highest and

70 Kettner (n 36) 37. See *Collingwood v Pays* (1656) 1 Sid 194; 82 ER 1052; *Foster v Ramsey* (1657) 2 Sid 51; 82 ER 1251; *Craw v Ramsey* (1670) Vaughn 274; 124 ER 1072.

71 *R v Manning* (1849) 2 Car & K 887; 175 ER 372, 900 [378].

72 *Daubigny v Davallon* (1794) 2 Anst 462; 145 ER 936, 468 (Macdonald CB).

73 John Mews, *The Digest of English Case Law: Containing the Reported Decisions of the Superior Courts and a Selection from Those of the Irish Courts to the End of 1911* (Sweet & Maxwell, 1911) vol viii, 195, citing *R v Manning* (1849) 1 Den CC 467; 169 ER 330.

74 *R v Burke* (1868) 32 JP 601; 11 Cox CC 138. See also Mews (n 73) 195; Henriques (n 1) 62.

75 *Gavin v Gibson* [1913] KB 379. See *Re Stepney Election Petition; Isaacson v Durant* (1886) 17 QB 54, 59.

76 Mews (n 73) 195, citing *Re Adams* (1837) 1 Moore PC; 12 ER 888.

77 *Joyce v DPP* [1946] AC 347, 366.

78 *Aeneas Macdonald's Case* (1747) 18 S T 858; Fost 59; 168 ER 30, 59 [30].

79 See William Forsyth, *Cases and Opinions on Constitutional Law; and Various Points of English Jurisprudence, Collected and Digested from Official Documents and Other Sources* (Stevens & Haynes, 1869) ch ix, 252.

80 *Re Bruce* (1832) 2 C & J 436; 149 ER 185. See also *Aeneas Macdonald's Case* (1747) 18 S T 858; Fost 59; 168 ER 30, 59 [30].

81 Kettner (n 36) 8.

greatest obligation of dutie and obedience',[82] as the relevant test so that birth 'within the liegeance'[83] of the King will make one '*indigenæ*, subject borne'.[84] A century later, Viner adopted this test, recognising an 'alien' as one 'born out of the Allegiance of the King',[85] with alienage signifying one 'born in a strange Country, under the Obedience of a strange Prince'.[86] Viner confirmed that persons 'born upon the English Seas are not Aliens',[87] and that the son of an alien born in England is, by that birth within the realm,[88] 'an Englishman, and not an Alien'.[89] Blackstone's *Commentaries* reaffirmed that natural-born subjects are 'born within the dominions of the crown … [and] … allegiance of the king',[90] with allegiance 'the tie, or *ligamen*, which binds the subject to the King'[91] in return for protection. Bacon also reaffirmed this position, noting that birth within allegiance makes one a natural-born subject.[92]

Taken together, it is clear that, at the close of the nineteenth century, the common law meaning of 'alien' was fixed and certain. An alien was one of foreign birth, 'born out of the allegiance of the King'.[93] Under the common law, the definition of alien as 'one who does not owe allegiance' has remained remarkably stable for 700 years.

4. No history of legislative alteration of this core meaning

Strikingly, there was no attempt to alter this core connection between allegiance and alienage at any point before federation. While the regulation of the consequences of alienage was a matter of clear legislative concern (as discussed below), the core definition remained stable. That is not to say that the issue of whether or not a person was a 'subject' was not the matter of legislative concern. Indeed, there are two major categories of legislative actions directed to whether a person may obtain the status of 'subject'.

82 Coke (n 17) 129a.
83 Ibid.
84 Coke (n 17) 8a.
85 Charles Viner, *A General Abridgement of Law and Equity; Alphabetically Digested under Proper Titles* (Aldershot, 1747) 262.
86 Ibid.
87 Ibid.
88 Ibid.
89 Ibid 261.
90 Blackstone (n 21) 366.
91 Ibid. See also Henry John Stephen, *New Commentaries on the Laws of England*, Edward Jenks (Butterworth & Company, 16th ed, 1914) vol 2, 538.
92 Mathew Bacon, *A New Abridgement of the Law*, ed Sir Henry Gwillim (A Strahan, 7th ed, 1832) 165.
93 John Bouvier, *A Law Dictionary; Adapted to the Constitution and Laws of the United States of America* (George W Childs, 12th ed, 1868) vol 1, 112.

First, it was clearly accepted that Parliament could receive a person into allegiance to the Crown by an act of naturalisation. The consequence of such an act would be to transform the status of that alien into a subject. This reception into the 'permanent allegiance of the Crown'[94] is recorded as early as 1295.[95] While the Crown would historically transform a person into a 'denizen' by prerogative, by the end of the fourteenth century, it was recognised that a personal Act of Parliament was needed to gain the full status of subject,[96] effectively treating the alien as if 'they were born within the King's territories'.[97] The first move to general Acts operated to allow naturalisation of a specific class of aliens, such as those serving on ships,[98] married women[99] and the children of royalists.[100] Eventually, these were replaced by more open general Acts, whereby naturalisation under statue replaced the system of naturalisation *by* statue.[101]

Second, Parliament could alter the conditions under which a person would be born owing allegiance to the Crown. For example, a number of Acts adopted elements of the *jus sanguinis* for children of subject parents.[102] The first such Act was passed in 1351,[103] which was interpreted as granting subjecthood.[104] Subsequent statutes unambiguously adopted this position, making subjects of children born out of allegiance by following descent.[105] However, the *jus sanguinis* of this statute law has always operated alongside the *jus soli* of the common law and did not displace it.[106] Strikingly, in no case did legislative action purport to alter the fundamental connection between subject–alien and the doctrine of allegiance. While an Act was

94 Salmond (n 4) 56.

95 *Elyas Daubeny's Case* (1295) I *Rotuli Parliamentorum* 135a.

96 Holdsworth (n 25) 76; Pollock and Maitland (n 27) 460; Hansard (n 18) 197. See also *Molyns v Fiennes* (1365) 'Select Cases before the Council' (Selden Society) 48–53.

97 Joseph Chitty, *A Treatise on the Law of the Prerogatives of the Crown and the Relative Duties and Rights of the Subject* (Joseph Butterworth & Sons, 1820) 14.

98 See *Duties on East Indies Goods* (1707) 6 Ann, c37.

99 *An Act to Amend the Law Relating to Aliens* (1844) 7 & 8 Victoria, c66.

100 *An Act for the Naturalizing of Children of His Majesty's English Subjects, Born in Foreign Countries during the Late Troubles* (1676) 29 Charles II, c6. See also Hansard (n 18) 21.

101 *An Act to Amend the Law Relating to Aliens* (1844) 7 & 8 Victoria, c66. See also Hansard (n 18) 6.

102 Price (n 11) 77.

103 *A Statute for Those Who Are Born in Parts beyond Sea* (*De Natis Ultra Mares*) (1350–1 & 1351–2) 25 Edward III, Stat 1.

104 *R v Eaton* (1627) Litt Rep 28–9; 124 ER 117. See also *Bacon v Bacon* (1641) Cro Car 601; 79 ER 1117, 602 [1118].

105 Hansard (n 18) 94–5. See, eg, *An Act for Naturalising Foreign Protestants* (1708) 7 Anne I, c5.

106 Price (n 11) 77–8.

passed to treat certain subjects as aliens for certain purposes,[107] at no time was an Act passed to make alien anyone born within the allegiance of the King, or to make aliens of subjects.

Indeed, until the latter half of the nineteenth century, no legislative actions even attempted to alter the permanence of allegiance. This common law doctrine of 'perpetual and unalienable'[108] allegiance held that no subject could severe the bond of allegiance: '*nemo potest exuere patriam*'.[109] Eventually, this allegiance was seen as 'inconsistent, self-contradictory, and riddled with ambiguities',[110] and led to a Royal Commission being established to examine the entire law of alienage and allegiance.[111] While the commission's report led to a softening of the perpetual and inalienable nature of allegiance, the core connection between alienage and allegiance remained unaffected.

The report accepted the core idea that all persons born within the dominions and allegiance of the Crown will be natural-born subjects, and those born outside that allegiance will be aliens.[112] The Royal Commission ultimately recommended retention of the *jus soli*, but also suggested the abandonment of the 'absolute and unbending'[113] nature of allegiance.[114] This recommendation was carried into effect under the *Naturalisation Act 1870*,[115] which allowed a natural-born subject to become a 'statutory alien',[116] either by being naturalised in a foreign State[117] or by making a declaration of alienage.[118]

107 *Customs Act* (1523) 14 & 15 Henry VIII, c4. See also Hansard (n 18) 10; Henriques (n 1) 55.
108 Bacon (n 92) 129.
109 'Once a subject always a subject': Salmond (n 4) 7.
110 Kettner (n 36) 45.
111 See United Kingdom, *Report of the Royal Commissioners for Inquires into the Laws of Naturalisation and Allegiance; with an Appendix Containing an Account of British and Foreign Laws, and of the Diplomatic Correspondence Which Has Passed on the Subject, Reports from Foreign States and Other Papers* (1869) being (1868–69) [4109] XXV 607.
112 Ibid 613.
113 Ibid 614.
114 Ibid 611.
115 *An Act to Amend the Law Relating to the Legal Condition of Aliens and British Subjects* (*Naturalisation Act)* (1870) 33 & 34 Victoria I, c14.
116 Henriques (n 1) 59.
117 *An Act to Amend the Law Relating to the Legal Condition of Aliens and British Subjects* (*Naturalisation Act)* (1870) 33 & 34 Victoria I, c14, s6. See also *Re Trufort, Trafford v Blanc* (1887) 36 Ch D 600.
118 *An Act to Amend the Law Relating to the Legal Condition of Aliens and British Subjects* (*Naturalisation Act)* (1870) 33 & 34 Victoria I, c14, ss3, 4. See also Henriques (n 1) 122–5.

Thus, while the absolute indelibility of allegiance was softened, the test for allegiance articulated in *Calvin's Case* was not altered. The clear acceptance of the common law and the Royal Commission, together with that absence of legislative alteration, means that there existed a fixed, certain and objective meaning of 'alien' at federation. An alien was one who was born out of the allegiance of the Crown.

5. Consequences of alienage

Under feudalism, rights and duties depended upon the holding of land and the personal bond of fealty between tenant and lord.[119] As Frederick Pollock and Frederick Maitland observe, this relationship was blind to nationality and origin. Feudalism is opposed to tribalism and even to nationalism: we become a lord's subjects by doing homage to him, and as this is done, the nationality of our ancestors and the place of our birth are insignificant.[120]

As medieval law developed, the personal fealty of feudalism was superseded by the 'absolute and unqualified' tie of allegiance between subject and King.[121] This bond of allegiance became the 'primary ligament' of society.[122] Under this new social contract, it began to make legal sense to differentiate on the basis of nationality: the 'included' subject owed allegiance to the Crown while the 'excluded' alien did not.[123] The territorial and personal basis underlying the doctrine of allegiance affected both the natural grant of the status and its acquisition and loss.[124] For medieval England, *allegiance* was the unifying concept in determining membership of the national polity.

6. Early restrictions on the rights of aliens

It is against this background that the significance of the concept of 'alien' began to take form as the excluded other—one who was exposed to certain liabilities purely as a result of that status. The reliance upon the concept of the 'alien other' as the basis for imposing domestic disabilities can be traced to the English loss of Normandy,[125] when political realities motivated laws

119 Holdsworth (n 25) 73.
120 Pollock and Maitland (n 27) 460.
121 Holdsworth (n 25) 77. Salmond observes that '[t]he term allegiance is a comparatively modern corruption of the ligeance (*ligeantia*), which is derived from the adjective liege (*ligius*) meaning absolute or unqualified': Salmond (n 4) 51.
122 Kettner (n 36) 3–4.
123 Holdsworth (n 25) 72.
124 Ibid 73.
125 Holdsworth (n 25) 72–4; Kettner (n 36) 4.

against aliens.[126] Prior to this point, as Pollock and Maitland have argued, no law of alienage could develop in the aftermath of the Norman conquest: a foreigner at the head of an army recruited from many lands conquered England, became King of England and endowed his followers with English lands. For a long time after this, there could be little law against aliens.[127]

However, once the Norman territories were lost, it began to make sense to distinguish between those with direct ties to England and those without such ties. The 'insider' status of subject, together with legal benefits and advantages, was granted to those in the faith and allegiance of the King, while the alien 'outsiders' were denied those benefits and became subject to a range of disabilities.[128]

King John's seizure of aliens' lands represents the first major imposition of disabilities upon aliens by restricting real property rights.[129] At first, this was as a 'dilatory exception'[130] arising from the 'enemy' status of the lost Normans: '[t]he Normans are traitors; the Frenchmen are enemies. All this will be otherwise if a permanent peace is ever established'.[131] But, as Pollock and Maitland observe, peace never came, and the exception became peremptory: '"You are an alien and your king is at war with our king", became "you are an Alien"'.[132]

In the following centuries, this approach led to aliens being treated as 'almost, if not wholly, rightless'.[133] First, aliens were effectively denied the right to securely hold real property: any real property held by an alien was liable to forfeiture to the King.[134] Second, aliens were limited in their capacity to enforce legal rights due to restrictions on their ability to access the King's courts to maintain actions.[135] Third, aliens were denied the ability to inherit[136] or to have inheritance traced through them.[137]

126 Pollock and Maitland (n 27) 461.
127 Pollock and Maitland (n 27) 460.
128 Keechang (n 23) 144.
129 Pollock and Maitland (n 27) 459. See also Viner (n 85) 257–8.
130 Pollock and Maitland (n 27) 462–3.
131 Ibid.
132 Ibid.
133 Holdsworth (n 25) 72.
134 Hansard (n 18) 3, citing *Perrogatiba Regis* (1324) 17 Edward II, c2, s12; Coke (n 17) 2b.
135 Coke (n 17) 129b.
136 Keechang (n 23) 113; citing *Petition of Petrus Malore* (1289) I *Rotuli Parliamentorum* 44; *Elyas de Rababyn* (1295) II *Rotuli Parliamentorum* 135; Coke (n 17) 8a.
137 *R v Philip de Beavais* (1321) in *The Eyre of London, 14 Edward II, Volume I* (Selden Society 1969) 86, 213ff. See also Keechang (n 23) 139–41.

Given the highly limited number of ways in which the State could directly interact with the individual in this period, these disabilities (regarding the holding of real property, maintaining actions and inheritance) effectively withheld from aliens the capacity to access some of the major benefits of being a member of society.

However, many of the rights we now regard as inherent aspects of citizenship—including rights of abode, right to work, right to enter territory—were not generally restricted for aliens. This was largely for the reason that such rights were simply not regulated in any way.

As can be seen, the identification of a person as an alien mattered because of the disabilities that could be imposed upon that person as a consequence of that status. The major concern was the extent of such consequences, not the definition of status.

7. Restrictions on aliens after *Calvin's Case*

Following *Calvin's Case*, there continued to be a stream of cases that examined the disabilities and restrictions of legal rights that were imposed on aliens by consequence of that status. These included:

- restrictions on inheritance[138]
- restrictions on protections offered by the Crown, including rights to bring actions[139] or hold copyright[140]
- limits on political rights[141]
- restrictions on enemy aliens[142] and subjects in enemy territory.[143]

138 *Kynnaird v Leslie* (1866) LR 1 CP 396; *Rittson v Stordy* (1855) 3 Sm v G 230; 65 ER 637; 3 Eq Rep 1039.
139 *Brown v Collins* (1883) 25 Ch D 56, 59.
140 *Low v Routledge* (1865) 1 Ch App 42.
141 *Cunningham v Tomey Homma* [1902] AC 151.
142 For effects of plea of enemy alien, see *Nicholas v Pawlett* (1695) Carth 302; 90 ER 778. See also *Daubigny v Davallon* (1794) 2 Anst 462; 145 ER 936; *Wells v Williams* (1697) 1 Ld Raym 282; 91 ER 1086; *Janson v Driefontein Consolidated Mines* [1902] AC 506.
143 *M'Connell v Hector* (1802) 3 Bos & Pul 113; 127 ER 61; 114 [62].

Throughout this time, Parliament continued to develop new consequences and disabilities that diminished the rights of aliens, including requirements for registration[144] and expulsion of aliens,[145] and restrictions on the holding of land[146] and the employment of alien servants[147] or apprentices.[148]

The regulation of trade was a common theme of these Acts, with a history of protecting the rights of alien merchants being traced back to the *Magna Carta*.[149] However, these Acts were more likely to impose restrictions on alien merchants[150] (both as to their merchandise[151] and their profits)[152] than to grant protection.[153] While some Acts granted benefits, such as bankruptcy[154] and trial by jury,[155] or removed common law disabilities,[156] the burdens imposed upon aliens remained substantial.

Being an alien exposed a person to a range of legal disabilities and, for this reason, many aliens sought to become subjects.[157] This is the principal connection between alienage and naturalisation.

144 The registration of aliens was a first temporary measure. See *Lord Grenville's Alien Act* (1793) 33 George III, c4, but the system maintained for many years, see *Act for the Registration of Aliens* (1826) 7 George IV, c54, before finally being repealed, see *Registration of Aliens Act* (1836) 6 & 7 William IV, c11.
145 *Alien Act* (1848) 11 & 12 Victoræ c20.
146 *Payment of Tithes of Aliens' Lands* (1403) 5 Henry IV, c11; *Confirmation of Liberties, Charters, and Statutes, Aulnage ect* (1407) 9 Henry IV, c7. See also *Concning Strangers* (1540) 32 Henry VIII, c16, s13.
147 *An Acte rateyinge a Decree made in the Sterre Chamber concninge Strungs Handicraftsmen inhitinge the Realme of Englonde* (1529) 21 Henry VIII, c16.
148 Hansard (n 18) 10. See *Thact concnying the takyng of apprentices by Straungers* (1523) 14 & 15 Henry VIII, c2.
149 (1297) 25 Edward I.
150 *Alien Merchants Act* (1439) 18 Henry VI, c4. See *Aliens Act* (1485) 1 Henry VII, c10; *Tillage Act* (1533) 25 Henry VIII, c13.
151 *The Ordinance of the Staples* (1353) 27 Edward III, Stat 2 c3 and *The Statute of the Twenty-Eighth Year of King Edward III,* (1354) 28 Edward III, c12, 13. For restrictions on the trade in weapons, see *Acte Concnyng the Bryngіng in of Bowestaves in to this Realme* (1514-5) 6 Henry VIII, c11.
152 See *Of the Statute Made at Westminster, in the Third year* (1379–80) 3 Richard II, c2; *Statute Made at Westminster in the Seventh Year* (1383) 7 Richard II, c12, which restricted the removal of profits from the Realm.
153 See, eg, *The Statute of the Twenty-Eighth Year of King Edward III* (1354) 28 Edward III, c12, 13; *Suing in Foreign Court* (1353) 27 Edward III, Stat 1, c6; *The Ordinance of the Staples* (1353) 27 Edward III, Stat 2, c2.
154 *Bankrupts* (1623) 21 James 1, c19.
155 *The Ordinance of the Staples* (1353) 27 Edward III, Stat 2 c8.
156 For example, removing the restrictions preventing tracing inheritance through aliens: *An Act to Enable His Majesties Naturall Borne Subjects to Inherite the Estates of theie Ancestors Either Lineal or Ccollateral Notwithstanding Their Father or Mother Were Aliens* (1698) 11 & 12 William III, c6. Similarly, aliens were granted, by statute, the right to hold land: see *An Act to Amend the Law Relating to the Legal Condition of Aliens and British Subjects (Naturalisation Act)* (1870) 33 & 34 Victoria I, c14.
157 Jones (n 41) 64.

8. Conclusions on the history of alienage

The common law maintained that the meaning of 'alien' was defined by reference to allegiance, with an alien not owing such allegiance to the Crown. This core definition of 'alien', contrasted to 'subject' by reference to allegiance, remained fundamentally unaltered from the time of Coke's articulation to federation. Allegiance remained the primary ligament of society and the defining concept of membership.

Parliament could extend (or contract) the class of subjects and confer allegiance through naturalisation. But the fundamental test for alienage remained unchanged: an 'alien' was one who did not owe permanent allegiance to the Crown and was, therefore, born out of the allegiance and protection of the Crown. In contrast, the consequences of alienage were seen to be entirely contingent upon the will of Parliament. The rights and disabilities of aliens contracted and expanded, depending on political concerns of the time.

III. The drafting history of the 'alien' power of the Commonwealth

This history of regulating the consequences of alienage make it entirely unsurprising that alienage has long been considered 'appropriate to central regulation in a federal system'.[158] Prior to federation, each of the colonies had separate laws about aliens,[159] but the treatment and exclusion of aliens was 'a common cause and a motivating force behind federation'.[160]

A. The early drafts of the Constitution

In early 1891, the two famous initial drafts of the Constitution by Andrew Inglis Clark and Charles Cameron Kingston recognised the need for the power to regulate aliens. Clark's draft, the more restrictive of the two in this respect, granted a power to regulate 'the immigration of Aliens', and an additional power to make 'a uniform law of the naturalisation of

158 Michael Pryles, *Australian Citizenship Law* (Law Book, 1981) 1.
159 See, eg, *Naturalization and Denization Act 1898* (NSW).
160 Rubenstein (n 15) 306.

Aliens'.[161] In contrast, Kingston's draft adopted a broader phrasing that extended beyond immigration, granting a power over 'Naturalization and Aliens'.[162] It was this latter approach that was subsequently referred to the Constitutional Committee in Sydney 1891.[163] As a consequence of this referral, the first official draft of the Constitution included such a power over 'Naturalization and Aliens'[164] and, while there were minor changes,[165] there were no substantive changes to the section during the early drafting process.

During the Easter 1891 voyage of the *Lucinda*,[166] only minor renumbering of that provision occurred.[167] However, an interesting insight into this section is found in a handwritten annotation. One of the drafts from the voyage contains an annotation, in Sir Samuel Griffith's handwriting, with an arrow prior to the word 'Aliens' pointing to the handwritten words 'the Status of', so that the power would have read: 'Naturalization and the Status of Aliens'.[168] This annotation demonstrates an awareness of the drafters that the power over aliens was not merely restricted to immigration, as in Clark's draft, but entailed a broader power over the status and rights of aliens. The subsequent crossing out of the annotation, and its absence from later drafts, does not necessarily negate this insight, for such removal is consistent with the drafters' frugality of words, if the addition was thought unnecessary.

Following the voyage on the *Lucinda*, the 'Naturalization and Aliens' power received remarkably little attention at the Sydney Constitutional Convention[169] and, while the Constitutional Committee added minor adjustments to the wording of the powers of Parliament,[170] the power remained fundamentally unchanged by the convention.[171] Six years later,

161 Andrew Inglis Clark, 'Bill for the Federation of the Australasian Colonies' (1891) in Samuel Griffith, *Successive Stages of the Constitution of the Commonwealth of Australia* (1891) Mitchell Library microfilm reel no. CY221, frame 27 and following. See John M Williams, *The Australian Constitution: A Documentary History* (Melbourne University Press, 2005) 85.

162 Charles Cameron Kingston, 'A Bill for An Act for the Union of the Australian Colonies' (1891) in Samuel Griffith, *Successive Stages of the Constitution of the Commonwealth of Australia* (1891) Mitchell Library microfilm reel no. CY221, frame 27 and following.

163 See Williams (n 161) 58.

164 Ibid 144.

165 Such as renumbering and the removal of the word 'federal': Williams (n 161) 174.

166 See generally David Clark, 'Kingston's Draft Constitution for United Australia' (2004) 7(1) *Constitutional Law and Policy Review* 1, 1.

167 See Williams (n 161) 195.

168 See 'The Constitution of the Commonwealth of Australia' The Voyage of the Lucinda, *Proof Revised for Printer*, 28 March 1891 (1891) in Williams (n 161) 195.

169 The provision was renumbered: compare Williams (n 161) 223 and 247.

170 See Williams (n 161) 273.

171 The provision again renumbered: compare Williams (n 161) 478, 303, 327, 423 and 447.

the Adelaide Constitutional Convention again altered the numbering and wording of the powers of Parliament, though the closest thing to a relevant substantive change was in the spelling of 'naturalisation'.[172] This new form carried through subsequent drafts in Adelaide,[173] in the Bill finally adopted[174] and in Samuel Griffith's critique.[175] Indeed, but for a slight renumbering by the Colonial Office,[176] this version emerged unchanged from the Sydney Convention.[177]

During the final Constitutional Convention in Melbourne, the wording of the powers of Parliament took final form,[178] and the spelling of naturalisation again altered.[179] A final renumbering[180] gave form to the Act as adopted by the Imperial Parliament:

> **Part V:** Powers of the Parliament
>
> **S 51.** The Parliament shall, subject to the provisions of this Constitution, have power to make laws for the peace, order and good governance of the Commonwealth, with respect to:
>
> ...
>
> **xix.** Naturalization and aliens;[181]

The language used in successive drafts of the 'Naturalization and Aliens' power reveal, firstly, an incredibly stable drafting history that, but for minor renumbering and spelling alteration, did not change during the entire drafting process; this highlights a non-controversial power. Secondly, the *Lucinda* draft reveals the applicability of this power to the regulation of the rights and status of aliens.

172 Williams (n 161) 510.
173 Ibid 567.
174 Ibid 595.
175 Ibid 649.
176 Ibid 747.
177 Ibid 778.
178 Ibid 875.
179 Ibid 875, 955, 1082.
180 Ibid 1129.
181 *The Constitution of the Commonwealth of Australia*, Commonwealth of Australia Constitution Act 1900 (UK) *63 & 64 Victoria c12*, London 6 July 1900.

B. The Constitutional Convention debates

This stability of the 'aliens' power becomes highly relevant when considered in light of the Constitutional Convention debates. The debates are particularly insightful for two purposes in understanding s 51(xix): helping to identify 'the mischief and defect'[182] towards which the relevant constitutional provision was directed',[183] and illuminating what the founders deliberately discarded.[184]

1. The 'mischief' of the alien power

At first glance, the Constitutional Convention debates shed little light on the resolution of the extent of the alien power, as there is remarkably little debate concerning it. Edmund Barton spoke to the significance of the power at the Melbourne Convention in language redolent of the race power, concluding that he was of the 'strong opinion that the moment the Commonwealth obtains any legislative power at all it should have the power to regulate the affairs of the people of coloured or inferior races who are in the Commonwealth'.[185] There is no record of debate on aliens, naturalisation or citizenship at the Adelaide[186] or Sydney constitutional conventions, where the power was adopted without debate.[187] The accepted position is that the power was not substantively debated.[188]

However, there were, in fact, highly illuminating discussions of the scope and purpose of the 'aliens' power at the Melbourne Convention. Critically, this discussion occurred in the context of whether the race power should be an exclusive power of the Commonwealth,[189] with the discussion helping to elucidate the mischief to which the 'aliens' power was directed.[190] This is seen in the interjection of Barton and Sir Isaac Isaacs:

---

182 *Baxter v Commissioner for Taxation (NSW)* (1907) 4 CLR 1087, 1104–6.

183 *Singh* (n 3) [54] (McHugh J); *Cheng v The Queen* (2000) 203 CLR 248, 292, 294–5 (McHugh J).

184 *Codelfa Construction Pty Ltd v State Rail Authority of New South Wales* (1982) 149 CLR 337, 346 (Mason J).

185 *Official Record of the Debates of the Australasian Federal Convention*, Melbourne, 25 January 1898, 228–9 ('Melbourne Convention Debate'). For records of all constitutional convention debates, see 'Records of the Australasian Federal Conventions of the 1890s, *Parliament of Australia* (Web Page) <www.aph.gov.au/About_Parliament/Senate/Powers_practice_n_procedures/Records_of_the_Australasian_Federal_Conventions_of_the_1890s>.

186 See *Official Record of the Debates of the Australasian Federal Convention*, Adelaide, 22 March – 5 May 1897.

187 *Official Record of the Debates of the Australasian Federal Convention*, Sydney, 22 September 1897, 1077.

188 Pryles (n 158) 1.

189 See Melbourne Convention Debate (n 185) 227–57.

190 Notably, the debate is referenced in the Index to Names as concerning 'Powers of the Parliament: Aliens': Melbourne Convention Debate (n 185) *Index to Names*.

> **Barton:** There is no subsection dealing with aliens except the one dealing with the naturalisation of aliens.
>
> **Isaacs:** The subsection is 'naturalisation and aliens'.

The fact that the 'aliens' power was discussed in debate regarding the race power highlights that it is the race power, and not immigration, with which the 'aliens' power is cousin. The framers were conscious of a sharp division between the regulation of the alien immigration and the regulation of aliens post-immigration, and saw the provision as directed towards this later use:

> **Reid:** I think the general idea all through has been that this subsection … was intended to deal with the admission of aliens.
>
> **Barton:** Not with the admission of aliens, but with aliens after they are here.[191]

Indeed, Richard O'Connor reveals that there was minimal substantive relationship between the aliens power and immigration, as he observed 'no necessary connection' between laws regulating the admission of aliens and laws regulating aliens once admitted:

> **O'Connor:** What possible connection is there between the making of a law preventing aliens from entering the state and the making of a law controlling their mode of living in that state? I can see no necessary connection between the two.[192]

The mischief to which the 'alien' power was directed was the regulation of the status and rights of aliens after their arrival in the Commonwealth. This proposition is clearly supported by the words of Isaacs:

> **Isaacs:** We have made the dealing with aliens … a power of the Commonwealth, and we have made … immigration a power of the Commonwealth, so that all those of the races who come into the community will not only enter subject to laws made in respect of immigration, but will remain subject to any laws … specially devise[d] for them.[193]

However unsavoury such uses may now appear, the debates make it clear that the aliens power was directed to such matters as the regulation of special licensing conditions of Afghan hawkers[194] and the restriction of

191 Ibid 241 (Edmund Barton).
192 Ibid 234 (Richard O'Connor).
193 Ibid 228 (Sir Isaac Isaacs).
194 Ibid 227 (Sir Isaac Isaacs).

mining rights to 'Asiatic or African aliens'.[195] While such regulation was not without controversy, with some delegates advocating that aliens ought to be treated fairly,[196] labelling it monstrous to degrade them with 'a brand of inferiority',[197] it was ultimately thought that central governance was better than a mishmash of State regulations.

This debate highlights that the mischief towards which the aliens power was directed was to the regulation of the rights and disabilities of aliens.[198] This regulation did not require the ability to define 'aliens' and operated most effectively when alienage was given a clear and objective meaning.

2. 'Omission': The relevance of the absent citizenship power

Second, the debates demonstrate a conscious decision to deny the Commonwealth a power over citizenship. The concept of citizenship acutely concerned the drafters, who made a 'conscious effort to exclude the term'.[199] The reasons for that exclusion were exhaustively debated[200] in response to a proposed amendment to prevent citizenship being a 'mere legal inference'[201] by granting an express power over 'Commonwealth citizenship'[202] and a power to legislate 'with reference to the rights and privileges'[203] of that citizenship. John Quick, the proponent of the ultimately unsuccessful amendment, argued that such an approach was potentially preferable to relying upon legal inference:

> **Quick:** Again, I ask are we to have a Commonwealth citizenship? If we are, why is it not to be implanted in the Constitution? Why is it to be merely a legal inference?

195 Ibid 240 (Sir John Forrest).

196 Ibid 246 (Charles Cameron Kingston).

197 Ibid 250 (Sir Josiah Symon).

198 It is worthwhile highlighting that there exists a logical nexus between the aliens power and the naturalisation power, for it is through naturalisation that the restrictions and disabilities would be removed.

199 Kim Rubenstein, 'Citizenship and the Centenary: Inclusion and Exclusion in 20th Century Australia' (2000) 24 *Melbourne University Law Review* 576, 580. See also John Chesterman and Brian Galligan (eds), *Defining Australian Citizenship: Selected Documents* (Melbourne University Press, 1999) 21–6 for discussion of the debates.

200 Chesterman and Galligan (n 199) 5. See also Melbourne Convention Debate n (185) 505, 664–91, 1750–68, 1780–1802, 2397–8.

201 Melbourne Convention Debate (n 185) 1767. See also discussion in Rubenstein (n 15) 24; Rubenstein (n 199) 579–83.

202 Melbourne Convention Debate (n 185) 1752 (John Quick).

203 Ibid 676 (Charles Cameron Kingston).

There were, however, both technical and ideological hurdles in the way of the adoption of the proposal. First, the delegates could not agree upon a definition of Commonwealth citizenship,[204] or indeed if a definition was necessary.[205] Second, delegates opposed the amendments on ideological grounds, concerned that they would give the Commonwealth too much power.[206] Concern was stated that the power could deprive people of their citizenship.[207] It was feared, with such a power, Parliament could affect the rights of natural-born subjects and even withdraw their birthright.[208]

Ultimately, the proposed power was rejected. The exclusion of a citizenship power was not a matter of neglect but choice,[209] a 'conscious decision of the delegates'.[210] The power was not rejected because it was already implicit but because it was felt inappropriate.

C. Conclusions regarding the drafting history

Taken together, the drafting history and relevant convention debates shed significant light on the mischief and purpose of s 51(xix). The 'aliens power' was directed to the regulation of the disability and rights of aliens—that is, the regulation of aliens once they were in Australia. Its closest analogue was the race power, not the immigration power. This was a power directed to the *consequences* of alienage.

While naturalisation may bring aliens within the membership of the Australian community, the mischief of the 'aliens' power concerns the potential disabilities of aliens prior to that inclusion. Given that the purpose was to regulate the consequence of someone holding the status of 'alien', this power did not demand that Parliament have the power to define the term 'alien'. The stable common law definition (regarding the absence of personal allegiance) was fully sufficient for this purpose.

204 Kim Rubenstein, 'Citizenship and the Constitutional Convention Debates: A Mere Legal Inference' (1997) 25(2) *Federal Law Review* 295, 301, doi.org/10.22145/flr.25.2.5.
205 See Melbourne Convention Debate (n 185) 1782 (Sir Josiah Symon), 1797 (John Alexander Cockburn), 196 (Sir Isaac Isaacs).
206 Rubenstein (n 204) 303.
207 Melbourne Convention Debate (n 185) 1761 (Sir Josiah Symon). See also Rubenstein (n 15) 30.
208 Ibid 1754, 1764. See also Pryles (n 158) 9.
209 Chesterman and Galligan (n 199) 7.
210 *Singh* (n 3) [101] (McHugh J).

At no time in the debates was it suggested that the 'aliens' power was related to a citizenship power.[211] The stable drafting history of the 'aliens' power, when contrasted with the quick abandonment of the citizenship power, shows that this was a relatively uncontroversial power. The 'aliens' power was never directed to the regulation of citizenship and was never seen as some form of de facto citizenship power.

IV. Conclusion: The alien other and the absence of an included 'we'

Fast forward a century and a bit, and we may be left wondering why this apparently archaic and discriminatory power has any significance for contemporary Australia, and why we should be discussing it in a book on national identity. This is a valid question and probably demands more attention than it attracts.

The legal history of the aliens power should make it clear that its purpose reflected the historical pattern of regulating the disabilities and curtailment of the rights of aliens. It was a power directed to the *consequences*, not the definition, of alienage.

However, over the last century (and particularly the last 20 years), the scope of this power appears to have radically transformed. The constitutional power to regulate 'naturalisation and aliens' in s 51(xix) has instead come to be seen as the hook upon which to hang the Commonwealth's power to regulate Australian nationality and citizenship.

A. The transition from consequences to definition

This transformation appears to have happened rather organically. In 1920, the Commonwealth Parliament sought to consolidate the *Immigration Restriction Act 1901* (Cth) (which regulated who could and could not physically enter Australia) and the *Naturalisation Act 1903* (Cth) (which regulated the process by which one could join the Australian polity) and

211 Their only relationship is their proposed proximity in the draft. The new power, s 21A, was proposed to follow on from the aliens power in s 21: see Melbourne Convention Debates (n 185) 1750.

unify them within a single Act.[212] The resultant *Commonwealth Nationality Act 1920* (Cth) adopted the significant nomenclature of 'nationality'. While the Act was clearly within constitutional limits, that language of nationality laid the groundwork for an Australian nationality and, in turn, citizenship. With a distinct Australian identity emerging through the two world wars, it was almost inevitable that a statutory concept of Australian citizenship would be created, as it was in 1948.[213]

Notably, when that citizenship was created, there was no recognition of the potentially constitutionally dubious (or at least unclear) foundation for that enactment. Neither in the Second Reading Speech introducing the *Nationality and Citizenship Act 1948* (Cth) nor in the preamble to the Act was any reference made to the constitutional power from which the legislation was sourced or to the constitutional concept of citizenship.[214] This is true also for the (renamed) *Australian Citizenship Act 1973* (Cth), and for amendments to this Act, which are similarly silent.[215]

The High Court has refused to properly engage with this ambiguity. For example, in *Shaw v Minister for Immigration and Multicultural Affairs*,[216] Gleeson CJ, Gummow and Hayne JJ, in discussing the historical emergence of the *Nationality and Citizenship Act 1948*, merely *observed* that '[u]ndoubtedly, to a significant degree, that statute depended upon the aliens power'.[217] Similarly, in *Koroitamana v Commonwealth*,[218] Gummow, Hayne and Crennan JJ accepted that it is now the 'settled position' that it is 'for the Parliament, relying upon para (xix) of s 51 of the Constitution, to create and define the concept of Australian citizenship'.[219]

212 *Commonwealth Nationality Act 1920* (Cth). This Act sought to 'consolidate decisions and legislation in the previous seventeen years concerning immigration and naturalisation': Alastair Davidson, *From Subject to Citizen: Australian Citizenship in the Twentieth Century* (Cambridge University Press, 1997) 61, doi.org/10.1017/CBO9780511518232.
213 See *Nationality and Citizenship Act 1948* (Cth).
214 Helen Irving, 'Still Call Australia Home: The Constitution and the Citizen's Right of Abode' (2008) 30 *Sydney Law Review* 131, 136, citing Commonwealth, *Parliamentary Debates*, House of Representatives, 30 September 1948, 1060 (Arthur Calwell, Minister for Immigration).
215 Irving (n 214) 136 citing Commonwealth of Australia, *Parliamentary Debates*, House of Representatives, 11 April 1973, 1312 (Al Grassby).
216 *Shaw v Minister for Immigration and Multicultural Affairs* (2003) 218 CLR 28.
217 Ibid 40 [21].
218 *Koroitamana v Commonwealth* (2006) 227 CLR 31.
219 Ibid 46 [48].

In only one case has the constitutional validity of the *Australian Citizenship Act 1948* (Cth) been directly considered by the High Court. In *Hwang v Commonwealth*,[220] McHugh J, sitting alone, rejected the charge of invalidity. His Honour drew together several threads to support this conclusion. While he relied in part on the 'emergence of Australia as an independent nation',[221] he placed great significance on s 51(xix), suggesting that the 'power to make laws with respect to naturalisation and aliens may itself be sufficient authority for the enactment of a citizenship Act'.[222] Given the legal history of that power, this seems an extraordinary claim without far greater justification and development.

It seems that part of this trend is accounted for by a failure to appreciate just how stable the concept of alienage was at federation, and that the focus of legislative power was on consequences not definition. For example, in *Singh v Commonwealth*[223] ('*Singh*'), a majority of the High Court held that a person born in Australia could be considered an alien (and therefore liable to deportation).[224] However, the decision in *Singh* lacks a clear ratio, with the Court forming three distinct blocks. The first of these denied an objective constitutional meaning to 'alien' and largely left the definition to Parliament.[225] The second and third blocks agreed that the Court must determine the meaning of 'alien', but differed in their definition regarding whether the determinative allegiance is that owed to this[226] or to a foreign State.[227] There was significant disagreement as to whether the term 'alien' had a fixed legal meaning at federation.[228] What is striking is the degree to which the focus of all justices was on definitions, not consequences, of alienage—the original driving purpose of this provision whitewashed from the discussion.

220 *Hwang* (n 2).
221 'The power of the Parliament to make laws with respect to citizenship does not depend upon international law. If it arises simply from the emergence of Australia as an independent nation, it is because of the fact that it is an independent sovereign nation and that other nations recognise it as such': ibid [8]–[9], [19].
222 *Hwang* (n 2) [18].
223 *Singh* (n 3).
224 It was a 5:2 majority with Gleeson CJ, the joint judgment of Gummow, Hayne and Heydon JJ, and Kirby J. In dissent was McHugh J and Callinan J.
225 See *Singh* (n 3) [4] (Gleeson CJ), [260]–[261] (Kirby J).
226 Ibid [49] (McHugh J), [315]–[316] (Callinan J).
227 *Singh* (n 3) [154] (Gummow, Hayne and Heydon JJ).
228 Compare ibid [157], [190] (Gummow, Hayne and Heydon JJ) with [38]–[39] (McHugh J).

I use that term advisedly. We cleanse the 'alien' power of its repugnant underlying purpose when we pretend that it is really a proto-nationality power. But the aliens power is cousin to the race power. It is about allowing Parliament the authority to impose (potentially extensive and repulsive) disabilities on the othered alien. Of course, such a use of the power is now rightly seen as incompatible with our modern liberal multicultural country. But this is exactly the point. This power had a clear purpose at federation, a clear focus on the consequences of alienage, not its definition. That our society has evolved to the point that such a purpose is no longer acknowledged is not, of itself, a justification for repurposing that power.

However, since *Singh*, the courts have largely condoned such repurposing, granting Parliament the full power to define alien,[229] and accepting that the word 'alien' is synonymous with 'non-citizen'.[230] Through this approach, the statutory non-citizen now defines the constitutional meaning of alien despite the circularity of the citizenship regime apparently depending upon the aliens power.

Only in the recent decision of *Love v Commonwealth*[231] does there appear to be the slightest turning of the tide against such a conception. In that case, the reasoning of some justices indicates a return to the core meaning of alien denoting an absence of belonging. This core meaning was, to some extent, determinative of their finding that an Australian Aboriginal person cannot be alien.[232] Even here, however, there is no genuine attempt to engage with that original purpose. The High Court remains obsessed with definition, perhaps because it has become taboo to delve into the ugly past.

229 *Taurino v Minister for Immigration and Multicultural and Indigenous Affairs* (2005) 143 FCR 1, [23]–[24] ('*Taurino*'). See also *Re Woolley; Ex parte Applicants M276/2003 by Their Next Friend GS* (2004) 225 CLR 1, 17 [38] (McHugh J).
230 *Taurino* (n 229) [29].
231 *Love* (n 3).
232 Ibid. This includes the reasoning of the majority justices: at [246]–[249] (Nettle J), [302] (Gordon J), [392]-[393], [404], [437] (Edelman J). Gageler J, in dissent, also adopted the meaning of alien as an absence of allegiance or belonging: at [93], citing Gaudron J in *Nolan v Minister for Immigration and Ethnic Affairs* (1988) 165 CLR 178, 189. Bell J, in the majority, did not refer nor rely on the historical meaning of alien but instead considered that the Australian Aboriginal could not fall within the aliens power as they could not be said to 'belong to another place': at [74].

B. The ugly past and national identity

The history of the Australian colonies and early federation involves an ugly obsession with exclusion and the curtailment of rights of any who were seen to be 'others'. The rollout of the White Australia policy as one of the first legislative priorities of the Commonwealth is only the most infamous illustration of this obsession. The 'aliens' power of the Commonwealth is entangled in this original sin. As a matter of history, its true analogue was the race power, not immigration, and certainly not citizenship. As I outline above, the power was designed to regulate the domestic disabilities of aliens (and the removal of those disabilities through naturalisation).

The juxtaposition is useful here. The opposite of an alien is not a citizen, no more than the opposite of a liability is not a right.[233]

An alien is one who does not owe allegiance. By consequence of that status, the alien is liable to suffer a broad range of domestic disabilities; they are at risk of having their property seized, their freedom curtailed, their legal protections removed, and their ability to enforce any remaining rights through the courts restricted. A subject is immune, by consequence of their bond of allegiance, to such disabilities.

A citizen is something more. A citizen is the included 'we' in the modern nation—celebrated, protected and consulted. A citizen in the modern liberal democracy is granted participatory rights in the governance of the State, is educated, nurtured and healed by that State. To be a citizen is to have rights that can be enforced against the State. This is substantially richer than merely being immune to certain liabilities.

In Australia, it is a consequence of our exclusionary, often racist, past that our federal Parliament does not have any express constitutional power over citizenship. There is no explicit power to create national rights of membership—to forge a positive new identity. Rather, there is only a power to exclude—to impose liabilities on the alien other. This is the dark, but true, purpose of s 51(xix).

233 As Hohfeld notes, the opposite of a liability is an immunity; the opposite of a right is a duty: Wesley Newcomb Hohfeld, 'Fundamental Legal Conceptions as Applied in Juridical Reasoning' (1917) 26 *Yale Law Journal* 710, doi.org/10.2307/786270.

Constitutions matter for many reasons, not least for the stories they tell us about the nation we wish to be. It should make us, as a nation, deeply uncomfortable that the High Court seems to have accepted a position that our citizenship is dependent upon this exclusionary power, a power that was never intended to be inclusive or generative. Of course, constitutions are living documents that can evolve, and it may well be that a modern citizenship power can be cobbled together from the scattered inferences in our founding document.

However, the aliens power ought to play no role in this construction. If we are, as a nation, to enrich our national identity, we must be open-eyed about the darkness of the past and the limitations that history carries forward to the future. It is no more appropriate to rest our national identity on the aliens power than on the race power: both are part of our past, but they should play no part in our future.

Australia aspires to be an open, inclusive, multicultural nation. The aliens power has no place in such a contemporary national identity. The constitutional legal history of that power is clear and it is devastating. This repugnant purpose needs to be openly acknowledged as an archaic relic of another time and its purported use abandoned.

If this means that we are left without a firm constitutional foundation for our national identity and citizenship, then so be it. Let us forge such an identity anew. Constitutions tell us the story of who we wish to be, and we, as a nation, deserve better than the exclusionary aliens power. Let us properly understand its history so that we can now consign that power to history.

9

The Failure of Cosmopolitanism? National Identity, Citizenship and Migration in an Age of Populism

Tiziana Torresi

In this chapter, I consider an old question in liberal political theory: what role does (or should) national identity play in our conception and practice of citizenship? And specifically in the Australian context, what role, if any, should the Australian Constitution play in shaping and reflecting national identity in relation to our conception and practices of citizenship? My interest here is centred around these debates in relation to migration and the role it plays in the growth of right-wing populism, a phenomenon also described in the literature as the migration–populism nexus.[1]

Right-wing populism has experienced a significant growth in many countries. In many Western European countries, few, if any, right-wing populist parties existed until recent decades and, where present, they received little support.[2] Yet in the early years of the twenty-first century, the

1 See, eg, Anna Visvizi, 'Querying the Migration–Populism Nexus: Poland and Greece in Focus' (Discussion Paper, Institute of European Democrats, July 2017).
2 This is not to say that populism is a new phenomenon in Western Europe but, rather, that recent circumstances have been particularly favourable to its resurgence, see Cas Mudde, 'Europe's Populist Surge: A Long Time in the Making' (2016) 95(6) *Foreign Affairs* 25.

Freiheitliche Partei Österreichs (FPÖ or Austrian Freedom Party) entered government. In 2001, a four-party government, containing populist Forza Italia and Lega Nord, was formed in Italy. In 2003, the Lijst Pim Fortuyn (LPF or Pim Fortuyn List) served in coalition in the Netherlands. Since 2008, we have seen right-wing populists in government in Italy, Finland, Greece, Norway, Denmark and the Netherlands,[3] as well as the particularly successful regimes in Hungary and Poland, and in East and Central Europe more generally.[4] Right-wing populist leaders were successful in India with the election of Narendra Modi, in Turkey with Recep Tayyip Erdogan, in the Philippines with Rodrigo Duterte, and Brazil with Jair Bolsonaro.[5] Anglophone countries have not been immune to this development, with the election of Donald Trump in the United States, and the success of Nigel Farrage and the Brexit campaign in the United Kingdom.[6]

3 Giuliano Bobba and Duncan McDonnell, 'Different Types of Right-Wing Populist Discourse in Government and Opposition: The Case of Italy' (2016) 21(3) *South European Society and Politics* 281, doi.org/10.1080/13608746.2016.1211239.

4 Jakub Szabó, 'First as Tragedy, then as Farce: A Comparative Study of Right-Wing Populism in Hungary and Poland' (2020) 13(2) *Journal of Comparative Politics* 24; Anna Kende and Péter Krekó, 'Xenophobia, Prejudice, and Right-Wing Populism in East-Central Europe' (2020) 34 *Current Opinion in Behavioral Sciences* 29, doi.org/10.1016/j.cobeha.2019.11.011.

5 Priya Chacko and Kanishka Jayasuriya, 'Asia's Conservative Moment: Understanding the Rise of the Right' (2018) 48(4) *Journal of Contemporary Asia* 529, doi.org/10.1080/00472336.2018.1448108; Julius Maximilian Rogenhofer and Ayala Panievsky, 'Antidemocratic Populism in Power: Comparing Erdoğan's Turkey with Modi's India and Netanyahu's Israel' (2020) 27(8) *Democratization* 1394, doi.org/10.1080/13510347.2020.1795135; Nicole Curato, 'Flirting with Authoritarian Fantasies? Rodrigo Duterte and the New Terms of Philippine Populism' (2017) 47(1) *Journal of Contemporary Asia* 142, doi.org/10.1080/00472336.2016.1239751; Tom Gerald Daly, 'Populism, Public Law, and Democratic Decay in Brazil: Understanding the Rise of Jair Bolsonaro' (Conference Paper, International Human Rights Researchers' Workshop: Democratic Backsliding and Human Rights. 2–3 January 2019) <clb.ac.il/wp-content/uploads/2018/12/Daly_Populism-Public-Law-Dem-Dec-Brazil_LEHR.pdf>. There is, of course, great diversity in the parties, movements and leaders that are variously defined as populist in different countries and regions. Thus, two specifications are necessary here. First, I am not interested in discussing or contributing to the vast literature that attempts to define and conceptualise more precisely what populism is. In this chapter, I am interested in discussing a very narrow aspect of the phenomenon, namely, the electoral success of right-wing movements that mobilise anti-immigration, anti-globalisation and anti-cosmopolitan narratives. These are mostly defined in the literature as right-wing populists. Second, the bulk of my analysis refers to Western liberal democracies, and particularly Europe and Australia.

6 Thomas Greven, 'The Rise of Right-Wing Populism in Europe and the United States: A Comparative Perspective' (Research Paper, Friedrich Ebert Foundation, May 2016) 1–8 <dc.fes.de/fileadmin/user_upload/publications/RightwingPopulism.pdf>; Ziya Öniş and Mustafa Kutlay, 'The Global Political Economy of Right-Wing Populism: Deconstructing the Paradox' (2020) 55(2) *The International Spectator* 108, doi.org/10.1080/03932729.2020.1731168.

In most of these cases, anti-immigration sentiment has been successfully used by right-wing populist movements in their campaigning and represents a key part of their political platform.[7] Right-wing populists seem to have been very successful in using perceived threats to national identity and sovereignty for their political ends. In fact, it has been argued that the contemporary political fault lines that characterise politics in many liberal democracies often centre around globalisation. Political cleavages can, often, no longer be fully captured along the classic redistributional left–right axis[8] and can, thus, be best characterised as a contest between cosmopolitanism and communitarianism—cosmopolis versus localised identities.[9] Populism, with its association with nationalism and authoritarianism, its often reactionary positions on gender, its anti-establishment, anti-globalisation and anti-immigration rhetoric, and its critical, if not outright hostile, stance towards supranational institutions, aligns with an anti-globalisation and anti-cosmopolitan stance, most clearly in its right-wing expressions. Part of

7 See, eg, Mauro Caselli, Andrea Fracasso and Silvio Traverso, 'Globalisation and Electoral Outcomes: Evidence from Italy' (2020) 32(1) *Economics & Politics* 68, doi.org/10.1111/ecpo.12147; Roger Waldinger, 'Immigration and the Election of Donald Trump: Why the Sociology of Migration Left Us Unprepared … and Why We Should Not Have Been Surprised' (2018) 41(8) *Ethnic and Racial Studies* 1411, doi.org/10.1080/01419870.2018.1442014; Todd Donovan and David Redlawsk, 'Donald Trump and Right-Wing Populists in Comparative Perspective' (2018) 28(2) *Journal of Elections, Public Opinion and Parties* 190, doi.org/10.1080/17457289.2018.1441844; Dani Rodrik, 'Why Does Globalization Fuel Populism? Economics, Culture, and the Rise of Right-Wing Populism' (Working Paper No 27526, National Bureau of Economic Research, July 2020), doi.org/10.3386/w27526; Birgit Sauer, 'The (Im) possibility of Creating Counter-Hegemony Against the Radical Right: The Case of Austria' in Birte Siim et al (eds), *Citizens' Activism and Solidarity Movements* (Springer International Publishing, 1st ed, 2019) 111–36, doi.org/10.1007/978-3-319-76183-1_5; Philipp Lutz, 'Variation in Policy Success: Radical Right Populism and Migration Policy' (2019) 42(3) *West European Politics* 517, doi.org/10.1080/01402382.2018.1504509. Mainstream political parties are not immune to the temptation of using anti-immigration sentiment as a way of deflecting public criticism around policy failures and challenges experienced by their polities. See, eg, Magdalena Lesińska, 'The European Backlash against Immigration and Multiculturalism' (2014) 50(1) *Journal of Sociology* 37, doi.org/10.1177/1440783314522189; Anna Śledzińska-Simon, 'Populists, Gender, and National Identity' (2020) 18(2) *International Journal of Constitutional Law* 447, doi.org/10.1093/icon/moaa047.

8 For example, many right-wing populist parties do not exhibit the conservative fiscal policies associated with the right, but rather support generous welfare schemes for the members of the national community. See, eg, Johan Nordensvard and Markus Ketola, 'Nationalist Reframing of the Finnish and Swedish Welfare States: The Nexus of Nationalism and Social Policy in Far-Right Populist Parties' (2015) 49(3) *Social Policy & Administration* 356, doi.org/10.1111/spol.12095.

9 Ruud Koopmans and Michael Zürn, 'Cosmopolitanism and Communitarianism – How Globalization is Reshaping Politics in the Twenty-First Century' in Pieter de Wilde et al (eds), *The Struggle Over Borders: Cosmopolitanism and Communitarianism* (Cambridge University Press, 2019) 1–34, doi.org/10.1017/9781108652698.001.

the success of this anti-globalisation and anti-immigration stance is thought to arise because of a perceived threat to national sovereignty and identity on the part of citizens of liberal democracies.[10]

If this analysis is correct, then a commitment to a cosmopolitan understanding of democratic institutions (and citizenship in particular), a commitment to supranational institutions (and even robust multilateral cooperation), and a policy of relatively open immigration, if perceived to undermine national identity and sovereignty, is conducive to a backlash that may eventually result in the political and electoral success of extreme right-wing movements, with the anti-liberal and anti-democratic consequences that this entails.

Echoes of these concerns are present in normative debates around how best to conceive of citizenship; liberal democracy and the social justice that liberal democratic theorists have, in the past decades, been engaging in; and the role that national identity plays (or should play) in these contexts. Communitarians, or liberal nationalists, long expressed a concern and issued a (prophetic?) warning: institutional sources of legitimacy alone cannot transcend self-interest in liberal democracies; a sense of national identity and a shared culture are, instead, key to the sustainability of liberal democracy, equal citizenship and social justice. Liberal democratic institutions require a shared culture and identity to be sustainable. Citizens need to perceive bonds that connect them to their fellow citizens to be willing to support policies of redistribution and social welfare, to understand and communicate with each other effectively in public debate, and to trust one another. Without the national identity 'glue', liberal democratic institutions, including equal citizenship, are unsustainable. Thus, beyond principled reasons to commit to special relations with compatriots and national self-determination, we have

10 There are, of course, many who are sceptical that immigration does significantly undermine national culture and identity; however, what is crucial in this argument is the perception that parts of the population have of the effects of immigration. See, eg, Jeremy Waldron, 'What Respect is Owed to Illusions about Immigration and Culture?' (Working Paper No 16–49, New York University School of Law, October 2016), doi.org/10.2139/ssrn.2851527. As long as the perception is of threat, then the populist strategy of harnessing anti-immigration sentiment could continue being effective.

good prudential reason to want to promote a communitarian conception of liberal polities that promote a shared culture and identity as the basis of liberal democratic institutions, including equal citizenship.[11]

Does the rise in populism experienced by many countries suggest there is truth in the communitarian warning? Does a perceived threat to national identity result in a movement away from open, solidaristic and progressive politics and towards extreme right-wing, xenophobic closure? If so, what are the implications for how we think about the role of national identity in liberal democratic societies? Should the liberal commitment to freedom of movement be sacrificed to avoid the collapse of liberal democratic institutions? Should institutions, and foundational documents such as the Australian Constitution, foster a sense of national identity? In particular, what are the implications for how we should conceive citizenship in the context of a normative paradigm that is defined by a continuum that stretches between cosmopolitan and communitarian poles? In this chapter, I will be considering some of these questions. There are, of course, other questions and considerations around this issue, among them questions of principle, but those are not the questions I am pursuing here.

I. Citizenship and national identity

In the twentieth century, the Westphalian order mandated State sovereignty as a dominant and unified political authority to control a territory. It also established a correlative understanding of membership as citizenship within political communities, based on two principles: exclusivity and congruence.[12] Citizenship was understood as membership in a distinct political community—a nation-state—defined in its 'national' dimension by a shared understanding of past history, shared identity and a common,

11 See, eg, David Miller, *On Nationality* (Clarendon Press, 1995); Will Kymlicka, *Multicultural Citizenship: A Liberal Theory of Minority Rights* (Clarendon Press, 1995), doi.org/10.1093/0198290918.001.0001; Will Kymlicka, *Politics in the Vernacular: Nationalism, Multiculturalism, and Citizenship* (Oxford University Press, 2001) vol 157; Yael Tamir, *Liberal Nationalism* (Princeton University Press, 1995); Patti Tamara Lenard, 'Can Multiculturalism Build Trust?' in Reza Hasmath (ed), *Managing Ethnic Diversity: Meanings and Practices from an International Perspective* (Routledge, 2011) 11–28; David Miller and Sundas Ali, 'Testing the National Identity Argument' (2014) 6(2) *European Political Science Review* 237, doi.org/10.1017/S1755773913000088.

12 Andrea Schlenker and Joachim Blatter, 'Conceptualizing and Evaluating (New) Forms of Citizenship between Nationalism and Cosmopolitanism' (2014) 21(6) *Democratization* 1091, doi.org/10.1080/13510347.2013.783820.

self-determined future. Political membership was based on the principle in international law that 'every person should have a nationality and should have one nationality only'.[13]

At the normative level, in the communitarian tradition, this understanding of citizenship also sees citizenship rights of individuals as grounded on their membership of the political community. Moreover, as an instantiation of the right of national political communities to self-determination, membership can only be distributed by members according to their own will, and their right to determine membership is only constrained by some obligation to admit refugees, for example.[14]

However, nation-states have been experiencing, for the past several decades, a challenge to this traditional 'Westphalian' model of sovereignty and, consequently, membership. The last few decades have seen the rise of a globalised economy characterised by the free flow of capital, goods, information and, to a lesser degree, labour, as well as the appearance of transnational and new international political actors. At the national level, increases in the pace and complexity of both migration and mobility have resulted in increasingly multicultural and diverse societies. This includes the presence of non-citizen permanent residents and, on the other hand, of holders of dual citizenships, as well as a growing number of temporary and circular migrants, who may never acquire citizenship at all.[15] The appearance of transnational diasporas means that many citizens possess complex identities and multiple allegiances, as well as living lives that span across different social and political spaces.[16] This complex reality—within the context of a normative paradigm to theorise membership and migration that is defined by a continuum that stretches between cosmopolitan and

13 *Convention on Certain Questions Relating to the Conflict of Nationality Law*, opened for signature 13 April 1930, 179 LNTS 89 (entered into force 1 July 1937).

14 Michael Walzer, *Spheres of Justice: A Defense of Pluralism and Equality* (Basic Books, 2008).

15 See, eg, Rainer Bauböck, 'Temporary Migrants, Partial Citizenship and Hypermigration' (2011) 14(5) *Critical Review of International Social and Political Philosophy* 665, doi.org/10.1080/13698230.2011.617127; Valeria Ottonelli and Tiziana Torresi, 'Temporary Migration and the Shortcomings of Citizenship' in Carlota Solé (ed), *Impact of Circular Migration on Human, Political and Civil Rights* (Springer, 2016) 153–72, doi.org/10.1007/978-3-319-28896-3_8.

16 Valeria Ottonelli and Tiziana Torresi, 'Inclusivist Egalitarian Liberalism and Temporary Migration: A Dilemma' (2012) 20(2) *Journal of Political Philosophy* 202, doi.org/10.1111/j.1467-9760.2010.00380.x.

communitarian poles—means that citizenship cannot today be theorised simply within the context of national communities, and we have, in fact, seen a proliferation of conceptualisations of citizenship along this continuum.[17]

In this chapter, I am not going to attempt to address this complexity comprehensively but will, rather, discuss what I suggest are two recognisable understandings of citizenship in the literature: the traditional understanding of citizenship as national citizenship, as defended by communitarian and liberal nationalist theorists, and a relatively more recent model, identified in the literature as 'postnational' citizenship. Each of these models is articulated along two dimensions: first, a normative framework to defend and ground rights and duties of citizens, and, similarly, of migrants. Second, a specific understanding of the sociological and political realities that are the basis of the citizenship practices of both individuals and States.

Scholars of postnational citizenship argue that the developments, at the national and international level sketched above, have broken down the simple, dyadic relationship between States and their citizens, if it indeed ever existed. Citizens are not anymore univocally committed to one nation-state and the State, on its part, constrained by globalised political and economic structures, cannot anymore embody the will and protect the interests of its citizens as effectively as it may once have. Many have spoken of a 'citizenship crisis', especially within the European context,[18] which calls for the redefinition of the concept of citizenship to keep up with changed, and still changing, political, economic and social conditions. These authors point to 'postnationalism' as embodying the 'reflexive transformation' of the conception of membership in liberal democracies; a transformation enacted as a response to the changes and challenges outlined above, and that switches the emphasis away from traditional understandings of sovereignty and citizenship towards a conception of shared sovereignty between different loci of authority—local, national and supranational—corresponding also to a new and multilayered conception of membership.[19]

17 For a taxonomy, see Schlenker and Blatter (n 12). See also Joachim Blatter and Andrea Schlenker, 'Between Nationalism and Globalism: Spaces and Forms of Democratic Citizenship in and for a Post-Westphalian World' (Working Paper No 6, University of Lucerne, Working Paper Series: Glocal Governance and Democracy, 1 January 2013), doi.org/10.2139/ssrn.3008495.

18 See, eg, Elizabeth Meehan, 'Citizenship and the European Community' (1993) 64(2) *The Political Quarterly* 172, doi.org/10.1111/j.1467-923X.1993.tb00325.x ; Dominique Schnapper, 'The European Debate on Citizenship' (1994) 126(3) *Dedalus* 199.

19 Gerard Delanty, *Citizenship in a Global Age* (Open University Press, 2000).

When thinking about these broad developments in relation to migration, we return to the most articulate discussion of postnational citizenship and migration yet written—the work of Yasemin Soysal.[20] Soysal's seminal research was a comparative analysis of the actual process of integration of migrants, detailing how liberal democratic citizenship has shifted from classical definitions of membership as 'national' membership, towards a postnational conception of membership, based on personhood and, hence, human rights. In her words: 'A new and more universal concept of citizenship has unfolded in the post-war era, one whose organising principles are based on universal personhood rather than national belongings.'[21]

Soysal distinguishes between two ways of understanding immigration and their two correlative and consequent models of migrants' integration. In the traditional model, foreigners are either considered as prospective members expected to integrate fully in the political and cultural life of the nation-state and, hence, be transformed into citizens and assimilated within the life of the polity, or else are not considered as part of the polity at all. In the 'post-war model' of immigration, however, migrants remain largely 'foreign' in the traditional sense sketched above—they do not greatly assimilate culturally, nor do they become members formally by acquiring citizenship—but are, nevertheless, granted many of the rights and privileges traditionally associated with citizenship, giving rise, therefore, to a new and recognised mode of 'belonging' to the political community.[22]

But how do these developments point to the emergence of a postnational conception of citizenship? To draw the connections, Soysal begins by referring to the *locus classicus* of discussions of the evolution of citizenship in liberal democracies: the seminal 1950s study by Thomas H Marshall.[23]

20 Yasemin Nuhoğlu Soysal, *Limits of Citizenship: Migrants and Postnational Membership in Europe* (University of Chicago Press, 1994); Yasemin Nuhoğlu Soysal, 'Citizenship, Immigration, and the European Social Project: Rights and Obligations of Individuality' (2012) 63(1) *The British Journal of Sociology* 1, doi.org/10.1111/j.1468-4446.2011.01404.x. See also Saskia Sassen, 'Towards Post-National and Denationalized Citizenship' in Engin F Isin and Bryan S Turner (eds), *Handbook of Citizenship Studies* (Sage Publishing, 2002) 277–92, doi.org/10.4135/9781848608276.n17; Linda Bosniak, 'Citizenship Denationalized' (2000) 7(1) *Indiana Journal of Global Legal Studies* 447, doi.org/10.2139/ssrn.232082; Christian Joppke, 'Transformation of Citizenship: Status, Rights, Identity' (2007) 11(1) *Citizenship Studies* 37, doi.org/10.1080/13621020601099831; Seyla Benhabib, *The Rights of Others: Aliens, Residents, and Citizens* (Cambridge University Press, 2004) vol 5, doi.org/10.1017/CBO9780511790799; A Aneesh and David J Wolover, 'Citizenship and Inequality in a Global Age' (2017) 11(5) *Sociology Compass* e12477, doi.org/10.1111/soc4.12477.

21 Soysal (n 20) 1.

22 Ibid 27.

23 Thomas H Marshall, *Citizenship and Social Class* (Cambridge University Press, 1950).

Marshall traces the development of the modern, liberal conception of citizenship along three consecutive 'generations' of rights. These clusters of entitlements were developed in different historical periods and in response to changing needs and conceptions of political community. Moreover, each new generation of rights was built on the achievement of the previous one, in a process that tended, through the struggles to expand democracy, towards full participation for all.

Soysal notes how what she defines as the new, contemporary model of integration of migrants within host societies and its subsequent pattern of rights' acquisition exactly reverses the order of acquisition of rights that Marshall describes as characteristic of the historical development of liberal citizenship; in this, it seems to also change the relationship of causality, loosely understood, among them.[24] In fact, according to Marshall's model, political rights precede, and are instrumental to, the acquisition of social and economic rights; that is, it is the acquisition of political rights that opens the way to full socio-economic rights. But in the case of migrants in the postwar period analysed by Soysal, economic and social rights are the first to be granted, with political rights sometimes following, but not always.

Soysal imputes this 'reversed' order in the granting of migrants' rights to the States' unwillingness or inability to deny to migrants basic rights associated with personhood—namely, civil liberties and rights to a basic level of economic and social welfare, such as health and education for migrant children. The reason why political rights would be less willingly conceded, Soysal continues, is their carrying *symbolic* significance, more strictly related to national identity and belonging. For this reason, political rights remain reserved largely to nationals. This is partially explained, according to Soysal, by an historical concurrence: political rights in the form of universal (male) suffrage and popular sovereignty were recognised at the time of the ideological apex of the conception of the nation-state, and are, therefore, more strictly associated with national identity. But how are these developments in the political practice of liberal democracies to be explained? Soysal argues that the extension of rights to 'foreignness' is only made intelligible by considering changes in the global institutional order and the impact they have on national institutions and policies.

24 Soysal (n 20) 130.

Soysal recognises, of course, that ideas of human rights are not new in Western political cultures. She notes, however, that they have only become an integral part of international relations and institutions in the twentieth century. This is why, she argues, the effects of human rights discourse on national institutions are being felt now. This institutionalisation of human rights influences national outcomes primarily in two ways: first, by creating 'collective cognitive maps' that function as a framework for individual and collective action; second, by defining new actors and collective interests that come to exert pressure on the already existing political, social and institutional systems.[25] Membership becomes multilayered, dissociated from national identity and predicated on human rights. It is, in this sense, cosmopolitan and 'procedural', based on universalist norms, not shared culture, identity and meaning. Postnationalists, therefore, do not deny the historical connection between the development of liberal democratic citizenship practices and the development of nation-states but claim this connection to be contingent, and advocate for the possibility and necessity of transcending this connection to move towards a postnational model.[26] What is at stake here is, therefore, both the normative framework of justification of membership rights, and their motivational, political and sociological basis. It is this latter I am interested in, in this chapter.

Liberal nationalists and postnationalists disagree on the socio-political basis necessary to sustain liberal democratic social justice institutions and practices of citizenship. For liberal nationalists, like David Miller, both democratic politics and distributive justice require a shared culture and identity to be sustainable; national identity is the glue that binds fellow citizens together and sustains those attitudes of trust and willingness to cooperate and share that are necessary to their success.[27] For postnationalists, it is the other way round: under the conditions of pluralism that have arguably always existed within nation-states, but particularly in contemporary societies characterised by the effects of globalisation, national identity cannot function as a suitable common identity and sustain liberal democratic politics. Rather, modern liberal democratic States should base their identity and practices upon more abstract and universalistic political and legal principles that transcend cultural difference. For some

25 Ibid 44.

26 Jürgen Habermas, 'The Inclusion of the Other: Studies in Political Theory', tr Ciaran Cronin (MIT Press, 1998).

27 Miller (n 11); David Miller, *Citizenship and National Identity* (OECD Publishing, 2000).

postnationalists, it is the democratic process itself, when engaged in, that produces solidarity, provided it achieves sufficient levels of social justice.[28] The claim, therefore, is both normative and empirical: liberal democracies have moved away from the traditional liberal nationalist model of citizenship and migrant integration, and this is a positive development.

The empirical part of this argument builds on the 'silent revolution' theory of value change, according to which the unprecedented high levels of existential security and prosperity experienced by people in developed Western societies during the postwar decades resulted in an intergenerational shift towards progressive values and principles. This shift generated rising support for movements advocating pacifism, environmental rights and protections, human rights, gender and racial equality, LGBTQIA+ rights, a fairer economic system nationally and globally, justice for indigenous peoples and the rectification of historic injustices, particularly in relation to colonialism. Most pertinently for the argument in this chapter, this change in values and principles included support for fairer terms of integration for migrants (as we have seen analysed in Soysal's work, discussed above), support for multiculturalism and a more open and generous immigration and asylum policy, if not the advocacy of outright open borders on the basis of a right to freedom of movement.

While it may have seemed, at times, that the postwar developments towards more progressive and cosmopolitan values, principles and identities represented a linear progression destined to grow and entrench, it has been clear from the start that sectors of the population in liberal democracies reacted to these developments by initiating forms of resistance to these changes that have been characterised as a retro backlash.[29] Especially prominent among the older generation, white men and less educated sectors, there is a clear rejection of progressive values and principles, resentment for the displacement of traditional, often religious norms, and a renunciation and denunciation of multiculturalism in favour of more traditional national identities and the revindication of sovereignty and national interest against cosmopolitan and supranational identities and institutions. These sectors

28 Jürgen Habermas, *The Postnational Constellation: Political Essays* (John Wiley & Sons, 2018).
29 Ronald F Inglehart and Pippa Norris, 'Trump, Brexit, and the Rise of Populism: Economic Have-Nots and Cultural Backlash' (Working Paper No RWP16-026, Harvard Kennedy School, August 2016), doi.org/10.2139/ssrn.2818659.

provide a pool of supporters potentially vulnerable to populist appeal that often include the denunciation of the erosion of economic and social standards, sovereignty and national identity.

However, the shift to progressive values in Western liberal democracies, explained here on the basis of unpresented existential security and prosperity in the postwar years, has been eventually coterminous in later decades with an erosion of that security and prosperity. Rising inequality and increased poverty, partially due to the effects of globalisation and the dominance of neoliberal policies have meant for many a diminution of their economic and social wellbeing.[30] This complex constellation of events, therefore, raises questions in relation to what explains the anti-progressive backlash that we see embodied in the success of right-wing populist movements. Does this development prove communitarians like Miller right? Does the rise of populism show the unfeasibility of cosmopolitan solidarity and a renewed vitality of localised identities and allegiances, or does it, rather, embody and dramatically prove the dangers of growing inequality and, indeed, the failure to realise principles of justice? What does it entail for projects of postnational and cosmopolitan citizenship and fairness in migration?

II. The rise of right-wing populism and the role of migration and identity

The success of populist parties, movements and leaders has received a lot of critical attention. Scholars have attempted to explain the significant success of populists, both on the left and the right, by considering a broad variety of factors. Pippa Norris and Ronald Inglehart group these explanations into accounts focused upon: (1) public opinion, (2) party strategies—this category can be broadened to include changes in political organisations

30 See, eg, Joseph E Stiglitz, *The Price of Inequality: How Today's Divided Society Endangers Our Future* (WW Norton & Company, 2012); Joseph Stiglitz, *The Great Divide* (Penguin UK, 2015); Thomas Piketty, *The Economics of Inequality* (Harvard University Press, 2015); François Bourguignon, *The Globalization of Inequality* (Princeton University Press, 2017), doi.org/10.2307/j.ctvc77hcm; Wolfgang Merkel and Michael Zürn, 'Conclusion: The Defects of Cosmopolitan and Communitarian Democracy' in Pieter de Wilde et al (eds), *The Struggle Over Borders: Cosmopolitanism and Communitarianism* (Cambridge University Press, 2019) 207–37, doi.org/10.1017/9781108652698.008.

including parties[31]—and (3) constitutional arrangements governing electoral rules.[32] Finally, much scholarship has concentrated on analysing the role social media plays in the electoral success of populist parties.[33]

In this chapter, I concentrate on two rival and dominant explanations of the success of populism that concentrate on the first of the accounts mentioned above, public opinion, to explain the roots of the undoubted success, with sectors of the population, of populist appeals to anti-immigration sentiment. Following Norris and Inglehart's analysis, I examine: (1) the *economic inequality* perspective and (2) the *cultural backlash* thesis.[34]

The economic inequality thesis points to a series of changes experienced in Western liberal democracies in the past few decades that have transformed the workforce and society. There is indisputable evidence of significant and growing income and wealth inequality, as well as absolute poverty in most Western liberal democracies. This trend is due to a complex constellation of factors, some of which were deliberate policy decisions, while others were developments in technology and society. Among the former, neoliberal austerity policies and the erosion of organised labour, with the systematic attack on trade unions, are key. This was followed by the casualisation of the workforce in many sectors and the creation of precarious work conditions and the gig economy. These new labour conditions were worsened by shrinking welfare safety nets that may have alleviated some of the negative effects of the crisis of work. A series of other developments also contributed to the worsening of conditions for many sectors of society: the rise of the knowledge economy, technological automation and the collapse of the manufacturing industry were significant contributing factors. In Australia, nationally, these developments took place in the wake of decades of globalisation, which meant an increase in global flows of labour, goods and capital. Migration over this period has been characterised by increased

31 Nadia Urbinati, 'Liquid Parties, Dense Populism' (2019) 45(9) *Philosophy & Social Criticism* 1069, doi.org/10.1177/0191453719872274.

32 Inglehart and Norris (n 29); Pippa Norris and Ronald Inglehart, *Cultural Backlash: Trump, Brexit, and Authoritarian Populism* (Cambridge University Press, 2019), doi.org/10.1017/9781108595841.

33 See, eg, Jamie Bartlett, 'Populism, Social Media and Democratic Strain' in Carla Sandelind (ed), *European Populism and Winning the Immigration Debate* (Fores, 2014) 99–116; John Postill, 'Populism and Social Media: A Global Perspective' (2018) 40(5) *Media, Culture & Society* 754, doi.org/10.1177/0163443718772186; Paolo Gerbaudo, 'Social Media and Populism: An Elective Affinity?' (2018) 40(5) *Media, Culture & Society* 745, doi.org/10.1177/0163443718772192; Sven Engesser et al, 'Populism and Social Media: How Politicians Spread a Fragmented Ideology' (2017) 20(8) *Information, Communication & Society* 1109, doi.org/10.1080/1369118X.2016.1207697; Mario Datts, 'Social Media, Populism, and Migration' (2020) 8(4) *Media and Communication* 73, doi.org/10.17645/mac.v8i4.3212.

34 Inglehart and Norris (n 29).

numbers and complexity. It involves a wider diversity of ethnic and cultural groups and is characterised by the replacement of, more or less, permanent migration by circulation as the dominant paradigm of global migration. (Circulation is characterised by the emergence of transnationalism and transnational communities.)[35] Moreover, growing refugee flows, often characterised as refugee crises, have also increased diversity within receiving societies, as well as focused public opinion on the perceived social, cultural and economic threat that immigration and asylum are represented to be.[36] The combined effect of these trends has meant significant changes for the worse for significant sectors of society. According to the economic inequality thesis examined here, rising inequality, economic and social deprivation, work precarity and, in some cases, absolute poverty has fuelled, among those affected, resentment of the political classes and to have made the less affluent and secure members of society susceptible to the anti-establishment, 'sovranist', nationalist and xenophobic anti-immigration rhetoric of populist movements, parties and leaders.

The cultural backlash thesis suggests, on the other hand, that populist parties' success can be explained, not as a result of economic inequality and insecurity, but, in large part, as a reaction against progressive cultural change. In Western societies, during the postwar decades, we witnessed an intergenerational shift towards what are perceived as more progressive values, such as cosmopolitanism and multiculturalism and support for environmental protection, human rights, gender and sexual equality, as well as a more open attitude to a greater number of immigrants. The development in conceptions of citizenship, from a more traditional national liberal conception to a postnational model predicated on human rights discussed above, can be inscribed within this more general value shift.

However, especially among the older generation, white men and less educated sectors, these developments were met with resistance strong enough to be considered a backlash. These sectors, according to this

35 Graeme Hugo, 'The New International Migration in Asia: Challenges for Population Research' (2005) 1(1) *Asian Population Studies* 93, doi.org/10.1080/17441730500125953; Bauböck (n 15).

36 See, eg, Eelco Harteveld, 'Blaming Brussels: The Impact of (News About) the Refugee Crisis on Attitudes towards the EU and National Politics' (2018) 56(1) *Journal of Common Market Studies* 157, doi.org/10.1111/jcms.12664; Pietro Castelli Gattinara, 'The "Refugee Crisis" in Italy as a Crisis of Legitimacy' (2017) 9(3) *Contemporary Italian Politics* 318, doi.org/10.1080/23248823.2017.1388639; Danilo Di Mauro and Vincenzo Memoli, 'The Role of Public Opinion in EU Integration: Assessing the Relationship between Elites and the Public during the Refugee Crisis' (2021) 59(5) *Journal of Common Market Studies* 1303, doi.org/10.1111/jcms.13183; Susan F Martin, 'The Global Refugee Crisis' (2016) 17(1) *Georgetown Journal of International Affairs* 5, doi.org/10.1353/gia.2016.0000.

line of argument, sense decline in their own values, principles, ideas and identities—including national, ethnic and religious identities—and, thus, actively reject progressive values. These are the sectors that, according to the cultural backlash thesis, provide a pool of supporters for populist movements, parties and leaders. As Norris and Inglehart put it, 'sectors once culturally predominant in Western Europe may react angrily to the erosion of their privileges and status'.[37] It is, therefore, the loss of cultural and identity dominance, rather than economic loss of privilege, that explains support for populist movements, particularly right-wing ones, which are more likely to resort to nativist, nationalist and xenophobic language that resonates with groups who perceive that their identities and culture are threatened.

Norris and Inglehart are the first to admit that the distinction drawn here between economic and cultural factors is somewhat artificial:

> Yet the analytical distinction drawn between economic inequality and cultural backlash theories may also be somewhat artificial. Interactive processes may possibly link these factors, if structural changes in the workforce and social trends in globalized markets heighten economic insecurity, and if this, in turn, stimulates a negative backlash among traditionalists towards cultural shifts. It may not be an either/or question, but one of relative emphasis with interactive effects.[38]

Yet, while admitting that it is not an 'either/or story', they insist that their evidence suggests that 'it would be a mistake to attribute the rise of populism directly to economic inequality alone'.[39]

It is, of course, important to recognise that re-vindications around equality are not exhausted by considerations of economic inequality and class cleavages, and we ought to be mindful of avoiding such reductionist arguments.[40] However, the importance of economic inequality, precarity and, in some cases, absolute poverty in explaining the success of right-wing populist parties and movements should not be dismissed. As Norris and Inglehart's own data, to a degree, demonstrate, and other studies show positively, economic insecurity functions as a trigger for the development of anti-immigration and anti-globalist attitudes through the arousal of

37 Inglehart and Norris (n 29) 3.
38 Ibid.
39 Ibid 30.
40 See, eg, Carol Johnson, *Social Democracy and the Crisis of Equality* (Springer, 2019) 1–22, doi.org/10.1007/978-981-13-6299-6_1.

emotions such as anger, fear and shame that, in turn, lead to support for populist parties and movements, who then have an incentive to exploit such sentiment, creating a vicious circle of supply and demand.[41]

III. The temptation to sacrifice migrants

The concern around immigration is not limited to right-wing populist parties and movements but has spread across the political spectrum and has regarded both the numbers and modes of migrant arrivals, and the principles and policies relating to the terms of their integration within political communities.

Multiculturalism as a political philosophy and a set of policies has come under assault since the turn of the century.[42] German Chancellor Angela Merkel proclaimed, in 2010, that the multicultural approach had 'utterly failed'.[43] Similar sentiments were echoed by Nicolas Sarkozy in 2011, when he commented that: 'We have been too concerned about the identity of the person who was arriving and not enough about the identity of the country that was receiving him.'[44] Merkel's and Sarkozy's comments were quickly supported by former Australian Prime Minister John Howard.[45] Similar language made its way also into official institutional spaces, such as the Council of Europe, whose 2008 White Paper stated:

41 Miguel Carreras, Yasemin Irepoglu Carreras and Shaun Bowler, 'Long-Term Economic Distress, Cultural Backlash, and Support for Brexit' (2019) 52(9) *Comparative Political Studies* 1396, doi.org/10.1177/0010414019830714; Mikko Salmela and Christian Von Scheve, 'Emotional Roots of Right-Wing Political Populism' (2017) 56(4) *Social Science Information* 567, doi.org/10.1177/0539018417734419; Duane Swank and Hans-Georg Betz, 'Globalization, the Welfare State and Right-Wing Populism in Western Europe' (2003) 1(2) *Socio-Economic Review* 215, doi.org/10.1093/soceco/1.2.215.

42 See, eg, Steven Vertovec and Susanne Wessendorf (eds), *The Multiculturalism Backlash: European Discourses, Policies and Practices* (Routledge, 2010), doi.org/10.4324/9780203867549; Will Kymlicka, 'The Rise and Fall of Multiculturalism: New Debates on Inclusion and Accommodation in Diverse Societies' (2010) 61(199) *International Social Science Journal* 97, doi.org/10.1111/j.1468-2451.2010.01750.x; Irene Bloemraad and Matthew Wright, '"Utter Failure" or Unity Out of Diversity: Debating and Evaluating Policies of Multiculturalism' (2014) 48(1) *International Migration Review* 292, doi.org/10.1111/imre.12135.

43 'Merkel Says German Multicultural Society has Failed', *BBC News* (Web Page, 17 October 2010) <www.bbc.com/news/world-europe-11559451>.

44 'Sarkozy Declares Multiculturalism "a Failure"', *France 24* (Web Page, 10 February 2011) <www.france24.com/en/20110210-multiculturalism-failed-immigration-sarkozy-live-broadcast-tf1-france-public-questions>.

45 Michael Peters and Tina Besley, 'Islam and the End of European Multiculturalism: From Multiculturalism to Civic Integration' (2014) 12(1) *Policy Futures in Education* 1, doi.org/10.2304/pfie.2014.12.1.1.

> Whilst driven by benign intentions, multiculturalism is now seen by many as having fostered communal segregation and mutual incomprehension, as well as having contributed to the undermining of the rights of individuals—and, in particular, women—within minority communities, perceived as if these were single collective actors. The cultural diversity of contemporary societies has to be acknowledged as an empirical fact. However, a recurrent theme of the consultation was that multiculturalism was a policy with which respondents no longer felt at ease.[46]

This shift away from support for more open immigration policies and multiculturalism has been experienced along the political spectrum. On immigration, differences between the mainstream left and right have become much smaller than they used to be. This is because mainstream left parties have distanced themselves from multicultural policies and expressed concerns around numbers and modalities of arrivals, and because conservatives have, sometimes, assumed pro-immigration views.[47] An example is Angela Merkel's opening of German borders to significant numbers of refugees during the 2015 crisis that cost her politically.[48] The position of some left-wing parties is well expressed by a report by the Tony Blair Institute for Global Change on the topic of immigration and integration, which explicitly calls the rise of populism into focus as a reason for progressive parties and movements to change their policies and general stance on immigration. This shift is perceived as a way of countering the electoral success enjoyed by right-wing populists on the basis of anti-immigration sentiment:

> With populism on the rise across the West, the challenge for progressives is to design immigration and integration policies that reconcile these concerns and secure the public confidence of a majority of citizens ... set out the basis of a balanced immigration framework that maximises the benefits of immigration economically, socially and culturally while addressing legitimate concerns about the management of migration flows.[49]

---

46 'White Paper on Intercultural Dialogue: Living Together as Equals in Dignity' (White Paper, 118th Ministerial Session, Council of Europe Ministers of Foreign, 7 May 2008).

47 Koopmans and Zürn (n 9).

48 Joyce Marie Mushaben, 'Wir Schaffen Das: Angela Merkel and the European Refugee Crisis' (2017) 26(4) *German Politics* 516, doi.org/10.1080/09644008.2017.1366988.

49 Harvey Redgrave et al, 'The Glue that Binds: Integration in a Time of Populism' (Report, Tony Blair Institute for Global Change, 21 April 2019) 5 <www.institute.global/insights/geopolitics-and-security/glue-binds-integration-time-populism>.

Another interesting example is the 'MoVimento 5 Stelle' in Italy. The movement has been considered by many as a populist movement. However, its characterisation as left or right has been more contested because it expresses positions traditionally held by both sides of politics. A breakdown of the members of the movement reveals that, while they hold progressive positions on many issues, they also exhibit anti-immigration and anti-EU and, therefore, anti-globalisation, 'sovranist' positions, which reflect the MoVimento's position on these issues, and its seating in the European Parliament with the Europe of Freedom and Direct Democracy Group, which brings together many of Europe's most right-wing and xenophobic parties.[50]

Progressive parties are, thus, tempted to adopt a rhetoric, such as that around the failure of interculturalism, which seeks to achieve a compromise, saving some degree of diversity and maintaining a commitment to welcoming new migrants, provided this inflow is 'controlled' and beneficial to the receiving country, while acknowledging the purported dangers of 'uncontrolled' or excessive immigration and the failures of multiculturalism. This is a dangerous tactic that risks reinforcing right-wing populist discourse.[51] The rise of right-wing populism seems, therefore, to represent a vindication of what has been called the new progressive's dilemma: a deep tension between diversity and solidarity, saving progressive, solidaristic politics from a right-wing drift, but at the price of sacrificing some commitment to open migration and multiculturalism.[52]

50 Lorenzo De Sio, 'Gli elettori M5S, PD e Lega e le Possibili Coalizioni: Uniti e Divisi da Economia, Immigrati, Europa' [M5S, PD and Lega Voters and Possible Coalitions: United and Divided by Economy, Immigrants, Europe] in Vincenzo Emanuele and Aldo Paparo (eds), *Gli Sfidanti al Governo: Disincanto, Nuovi Conflitto e Diverse Strategie dietro il Voto del 4 Marzo 2018* [*The Challengers to the Government: Disenchantment, New Conflict and Diverse Strategies behind the Vote of 4 March 2018*] (Centro Italiano Studi Elettorali, 2018) 187–91; Roberto Biorcio and Paolo Natale, *Il Movimento 5 Stelle: Dalla Protesta al Governo* [*The 5 Stars Movement: From Protest to Government*] (Mimesis, 2018).

51 Will Kymlicka, 'Defending Diversity in an Era of Populism: Multiculturalism and Interculturalism Compared' in Nasar Meer, Tariq Modood and Ricard Zapata-Barrero (eds), *Multiculturalism and Interculturalism: Debating the Dividing Lines* (Edinburgh Scholarship Online, 2016) 158–77, doi.org/10.1515/9781474407106-009. See also Nasar Meer and Tariq Modood, 'How Does Interculturalism Contrast with Multiculturalism?' (2012) 33(2) *Journal of Intercultural Studies* 175, doi.org/10.1080/07256868.2011.618266; Geoffrey Brahm Levey, 'Interculturalism vs Multiculturalism: A Distinction without a Difference?' (2012) 33(2) *Journal of Intercultural Studies* 217, doi.org/10.1080/07256868.2012.649529.

52 Nicholas Pearce, 'Diversity versus Solidarity: A New Progressive Dilemma' (2004) 12(3) *Renewal* 79–87; David Goodhart, 'Too Diverse?' (2004) 95(30) *Prospect Magazine* 7.

The dangers inherent in this strategy are exemplified by the story of Jilmar Ramos-Gomez, who served in the Marines and saw combat in Afghanistan. Born in Grand Rapids, Michighan, he is indisputably a US citizen. Nevertheless, in December 2018, federal immigration authorities took him into custody to face possible deportation. This was as a result of an arrest on unrelated matters. In November 2018, Gomez was arrested for trespassing onto the helipad area on the roof of a local hospital. He was, at the time, undergoing psychiatric treatment for post-traumatic stress disorder, not uncommon for veterans. After the incident, he pleaded guilty in court, and a local judge ordered him released. But instead of releasing him, the county jail turned him over to the custody of the US Immigration and Customs Enforcement ('ICE'), a federal law enforcement agency under the US Department of Homeland Security. The county did that based on a request from ICE, which claimed Gomez was in the country illegally, even though the evidence that Gomez was a citizen seems to have been presented to the police at the appropriate time.[53]

This story, one of many similar ones,[54] serves to remind us of a point that can be lost when discussing how national identity serves to shape our politics as I am doing here. The reverse is also true, namely, that politics shapes our national identity as well. The way that we talk about and debate political membership shapes our understanding of who belongs and who does not. Thus, the way we talk about certain groups—for example, Mexican immigrants—shapes our understanding of whether somebody belongs securely or not. Similarly, the way we police and enforce citizenship rules serves not just to mirror but to shape membership.[55] Therefore, a rhetoric that stigmatises certain groups and concentrates on the negative effects of their presence in the polity works also to undermine inclusive equality by reproducing and reinforcing stereotypes around who belongs and who does not that do not map formal citizenship but racialised identities and

53 Nearly a year later, the Grand Rapids City Commission unanimously agreed to award Ramos-Gomez US$190,000 in a settlement over the wrongful detainment. See Alex Horton, 'Police Knew a War Veteran was a US Citizen. ICE Detained Him Anyway' *Washington Post* (online, 15 November 2019) <www.washingtonpost.com/national-security/2019/11/14/police-knew-war-veteran-was-us-citizen-ice-detained-him-anyway/>.

54 See, eg, Mary Romero, 'Keeping Citizenship Rights White: Arizona's Racial Profiling Practices in Immigration Law Enforcement' (2011) 1(1) *Law Journal for Social Justice* 97; Alpa Parmar, 'Arresting (Non)Citizenship: The Policing Migration Nexus of Nationality, Race and Criminalization' (2020) 24(1) *Theoretical Criminology* 28, doi.org/10.1177/1362480619850800.

55 Leo Chavez, *The Latino Threat: Constructing Immigrants, Citizens, and the Nation* (Stanford University Press, 2013), doi.org/10.1515/9780804786188; Rachel E Rosenbloom, 'The Citizenship Line: Rethinking Immigration Exceptionalism' (2013) 54(4) *Boston College Law Review* 1965.

xenophobic prejudice. Thus, anyone concerned with equal citizenship ought to tread carefully when engaging in discussions around national identity and migration.

Attempts to move us back from a cosmopolitan, postnational understanding of citizenship towards one based more on a shared national identity and culture risks undermining the very idea of inclusive, equal citizenship by unwittingly sustaining a divisive, xenophobic rhetoric that is the basis of the right-wing, populist success in the first place. This does not, of course, resolve the debate around national versus postnational citizenship as, among other things, it does not show that any attempt at defining and defending some form of national identity would be equally divisive, nor does it indicate how to counteract the growing success of anti-immigration platforms with some sectors of the public. It does, however, suggest caution in the way that we approach discussions around migration, multiculturalism, citizenship and identity.

IV. Conclusion: Citizenship, identity and equality

What, then, are the implications of the preceding discussion for the questions I am considering here? Namely, what role does national identity play in our conception of citizenship and what role should it play? If, in considering this question, we conclude that the fostering of a shared national identity and culture is desirable, could the Australian Constitution play a role in reflecting and fostering such a shared culture and identity? What I have wanted to consider here is whether the rise of right-wing populism, given its successful use of anti-immigration sentiments, gives us a reason to want to conceive of citizenship as shaped and steeped in a shared national identity, as the communitarians suggest, rather than as a cosmopolitan institution based on an idea of shared humanity. In other words, should we engage in a process of reversal of the movement from national to postnational forms of citizenship, as described by Soysal and discussed above, to avert the danger of the undermining of an ideal of liberal egalitarian justice and equal citizenship altogether? Indeed, has such a reversal not actually already happened in the hearts and minds of many citizens of liberal democracies and has the perceived refusal, on the part of social, economic and political elites, to accept this change been pivotal to the success of right-wing populism?

While Australia seems to be somewhat less vulnerable to these forms of backlash than other Western democracies, it is, nevertheless, not immune to these trends. Thus, these questions should be given careful consideration.[56] The evidence supports quite strongly the fact that anti-immigration and anti-cosmopolitan sentiments are part of the picture in explaining the electoral success of right-wing populist parties and movements. However, the evidence, when considered carefully, also indicates two other important points. First, growing inequality and poverty in Western liberal democracies, in the past decades, contributes significantly to the feelings of insecurity that motivate anti-immigration and anti-cosmopolitan sentiment. Migrants, unfortunately, are seen as both an economic and cultural threat by the most socially and economically insecure sections of society, creating very fertile ground for anti-immigration propaganda. Second, the adoption of a negative stance—even only cautiously—on immigration and multiculturalism favours the development of an understanding of who belongs and who does not, which fails to be truly inclusive. Thus, attempts on the part of progressive parties and movements to hit a middle ground and assuage popular fears around immigration end up undermining the ideal of equal citizenship central to liberal egalitarian political principles and practices.

In the Australian context, at least from the perspective discussed here (which is obviously not exhaustive), the careful affirmation of a multicultural identity that is truly inclusive may be appropriate and justified, given that there is some evidence that the cultivation of a shared identity that affirms a commitment to multiculturalism may be helpful in fostering unity and trust.[57] This affirmation may usefully happen in the Constitution. It would have to be crafted to avoid reification of a specific, narrow and thickly substantive identity, which is inevitably going to be resemblant of majority culture and identity and, therefore, to be exclusionary, in some regards, for those who do not share its characteristics. Such a reified and calcified identity may be limiting of the normal cultural progression and change in the ways and norms of a polity due to many factors, of which immigration is but one. How postnational or cosmopolitan, if at all, this identity need be to achieve these ends is, of course, a very difficult empirical question, and

56 In fact, post-multiculturalism itself is predicated here on the basis of multiculturalism having been a success, not a failure, so much so that we do not need to worry about these questions anymore. For a discussion, see Geoffrey Brahm Levey, 'Australia's "Liberal Nationalist" Multiculturalism' in Richard T Ashcroft and Mark Bevir (eds), *Multiculturalism in the British Commonwealth Since 1945: Comparative Perspectives on Theory and Practice* (University of California Press, 2019) 83–103, doi.org/10.1515/9780520971103-006.

57 Lenard (n 11).

even more contested normatively. I do not attempt to answer this question here beyond the considerations I have expressed already. It may even be that, to avoid the stigmatising and divisive effects of anti-immigration rhetoric described above, such an instituted shared culture and identity would also have to include a commitment to a fairly open migration policy and the recognition of what we may consider a duty to take migrants needs and rights seriously at the point of entry, as well as a commitment to multiculturalism, once migrants are admitted. This may fall short of a commitment to open borders, of course, since there are many elements and duties that compose a just immigration policy, but it would impose some limits on acceptable policy in this area.

However, perhaps more importantly, the evidence around the rise of right-wing populism supports the protective value of instituting mechanisms to achieve substantive equality, including, and with great emphasis on, socio-economic rights. Such a commitment would aim to stem and reverse the growth of inequality and poverty that, as we have seen, leads to support for right-wing parties, which furthers erodes progressive economic policies and, in their turn, creates more inequality and poverty in a vicious circle.[58] What role can the Australian Constitution play in achieving these provisions? There are, of course, numerous options. One possible route would be for the Constitution to affirm a principle of substantive equality—to be articulated, for example, through the recognition of a right to work or to a universal basic income.[59] The institution of such provisions to achieve substantive equality is likely to have a protective effect against right-wing populist political success greater (if the evidence reported here is correct) than the mere affirmation of a shared national identity and culture. To be resolved, the new progressive dilemma requires a renewed commitment to substantive socio-economic equality at the core of equal citizenship.

58 Patti Tamara Lenard, 'Rebuilding Trust in an Era of Widening Wealth Inequality' (2010) 41(1) *Journal of Social Philosophy* 73, doi.org/10.1111/j.1467-9833.2009.01479.x.

59 For a discussion of these ideas, see, eg, Jon Elster, 'Is There (or Should There Be) a Right to Work?' in Amy Gutmann (ed), *Democracy and the Welfare State* (Princeton University Press, 2021) 53–78, doi.org/10.2307/j.ctv14163mz.8; Philip Harvey, 'Right to Work and Basic Income Guarantees: Competing or Complementary Goals' (2005) 2(1) *Rutgers Journal of Law & Urban Policy* 8; Karl Widerquist and Michael Anthony Lewis, *The Ethics and Economics of the Basic Income Guarantee* (Routledge, 2017), doi.org/10.4324/9781315239934.

10

National Identity and Australian Federalism

Robyn Hollander

In 1901, the Australian Constitution became law. Although an Act of the British Parliament, our constitution articulated the aspirations of colonial lawmakers and an electorate of primarily male British subjects—an Australia that was proudly white, male, British and Christian. As a statement of Australian identity, this vision was far from inclusive and has become increasingly less so over the decades as the Australian community has become even more diverse. Indeed, Australia is arguably characterised by a national intersectionality. This makes it timely for a project such as this to revisit this nineteenth-century constitutional version of national identity and consider ways in which it might be made relevant for our twenty-first-century nation. There is, however, one aspect that, somewhat paradoxically, remains fit for purpose, and that is our federal structure. This chapter argues that federalism provides some capacity to recognise and reflect the multiplicity of Australian identities, albeit in an incomplete way. For this reason, I argue that that the federal structure, adopted by the founders, continues to be of value despite a century of increasing centralisation.

The link between federalism and diversity is hardly controversial. It is well accepted that federalism provides an institutional framework that accepts and accommodates territorial or place-based diversity where there are marked differences in religion, language, ethnicity and culture. So much is uncontested and supports the continued relevance of federalism in countries across the globe from Switzerland and Canada to India and Ethiopia.

In many countries, differences are clearly place-based, but we have also seen the emergence of 'non-territorial federalism' to accommodate spatially dispersed communities.[1] The Belgian federal structure is an attempt to add cultural difference over a more traditional federal structure. Thus, territorial 'Regions' (which have responsibilities in relation to the economy, employment and infrastructure) sit beneath cultural 'Communities' (which are responsible for education and language and a range of social policy areas).[2]

In Australia, however, critics of federalism contend that there are no comparable cleavages and, thus, federalism has long outlived its usefulness because there is but a single uniform Australian identity. Former Prime Minister John Howard was clearly of this view, arguing that our shared *Australian* identity overrode all other attachments. While other federal leaders, such as Gough Whitlam, have been strong centralists, they have been less strident in their rejection of the notion of States as cultural identities. Howard's centralism was part of his 'one nation' rhetoric, which served to deny the existence of difference and the multiplicity of allegiance. For Howard, the two connections that were most relevant in modern Australia were to the nuclear family and to country. Allegiances to place, class and ethnicity were simply artefacts of an earlier time or other place.[3] Thus, he saw existing State and Territory boundaries as geopolitical constructs rather than cultural communities, and maintained that such boundaries simply hampered economic growth and individual mobility.[4]

This characterisation obscures the more fine-grained, socio-economic variations between the States and Territories. As has been argued elsewhere,[5] each of the States and Territories in the federation is distinctive, displaying

1 Dietmar Kneitschel, 'Federalism and Non-Territorial Minorities' in Aviezer Tucker and Gian Piero de Bellis (eds), *Panarchy: Political Theories of Non-Territorial States* (Routledge, 2016).

2 'Belgium, A Federal State', Belgium.be: Official Information and Services (Web Page) <www.belgium.be/en/about_belgium/government/federale_staat>.

3 See, eg, Carol Johnson, 'John Howard's "Values" and Australian Identity' (2007) 42(2) *Australian Journal of Political Science* 195, doi.org/10.1080/10361140701319986; Nick Dyrenfurth, 'John Howard's Hegemony of Values: The Politics of "Mateship" in the Howard Decade' (2007) 42(2) *Australian Journal of Political Science* 21, doi.org/10.1080/10361140701319994; Stefano Gulmanelli, 'John Howard and the "Anglospherist" Reshaping of Australia' (2014) 49(4) *Australian Journal of Political Science* 581, doi.org/10.1080/10361146.2014.965658.

4 Robyn Hollander, 'John Howard, Economic Liberalism, Social Conservatism, and Australian Federalism' (2008) 54(1) *Australian Journal of Politics and History* 85, doi.org/10.1111/j.1467-8497.2008.00486.x.

5 See, eg, Nicholas Aroney, Scott Prasser and Alison Taylor, 'Federal Diversity in Australia: A Counter-Narrative' in Gabrielle Appleby, Nicholas Aroney and Thomas John (eds), *The Future of Australian Federalism: Comparative and Interdisciplinary Perspectives* (Cambridge University Press, 2012), doi.org/10.1017/CBO9780511902550.020; Rodney Smith, *Australian Political Culture* (Pearson, 2001).

longstanding and newly emerging differences that are frequently reflected in politics and policy. The 'one Australia' rhetoric not only ignores these differences but also denies the existence of differences and allegiances associated with gender, sexuality, ethnicity and belief that are not neatly contained within State borders. Such differences, both between and within States, mean that Australia's federal framework is still relevant. This is because of the way it can provide opportunities to recognise and accommodate diversity. It does this through the duplication and overlap that inevitably characterise all federal systems. In particular, I argue that federalism and the overlap and duplication it creates allows for our multiplicity of identities to manifest in different policy choices and, in particular, enables minorities to gain hard-won successes in pursuing social change.

In the first part of this chapter, I expand on the argument that federal duplication and overlap has both strengths and weakness. In the second part, I put this argument to the test through the use of two case studies of the various approaches to decriminalisation of homosexuality (in which I focus on four key jurisdictions because they exhibit very distinctive trajectories) and the recognition of same-sex relationships.

These case studies demonstrate two important conclusions in understanding the relevance of federation for twenty-first-century Australian identity. First, the path to decriminalisation of homosexuality demonstrates that, for the most part, decriminalisation was achieved through a focus on *regional issues and politics*, and changes reflected the way in which the different States and Territories conceptualised themselves and their collective identity. It was this that facilitated change in most cases where it was not a straightforward 'follow the leader' process. Nor was it something that could have been achieved by a national government even if it had had the power to act unilaterally because of the strength and geographical distribution of opposition. The national dimension was not irrelevant, however, and played a significant part in the process of change in Tasmania. This chapter finds that, in the case of decriminalisation, the twin roles of duplication and overlap provided the context to achieve decriminalisation across Australia.

Second, in the case of the recognition of same-sex relationships, federalism was important because it provided a multitude of spaces for minority groups to achieve more expansive recognition, particularly as the Commonwealth was recalcitrant. This is because the smaller State and Territory polities were more accessible, and governments could benefit from policy experimentation and diffusion.

I. Duplication, overlap and difference

To understand how federalism can facilitate the recognition of diversity, we need to come to grips with two fundamental dimensions of federalism: duplication and overlap. Although frequently referenced, these factors are rarely, if ever, defined and analysed in a serious and systematic way. This is particularly so in the Australian context but also in the theoretical and empirical federalism literature more generally. The upshot of this neglect is that the way duplication and overlap can impact on politics and policymaking, both positively and negatively, is rarely examined as a whole despite an abundance of empirical work on federalism and specific policies, particularly in the US, and in non-scholarly critiques of federal systems.

This section examines the costs and benefits of duplication and overlap. Before proceeding it is useful to define the meaning of duplication and overlap more precisely. To do so, we need to look outside political science to the literature on complex machine systems.[6] In this field, duplication is defined as occurring when systems with the *same* functions operate independently of each other. In federations, duplication exists, by definition, because of the existence of multiple jurisdictions with the same (or broadly similar) powers. Overlap exists when systems intersect despite having different purposes and core activities. In federations, overlap (otherwise known as concurrency) occurs because some powers are shared usually between central and sub-national governments. Such power sharing is inescapable because of the complexities of governing. While political leaders may yearn for 'clean lines' in relation to roles and responsibilities, such aspirations have proved to be illusory as former Prime Minister Tony Abbott's white paper process demonstrated.[7] It is simply not possible to disentangle the intricate web of intergovernmental relationships.

Just as duplication and overlap are inevitable, so are the outcomes, which are redundancy, inconsistency and fragmentation: redundancy because of replication of institutions, roles and responsibilities either through duplication or overlap; inconsistency because jurisdictions can and do

6 See, eg, Allan W Lerner, 'There Is More than One Way to be Redundant: A Comparison of Alternatives for the Design and Use of Redundancy in Organizations' (1986) 18(3) *Administration and Society* 334, doi.org/10.1177/009539978601800303; Martin Landau, 'Redundancy, Rationality, and the Problem of Duplication and Overlap' (1969) 29(4) *Public Administration Review* 346, doi.org/10.2307/973247.

7 Mark Bruerton and Robyn Hollander, 'Introduction' in Mark Bruerton et al (eds), *A Peoples Federation* (Federation Press, 2017).

exercise their decision-making powers to implement different processes and achieve different outcomes; and fragmentation because authority and responsibility are dispersed. These are commonly seen as negatives: redundancy is wasteful, inconsistency confusing and fragmentation unaccountable. However, I argue that they should not be so easily condemned. Rather, they should be seen as providing opportunities to incorporate the multiple identities that constitute the Australian nation into decision-making processes. This applies to those identities that are place-based and those that are more dispersed.

A. Redundancy

Redundancy is one way in which federal duplication and overlap create space for policy tailored to meet the needs of national minorities through experimentation and learning. James Bryce, an early federalist scholar, certainly thought this a benefit of federalism. He believed that federations could prompt positive change because they allowed for State-based experimentation. State-based policy could show us what worked and what did not. He characterised it thus:

> A comparatively small commonwealth like an American state easily makes and unmakes its laws; mistakes are not serious, for they are soon corrected; other states profit by the experience of a law or a method which has worked well or ill in the state that has tried it.[8]

In the 1930s, US Supreme Court Justice Louis Brandeis did much to promote this idea of laboratory federalism. He saw his country's federal structure as a mechanism for resolving pressing problems because it provided secure venues for 'political and social invention' and, thus, could afford both positive and negative examples of policy performance.[9]

While much of the discussion has focused on the potential for federalism to promote 'technical progress' in public policy,[10] more important from our perspective is the opportunity to craft policy more directly responsive to local concerns and acceptable to particular constituencies.[11]

8 James Bryce, *The American Commonwealth* (Macmillan, 1893) 353.

9 EE Steiner, 'A Progressive Creed: The Experimental Federalism of Justice Brandeis' (1983) 2(1) *Yale Law and Policy Review* 1.

10 Wallace E Oates, 'An Essay on Fiscal Federalism' (1999) 37(3) *Journal of Economic Literature* 1120, doi.org/10.1257/jel.37.3.1120.

11 John Kincaid, 'Foreword: The New Federalism Context of the New Judicial Federalism' (1995) 26(4) *Rutgers Law Journal* 913.

The COVID-19 pandemic provides a striking example of the ways in which the different Australian States and Territories adopted different policy settings and approaches based on their specific circumstances and demands. These measures extended to closing their borders. Arguably, the autonomy available to sub-national jurisdictions in federations such as Australia, Canada and even the US has been extremely valuable in efforts to mitigate against the worst effects of the pandemic.

Moreover, successful policy initiatives often provide models for other States to emulate. The parallel systems provided through duplication allow policymakers to compare and contrast, thereby diffusing successes (and failures). This diffusion of policy can occur between States (horizontal) or between States and the central government (vertical) and through a variety of channels: through competition between States, via purposeful learning or lesson drawing, by emulation or through imposition.[12] Recent Australian examples of policy experimentation and learning include the development of legislation around discrimination, human rights and civil unions.

We can also find benefits in the apparent redundancy in overlapping roles and responsibilities because it can allow governments to step in to address policy failures or gaps. Thus, in 1967, after a successful referendum, the Commonwealth was able to take the initiative in Aboriginal affairs after decades of State policy failure. More recently, States, most notably Victoria, have taken the initiative in the negotiation of treaties with First Nations in the face of Commonwealth intransigence. Leadership in environmental protection has oscillated between governments. In the 1980s, it was the Commonwealth that assumed the lead, using the overlap provided for in the Constitution to extend protection to significant wilderness areas in Tasmania and Queensland. In the 1990s, by contrast, Western Australia and Queensland stepped in to protect old-growth forests when the Commonwealth was advocating extensions to logging. In the early 2000s, the Australian government showed little interest in climate change, and the States and Territories took the initiative in developing and implementing policies to reduce carbon emissions. These are all examples of where overlap, characterised by the *shared* nature of responsibility, has allowed other views to be heard and influence another level of government to step up.

12 Charles R Shipan and Craig Volden, 'Policy Diffusion: Seven Lessons for Scholars and Practitioners' (2012) 72(6) *Public Administration Review* 788, doi.org/10.1111/j.1540-6210.2012.02610.x.

B. Inconsistency

Allowing States to make their own laws is one way in which federalism accommodates difference. Another is to facilitate mobility. In normal times, State borders are relatively porous and citizens can freely move between them. For the theoretical economist, Charles Tiebout, the advantages are clear.[13] In a federation, individuals and groups can utilise the option of free exit to choose the jurisdiction that best suits their policy preference. Put more simply, federalism offers people more political and policy choices than those available under a unitary regime and all this without any need to leave the country. According to Tiebout's model, based on the US experience, federalism allows firms and individuals to find their ideal tax–service mix. Those who wanted higher levels of government services and were prepared to pay the necessary higher taxes could choose those States that offered their preferred mix. Others willing to forgo the services in exchange for lower taxes would be able to find a jurisdiction that matched this preference. This 'sorting' or 'shifting' ensured that all could find their optimum combination. It also worked for firms because it allowed them to find their own individual ideal mix—low taxes, low wages, lax health and safety regulation and environmental standards versus a highly interventionist State providing quality infrastructure and a highly educated, healthy workforce. Competitive federalism scholars suggest that such differences in economic policy settings do not last, but instead create pressures leading to a 'race to the bottom' or, less commonly, a 'race to the top' as jurisdictions compete to attract businesses. By this reasoning, such competitive pressures lead to long-term homogeneity.[14]

The reductionist scenario provided by classical economics relies on the assumption that firms and individuals are infinitely mobile—that is, free to move to secure their preferred policy mix. In practice, mobility is constrained. There are obvious barriers to exit: relocation is not costless, and family and familiarity hold people to locations. Similarly, competitive 'races', in either direction, are not inevitable but, rather, are context specific. For example, in Australia, there is no evidence that interstate competition affected State workers' competition schemes before the 1990s. More recently, however, the

13 Charles M Tiebout, 'A Pure Theory of Local Expenditures' (1956) 64(5) *Journal of Political Economy* 416, doi.org/10.1086/257839.

14 For a review of the literature, see Robyn Hollander and Louise Thornthwaite, 'Competitive Federalism and Workers' Compensation: Do States Race to the Bottom?' (2018) 53(3) *Australian Journal of Political Science* 336, doi.org/10.1080/10361146.2018.1477115.

rise of neoliberal ideology has seen a policy convergence both between and within nations.[15] Despite these caveats, there are examples of both persistent State diversity and citizens exercising the option of interstate mobility. The most striking example of this is the 'great migration' of African Americans from the oppressive Jim Crow south to northern cities across the US in the twentieth century.

While diversity can provide citizens with choice and offer opportunities for 'progress' in public policy, it also presents the possibility of a deeper, more profound problem: can (and does) it allow for bad policy? Indeed, there are good theoretical reasons to think that smaller jurisdictions are more, rather than less, likely to enact policy that is ineffective, unfair and even destructive. The causes of this are diverse: smaller polities are open to capture by specific interests, they can struggle to attract political and policy talent, or they may lack the resources to pursue sound policy. More profoundly, the independence of State and Territory governments allows them to enact oppressive policy. Two centuries ago, the French philosopher and scientist Nicholas de Condorcet declared:

> As truth, reason, justice, the rights of man, the interests of property, of liberty, of security, are in all places the same; we cannot discover why all the provinces of a state, or even all states, should not have the same civil and criminal laws, and the same laws relative to commerce. *A good law should be good for all men.* A true proposition is true everywhere.[16]

In other words, States' rights should never trump human rights. Yet there is compelling evidence to suggest that some sub-national governments, when given the capacity to do so, will enshrine gross violations of individual freedoms and impose harsh sanctions on those who resist them, as will central governments. This, for many, is federalism's biggest failing; give local polities autonomy (or central governments concentrated power) and face the risk that they will use it to oppress minorities in their midst.

15 Ibid; Beth A Simmons, Frank Dobbin and Geoffrey Garrett, 'Introduction: The International Diffusion of Liberalism' (2006) 60(4) *International Organization* 781, doi.org/10.1017/S0020818306060267.

16 Jacob T Levy, 'Federalism, Liberalism, and the Separation of Loyalties' (2006) 101(3) *The American Political Science Review* 459, 463, doi.org/10.2139/ssrn.739448, citing Marie Jeane Antoine Nicolas de Caritat, Marquis de Condorcet, *Observations on the Twenty-Ninth Book of the Spirit of the Law* (1969) appended to Destutt de Tracy, *A Commentary and Review of Montesquieu's The Spirit of the Laws*, tr Thomas Jefferson (Burt Franklin, 1811) (emphasis added).

But what if we are unable to agree on what is good and true? And can we always assume that what is good and true in one place, and at one time, is equally as good in another place and time, particularly in relation to thorny issues related to values and beliefs? Christopher Z Mooney argues that it is the 'genius' of federalism that it recognises and facilitates the policy heterogeneity essential to maintaining social harmony when there are no clear and agreed answers.[17] As such, the duplication that characterises federalism is uniquely equipped to manage a heterogeneous population characterised by diverse, and divergent, values. Thus, not only can individuals choose to live in communities that share their preferred tax–service mix, but they can also match their value preferences.

For universalists, this argument is hardly satisfactory. Surely there are some rights that are inviolable irrespective of the preferences of a State or provincial majority? Here, too, federalism can provide the answer once we add overlap to the mix. If duplication allows difference, overlap mitigates against bad policy. The argument is as follows: a coordinated style of federalism, whereby each level of government is confined to its own sphere, can allow poor policy to thrive, but in concurrent arrangements, areas of overlap enable central governments or federal courts to override or undermine oppressive sub-national measures. While most federal constitutions give primacy to national institutions, overlap can also allow State regimes to diverge from or exceed centrally determined standards. The value of this tension is clearly evident in relation to environmental policy in federations where we find examples of both federal and State leadership.[18]

While federal overlap and duplication might provide a fail-safe and offer diversity, it has also been accused of making it harder to hold governments to account and this is what we now examine.

17 Christopher Z Mooney, 'The Decline of Federalism and the Rise of Morality – Policy Conflict in the United States' (2000) 30(1) *Publius: The Journal of Federalism* 171, 180, doi.org/10.1093/oxfordjournals.pubjof.a030059.

18 See, eg, Barry G Rabe, 'States on Steroids: The Intergovernmental Odyssey of American Climate Policy' (2008) 25(2) *Review of Policy Research* 105, doi.org/10.1111/j.1541-1338.2007.00314.x; Robyn Hollander, 'Rethinking Overlap and Duplication: Federalism and Environmental Assessment in Australia' (2009) 40(1) *Publius: The Journal of Federalism* 136, doi.org/10.1093/publius/pjp028.

C. Fragmentation

The fragmentation associated with duplication and overlap provides the most obvious way in which federalism supports diversity by providing more opportunities for political engagement both territorially and non-territorially. The territorial case that federalism allows for a broader range of voices to be heard is built on duplication, and is relatively straightforward. State electorates in Australia are much smaller than their federal counterparts. The smaller electorates can be more cohesive because there is less need to agglomerate different communities. The smaller scale also means that the institutions of government are geographically closer than their national counterparts. There are even suggestions that sub-national representatives are more diverse—that is, that there are more women or minorities in State parliaments because of scale, electoral cohesiveness and proximity.[19] These elements mean that, conceivably, citizens can engage more closely with their elected officials and the bureaucracy. One of the problems of this line of argument can be summed up in one word: scale. While this argument might hold for some jurisdictions, Australian State government electorates are still large, and they can be geographically dispersed and far from the centres of power. Nevertheless, as noted above, there are subtle but distinct differences between the States and Territories, and duplication can provide opportunities for groups and interests that are geographically concentrated to make their voices heard.

Overlap and duplication also provide multiple opportunities for political engagement. Whereas unitary governments provide citizens with single points of contact, federations and, in particular, concurrent federations offer much more. Duplication means that advocacy groups can choose to campaign in the most sympathetic jurisdictions. While Tiebout emphasised the potential for people and organisations to move in search of their ideal policy mix, other scholars have focused on the movement of campaigns and aspirations seeking a sympathetic ear. Duplication means that interest groups can 'forum shop', selecting jurisdictions that offer the highest chance of success. Such strategies are particularly important for 'outsider' groups who can find it difficult to break into well-entrenched policy networks and communities.[20] Venue selection can be critical to the success or failure

19 See, eg, Marian Sawer and Marian Simms, *A Woman's Place: Women and Politics in Australia* (Allen & Unwin, 2nd ed, 1993).

20 Keith E Hamm, 'The Role of "Subgovernments" in US State Policy Making: An Exploratory Analysis' (1986) 11(3) *Legislative Studies Quarterly* 321, doi.org/10.2307/439840.

of a cause and 'lobbyists … frequently speak of designing their advocacy strategies as if they were preparing for war, carefully selecting battlefields that play to their strengths at the expense of their enemies'.[21] It is especially important when issues are strongly ideological and highly conflictual, but is also closely linked to political and economic context, interest group resources and institutional design.[22] Overlap also offers advantages by providing multiple fora for political action; if one level of government is unresponsive, advocates may find the other more receptive. In this way, federalism can provide a powerful pluralistic antidote to undemocratic alliances between government and those who exert strong influence. One of federalism's great strengths, therefore, is that it 'offers citizens multiple points of access to public power [and] opportunities to appeal to other governments on certain matters when one is unresponsive'.[23] If citizens cannot gain traction with one level of government, overlap means that they can campaign at another level. The resulting pluralism, 'with multiple points of access and manoeuvre, both horizontally and vertically, has produced cycles of activism alternating between the National Government and the States, depending on conditions and values in the society'.[24] Morton Grodzins characterised such activity as utilising the 'cracks' that exist in his famous federal marble cake of overlapping roles and responsibilities.[25]

This section has argued that federal duplication and overlap, and the resulting redundancy, inconsistency and fragmentation, offer the potential to recognise diversity and build a more inclusive polity. The next section puts this argument to the test by examining how Australian federalism facilitated the recognition of LGBTQIA+ Australians. It focuses on two key policy reforms: decriminalisation of homosexuality and same-sex relationship recognition.

21 Thomas Holyoke, 'Choosing Battlegrounds: Interest Group Lobbying Across Multiple Venues' (2003) 56(3) *Political Research Quarterly* 325, 325, doi.org/10.2307/3219792.

22 John Constantelos, 'Playing the Field: Federalism and the Politics of Venue Shopping in the United States and Canada' (2010) 40(3) *Publius: The Journal of Federalism* 460, doi.org/10.1093/publius/pjq010; John Constantelos, 'Lobbying across the USA: From State Vetoes to Federal Venues' (2018) 7(1) *Interest Groups and Advocacy* 19, doi.org/10.1057/s41309-018-0028-2.

23 Kincaid (n 11).

24 Richard P Nathan, 'Updating Theories of American Federalism' (Speech, Annual Meeting of the American Political Science Association, 2 September 2006) 5 <rockinst.org/wp-content/uploads/2018/02/2006-09-02-updating_theories_of_american_federalism.pdf>.

25 Morton Grodzins, 'The American Federal System' in Robert A Goldwin (ed), *A Nation of States: Essays on the American Federal System* (Rand McNally, 1961).

II. Decriminalisation, recognition and the sub-national path to same-sex marriage

Kees Waaldijk argues that full citizenship for LGBTQIA+ people proceeds in a series of stages beginning with political rights to speak out, to organise and to associate.[26] This is followed by decriminalisation, an end to discrimination and, finally, recognition of relationships and marriage. This section examines two of these stages—the decriminalisation of homosexuality and the path to same-sex relationship recognition—and, in particular, the importance of duplication and overlap in facilitating change. It shows how duplication (the existence of multiple States with the same roles and responsibilities) allowed the various governments to respond differently in accordance with local imperatives and pressures and in line with the preferences of their own communities. While responding to internal pressures, there was still evidence of policy learning; community actors, in particular, did not operate in a vacuum and were aware of, and influenced by, developments in other States in relation to both decriminalisation and relationship recognition. While policymakers explicitly acknowledged the influence of other jurisdictions in relation to relationship recognition, it does not appear to have been important in relation to decriminalisation. Overlap was also significant because it provided opportunities to overcome policy blockages at one level of government by appealing to another. In these ways, the redundancy, inconsistency and fragmentation allowed for the development of a more inclusive polity.

A. Decriminalisation and the twin factors of duplication and overlap

In the carve up of roles and responsibilities under the Australian Constitution, the States retained control of the criminal law. This included its provisions, inherited from the United Kingdom, prohibiting sexual relations between men.[27] While there were some differences between the States—for example, Victoria retained the harshest of penalties for buggery much longer than the other States—sexual relations were illegal in all jurisdictions until 1975, when South Australia (SA) became the first State or Territory to decriminalise

26 Kees Waaldijk, 'Civil Developments: Patterns of Reform in the Legal Position of Same-Sex Partners in Europe' (2000) 17(1) *Canadian Journal of Family Law* 62.

27 Graham Carbery, *Towards Homosexual Equality in Australian Criminal Law: A Brief History* (Australian Lesbian & Gay Archives, 2nd ed, 2014) 2.

homosexual acts between consenting adult males. Other jurisdictions followed: the Australian Capital Territory (ACT) in 1976, Victoria in 1980, the Northern Territory (NT) in 1983, New South Wales (NSW) in 1984, Western Australia (WA) in 1989 and Queensland in 1990.[28] Tasmania did not decriminalise homosexual acts between consenting adults until 1997. This piecemeal pattern of change was largely the product of intrastate political struggles and demonstrates the importance of duplication, and also overlap, in facilitating change. I argued above that one of the strengths of duplication is that it allows for inconsistency between jurisdictions. This means that individual jurisdictions can be more responsive to the policy preferences of their citizens, the activities of policy entrepreneurs and the impact of local policy disruptions or shocks. This is evident in the examination of the process of change in SA, NSW and Queensland undertaken below. By contrast, in Tasmania federal overlap proved to be crucial. I have chosen to focus on these four States, partly for brevity and partly because each adopted a distinctive path to decriminalisation.

1. South Australia

In SA, decriminalisation was driven by a specific event that occurred within an increasingly receptive political and policy context. Decriminalisation had been on the Australian Labor Party (ALP) government's agenda from the mid-1960s when the then Attorney-General Don Dunstan requested his department draft a Bill. While he did not proceed with that Bill, he was unwilling to let the issue drop, and the government included it in the terms of reference of a 1971 inquiry into the operation of the State's criminal law.[29] The LGBTQIA+ community had also begun to mobilise, albeit on a very modest scale, with the formation of a branch of Campaign Against Moral Persecution (CAMP), established in 1971. CAMP was not politically oriented and its limited reform impetus was underpinned by its commitment to civil liberties.[30] It is unlikely that these factors alone, without a disruptive event, would have led to decriminalisation in 1975. It took a very specific event to propel the issue of decriminalisation to centre stage.

28 Melissa Bull, Susan Pinto and Paul Wilson, 'Homosexual Law Reform in Australia' (Briefing Paper No 29, Australian Institute of Criminology, January 1991) 2 <eprints.qut.edu.au/128198/1/7c5c1e7daf802d9c49c6f2e259991d3d0ca8.pdf>.

29 Carbery (n 27) 6.

30 Claire Parker, 'Abortion, Homosexuality and the Slippery Slope: Legislating "Moral" Behaviour in South Australia' (PhD Thesis, University of Adelaide) 159.

In 1972, Dr George Duncan, a newly appointed academic at the University of Adelaide, was found drowned in the River Torrens. It quickly transpired that the police had been involved in his death as part of their ongoing entrapment operation in the surrounding parklands. The resulting scandal generated significant pressure for change from diverse sectors of the community and mainstream media.[31] The heightened interest provided opportunities for reform groups to exert political influence. CAMP and a newly formed chapter of Gay Liberation sought to influence the course of change.[32] However, the first Bill, proposed by renegade Liberal Murray Hill, passed a year later in 1972, merely allowed consent to be considered as a defence while leaving the acts themselves illegal.[33] This proved to be a temporary setback and, in 1975, SA became the first Australian jurisdiction to effectively decriminalise homosexuality. In SA, the dynamic of change was driven by events. Prior to this, while there was some support for change at the highest levels of government, there was little LGBTQIA+ activism or community interest.

2. New South Wales

Change followed a very different trajectory in NSW. The context differed in several important ways. First, there was a sizeable and highly visible LGBTQIA+ community. Second, there were longstanding, organised and politically active community groups including CAMP and the Gay Rights Lobby. Third, the community was subject to heavy-handed and highly visible policing.[34] However, despite the existence of these three important elements, legislators were slow to act. This was because of the strength and influence of those opposed to decriminalisation, particularly inside the Parliament. The Reverend Fred Nile was a vocal and influential presence in the Legislative Council. In addition, unlike its counterparts in Victoria and Queensland, the NSW ALP had a significant conservative Catholic wing. Together, these forces ensured the defeat of several very modest private members Bills in 1981 and 1982.[35] While efforts to repeal the law appeared stalled, the ALP government's commitment to equality more broadly, and women's equality in particular, offered some unexpected opportunities.

31 Carbery (n 27) 6.

32 Parker (n 30) 170–8.

33 Graham Willett, 'Australia: Nine Jurisdictions, One Long Struggle' in Corrine Lennox and Matthew Waites (eds), *Human Rights, Sexual Orientation and Gender Identity in the Commonwealth: Struggles for Decriminalisation and Change* (University of London Press, 2013) 214.

34 Ibid 217.

35 Carbery (n 27) 29.

In 1977, the Parliament enacted broad anti-discrimination measures that outlawed discrimination on the basis of race, sex and marital status. It also charged the newly established Anti-Discrimination Board with the task of investigating and reporting on discrimination on the grounds of age, political or religious conviction, disability, trade union membership and, somewhat ironically, homosexuality.[36] Thus, the paradoxical situation existed whereby the government simultaneously promoted the 'equal treatment of all human beings' including homosexuals while continuing to support the prosecution of those engaged in male homosexual acts.

The situation was to become still more anomalous. In 1981, changes to the NSW sexual assault laws included gender neutral terminology. The result was that non-consensual sex between adults, irrespective of gender, attracted a maximum penalty of seven years imprisonment, while consensual sex between consenting adult males continued to attract a maximum penalty of 14 years.[37] Gay rights activists and their supporters in Parliament used this as an opportunity to advocate for decriminalisation. However, while the ALP still allowed its parliamentary members a conscience vote on the issue, all attempts to repeal or even modify the existing laws were doomed to defeat. In 1984, following yet another election victory, Premier Neville Wran removed the conscience vote and ushered a Bill through the Parliament decriminalising homosexual acts between consenting males over the age of 18. Full equality had to wait until 2003, however.[38]

3. Queensland

As in SA and NSW, the Queensland trajectory was driven by distinctive local circumstances. The State had long been governed by a conservative government led by Joh Bjelke-Petersen. In the 1980s, while other States were considering liberalisation, the Queensland Government was becoming increasingly repressive. Neither widely publicised heavy-handed police actions, the public health concerns surrounding the AIDS epidemic nor the nascent gay rights organisations had any impact.[39] In fact, in dealing with AIDS, Altman argues that the Queensland government was 'both punitive and uncooperative in dealing with the homosexual community',[40]

36 *Anti-Discrimination Act 1977* (NSW) s 119.

37 Carbery (n 27) 27.

38 Ibid 27–35.

39 Willett (n 33) 221–3.

40 Shirleene Robinson, 'Responding to Homophobia: HIV/AIDS, Homosexual Community Formation and Identity in Queensland, 1983–1990' (2010) 41(2) *Australian Historical Studies* 181, doi.org/10.1080/10314611003716879.

denouncing homosexuals for spreading disease. It used its censorship laws and street march bans to supress any opposition. The government even contemplated criminalising lesbianism[41] and passed legislation prohibiting licensed venues from serving alcohol to homosexual customers in an attempt to close down gay bars.[42] While the law was unenforceable, it indicates the prevailing level of government opposition to decriminalisation. The mid-1980s marked the highpoint of the National Party's dominance in Queensland. In 1987, the government was forced to establish a Commission of Inquiry into Police Corruption. Although the terms of reference were narrow, Commissioner Tony Fitzgerald used the opportunity to expose wrongdoing and mismanagement at the highest levels. The Fitzgerald Inquiry was a major turning point for the State. Ministers and senior police officers were jailed and, in 1989, the National Party government, which had dominated the State for three decades, was swept away.[43]

While Fitzgerald had not addressed the question of decriminalisation explicitly, his report recommended a parliamentary inquiry into the State's criminal law with particular attention to 'voluntary sexual or sex-related behaviour', the costs of policing and the option of decriminalisation.[44] The task was taken up after the election by the newly formed Parliamentary Criminal Justice Committee; it recommended decriminalisation and legislation swiftly followed.[45] Graham Willett argues that change was able to proceed with relatively little community opposition compared to other States because there was no imperative to organise prior to 1989.[46]

4. Tasmania

Duplication and the opportunity it provided for individual States to follow their own trajectories was important to reform in most States. However, none of the factors that had propelled change in the other States dented

41 Shirleene Robinson, 'Homophobia as Party Politics: The Construction of the "Homosexual Deviant" in Joh Bjelke-Petersen's Queensland' (2010) 17(1) *Queensland Review* 29, 29, doi.org/10.1017/S1321816600005249.
42 Ibid 39–40.
43 Janet Ransley and Richard Johnstone, 'The Fitzgerald Symposium' (2009) 18(3) *Griffith Law Review* 531, doi.org/10.1080/10854653.2009.10854653.
44 Queensland Commission of Inquiry into Possible Illegal Activities and Associated Police Misconduct, *Report of a Commission of Inquiry Pursuant to Orders in Council* (Report, 3 July 1989) 377.
45 Criminal Justice Committee, Parliament of Queensland, 'Reforms in the Laws Relating to Homosexuality: An Information Paper' (Report No 2, 5 June 1990).
46 Willett (n 33) 221.

successive Tasmanian Parliaments' determination to retain its criminal sanctions. Despite the changed social and political climate, it was federal overlap that proved decisive in Tasmania.

In the early 1970s, the Commonwealth had demonstrated some commitment to homosexual law reform. In 1969, the federal conference of the ALP committed to law reform.[47] In 1973, the Commonwealth passed a motion with bipartisan support in the federal Parliament declaring that homosexual acts between consenting adults not be subject to criminal law. However, the motion had no authority, except in the ACT where a proposed legislative change lapsed in 1975.[48] The federal Parliament also established a Royal Commission into Human Relationships. The Commission's final report, delivered in 1977, contained wide-ranging recommendations, including decriminalisation, an end to discrimination, same-sex education in schools and the introduction of some relationship rights (but not same-sex marriage or adoption). It also urged the Commonwealth to set an example by ending discrimination in the Commonwealth Public Service and Defence Force.[49] This was indicative of the Commonwealth's authority. However, even if the Commonwealth had had aspirations to see homosexuality decriminalised Australia wide, it appeared to be powerless until the early 1980s. The cases of *Koowarta v Bjelke-Petersen* ('*Koowarta*')[50] and *Commonwealth v Tasmania* ('*Tasmanian Dams Case*')[51] in 1982 and 1983, respectively, revealed a hitherto unrecognised overlap in lawmaking authority, because they confirmed that the Commonwealth had the authority to make laws in areas of State responsibility if it was needed to meet international treaty obligations. This offered those seeking change in Tasmania a way forward.

Some barriers remained, however. The *International Covenant on Civil and Political Rights*[52] (ICCPR), to which Australia was a signatory, did not address sexual orientation explicitly, although it could be read into its emphasis on equality, anti-discrimination and rights to privacy. A more significant problem was the absence of any mechanisms to ensure that governments acted on these principles. This changed in 1991 when the Commonwealth

47 Graham Willett, 'Minorities Can Win: The Gay Movement, the Left and the Transformation of Australian Society' [1997] (149) *Overland* 64, 66.
48 Carbery (n 27) 25.
49 *Royal Commission into Human Relationships* (Report, November 1977) 93–105.
50 *Koowarta v Bjelke-Petersen* (1982) 153 CLR 168.
51 *Commonwealth v Tasmania* (1983) 158 CLR 1.
52 *International Covenant on Civil and Political Rights*, opened for signature 16 December 1966, 991 UNTS 171 (entered into force 23 March 1976).

signed the First Optional Protocol to the ICCPR. The protocol allowed individual citizens to highlight violations of human rights in member countries before the UN Human Rights Committee (HRC). With change blocked at the State level, Tasmanian reformers seized the opportunity and a member of the Tasmanian Lesbian and Gay Rights Group, Nick Toonen, lodged a complaint with the HRC. The HRC accepted the premise that Toonen's human rights had been violated, thereby placing Australia in breach of its obligations. While the HRC could not compel the Commonwealth Government to act, its finding exerted moral suasion and, in 1994, the Commonwealth passed legislation overriding the provisions of Tasmanian Criminal Code. While some members of the Tasmanian Legislative Council were initially determined to resist this challenge to their sovereignty, they ultimately acquiesced, abandoning their State's prohibition and allowing the repeal measures through.[53]

This section has argued that duplication was central to the trajectory of decriminalisation because it made it possible for individual States to follow their own paths. While local chapters of groups such as CAMP and Gay Liberation learnt from each other, and advocates could point to successes in other States, there is little indication of policy diffusion; each State adopted its own distinctive provisions in relation to key elements such as the age of consent. There is also some indication that developments in other States led to a hardening of policymakers' intransigence. In Queensland, for example, Premier Joh Bjelke-Petersen condemned NSW for legalising homosexuality and called for homosexuals in his State to go back to NSW where they came from.[54]

To critics of federalism, the inconsistency around the timing and detail of legislative change bolsters arguments for a uniform national approach. This argument, however, assumes that if the Commonwealth Government had had responsibility for this area of policy, decriminalisation would have been achieved much earlier, and that federalism retarded reform. However, while the Commonwealth did show some early signs of commitment to reform, it is not clear that any other outcome would have been achieved. In the early 1970s, there was still significant opposition to change, especially in NSW, Queensland, WA and Tasmania, and there is no guarantee that these political

53 Tim Tenbensel, 'International Human Rights Conventions and Australian Political Debates: Issues Raised by the "Toonen Case"' (1996) 31(1) *Australian Journal of Political Science* 7, doi.org/10.1080/10361149651247; Alexandra Purvis and Joseph Castellino, 'A History of Homosexual Law Reform in Tasmania' (1997) 16(1) *University of Tasmania Law Review* 12.

54 Robinson (n 41).

forces would not have prevailed. It is quite possible that the Commonwealth would have been held back from action by the same political pressures that delayed change. Two decades later, the Commonwealth seemed to have little appetite for tackling LGBTQIA+ discrimination. Further, if one considers the trajectory of Commonwealth anti-discrimination legislation, such change at the federal level would appear unlikely. By the end of the 1990s, all States and Territories had prohibited discrimination on the basis of sexual orientation or lawful sexual activity; however, it was not until 2012 that the Gillard ALP government amended the *Sex Discrimination Act 1984* (Cth) to provide a similar standard of protection at the federal level.

Duplication and overlap allowed the States to follow their own trajectories and connect the timing and rationale for change to prevailing State social cultures and political imperatives. Thus, in Queensland, a notoriously socially conservative State, the debates and rationale for change stemmed from issues in police corruption rather than any commitment to civil liberties (as in SA), or campaign from affected individuals and concern for women's rights (as in NSW). In Tasmania, the campaign to change the law was a manifestation of a more explicit contest over identity. The *Toonen Case*[55] was not simply about anti-discrimination and privacy but 'sought to … broaden the concept of what it means to be Tasmanian'.[56] Its success paved the way for a more inclusive community, as evidenced below. In this way, changes to the way we see ourselves as Australians were affected at the State level.

B. Relationship recognition, redundancy and policy diffusion

The previous section highlighted the value of the inconsistency and fragmentation that result from duplication and overlap. This section focuses on the importance of redundancy and the opportunities it provided for States to learn from each other, and for inaction at the Commonwealth level to be compensated for.

55 Human Rights Committee, *Views: Communication No 488/1992*, 50th sess, UN Doc CCPR/C/50/D/488/1992 (4 April 1994).

56 Wayne Morgan, 'Identifying Evil for What It Is: Tasmania, Sexual Perversity and the United Nations' (1994) 19(3) *Melbourne University Law Review* 740, 746.

Legislative responsibility for recognising relationships is divided between the Commonwealth and the States. Sections 51(xxi) and 51(xxii) of the Constitution designates marriage (as well as divorce and parental rights) as a Commonwealth responsibility (although it was content to leave this responsibility with the States until 1961, in the case of marriage, and 1972, in the case of divorce). However, the Commonwealth's constitutionally enumerated power did not extend to de facto relationships and the related issues of partner rights and the distribution of property following a relationship breakdown. These remained State responsibilities. This overlap proved to be significant, as we shall see below.

The Commonwealth's sentiments regarding same-sex marriage became evident in 2004 when it passed an amendment to the *Marriage Act 1961* (Cth) ('*Marriage Act*'). The Act explicitly limited marriage to 'the union of a man and a woman to the exclusion of all others, voluntarily entered into for life' and equally explicitly prohibited any recognition of same-sex marriages performed outside Australia.[57] The amendment was a response to a case brought before the Family Court by two same-sex couples who had married in Canada and sought to clarify their status in Australia. For over a decade, successive Commonwealth governments had stood firm against proposals to recognise same-sex marriage. Between 2004 and 2018, no less than 23 Bills dealing with marriage equality were introduced in the federal Parliament by members from across the political spectrum. Few were debated and only four came to a vote, in 2010, 2012 and 2013: all were defeated.[58]

1. De facto recognition and civil unions

Commonwealth inaction left a significant gap during this period; however, advocates of reform began to have some success in having their relationships recognised in a different way. As mentioned, the Commonwealth's constitutional power did not extend to de facto relationships, and it was in this space that States began to exhibit distinctive approaches to the recognition of same-sex relationships. In 1984, NSW passed comprehensive legislation to deal with disputes within de facto relationships, and other jurisdictions followed. State governments also moved to reduce discrimination against men and women in de facto relationships in a host of other areas, including

57 Kristen Walker, 'The Same-Sex Marriage Debate in Australia' (2007) 11(1–2) *International Journal of Human Rights* 109, doi.org/10.1080/13642980601176290.

58 Deirdre McKeown, 'Chronology of Same-Sex Marriage Bills Introduced into the Federal Parliament: A Quick Guide' (Research Paper, Parliament of Australia, 15 February 2018) <parlinfo.aph.gov.au/parlInfo/download/library/prspub/3921906/upload_binary/3921906.pdf>.

compensation, superannuation and other entitlements. The result was that 'Australian law … treated people in cohabiting (though unregistered) heterosexual relationships in ways almost identical to married couples'.[59]

The States gradually extended the framework to cover same-sex couples across all jurisdictions, beginning in NSW in 1999, Victoria in 2001, Queensland in 2002, WA in 2002 and 2003, the NT in 2003, Tasmania in 2003, the ACT in 2003 and 2004, and SA in 2006. By the mid-2000s, all of the States and Territories (except WA) had referred their powers to the Commonwealth and responsibility for the regulation of de facto relationships was incorporated into the *Family Law Act* in amendments in 2009. Tellingly, the Commonwealth initially refused to accept responsibility for same-sex relationships despite the States making it clear that their definitions of de facto relationships included same-sex couples.[60]

De facto recognition was significant but limited, because de facto couples did not have simple ways of proving their relationship. Instead, they were obliged to rely on the application of one or more 'tests', such as duration, cohabitation, caring for children, and shared income and assets, to establish the existence of their relationship. They were, thus, denied the same automatic rights as married couples. This was addressed through relationship registration schemes in Victoria and the ACT in 2008, NSW in 2010, Queensland in 2011 and SA in 2016.

Tasmania was the first to introduce a relationship registration scheme. In 2003, a scant six years after homosexuality was decriminalised in that State, the Tasmanian Parliament introduced a scheme to recognise 'significant relationships'. The scheme provided an a priori way of formally recognising a relationship between two consenting unmarried adults who were not related to each other in any other way. While not solely focused on same-sex couples, the measure represented an important significant step because, as opponents pointed out, it had many of the features of traditional marriage. It imposed rights and obligations in relation to property and maintenance, and it removed many of the discriminatory measures contained in State legislation around such things as hospital access, superannuation, wills and property division, and employment conditions. There were, however, important differences. Those in registered significant relationships were not

59 Reg Graycar and Jenni Millbank, 'From Functional Family to Spinster Sisters: Australia's Distinctive Path to Relationship Recognition' (2007) 24(1) *Washington University Journal of Law and Policy* 121, 124.
60 Donna Cooper, 'For Richer for Poorer, in Sickness and in Health: Should Australia Embrace Same-Sex Marriage?' (2005) 19(2) *Australian Journal of Family Law* 153, 164.

allowed to adopt children unless the children were already related to them. Importantly, registration did not incorporate any ceremonial aspects and relied on the completion of a simple form to be lodged with the Tasmanian registry of births, deaths and marriages. It was not marriage.[61]

Other States used the Tasmanian legislation as a model. In 2008, Victorian legislators made their debt to Tasmania explicit and replicated the title and many of the Tasmanian provisions.[62] Like the Tasmanians, they did not include any provisions for a formal ceremony despite pressure from some members of Parliament and the Victorian Gay and Lesbian Rights Lobby;[63] nor did they include provisions to recognise relationships registered in other States on the rather curious grounds that it was not in the Tasmanian template. The ACT, NSW and Queensland also referenced the Tasmanian and Victorian precedents when introducing their own schemes and provided for mutual recognition.

Duplication allows for more than the simple transfer of policy. It can also allow governments to learn from the experience of others, and to adapt and improve on the original model. There is some indication that this occurred. The Tasmanian, Victorian and NSW Acts did not acknowledge the cultural and symbolic dimensions commonly associated with marriage in their terminology or processes. As one critic put it: 'I marry (or wed) my beloved. I register my dog … [r]egistered relationships … next you get a little plastic tag to wear and an ear tattoo'.[64] The difference is significant: 'registration' represented official recognition of an existing relationship while the act of 'union' created a new and distinctive bond.[65] The ACT's *Civil Union Act 2006* (ACT) incorporated the cultural and symbolic dimensions in the language of the legislation, and in the inclusion of an official ceremony conducted by an authorised celebrant. In introducing the Bill, the Chief Minister acknowledged the Tasmanian Act but emphasised the social

61 Olivia Rundle, 'An Examination of Relationship Registration Schemes in Australia' (2011) 25(2) *Australian Journal of Family Law* 121, 127–9.

62 Victoria, *Parliamentary Debates*, Legislative Assembly, 6 December 2007, 4393 (Rob Hulls, Attorney-General).

63 Ibid; 'A Relationship Register for Victoria: Information Paper', *Victorian Pride Lobby* (Web Page) <humanrights.gov.au/sites/default/files/content/human_rights/samesex/inquiry/submissions/256.pdf>.

64 Robyn Ironside, 'Newman Government Renames and Amends Civil Partnerships Act in Parliament', *The Courier Mail* (online, 21 June 2012) <www.couriermail.com.au/news/same-sex-couples-in-queensland-lose-civil-unions/news-story/fccfc0079fb2c76ff6c03ba1f3fa0e5c>.

65 Normann Witzleb, 'Marriage as the "Last Frontier"? Same-Sex Relationship Recognition in Australia' (2011) 25(2) *International Journal of Law, Policy and the Family* 35, doi.org/10.1093/lawfam/ebr007.

dimensions of the proposed law in the ACT.[66] It was clear that others also recognised this. The opposition accused the government of introducing gay marriage by stealth and put up an alternative proposal replicating the Tasmanian legislation.[67] The Commonwealth Government was also concerned and overturned the Act. It was replaced by the *Civil Partnerships Act 2008* (Cth). Under intense pressure from the Commonwealth, the ACT government emphasised that its measure was a simple, practical device, quite unlike marriage, although it still provided for an official ceremony conducted by a registered notary.[68]

Queensland followed the ACT in incorporating an official ceremony and commemorative certificate in its *Civil Partnerships Act 2011* (Qld). The Queensland measure was unique in that, to terminate the partnership, the parties were required to apply to the District Court and declare that they had lived apart for 12 months and that the relationship had broken down irreconcilably.[69] Elsewhere, it involved the simple lodgement of a form with the registry. As in the ACT, opponents had argued for the barebones registration model, and they succeeded when the incoming Liberal National government removed the symbolic elements and any significant hurdles to termination.

Duplication allowed the States to learn from each other; however, overlap was also critical. As argued above, although responsible for marriage, the Commonwealth's dominance in regulating relationships was not complete and the States used their constitutional space outside marriage to extend formal recognition to same-sex relationships. This kept the issue alive and served to allay some of the fears in the community.

In Tasmania, NSW and SA, individual members of Parliament attempted to challenge the Commonwealth's authority by proposing State marriage Bills. Some believed that there were genuine constitutional gaps that the States could legitimately use to provide for same-sex marriage because the Australian Constitution was silent on gender and simply referred to 'marriage'. They argued that, by defining marriage as a union between a man and a woman, in the 2004 amendment to the *Marriage Act*, the

66 Australian Capital Territory, *Parliamentary Debates,* Legislative Assembly, 28 March 2006, 655–9 (John Stanhope, Chief Minister).

67 Rundle (n 61) 130.

68 Ibid 140–1; Aleardo Zanghellini, 'Marriage and Civil Unions: Legal and Moral Questions' (2011) 35(2) *Federal Law Review* 265, 265–6.

69 *Civil Partnerships Act 2011* (Qld) s 15.

Commonwealth had delimited its authority and suggested that same-sex marriage could be seen as a distinctly different type of relationship and thus not covered by the Constitution. While the argument was not necessarily persuasive, some State legislators maintained that their actions were worthwhile because they provided an important signal to Commonwealth legislators and the community. According to one Tasmanian Member of the Legislative Council: 'If the possibility of an invalid bill stopped us from legislating, very little reform could be undertaken ... Leadership is about challenging the status quo.'[70] His argument failed to win over his colleagues and the Bill failed, as did similar efforts in other States.

The ACT government was the only one that pushed ahead, making use of Commonwealth changes to the way in which it oversaw Territory lawmaking. In 2012, it reinstated its earlier civil unions legislation and, in 2013, took the further step of embracing marriage equality. The legislation passed in October and the first marriages took place on 7 December. The Commonwealth wasted no time in launching a challenge in the High Court. The Court handed down its decision, invalidating the ACT law, on 12 December.[71]

In the case of same-sex marriage, the redundancy created by duplication and overlap allowed the States to step into the breach left by the Commonwealth and develop a more inclusive framework. While the Constitution deemed marriage a Commonwealth responsibility, the States used their power over de facto relationships to recognise and even celebrate same-sex relationships. While these efforts all fell short of marriage, they were significant for several reasons: first, they offered a higher level of recognition; second, they put paid to fears that recognising same-sex relationships somehow threatened more traditional relationships; third, they helped sustain LGBTQIA+ activism; and, finally and most importantly, they ensured that the issue remained on the national government's agenda. The changes in the legal status of same-sex couples pioneered at State and Territory level distilled the issue at Commonwealth level to one of symbolism and identity, paving the way for the changes to the *Marriage Act* in 2017 that gave same-sex couples the same rights and obligations as opposite-sex couples. The 1901 Constitution, in acknowledging marriage, articulated a particular conception of familial

70 Tasmania, *Parliamentary Debates*, Legislative Council, 27 September 2012, 26 (Mike Gaffney).

71 *Commonwealth v Australian Capital Territory* (2013) 250 CLR 441.

relationships. Over time, this conception has had to expand to recognise a broader range of relationships. As we have seen, federalism and, in particular, duplication and overlap have facilitated this expansion.

III. Conclusion

The inevitable duplication and overlap in federal systems generates redundancy, inconsistency and fragmentation. These are often counterproductive, but they can also create opportunities to build a more inclusive national community, as demonstrated in our examination of two milestones on the road to full equality for LGBTQIA+ Australians: decriminalisation and same-sex marriage. In both cases, duplication and overlap were significant. Duplication and, in particular, the capacity for States to follow their own paths was important in the decriminalisation of homosexuality. Change may have been painfully slow in some jurisdictions but it also allowed others to proceed in advance of the majority. Overlap provided the mechanism to overcome the final barriers. Both duplication and overlap were important in achieving same-sex marriage. While formal responsibility for marriage lay with the Commonwealth, this did not preclude State-based initiatives to recognise same-sex relationships. As we saw, the States learnt from each other and their initiatives helped to maintain pressure on the Commonwealth.

Taken together, the apparent limitations of duplication and overlap—redundancy, inconsistency and weak accountability—have the capacity to offer something more than their individual parts, something that reflects the multiple identities that compose contemporary Australia. In this way, federalism, with its inevitable duplication and overlap, can give voice to minorities and provide diverse opportunities to reconceptualise Australia's national identity from both the top-down and the bottom-up.

Part Three

11

Indigenous Sovereignty and Constitutional Reform

Lydia McGrady

Sovereignty is a source of political authority. The Uluru Statement from the Heart asserts the continuation of Indigenous sovereignty.[1] A principle that emerged from the Referendum Council's report, which followed, was the necessity for structural reform.[2] Within law, sovereignty has been a vague and partial political concept. From its origins as a remit to the power of the Crown to its use as a source for claiming the unlimited power of parliaments, national sovereignty has been used within law as an invisible adjudicator of human rights. Sovereignty can and should be able to reflect the full composition of all peoples of the land. This chapter questions concepts of sovereignty that are often held immutable. It claims that national sovereignty is an evolving reflection of the people and only legally applicable in international law. Therefore, sovereign power should be vested in the people, not merely the Parliament, as it is a multifaceted concept.

This chapter discusses the concept of sovereignty as applied in Australian law and argues for a reconsideration of the conventional characterisation of sovereignty. The concept of sovereignty in the law of Australia has been applied legally, politically and symbolically to limit the ability of Indigenous

1 'The Uluru Statement from the Heart', *The Uluru Statement* (Web Page, 26 May 2017) <ulurustatement.org/the-statement/view-the-statement/>.

2 Referendum Council, *Final Report of the Referendum Council* (Final Report, 30 June 2017) 23 <ulurustatemdev.wpengine.com/wp-content/uploads/2022/01/Referendum_Council_Final_Report.pdf>.

peoples to assert self-determination. Indigenous sovereignty, a distinct form of sovereignty, is an essential element of Indigenous rights. It encompasses the source of the embodiment of law for Indigenous peoples and is a distinct authority that was never ceded and exists alongside the Australian Constitution. This chapter questions how the term sovereignty has been employed and examined to both limit and promote Indigenous peoples. In doing so, it reaffirms the importance of sovereignty to Indigenous peoples and its relevance to debates on constitutional reform.

I. Are constitutions political or legal?

It is essential to first contextualise the purpose of constitutions to establish their connection with sovereignty. It must be determined whether constitutions are political or legal instruments in the practice of a nation-state. The supremacy of a constitution as a founding legal document is regularly held to be indisputable. As such, it is often described as the founding law of a nation-state. Constitutional law has been used as, a priori, the 'establishment' of a nation-state. Massimo La Torre suggests that constitutional law can only be law if it is shaped and regulated by political power.[3] There have been varying views of the balance of this political power.

Edmund Burke proposed that a constitution was a statement of custom and history[4]—a stagnant and fixed innate law. It was immutable and not disturbed by social concerns. In contrast, Thomas Paine, in his response to Burke, claimed that a constitution was a source of government, not a statement of government.[5] Since, in this way, a constitution limits state power, it can be seen as a human rights–based theory. Hans Kelsen viewed a theory of norms as the first historic trace of a legal principle that was constituted.[6] HLA Hart rejected this theory, instead presupposing recognition that the validity of law could change over time.[7] His views on positivism have been used by Australian courts to limit recognition of Indigenous law. International law allows for Indigenous rights to be a distinct category of recognised law, but there has been a lag in the adoption of this international legal recognition of Indigenous law and political rights in Australia.

3 Massimo La Torre, *Constitutionalism and Legal Reasoning: A New Paradigm for the Concept of Law* (Springer, 2007) 4.
4 Edmund Burke, *Reflections on the Revolution in France* (Yale University Press, 2003).
5 Thomas Paine, *Rights of Man* (Project Gutenberg, 1792).
6 Hans Kelsen, *The Communist Theory of Law* (Scientia, 1976).
7 HLA Hart, *The Concept of Law* (Oxford University Press, 1961).

II. Indigenous rights in constitutions

Various constitutions across the world acknowledge Indigenous political rights. These can be rights that recognise or regulate Indigenous political institutions. In regions such as Latin America and Africa there are increasing numbers of constitutional provisions relating to Indigenous group rights and Indigenous political organisations. The inclusion of Indigenous peoples in constitutions provides a mechanism for Indigenous peoples to have our unique position acknowledged and respected.

Why some Indigenous peoples are recognised and not others can be explained with reference to the relative political position of Indigenous groups. In this light, it is important to consider the role of a constitution. Jean Jacques Rousseau described a constitution as a social contract between individuals and the State.[8] This may be questionable, as there is no agreement made between the people and the State. Thus, John Rawls suggested, following Immanuel Kant, that it was a hypothetical contract.[9] There is a moral impetus for the state to uphold this relationship with the people. In this regard, a constitution should serve to protect the rights of individuals or distinct groups, such as Indigenous peoples or minority groups.

Some scholars, such as Tom Ginsburg, describe constitutions as contracts made through elite bargaining power.[10] In this context, the political will of Indigenous communities remains limited unless there is enthusiasm from the government to respond to each Indigenous communities' political concerns. Comparative studies of the constitutional inclusion of Indigenous peoples in various nations by Katharina Holzinger et al drew on both Ginsburg's and Ran Hirschl's distinction of constitution-making as a political power game.[11] Unlike the aforementioned scholars, and drawing

8 Jean Jacques Rousseau, *The Social Contract* (Dent, 1913).

9 John Rawls, *A Theory of Justice* (Leiden, 2013).

10 Tom Ginsburg, Daniel Lansberg-Rodriguez and Mila Versteeg, 'When to Overthrow Your Government: The Right to Resist the World's Constitutions' (2013) 60(5) *UCLA Law Review* 1184, doi.org/10.2139/ssrn.2125186.

11 Katharina Holzinger et al, 'The Constitutionalization of Indigenous Group Rights, Traditional Political Institutions, and Customary Law' (2019) 52(12) *Comparative Political Studies* 1775, 1782, doi.org/10.1177/0010414018774347; Tom Ginsburg, *Judicial Review in New Democracies: Constitutional Courts in Asian Cases* (Cambridge University Press, 2003), doi.org/10.1017/CBO9780511511189; Ran Hirschl, *Towards Juristocracy: The Origins and Consequences of the New Constitutionalism* (Harvard University Press, 2004).

on work by Jeffrey Harden, they included the citizenry as essential actors.[12] Groups of citizens, such as Indigenous peoples, meet with constitutional actors and, through political means, create effective rights guarantees in the constitutional provisions created.[13] A 2019 study of 193 UN member states found that the mere presence of demand for constitutional change may not cause constitutional actors to grant Indigenous rights.[14] Due to its broad scope, its conclusions varied, but it nevertheless asserted the importance of democracy to the granting of Indigenous rights. Indeed, it found a correlation between levels of democracy and the acknowledgement of Indigenous peoples' rights. Contrasting the constitutional inclusion of Australian Indigenous peoples with similar Indigenous minority groups, such as in Canada and the United States, it highlighted the problem of examining concepts of democracy. It reveals that Australia does not provide a mechanism for Indigenous peoples to be seen as a unique polity, despite the country's democratic character. This is due, in part, to Indigenous peoples' rights not being included in the Constitution. There must be a political and legal shift in ideology to combat this—a national shift to asserting more than one identity. Kymlicka provides a way of understanding democracies as multinational—a concept that highlights issues of sovereignty.[15]

III. Sovereignty

In Australia, the concept of popular sovereignty has had wavering support in the High Court.[16] Its application is often sourced to GJ Lindell, cited in *Australian Capital Television Pty Ltd v Commonwealth* ('*ACTV Case*'), who posited popular sovereignty as a way to address the legal authority of the Constitution after the Australia Acts were legislated.[17] Jeffrey Goldsworthy suggests that there need not be justification for the legal authority behind the Constitution in Australia, asserting 'no good reason has been stated

12 Holzinger et al (n 11) 1783; Jeffrey J Harden, *Multidimensional Democracy: A Supply and Demand Theory of Representation in American Legislatures* (Cambridge University Press, 2016), doi.org/10.1017/CBO9781316442920.

13 Holzinger et al (n 11) 1783.

14 Ibid 1800.

15 Will Kymlicka, 'Multicultural Citizenship within Multination States' (2011) 11(3) *Ethnicities* 281, doi.org/10.1177/1468796811407813.

16 See *Nationwide News Pty Ltd v Wills* (1992) 177 CLR 1, 70 (Deane and Toohey JJ) ('*Nationwide News*'); *Theophanous v Herald & Weekly Times Ltd* (1994) 182 CLR 104, 180 (Deane J); *Ridgeway v The Queen* (1995) 184 CLR 19, 91; *McGinty v Western Australia* (1996) 186 CLR 140, 237 (McHugh J) ('*McGinty*').

17 (1992) 177 CLR 106, 137–8 (Mason CJ) ('*ACTV Case*').

that the Constitution must rest on some deeper legal foundation'.[18] Goldsworthy also notes that the maxim of parliamentary sovereignty in Britain is being upheld through legal actors, such as judges.[19] The judiciary are the means by which the concept of parliamentary sovereignty continues to be observed in Australia as well. The complicated relationship between parliamentary sovereignty and the rule of law is obvious and a continuing logical dilemma. What must be discussed instead is the authority by which claims of parliamentary sovereignty have been used as a limitation rather than an indication of legal validity. If legal authority is the Constitution itself, what must be determined is the source of this authority.

It is important to distinguish between international law sovereignty (or external sovereignty) and internal sovereignty. Often these terms are used interchangeably, but they are quite separate. The former has its 'legality' in international law as an actor, the latter within the state. These are modern concepts. Sovereignty is often misplaced in international law as merely external. Internal sovereignty is often thought to be the supreme authority within a nation-state, such as a constitution. However, this authority is limited by mechanisms to alter the constitution and the delegating of shared powers. Indigenous sovereignty has connections to both external and internal sovereignty. Most of the customary norms of internal Indigenous self-determination are noted in international law declarations of the United Nations. What is less discussed is the internal form of sovereignty and its relationship to the nation-state.

There are varying modern philosophical concepts of sovereignty. The Hobbesian view describes the nation-state as defined by its borders, making sovereignty a legal status. Carl Schmitt posited that the Hobbesian shift was the beginning of modern sovereignty.[20] Burke, extending on Thomas Hobbes, asserted that there must be a singular sovereign.[21] John Locke, conversely, extended sovereignty to protect private property. It was this extension that justified colonial iterations of denials of Indigenous sovereignty. Thus, imperial constitutional law was the basis from which

18 Jeffrey Goldsworthy, *Parliamentary Sovereignty: Contemporary Debates* (Cambridge University Press, 2010) 48, doi.org/10.1017/CBO9780511781490.

19 Ibid 5.

20 Carl Schmitt, *Dictatorship from the Origin of the Modern Concept of Sovereignty to the Proletarian Class Struggle* (Polity Press, 2014).

21 Richard Bourke, 'Discussion: Sovereignty, Opinion and Revolution in Edmund Burke' (1999) 25(3) *History of European Ideas* 99, doi.org/10.1016/S0191-6599(99)00026-1.

sovereignty was acquired in Australia, but this did not extinguish Indigenous sovereignty. A concept of parliamentary sovereignty, namely the Imperial Parliament, emerged from this ideology.

AV Dicey devised parliamentary sovereignty as a means to categorise Britain's constitutional position.[22] This was an important characterisation, as it shaped Australia's vision of parliamentary sovereignty; however, it is misplaced in Australia and is no longer relevant to modern law. Dicey distinguished between political and legal sovereignty[23]—political sovereignty was vested in the people and legal sovereignty in the Parliament—and gave credence to the idea of a unitary legal authority, namely the British Parliament. The US was founded on an attempt to clarify a source of sovereign power. That power came to be vested in the US Constitution and is interpreted as being that of the people. It combines the categories of legal and political authority into one source. However, there has been a shift in Britain from the Parliament to the electorate or the executive, making, as some claim, parliamentary sovereignty a fiction.[24] Following on from this, I argue that the term parliamentary sovereignty is not applicable in Australia.

Dicey's initial principle of parliamentary sovereignty was founded on two precepts. First, that Parliament, and only Parliament, can make and amend any law.[25] Second, that no other institution, such as the judiciary, can limit any legislation.[26] Dicey also asserted that Parliament cannot limit itself to make any law and no Parliament can bind further parliaments. In this way, Parliament was personified as a legal actor. Dicey did not intend for parliamentarians to act as trustees.[27] Parliamentary sovereignty was accepted as the manner in which law was made. While the Parliament practised these principles, Dicey, objecting to the party system, began to reluctantly advocate for a referendum process. He felt that political parties were flawed. This underlines Dicey's ultimate concern with the theory of parliamentary

22 AV Dicey, *An Introduction to the Study of the Law of the Constitution* (Macmillon, 10th ed, 1959).
23 Ibid.
24 RL Borthwick, 'What Has Happened to the Sovereignty of Parliament?' in Laura Brace and John Hoffman (eds), *Reclaiming Sovereignty* (Bloomsbury Publishing, 2016) 28, doi.org/10.5040/9781474288477.ch-002.
25 Dicey (n 22).
26 Ibid.
27 Ibid.

sovereignty—namely, that the will of the people was being usurped by a party system.[28] However, his traditional theory remained substantially more influential than his later qualified objections.

In Australia, the concept of parliamentary sovereignty emerged from Dicey.[29] However, as asserted by David Kinley, the concept has never represented the constitutional system.[30] Parliamentary sovereignty is always subject to social and political mores.[31] It is also inaccurate to use, interchangeably, the terms parliamentary sovereignty and parliamentary supremacy.[32] This is because the Parliament is limited by the Constitution, refuting Dicey's second rule. As such, parliamentary supremacy, or the legislature subject to social checks and balances, is the only term that is relevant to Australia. To be clear, parliamentary supremacy should not be equated with parliamentary sovereignty. Nevertheless, the concept of parliamentary sovereignty continues to be used in legal discourse as a mechanism to deny Indigenous rights.

It is important to distinguish between different definitions of sovereignty, as their complexity and overlap is often overlooked. As Denis J Galligan notes, sovereignty is the source of political authority.[33] Galligan also notes, broadly, that there may be three types of internal sovereignty: legal, political or constitutional.[34] The legal category refers to the paramount authority of a legal order, that often associated with parliamentary sovereignty in the imperial sense. In a constitutional sense, however, sovereignty lies in the authority that makes the constitution and the constituted bodies within.[35] This is where the concept of direct popular sovereignty is applicable: sovereignty of the people as authority. Galligan categorises the Australian Constitution in this way. Although no reference to sovereignty is made in the Australian Constitution, sovereignty is assumed to be within the people.[36] This is referred to as political sovereignty. This political sovereignty would

28 Rivka Weill, 'Dicey was Not Diceyan' (2003) 62(2) *The Cambridge Law Journal* 474, 484, doi.org/10.1017/S000819730300638X.

29 David Kinley 'Constitutional Brokerage in Australia: Constitutions and the Doctrines of Parliamentary Supremacy and The Rule of Law' (1994) 22(1) *Federal Law Review* 195, doi.org/10.1177/0067205X9402200107.

30 Ibid.

31 Ibid 196.

32 Ibid 197.

33 Denis J Galligan, 'The Sovereignty Deficit of Modern Constitutions' (2013) 33(4) *Oxford Journal of Legal Studies* 703, 704, doi.org/10.1093/ojls/gqt025.

34 Ibid 705.

35 Ibid.

36 Ibid.

be that of representative democracy. As such, it is pertinent to discuss why there has been a reluctance to vest direct power in the people in case law despite references to s 128.[37]

Such political and legal distinctions, as noted earlier, are essential for the discussion of sovereignty. In this discussion, I will be making broad legal claims. For Australia, the conventional view is that the legality of the Constitution derived not from the Constitution itself but from Westminster.[38] The removal of the legal aspect of this initial power did not occur until 1986.[39] George Winterton argues that, although popular sovereignty existed, as evidenced by s 128, it was political sovereignty.[40] Leslie Zines also makes this distinction.[41] In this way, parliamentary sovereignty is obviated by the creation of a new source of authority for the sovereign: the Australian people. However, this popular sovereignty has been used to vest power, paradoxically, back in the Parliament through representative democracy by replacing the Imperial Parliament with the Australian Parliament. This obscures the legal conundrum of the source of the Constitution's legal authority.

The High Court has occasionally promoted the concept of direct popular sovereignty. Murphy J suggested in 1976 that the authority of the Constitution was vested in the people.[42] Deane J similarly argued for popular sovereignty as the source of authority of the Constitution.[43] Both, however, applied this popular sovereignty as legitimating parliamentary sovereignty, but assumed that this power derived from the people by way of the Constitution. Murphy J expanded this to include individual rights.[44] This was the ability of the people as collective individuals to contain authority, as confirmed in *Nationwide News Pty Ltd v Wills* where Deane and Toohey JJ stated that the role of the government was to represent the

37 Australian Constitution.

38 Peter C Oliver, *The Constitutions of Independence: The Development of Constitutional Theory in Australia, Canada and New Zealand* (Oxford University Press, 2005) 267.

39 George Winterton, 'Popular Sovereignty and Constitutional Continuity' (1998) 26(1) *Federal Law Review* 1, 6, doi.org/10.22145/flr.26.1.1.

40 George Winterton, 'The Constitutional Implications of a Republic' in MA Stephenson & Clive Turner (eds), *Australia, Republic or Monarchy? Legal and Constitutional Issues* (University of Queensland Press, 1994) 15.

41 Leslie Zines, *The High Court and the Constitution* (Butterworth, 4th ed, 1997).

42 See discussion in Brendan Lim, *Australia's Constitution after Whitlam* (Cambridge University Press, 2017) 146.

43 Ibid 147.

44 Ibid 148.

people.[45] This view, that constitutional power derived from the people, was an expansion of both judges' ideologies of common law rights. This was affirmed by Mason CJ, in the *ACTV Case*, who described the people as a sovereign power, with such power stemming from the Constitution despite its imperial origins.[46] Dawson J, in the *ACTV Case,* contested this view, distancing himself from constitutional concepts that relied on the will of the people and comparisons to the US Constitution.[47] In *McGinty v Western Australia*, Mason CJ's view was reiterated, with caution, by McHugh J, who stated that the political and legal sovereignty of Australia was vested in the people following the removal of the UK Parliament.[48] This power was vested in s 128.[49]

A number of cases followed that seemed to distance themselves from the popular sovereignty argument.[50] Brennan CJ argued, in *Kruger v Commonwealth*, that popular sovereignty was present at the time of the enactment of the Constitution through its preamble.[51] Further decisions have reinforced the supremacy of the Australian Constitution in regard to matters of Australian law.[52] Despite this, there has been judicial reluctance to endorse direct popular sovereignty and, indeed, in some instances, outright refusal. Assertions of political sovereignty in recent cases assume a weaker form of popular sovereignty.[53] However, the foundation of the Constitution is still grounded in popular sovereignty, as asserted in *McCloy v New South Wales*, albeit in a weaker form.[54]

As noted by Duke, applications of popular sovereignty in the High Court have been relegated to 'weaker' popular sovereignty associated with representative democracy rather than the actual will of the people.[55] This weaker popular sovereignty is internal to the Constitution and relates to

45 *Nationwide News* (n 16).
46 *ACTV Case* (n 17) 137–8.
47 Ibid 181.
48 *McGinty* (n 16) 230.
49 See Gummow J's judgment: Ibid 178.
50 See *Kruger v Commonwealth* (1997) 190 CLR 1 ('*Kruger*'); *Levy v Victoria* (1997) 189 CLR 579; *Lange v Australia Broadcasting Corporation* (1997) 189 CLR 520.
51 *Kruger* (n 50) 41–2.
52 *Sue v Hill* (1999) CLR 462; *Love v Commonwealth* (2020) 270 CLR 152.
53 *McCloy v New South Wales* (2015) 257 CLR 178, 207 ('*McCloy*'); *Unions NSW v New South Wales* (2013) 252 CLR 530.
54 *McCloy* (n 53).
55 George Duke, 'Popular Sovereignty and the Nationhood Power' (2017) 45(3) *Federal Law Review* 415, doi.org/10.22145/flr.45.3.3.

democratic processes.[56] The stronger view, originated by Schmitt as actual political will or direct popular sovereignty, sees the people as having the authority to create a constitution.[57] The will of the people is superior to any constitution or form of democracy. The High Court has variably acknowledged s 128 as being a possible source of such authority, but this source is often connected to such authority being present in representative government. Further, it is suggested that even s 128 is invariably subject to parliamentary will by the referendum process.[58] But this ignores one aspect of constitutional reform—that movements to change the constitution often take place beyond the parliamentary realm. Therefore, internal sovereignty is, according to Australian law, only political, not legal. This is due to the legal foundation of the Constitution—that is, popular sovereignty—amounting to a theory regulated to representative democracy rather than the actual will of the people. As the Constitution cannot bind itself, its legal authority has not been established beyond this imbued arrangement.

As seen in the above analysis, there has been a reluctance to assert direct popular sovereignty, and operational popular sovereignty has been regulated to representative democracy (or political sovereignty to use Dicey's term). The legality of popular sovereignty has been anchored in the Constitution. However, the legal foundation of the Constitution remains contestable. This foundation implies shared sovereignty. Due to this conundrum, national sovereignty and the manner of its acquisition has been termed non-justiciable. This is through no distinction being determined between external and internal sovereignty. However, the concept of internal sovereignty, as termed by international law, provides a solution; it does not require singular authority. This concept of shared authority, therefore, can and must also include Indigenous sovereignty. This is through the ability of internal sovereignty to be shared within a nation-state. Therefore, constitutional reform must be understood to recognise Indigenous sovereignty in a way that is consistent with international law. If power is assumed to be vested in the Australian people, rather than an institution, it must be reflective of such people.

56 Ibid 423.

57 Ibid; Carl Schmitt, *Constitutional Theory* (Duke University Press, 2008) 125.

58 *McGinty* (n 16) 272.

Indeed, it may be claimed that Dicey intended popular sovereignty to be the source of power for parliamentary sovereignty.[59] However, this occurred more substantially after a realisation of the limitations of parliamentary sovereignty. The tenuous concept of sovereignty is linked to the issue of 'defining' the State. John Hoffman argues that postmodern scholars such as Jens Bartelson and Max Weber are prevented from defining sovereignty due to its highly contestable nature.[60] Hoffman argues instead for a 'post-statist' sovereignty that may be legitimised by the fact that it is not imposed.[61] Indigenous sovereignty and national sovereignty could coexist under such a concept.

IV. Indigenous sovereignty

The idea of sovereignty has been used as a political tool to limit the rights of Indigenous peoples by political actors. Additionally, as noted by Beth McKenna and Ben Wardle, Indigenous sovereignty has been denied in Australia by a series of legal fallacies.[62] McKenna and Wardle show how judicial processes underpin the claim that sovereignty is non-justiciable.[63] International law, as it existed in Europe, was used as a means to judicially deny Indigenous sovereignty. Yet, Indigenous sovereignty was often recognised in other nations, such as the US.[64]

Mabo v Queensland (No 2) ('*Mabo (No 2)*') held that there was an acquisition of sovereignty by the Crown, but that it took the form of radical title of occupied territory.[65] This stated that the Indigenous rights that existed were not removed by the common law at settlement but by the subsequent acts of a sovereign government. The *Mabo (No 2)* presented a statement of inherent Indigenous rights pre-existing in Australia and the legal fallacy of terra nullius was overturned. In a subsequent case, Mason CJ reiterated Gibbs J's earlier finding in *Coe v Commonwealth*, that although Indigenous

59 Lim (n 42) 28.
60 John Hoffman, 'Is it Time to Detach Sovereignty from the State?' in Laura Brace and John Hoffman (eds), *Reclaiming Sovereignty* (Bloomsbury Publishing, 2016) 20, doi.org/10.5040/9781474288477.ch-001.
61 Ibid.
62 Beth McKenna and Ben Wardle, 'Usurping Indigenous Sovereignty through Everchanging Legal Fictions' (2019) 28(1) *Griffith Law Review* 37, doi.org/10.1080/10383441.2019.1682959.
63 Ibid 38.
64 Ibid 43.
65 (1992) 175 CLR 1 ('*Mabo (No 2)*').

sovereignty may exist, there are no legal organs by which to exercise it.[66] *Milirrpum v Nabalco*, however, asserted that Aboriginal people existed through a 'government of laws'.[67] To acknowledge the rights emerging from traditional law is to recognise that law. This presupposition infers that, as an Indigenous legal system exists, there may be Indigenous sovereignty separate from, and prevailing over, Australian sovereignty. The *Mabo (No 2)*, by its acknowledgement of a change in sovereignty, recognises the pre-existing sovereignty of Indigenous peoples.[68]

As many authors have noted, the national narrative holds that Indigenous sovereignty was extinguished as a consequence of colonisation.[69] This is asserted in *Members of Yorta Yorta Aboriginal Community v Victoria*, which states that, as there can be no plural law, Indigenous sovereignty was superseded.[70] However, on closer analysis, these are not denials of Indigenous sovereignty but assertions of parliamentary supremacy. To put this another way, Indigenous sovereignty exists but, without recognition of Indigenous peoples as sharing internal legal jurisdiction, there is no legal avenue by which to exercise it.

The Australian Constitution was created to negate Indigenous sovereignty. Indeed, it is often used as the legal foundation to assert that Indigenous sovereignty can never be recognised. This is a misunderstanding of both sovereignty and constitutional law. Australia has the ability to recognise Indigenous sovereignty. Indigenous sovereignty can be described as a form of sovereignty with fundamental authority.[71] In this way, it aligns with calls for authority. Therefore, claims to the contrary are misguided. There are precedents for the recognition of Indigenous sovereignty in many nations across the world. Sovereignty has an intertwined connection with treaty-making. It would be nonsensical to provide for state-led treaty-making, which acknowledges the underlying sovereignty of Indigenous peoples, but to refute this in national law.

---

66 *Coe v Commonwealth* (1993) 118 ALR 193; *Coe v Commonwealth* (1979) 24 ALR 118.
67 *Milirrpum v Nabalco Pty Ltd* (1917) 17 FLR 141, 267.
68 *Mabo (No 2)* (n 65) 426.
69 Alison Vivian et al, 'Indigenous Self-Government in the Australian Federation' (2017) 20(1) *Australian Indigenous Law Review* 215.
70 *Members of the Yorta Yorta Aboriginal Community v Victoria* (2002) 214 CLR 422.
71 Sean Brennen et al, '"Sovereignty" and its Relevance to Treaty-Making Between Indigenous People and the Australian Government' (2004) 26(3) *Sydney Law Review* 307, 314.

The US is but one example where shared sovereignty with Indigenous peoples is recognised. Such recognition poses no threat to the US as a nation-state and has little impact on the stability of the nation-state as a whole. It is recognised in the US Constitution, which establishes Indigenous peoples as the First Peoples of the land. Numerous US presidents have recognised the concept of shared internal sovereignty, including Republican presidents such as George W Bush, who described the work between Indigenous peoples and the nation as work between 'sovereigns'.[72] The Marshall decisions in the US comprise hundreds of signed treaties that establish the ability of native sovereigns to be recognised. It must be noted, however, that many of these treaties were signed with unfair stipulations and need to be adapted to modern circumstances. Similar recognition of Australian Indigenous peoples as the First Peoples may also be conducive to treaty-making. Although such recognition has previously been described as merely symbolic, this is to view national sovereignty as an immutable fact rather than a variable concept. Many Australian States and Territories have already begun the treaty-making process with Indigenous peoples.

There is an unresolved tension between Indigenous sovereignty and constitutional recognition in Australia for both Indigenous peoples and the state. Some scholars claim that any form of constitutional recognition will cede Indigenous sovereignty,[73] as the Constitution would formally recognise the place of Indigenous Australians as subject to specific constitutional law. There needs to be a measured approach. Some constitutional scholars, such as George Williams, suggest that the issue of sovereignty can be affirmed and aligned with constitutional reform.[74] Indeed, Williams claims that it could promote sovereignty.[75] The combining of States to a federal system can recognise shared sovereignty. Indigenous 'states' and polity can similarly exist within a federal system. This is to suggest that Indigenous sovereignty, as it exists, can be another form of sovereignty subject to the States as the States are subject to the Commonwealth. It is worth noting that this form of sovereignty would not require laws that are in conflict with State law. Instead, it would be compatible with the Parliament as subject to the Constitution. The distinct character of Indigenous sovereignty allows for its existence to be continuous, as seen in case law. There must be a system by which Indigenous

72 Ibid.

73 George Williams, 'Does Constitutional Recognition Negate Aboriginal Sovereignty' (2012) 8(3) *Indigenous Legal Bulletin* 10, 11.

74 Ibid.

75 Ibid.

sovereignty is recognised alongside the sovereignty of the Australian States and Commonwealth. Self-determination is described by Anaya as an emerging customary norm of international law.[76] It should be noted that Indigenous legal systems have been acknowledged in literature and case law. A key element of constitutional reform is the concept of self-government. Its connection to self-determination is essential. Self-determination is at the core of Indigenous people's inclusion in constitutions across the world. As such, it should also be recognised as the core of constitutional reform for Indigenous peoples in Australia. Self-determination can be expressed through measures of self-government that may be asserted by acknowledging the political authority of Indigenous peoples.

Parliamentary sovereignty is often cited as a reason for rejecting Indigenous constitutional recognition.[77] As noted above, parliamentary sovereignty in Australia is more accurately termed popular sovereignty and parliamentary supremacy. The idea of parliamentary sovereignty stems from Dicey and others who advocated for a constitutional Parliament. But, as discussed by Peter C Oliver, it is a tenuous concept.[78] To question Parliament's supremacy is a fraught exercise, as the character of the Australian Constitution is said to give Parliament its power. But when the source of this power is examined through its origin in sovereignty, it becomes less persuasive.

There is a tension between the symbolic and the legal proposals for Indigenous constitutional reform. The view of the Referendum Council and many Indigenous leaders is that it would be impertinent to merely create a symbolic gesture rather than a legal obligation. Sovereignty has been used as a substitute for national identity, and as a vehicle for limiting the rights of Indigenous Australians through a denial of Indigenous sovereignty. Australian notions of sovereignty must be reimagined to encompass Indigenous peoples' sovereignty as a continuing and an important element of Australia's national identity. As noted above, constitutional reform is one way in which to achieve this. But there are many elements that must be part of this process, such as truth-telling, as suggested by Megan Davis

76 SJ Anaya, 'The Emergence of Customary International Law Concerning the Rights of Indigenous People' (2005) 12 *Law and Anthropology* 138.

77 Shireen Morris, 'Lessons from New Zealand: Toward a Better Working Relationship Between Indigenous People and the State' (2014) 18(2) *Australian International Law Review* 67.

78 Oliver (n 38).

and Gabrielle Appleby.[79] The importance of recognising this Indigenous sovereignty and its connection to self-determination must not be underestimated.

V. Symbolic versus legal

The tension between symbolic and legal rights is relevant to Australian Indigenous peoples. What is evident in calls for constitutional recognition is the necessity for legal substantive rights rather than merely symbolic gestures. Symbolic rights are often found in the context of constitutional law in constitutions that contain emotive or poetic sentiment, such as the US Constitution. The Australian Constitution was not founded on such romanticised ideals of 'equality' and 'freedom'. Instead, it was a pragmatic document freed from such lofty aspirations. The language employed is intended to be easily applicable and non-threatening to the Crown. This has been a detriment to the inclusion of morality—an element of intangible weight that shapes political processes. The absence of flourish in the Australian Constitution has limited its ability to be amended, leaving it rigidly and pragmatically grounded in its established principles. These principles are deemed to be 'correct' and any delineation is seen as a threat to the stability of the nation it addresses.

Many observers take a stagnant view of the Australian Constitution. Dylan Lino, in his critique of the Constitution's apparent lack of symbolism, urges that this view must be changed.[80] The problem is not within the document itself. As Lino notes, the traditional view is that it is not encased in universal political philosophy and is instead structural.[81] This is because it does not address many elements of individual human rights. Universal political philosophy includes such elements. The philosophical element must, therefore, be imposed. Lino suggests that the symbolic element is a reflection of 'Australian' citizenry.[82] Yet it should explore what is possible in questioning basic principles and their philosophical underpinnings. The absence of rights or rights protection in the Constitution has impacted its lack of philosophical imagining. As Lino attests, the purpose of the Australian

79 Megan Davis and Gabrielle Appleby, 'The Uluru Statement and the Promises of Truth' (2018) 49(4) *Australian Historical Studies* 501, doi.org/10.1080/1031461X.2018.1523838.
80 Dylan Lino, 'The Australian Constitution as Symbol' (2020) 48(4) *Federal Law Review* 543, 543, doi.org/10.1177/0067205X20955076.
81 Ibid.
82 Ibid 544.

Constitution should be to reflect and reconcile competing values.[83] To view it as stagnant—that is, stuck in its original liberal conservative form—fails to acknowledge political and judicial interpretations of its meaning.

In this regard, there is space to respect Indigenous peoples and our rights in the Constitution. Much of the criticism of Indigenous constitutional reform has rested on the ideal of equality. The argument is that equal rights should be afforded to all citizens, irrespective of race. Any special provisions would infringe on the Australian national identity and its commitment to equality. This type of criticism points to the need to question what Australian national identity entails. For the Australian Constitution, objections to Indigenous constitutional reform have been based on an understanding of the document as pragmatic. This argues that any such amendment would taint its pragmatism. But this is a misunderstanding of what is sought by Indigenous constitutional recognition. It is not meant to embody symbolic declarations but to give pragmatic power to Indigenous peoples. Indeed, rather than address racial discrimination, this liberal conservative view is what shaped the initial foundations of an Indigenous representative body to Parliament.[84] Early calls by government for constitutional recognition for Indigenous peoples sought symbolic acknowledgement only. From this emerged a call for substantive legal recognition in addition to calls for truth-telling and treaties.

The Expert Panel on Constitutional Recognition of Indigenous Australians recommended repealing the race provisions of ss 25 and 51(xxvi). This then led to suggestions for amendments on racial discrimination. However, as such recommendations fall short of addressing more serious Indigenous issues, they were rejected as not offering significant structural benefits. The idea of equality is often put forth as a denial of Indigenous constitutional reform. This is because the character of the document has been interpreted as a symbol of equality. This draws attention to the concept of equality put forth by many constitutions around the world. Despite containing an underlying norm of equality, the practice of equality as suggested by liberalism does not address practical inequality. This is how equality has been used within political discourse to deny human rights and ignore minorities and Indigenous peoples. This is a question not of equal law or equal access to law, but of law that promotes equality, a distinction that is often overlooked. Any legal reform that is proposed must be able to

83 Ibid 548.
84 Ibid 550.

promote equality by first addressing the inequality that affects Indigenous populations. The issues of Indigenous peoples are unique to the context in which they operate.

Debates about political morality for Australia are taken up in the political realm.[85] Goldsworthy suggests that principles such as the rule of law are only implicit to lawyers in the Constitution.[86] In a similar process, the High Court has suggested that there is no implied right of equality.[87] Duncan Ivison notes that Indigenous self-government should be connected to equality.[88] Mason CJ rejected that Aboriginal law could be found to exist separate to Australian law in *R v Walker* on the basis of equality before the law.[89] However, as noted by Ivison, equality before the law should not be synonymous to identical before the law.[90] It is precisely the opposite, as Indigenous claims can only be considered equally when consideration is given to Indigenous peoples' unique historical and social circumstances.

While parliamentary supremacy allows for the creation of laws, such laws are subject to social and ethical mores. Popular sovereignty is the source of this political authority. This popular sovereignty is a form of internal sovereignty. As internal sovereignty can be shared, Indigenous sovereignty may also be present as a source of inherent authority. Therefore, Indigenous people must be afforded more political authority in the making of laws relevant to Indigenous peoples and this inherent and prevailing Indigenous sovereignty.

VI. Conclusion

The positive aspects of constitutional reform are practical outcomes, not symbolic. Government objectors to constitutional reform hope to maintain the current constitutional schema. But, as evidenced here, in doing so, such objectors erroneously assert parliamentary sovereignty. Indigenous sovereignty exists. Therefore, it is essential for the nation to acknowledge

85 Jeffrey Goldsworthy, 'Constitutional Cultures, Democracy and Unwritten Principles' [2012] (3) *University of Illinois Law Review* 683, 685.
86 Ibid.
87 Goldsworthy (n 18) 101–102.
88 Duncan Ivison, 'Decolonizing the Rule of Law: Mabo's Case and Postcolonial Constitutionalism' (1997) 17(2) *Oxford Journal of Legal Studies* 253, 255, doi.org/10.1093/ojls/17.2.253.
89 *R v Walker* (1994) 182 CLR 45, 46.
90 Ivison (n 88) 272.

Indigenous sovereignty in the political sphere. Kim Rubenstein asserts that Australians were British citizens prior to 1986, a point that marked a change in legal sovereignty from the imperial courts to the Australian nation.[91] But if the imperial courts' acquisition of sovereignty is contestable and initially a judicial creation, the primacy of such sovereignty is unresolved. There must be an acknowledgement, therefore, that sovereignty is a multifaceted concept. Modern Australian sovereignty only 'exists' in international law, and international legal norms acknowledge the existence of Indigenous self-determination. In reference to internal sovereignty as a concept, Australia never legally acquired its own form of 'parliamentary sovereignty'. Instead, a form of popular sovereignty was created in the Constitution. Again, as stated in international law, this popular sovereignty, or political sovereignty, may exist alongside other forms of sovereignty such as Indigenous sovereignty.[92] Therefore, as I have argued, it is possible for Indigenous sovereignty to be recognised by the state. Political recognition may allow for a flow of morality that aligns with progressive lawmaking. Indigenous rights may be recognised in alignment with political constitutional reform.

The Uluru Statement clearly asserts the pre-existence of Indigenous sovereignty. As such, it is logical to formulate a statement, under both international law and national law, that Indigenous sovereignty was never ceded. It is important to understand that a denial of Indigenous sovereignty is a denial of Australia's national identity.[93] A representative body is a solution. It is intended as a way to express Indigenous inclusion in political discourse. This has been interpreted as such by political actors. However, it was not without its drawbacks and has been misunderstood and mischaracterised. It has also been suggested that such a body rejects the principles of equality, but the Constitution currently enables law on the basis of race in s 51(xxvi) and s 122. Allowing Indigenous peoples recourse to the law, in fact, recalibrates the inherent inequality present in the Constitution.

91 Kim Rubenstein, 'Power, Control and Citizenship: The Uluru Statement of the Heart as Active Citizenship' (2018) 30(1) *Bond Law Review* 19, 23, doi.org/10.53300/001c.5659.

92 Brennen et al (n 71) 319.

93 McKenna and Wardle (n 62) 56.

What has to be called into question is the salience of Australian concepts of sovereignty, their origins and their place in modern Australia. As stated, this is a question of both national identity and national morality. The notions of popular sovereignty and shared internal sovereignty can align with the goals of Indigenous peoples and our inclusion in the Constitution.

12

The Potential Moral Power of a New Australian Constitutional Preamble

Benjamin T Jones

At first glance, 'moral power' might seem an oxymoron. If not oppositional concepts, the former is often seen as a restriction or intangible handbrake on the latter. However, this is not necessarily the case. Power, in its most basic form, is the ability to get what you want and, often, the ability to get others to do what you want. This can apply to individuals or to groups or to States. Joseph Nye notes that nations that are sufficiently powerful and wealthy can use hard power to get what they want (meaning the threat of military force or sanctions), but they can also use soft power (which essentially means that if a nation is popular and respected it can influence others).[1]

This chapter applies the work of sociologist Dennis Wrong to the Australian Constitution. Wrong distinguishes between 'power over' and 'power to'.[2] 'Power over' is coercive; it involves control that can be exercised over a person or group. In Nye's taxonomy, 'power to' is a kind of soft power. Characterised by influence, it is when you can inspire or encourage a person or group to act in the ways you want them to. It will be argued in this chapter that a constitutional preamble has a form of moral 'power to'. This kind of morality is distinct from personal or religious variations. A constitutional preamble offers a form of civic morality tied to notions of good citizenship

1 Joseph S Nye Jr, 'Get Smart: Combining Hard and Soft Power' (2009) 88(4) *Foreign Affairs* 160.

2 Dennis Wrong, *Power: Its Forms, Bases, and Uses* (Transaction, 2009).

and pursuing the greater good over individual gain. The key to moral power, to channel Marshall McLuhan, is in the medium rather than the message.[3] If an individual, group or government is seen to hold moral authority, they have a form of 'power to' and can influence behaviour in a way others cannot. Similarly, the moral power of a constitutional preamble exists only to the extent that the Constitution itself is popularly respected.

As the rule book under which Australia's States and Territories operate, the Australian Constitution carries supreme legal power. The preamble does not have 'power over' but rather 'power to'. It has the power to articulate national values and to give certain concepts and ideals national significance. It can be argued that it also has the power to influence courts by providing an interpretative lens through which the Constitution can be viewed. Constitution drafters John Quick and Robert Garran believed that the Australian preamble might provide a 'valuable service' to the courts.[4] In practice, however, the preamble has rarely been used as an interpretive guide with the 1988 Constitutional Commission noting that it lacked legal power.[5] When alternative preambles were being earnestly debated in the 1990s, it was widely accepted that the purpose of a new preamble would be symbolic only. The 1998 Constitutional Convention resolved that a new preamble was appropriate but that a stipulation should be inserted into ch 3 of the Constitution to explicitly state that the preamble is not a tool for interpreting provisions in the Constitution.[6] The symbolic nature of a preamble does not mean it is unimportant. As Liav Orgad notes: 'For individuals, preambles are the national consciousness: they define the constitutional identity and, as such, they define who the "we" is.'[7]

Spurred by the prospect of a referendum on the republic in 1999, the 1990s witnessed a period of national self-reflection and debate over national identity. In this atmosphere, a flurry of alternate preambles were drafted by conservative and progressive politicians, historians, Indigenous activists and other citizens. Because of the gravitas of the Constitution, the preamble,

3 Robert Logan, *Understanding New Media: Extending Marshall McLuhan* (Peter Lang, 2010) 353.

4 John Quick and Robert Garran, *The Annotated Constitution of the Australian Commonwealth* (Angus and Robertson, 1901) 286.

5 However, there is some debate over the preamble's legal status, with the 1993 Republic Advisory Committee suggesting that a minor role cannot be assumed: see Mark McKenna, 'First Words: A Brief History of Public Debate on a New Preamble to the Australian Constitution 1991–99' (Research Paper No 16, Parliament of Australia, 4 April 2000) <parlinfo.aph.gov.au/parlInfo/search/display/display.w3p;query=Id%3A%22library%2Fprspub%2FFV716%22>.

6 John Warhurst and Malcolm Mackerras, *Constitutional Politics: The Republic Referendum and the Future* (University of Queensland Press, 2002) 8.

7 Liav Orgad, 'The Preamble in Constitutional Interpretation' (2010) 8(4) *International Journal of Constitutional Law* 738, doi.org/10.1093/icon/mor010.

although devoid of legal power, nevertheless has potential moral power. The reason this power is only 'potential' is because the current preamble is not used as a statement of national values. Technically, the Australian Constitution does not have a preamble at all. Rather, there is a preamble to the *Commonwealth of Australia Constitution Act 1900* (UK) that approved the Constitution.[8] Strictly speaking, what is commonly called the Australian constitutional preamble is an introduction to a piece of British legislation. For the sake of clarity, however, this chapter will use the popular term, preamble. Nevertheless, understanding that it was never written to be the foundational text of a new nation goes some way to explaining why it is so bland and uninspiring when held against the relative refulgence of other nations' preambles. It also explains why so many diverse groups in the 1990s saw value in changing it despite their different stances on what should be included and excluded. The current preamble was never intended to fulfil this high function of exerting moral power and proclaiming the values of the nation. Indeed, the men who wrote and passed it did not see themselves as founding fathers so much as facilitators of Australia's elevation in status from a collection of British colonies to a unified dominion of Empire.

Gregory Craven notes that there is a 'deadening contrast' between the jejune banality of the Australian Constitution and the emotive rhetoric of others.[9] The Australian preamble drily states:

> WHEREAS the people of New South Wales, Victoria, South Australia, Queensland, and Tasmania, humbly relying on the blessing of Almighty God, have agreed to unite in one indissoluble Federal Commonwealth under the Crown of the United Kingdom of Great Britain and Ireland, and under the Constitution hereby established:
>
> And whereas it is expedient to provide for the admission into the Commonwealth of other Australasian Colonies and possessions of the Queen:
>
> Be it therefore enacted by the Queen's most Excellent Majesty, by and with the advice and consent of the Lords Spiritual and Temporal, and Commons, in this present Parliament assembled, and by the authority of the same, as follows.[10]

8 Nicholas Aroney, *The Constitution of a Federal Commonwealth: The Making and Meaning of the Australian Constitution* (Cambridge University Press, 2012) 1.

9 In particular, he contrasts the Australian Constitution with the famous opening to the US preamble, 'We the People': see Greg Craven, *Conversations with the Constitution: Not Just a Piece of Paper* (University of New South Wales Press, 2004) 11.

10 Australian Constitution, preamble.

For modern readers, the preamble might appear jarring and alien with the States of the Commonwealth described as 'possessions of the Queen'. There is no declaration of independence or sovereignty, a usual inclusion in a preamble.[11] The best-known phrase in this poorly known document is 'indissoluble Federal Commonwealth'. The words immediately following it, however—'under the Crown of the United Kingdom'—are equally important.

It is not just the included text but what is missing from the preamble that is significant. Ideas like freedom, democracy and equality are all absent. High-minded but abstract concepts are common staples of preambles around the world. Their absence in Australia is because the preamble was not crafted to exert moral power. It is not simply the case that the constitution writers of the late nineteenth century and Australians today have a different concept of patriotism and a different understanding of Australia's place in the world and its relationship with Britain (although this is certainly the case). For the constitution writers, the objective of the preamble was not to provide an origin myth—they looked to their British heritage for such things—but to introduce the document and to potentially provide clarity if some words or phrases become 'obscured by the raising of unexpected issues and by the conflict of newly emerging opinions'.[12] The Australian preamble does not exert moral power, but there is value in considering some that do and what a new Australian preamble might look like.

This chapter will briefly consider some constitutional preambles that exert moral power before exploring the often overlooked second question in Australia's 1999 republican referendum that proposed a new preamble. It will also explore the interplay between preamble writing and seeking justice for First Nations peoples. Finally, it will discuss two proposed preambles to the Australian Constitution: one composed by the author and the other drafted by a group of senior school children. Ultimately, the chapter argues that it is not only possible but also desirable for Australia to replace the current constitutional preamble with a new one. The wording of any new preamble will draw criticism and the ensuing debates will likely be tempestuous. This is not necessarily a bad thing. At a national level, as WEH Stanner argued in his famous Boyer Lectures of 1968, uncomfortable discussions are preferable to great silences.[13] This is a piece of intellectual infrastructure worth fighting

11 Orgad (n 7) 716.

12 Quick and Garran (n 4) 286.

13 WEH Stanner, *After the Dreaming Black and White Australians: An Anthropologist's View* (ABC, 1969) 18.

for and, crucially, compromising for. Producing a new preamble that better reflects the modern nation and is specifically designed to exert moral power is not beyond Australia's creative and academic capability.

I. Preamble with moral power

The primary purpose of most constitutional preambles is to serve as a national mission statement and articulate the values of an imagined community.[14] This can be accompanied by a secondary function of guiding the interpretation of the constitution (though, as noted earlier, the Australian preamble is generally not used in this way).[15] A preamble can set the stage and establish the historical context for the constitution to follow. Some are dry and legalistic, others poetic and uplifting. One of the oldest and most influential constitutions is that of the French Republic. Unlike in Australia, the French preamble is considered to be incorporated into the constitution.[16] Significantly, the French preamble also contains references to other important national documents, including the 1789 Declaration of the Rights of Man, and places itself in a specific historical context. The second half of the text speaks to national values. It reads:

> By virtue of these principles and that of the self-determination of peoples, the Republic offers to the overseas territories which have expressed the will to adhere to them new institutions founded on the common ideal of liberty, equality and fraternity and conceived for the purpose of their democratic development.[17]

However well or poorly you may think the French State lives up to these ideals (or if you think the ideals are worthy or not), their strategic position in the preamble gives them a moral authority that has, in turn, shaped policy and perceived national values. In particular, the French tripartite motto, born in the eighteenth-century revolution, has influenced nations around the world.

14 To borrow Benedict Anderson's well-known phrase: Benedict Anderson, *Imagined Communities: Reflections on the Origin and Spread of Nationalism* (Verso, 1983).

15 Mark McKenna, Amelia Simpson and George Williams, 'First Words: The Preamble to the Australian Constitution' (2001) 24(2) *University of New South Wales Law Journal* 382, 382–3.

16 David Marrani, *Dynamics in the French Constitution: Decoding French Republican Ideas* (Routledge, 2013) 47, doi.org/10.4324/9780203798652.

17 Anne Wagner and Malik Bozzo-Rey, 'French Commemorative Postage Stamps as a Means of Legal Culture and Memory', in Anne Wagner and Richard K Sherwin (eds), *Law, Culture and Visual Studies* (Springer, 2014) 321, doi.org/10.1007/978-90-481-9322-6_15.

The other great revolution of the eighteenth century has been similarly influential. The first three words of the United States constitutional preamble, 'We the people', have had a great influence on that nation and others.[18] This opening line places the emphasis on the people and removes it from either the monarchy or an imagined divinity. Contrast this with the preamble of the Republic of Ireland, which begins: 'In the name of the Most Holy Trinity, from Whom is all authority and to Whom, as our final end, all actions both of men and States must be referred.'[19] It goes on to specifically recognise Christianity as the national religion with a reference to 'our Divine Lord, Jesus Christ'.[20] The Australian preamble has echoes of both with references to 'the people' and 'Almighty God'. In Australia, the word 'God' was included at the 1898 Constitutional Convention but is counterbalanced by s 116 of the Constitution, which prohibits the establishment of a State religion or the use of any religious test to hold public office. As we will see, despite Australians in 1998 being far less religious than in 1898 (and even less religious today), many of the proposed alternative preambles, including the one put to a referendum, maintained a reference to 'God'.

The French and American preambles have influenced other democratic nations around the world. Perhaps the clearest example is the preamble of India, which presents a quartet of national values. With allusions to France and the United States, it notes:

> WE, THE PEOPLE OF INDIA, having solemnly resolved to constitute India into a SOVEREIGN SOCIALIST SECULAR DEMOCRATIC REPUBLIC and to secure to all its citizens:
>
> JUSTICE, social, economic and political;
>
> LIBERTY of thought, expression, belief, faith and worship;
>
> EQUALITY of status and of opportunity;
>
> And to promote among them all
>
> FRATERNITY assuring the dignity of the individual and the unity and integrity of the Nation;

18 Orgad (n 7) 714.

19 Donal K Coffey, *Drafting the Irish Constitution, 1935–1937: Transnational Influences in Interwar Europe* (Palgrave, 2018) 41, doi.org/10.1007/978-3-319-76246-3_2.

20 Ibid.

> IN OUR CONSTITUENT ASSEMBLY this twenty-sixth day of November, 1949, do HEREBY ADOPT, ENACT AND GIVE TO OURSELVES THIS CONSTITUTION.[21]

In this short passage, several important concepts are highlighted. Each of the five descriptors of the Indian State are significant, as is the order. First and foremost, having endured centuries of British colonisation, the preamble declares that it is, above all, a sovereign State. The words 'socialist' and 'secular' were inclusions by Prime Minister Indira Gandhi as part of the wide ranging 40-second amendment in 1977, but the terms had been popularly used since independence.[22] Finally, the Indian State will adhere to democratic principles and adopt a republican form. If the word republic was swapped for federation, then all five would describe the Australian State (provided 'socialist' was understood in its broad meaning, as used in India). Instead, Australia's preamble uses the outdated term 'possessions'.

As well as articulating four key national values, the Indian preamble serves as a declaration of decolonisation. This is a common theme in the constitutions of the many nations in Asia and Africa that gained independence from European empires in the wake of World War II. The preamble to the Indonesian Constitution explicitly condemns the negative impact of Dutch colonisation and speaks to the right of nations to self-determination. It begins with the emotive line: 'Whereas freedom is the inalienable right of all nations, colonialism must be abolished in this world as it is not in conformity with humanity and justice.'[23] The South African preamble also highlights historical wrongs and offers a set of values to guide the nation into the future. It recognises the 'injustices of our past' and suggests part of the constitution's role is to help '[h]eal the divisions of the past'.[24] Again, the contrast with Australia's preamble is stark. It was composed by colonists and reflects British imperialism of the late nineteenth century. It does not recognise past injustices against First Nations or include any desire to provide healing. These concepts would have made no sense to the constitution writers but are clearly relevant to modern Australia.

21 Stuart Corbridge and John Harriss, *Reinventing India: Liberalization, Hindu Nationalism and Popular Democracy* (Polity Press, 2006) ch 2.

22 Rachel Fell McDermott et al, *Sources of Indian Traditions: Modern India, Pakistan, and Bangladesh*, (Columbia University Press, 3rd ed, 2014) vol 2, 885, doi.org/10.7312/mcde13828.

23 Denny Indrayana, *Indonesian Constitutional Reform, 1999–2002: An Evaluation of Constitution-Making in Transition* (Kompas, 2008) 431.

24 Hennie PP Lötter, *Injustice, Violence and Peace: The Case of South Africa* (Rodopi, 1997) 120, doi.org/10.1163/9789004458963.

The inclusion in a preamble of lofty notions like freedom and equality does not mean that the nation will live up to them; nor does the denunciation of past wrongs mean that they will not be repeated. The people of Timor-Leste may have seen some hypocrisy in the Indonesian preamble when they fought for their own independence from the 1970s to the early 2000s. This view was shared by some Indonesian leaders, especially Dewi Fortuna Anwar, who argued for a policy shift to realign the Habibie administration with the spirit of the preamble.[25] With the resurgence of Hindu nationalism under Prime Minister Narendra Modi, India's commitment to secularism can be questioned.[26] Conservative Catholics might see Ireland's decision to legalise same-sex marriage in 2015 and abortion in 2018 as a deviation from the spirit of their preamble (while progressives may counter that it is the preamble that should change). More generally, with the rise of right-wing populism and anti-immigration political parties around the world, many nations with preambles that refer to 'the people' are negotiating who exactly this includes and excludes. It is worth reiterating that a constitutional preamble offers a moral 'power to' not a 'power over'. It has the power to articulate a certain national vision and to influence the way citizens interact, and even how the constitution itself should be interpreted. It is, however, a limited form of soft power, and other influences may well prove greater at any particular moment in history.

The preambles of the nations mentioned above, and many others besides, do exercise a form of moral power. They set out the key principles for their societies and provide a historic context through which the constitution proper can be read. Whether secular like India or religious like Ireland, because of the legal gravitas of the constitution itself, the words in the preamble carry moral weight. In Australia's case, they do not because they were never designed to serve this function. The Australian preamble is not memorised by school children, recited at citizenship ceremonies or embedded in the popular consciousness. While its lack of moral power does not impact the functioning of the Constitution, it is a missed opportunity and, as the passionate debates of the 1990s demonstrate, many feel strongly that a new preamble is appropriate. The potential moral power of a new preamble has been recognised, not only by progressive reformers but also by

25 Lena Tan, 'From Incorporation to Disengagement: East Timor and Indonesian Identities, 1975–1999', in Daniel Rothbart and Karina V Korostelina (eds), *Identity, Morality, and Threat: Studies in Violent Conflict* (Lexington, 2006) 201.

26 See Ian Hall, *Modi and the Reinvention of Indian Foreign Policy* (Bristol University Press, 2019) 41–60, doi.org/10.1332/policypress/9781529204605.003.0003.

conservatives. It was Prime Minister John Howard, leader of the conservative Liberal Party, who insisted on a secondary debate about a new preamble to accompany the republic debate leading up to the 1999 referendum.

II. The preamble referendum, 1999

The Australian referendum on 6 November 1999 is often called the republic referendum, and the issue of severing constitutional ties with the British monarchy certainly dominated the debate. Nevertheless, it was a two-part referendum, and the second question asked Australian citizens if they approved an alternative preamble. Despite actively campaigning against the republic, Howard authored a constitutional preamble with help from poet Les Murray, conservative historian Geoffrey Blainey and two of his staff members, Catherine Murphy and Michael L'Estrange.[27] The new preamble was to serve as a statement of values for the Australian nation. Cynics may argue that, as a staunch monarchist and shrewd politician, the inclusion of a second question was a tactical move to obfuscate discussion on the republic. In January 1999, the Australian Republican Movement and the Australian Labor Party (which officially endorsed Australia becoming a republic) argued that the preamble question should be dropped as it was a distraction.[28] Given how passionately Howard advocated for the preamble and the personal interest he showed in the issue, it is more likely that he genuinely believed the preamble held potential moral power that should be tapped into (provided he could dictate the terminology).

Australian politics in the 1990s was dominated not only by the republic debate but also by discussions of the historic and ongoing injustices faced by Australia's First Nations. Under the Labor prime ministership of Paul Keating, who delivered the historic Redfern address in 1992, there were hopes that the 1990s would be the decade of reconciliation between Indigenous and non-Indigenous Australians. The Keating government established the Council for Reconciliation, passed the *Native Title Act 1993* (Cth) and instigated a national inquiry into the Stolen Generations. When Howard and the Liberals were swept to power in 1996, it was against this backdrop of serious conversations about reconciliation and how Indigenous Australians

27 Mark McKenna, Amelia Simpson and George Williams, 'With Hope in God, the Prime Minister and the Poet: Lessons from the 1999 Referendum on the Preamble' (2001) 24(2) *University of New South Wales Law Journal* 406.
28 McKenna (n 5).

should be recognised. Howard faced sustained criticism for his refusal to offer an apology to members of Stolen Generations—a recommendation from the *Bringing Them Home Report* endorsed by the Council for Reconciliation and enacted by all State and Territory governments—and was seen as being out of step with public sentiment.[29] Howard felt strongly that a so-called 'black armband' view of history, a phrase coined by Blainey, dominated public consciousness in the early 1990s.[30] In response, he sought language that presented the Australian story as one of 'heroic and unique achievement against great odds'.[31] This partly explains why he insisted on a 'statement of regret' rather than an apology on behalf of the federal government. As Jacob Levy notes, Howard's personal statement was 'no more than the expression of sorrow of an onlooker to a tragedy' and it was specifically worded to deny any responsibility of behalf of the government.[32]

Turning to the proposed preamble, Howard explained that recognition of First Nations in the Constitution was part of the raison d'être. He claimed in Parliament that:

> I think that as we approach the Centenary of Federation there are a growing number of Australians—Liberal and Labor, republican and anti-republican alike—who would like to see embedded in the basic document of this country some recognition of the prior occupation of the landmass of Australia by the indigenous people.[33]

A few days before the 1999 referendum, he spoke with 2GB Radio's Mike Jefferies about why he supported a new preamble despite opposing Australia becoming a republic. He again stated that recognition of First Nations was his primary motivation in pursuing a new preamble:

> I would like to see the republic defeated but I would like to see the preamble succeed. The great advantage of the preamble, and bear in mind all your listeners, a preamble is just a simple statement of basic values and beliefs. It doesn't have any legally binding effect and

29 Wayne Warry, *Ending Denial: Understanding Aboriginal Issues* (University of Toronto Press, 2007) 63. See also Danielle Celermajer, *The Sins of the Nation and the Ritual of Apologies* (Cambridge University Press, 2009) 174–5, doi.org/10.1017/CBO9780511581502.

30 Paul Kelly, *The March of Patriots: The Struggle for Modern Australia* (Melbourne University Press, 2010) 335–6.

31 'Sir Thomas Playford Memorial Lecture, Adelaide Town Hall', *Department of Prime Minister and Cabinet* (Web Page, 5 July 1996) 1–2 <pmtranscripts.pmc.gov.au/release/transcript-10041>.

32 Jacob T Levy, *The Multiculturalism of Fear* (Oxford University Press, 2000) 246, doi.org/10.1093/0198297122.001.0001.

33 Commonwealth, *Parliamentary Debates*, House of Representatives, 8 February 1999, 2061 (John Howard).

> it talks about things like recognising the place of the aborigines as the first people of the nation. It talks about the sacrifice of people in war about the common values that bind us together as Australians.[34]

As with the statement of regret, Howard appeared willing, even enthusiastic to recognise First Nations, but only, and ironically, if he was able to dictate the terms to them and choose the language to be used.

The initial draft of Howard's preamble was released to the press on 23 March 1999 and received widespread criticism from Indigenous rights activists and many others.[35] It was seen as insufficient for only noting that First Nations 'inhabited' Australia, with no reference to their continuing role as custodians of their traditional lands. Overwhelmingly, Indigenous leaders refused to support the preamble (in either this form or its final draft), with several calling for the second referendum question to be dropped altogether.[36] Howard's preamble also included a line perceived as 'blokey' if not sexist: 'We value excellence as well as fairness, independence as dearly as mateship.'[37] The inclusion of the word 'mateship' was impolitic but something Howard felt strongly about. The following month, Murray claimed, in an open letter published in *The Sydney Morning Herald*, that, on mateship, he 'bowed to the Prime Minister's preference'.[38] Speaking to John Laws, Howard defended its inclusion, noting: 'whatever its male origins might be, it has acquired a generic meaning'.[39] Nevertheless, criticism from many high-profile women, including Meg Lees, whose Democrats Party held the balance of power in the federal Senate after July, saw the phrase removed.[40]

34 'Transcript of the Prime Minister the Hon John Howard MP Radio Interview with Mike Jeffries (2GB)', *Department of Prime Minister and Cabinet* (Web Page, 1 November 1999) <pmtranscripts.pmc.gov.au/release/transcript-10989>.

35 For example, former chairperson of the Aboriginal and Torres Strait Islander Commission Lowitja O'Donoghue called the preamble 'pathetic': see 'Preamble Pathetic', *The Sydney Morning Herald*, 16 April 1999, 7. See also McKenna (n 5).

36 Mark McKenna, *This Country: A Reconciled Republic* (University of New South Wales Press, 2004) 58.

37 Les Murray, 'Mates Lost and Saved: Drafting the Constitutional Preamble', in John Warhurst and Malcolm Mackerras (eds), *Constitutional Politics: The Republic Referendum and the Future* (University of Queensland Press, 2002) 82–3.

38 Ibid 84.

39 'Transcript of the Prime Minister the Hon John Howard MP Interview with John Laws—Radio 2UE', *Department of Prime Minister and Cabinet* (Web Page, 23 March 1999) <pmtranscripts.pmc.gov.au/release/transcript-11116>.

40 Wayne Errington and Peter Van Onselen, *John Winston Howard: The Definitive Biography* (Melbourne University Press, 2008) 286.

Beyond these points, the initial draft was also criticised for ignoring many of the recommendations of the Constitutional Convention and, despite the assistance of Howard's celebrated co-author, containing the odd solecism (the term 'woven together' was often singled out).[41] Addressing Parliament on 24 March 1999, senior Labor figure and former Foreign Minister Gareth Evans gave a scathing rebuke of Howard's preamble, accusing the prime minister of being too controlling and refusing to listen to the broader Australian public. Dismissing it as a 'clunker of a document which has satisfied practically no one in this country', Evans stated:

> If he had listened for a start to Aboriginal and Torres Strait Islander Australians, they would have told him that his flora and fauna type references ... and his theme park reference to their cultures were just not good enough ... if he had listened to Australian women, he would not have put into his draft a word like 'mateship' ... If he had listened again to the delegates to his own Constitutional Convention ... [he] would have had a reference to custodianship. He would have had 'We the people of Australia' language in there. He would have had an affirmation of respect for our unique land and environment.[42]

In the face of such a backlash, Howard was compelled to either abandon the preamble or undertake a substantial rewrite. He chose the latter, but did not involve Murray. Instead, he sought advice (and much-needed political support) from the new Democrats Senator and Gumbaynggirr man Aden Ridgeway.

The final version of the preamble read:

> With hope in God, the Commonwealth of Australia is constituted as a democracy with a federal system of government to serve the common good.
>
> We the Australian people commit ourselves to this Constitution:
>
> proud that our national unity has been forged by Australians from many ancestries;
>
> never forgetting the sacrifices of all who defended our country and our liberty in time of war;

41 McKenna, Simpson and Williams (n 15).

42 'Address by the Hon Gareth Evans QC MP to the House of Representatives, Canberra', *Gareth Evans* (Web Page, 24 March 1999) <www.gevans.org/speeches/old/1998-1999/240399_preamble_australian_constitution.pdf>.

> upholding freedom, tolerance, individual dignity and the rule of law;
>
> honouring Aborigines and Torres Strait Islanders, the nation's first people, for their deep kinship with their lands and for their ancient and continuing cultures which enrich the life of our country;
>
> recognising the nation building contribution of generations of immigrants;
>
> mindful of our responsibility to protect our unique natural environment;
>
> supportive of achievement as well as equality of opportunity for all;
>
> and valuing independence as dearly as the national spirit which binds us together in both adversity and success.[43]

As Mark McKenna notes, this version was generally seen as an improvement but still faced much criticism.[44] Even Les Murray said he would not vote for it.[45] Perhaps the most consistent objection was that Howard had failed to consult with Indigenous leaders or use the word 'custodians' in reference to the traditional owners.[46] In March, a journalist had asked Howard 'why did [you] feel unable to go the extra step and mention the word custodianship especially given that this is going to have no legal implications?'[47] His response was simply that 'I think this better expresses what happened and in a more poetic flowing fashion'.[48] It is difficult to accept that Howard refused to include the word in either the first or final draft purely for poetic reasons. Like his insistence on 'regret' rather than 'apology', he chose his words with care and wanted to stamp his conservative seal on the foundational national document. Further amendments suggested by Labor and the Greens were rejected and, with support from the Democrats, the above version was put to the people on 6 November.

43 Les Murray, 'Mates Lost and Saved: Drafting the Constitutional Preamble', in John Warhurst and Malcolm Mackerras (eds), *Constitutional Politics: The Republic Referendum and the Future* (University of Queensland Press, 2002) 84–5.

44 McKenna (n 5).

45 Murray (n 37) 85.

46 McKenna (n 5).

47 'Transcript of the Prime Minister the Hon John Howard MP Press Conference Prime Minister's Courtyard, Parliament House', *Department of Prime Minister and Cabinet* (Web Page, 23 March 1999) <pmtranscripts.pmc.gov.au/release/transcript-11109>.

48 Ibid.

The result of the 1999 referendum was a double defeat. The proposed republic failed with 45.1 per cent of voters supporting it while the preamble was backed by just 39.3 per cent.[49] In a sense, the result is the opposite of what one might expect. The republic issue was far more divisive and complex, whereas, in principle at least, a broad cross-section of Australians across the political spectrum believed that the preamble should be updated. The low result for the preamble should not be entirely placed on inadequacies in the document itself. As Wayne Errington and Peter Van Onselen note, in the combative political environment of the late 1990s, 'opposing the preamble became a shorthand way of opposing Howard's values'.[50] One lesson that emerges from the 1990s debates is that language matters and, even without legal power, the constitutional preamble does have a potential moral power. This helps explain the heated debate over the wording. The language of the current preamble is so antiquated that it can be seen as politically neutral. In contrast, Howard's preamble became both politically partisan and embroiled in a larger culture war. Howard's preamble was defeated in 1999 as much for its author as its content, but the potential to exert moral power through the Constitution remains worthy of consideration.

III. A minimalist preamble

Although Howard's preamble was the only one to go to a referendum, the 1990s saw a raft of alternative compositions put forward. Despite many worthy options being in the public arena, in 2018, I published my own alternative preamble in a book called *This Time: Australia's Republican Past and Future.*[51] It was with some trepidation that I made another offering to a crowded marketplace, but my logic was that it is pernicious to criticise either Howard's preamble or the current preamble without suggesting an alternative. My preamble reads:

> We, the Australian people, hold these three dear: democracy, meritocracy and community.
>
> We cherish the ancient and continuing cultures that belong to this land,

49 George Williams and David Hume, *People Power: The History and Future of the Referendum in Australia* (University of New South Wales Press, 2010) 195.

50 Wayne Errington and Peter Van Onselen, *John Winston Howard: The Definitive Biography* (Melbourne University Press, 2008) 286.

51 Benjamin Jones, *This Time: Australia's Republican Past and Future* (Redback, 2018).

> We honour those who have served this nation in war and in peace,
>
> And we commit ourselves to one guiding principle: all citizens of this indissoluble Commonwealth are equal.
>
> With respect for country and love for justice, liberty and freedom, we pledge to stand truly by each other to defend our constitution.[52]

As I stress in the book, my primary purpose in composing a new preamble is to prompt discussion. One of the startling features of the 1999 referendum is how little time for public discussion was allowed on the second question. With a fixed timeline in place, Howard's preamble was offered in a 'take it or leave it' fashion. Australians chose the latter, but that does not mean a new, inclusive national discussion could not be fruitful.

My preamble is clearly minimalist in style. I resisted the urge to try to comprehensively cover all aspects of Australian history and cultural life, and to squeeze every national value into one document. My preamble does not include all the elements suggested at the 1998 Constitutional Convention but attempts to be a concise statement of civic values that could serve as a national oath as well as an introduction to the Constitution. References to the Crown and to God are replaced by the Australian people. Although there was agreement in 1998 that the words 'Almighty God' should be maintained, Australia's religious demographics have changed substantially. Between 2011 and 2021, Australians professing 'No Religion' rose from 22.3 to 38.9 per cent.[53] In 2017, the Australian Bureau of Statistics noted that the number of people without religion was 'rising fast'.[54] Recognising this trend, a reference to 'God' is more likely to be more divisive than unifying. Similarly, references to the Queen and monarchy are replaced with democracy and meritocracy. Even if this preamble were adopted without Australia becoming a republic, this is still a more accurate reflection of how Australia operates.

My version includes a nod to the current preamble with the words 'indissoluble Commonwealth' and also to the Eureka Stockade, the mythical birthplace of Australian democracy, with the 'pledge to stand truly by each other'. The line honouring First Nations is, perhaps, the most likely to attract

52 Ibid 120.

53 'Religion in Australia', *Australian Bureau of Statistics* (Web Page, 2021) <www.abs.gov.au/media-centre/media-releases/2021-census-shows-changes-australias-religious-diversity>.

54 Anthony Mellor, *Karl Rahner, Culture and Evangelization: New Approaches in an Australian Setting* (Brill, 2019) 57, doi.org/10.1163/9789004400313.

criticism. It states that Indigenous connection to the land is both ancient and ongoing and that this should be cherished by all Australians. Much more could justifiably be included. The phrasing of Lowitja O'Donoghue's proposed preamble is particularly worthy of consideration. Her draft includes the line: 'Australia recognises the Aboriginal peoples and Torres Strait Islanders as its indigenous peoples with continuous rights by virtue of that status'. The brevity of my acknowledgement is in keeping with the minimalist style of the whole preamble, but I would certainly welcome edits and improvements, particularly from Indigenous leaders. As stated above, its purpose is to act as a conversation starter, and any conversation on a new preamble must include First Nations peoples.

The clear theme in my preamble is the equality of Australian citizens. This is a principle that reaches across the political divide and sits at the heart of Australian democracy. It is for others to judge the shortcomings of this preamble, but I have some confidence that it at least holds up well against the current one and offers a better reflection of Australian civic values. Further, it offers a moral power that can be drawn upon. During the debates over marriage equality, for instance, would it have had any impact if campaigners could point to the preamble and note the guiding principle of equality? Or consider supporters of the Uluru Statement (I count myself in this camp). Would it make the case for a treaty and Voice to Parliament stronger if campaigners could point to the constitutional preamble and remind politicians that they are morally bound to cherish the ancient and continuing cultures that were here for tens of thousands of years before British colonisation? In both cases, the preamble would not have legal 'power over' and could not compel legislative change. A preamble such as mine would, however, exert a moral 'power to' and play some role in influencing opinions.

IV. The voice of the young

The 24th National Schools Constitutional Convention took place in Canberra from 19 to 21 March 2019. One hundred and twenty high school students from around Australia were selected to take part and discuss the constitutional preamble and debate if it should be changed. The convention included guest speakers (of which I was one), set readings and a chance to compare Australia's preamble to that of other nations. By far the most exciting part for students and facilitators alike was when the students broke up into small working groups and drafted alternative preambles. After these were presented, the students voted on their preferred draft. Once an initial winner was selected, all students could propose amendments and edits that were voted upon until their draft reached a final form.

The final version read as follows:

> We the Australian people, united as an indissoluble Commonwealth, commit ourselves to the principles of equality, democracy and freedom for all and pledge to uphold the following values that define our nation.
>
> We stand alongside the traditional custodians of the land and recognise the significance of Aboriginal and Torres Strait Islander cultures in shaping the Australian identity, their sovereignty was never ceded.
>
> As a nation and indeed community, we are united under the common goal to create a society catered to all, regardless of heritage or identity.
>
> We pledge to champion individual freedom and honour those who have served and continue to serve our nation.
>
> As Australians, we stand for the pursuit of a democratic State that upholds the fundamental principles of human values as set out by this Constitution.[55]

After three days of robust discussion, students took part in one final vote to ratify their constitutional preamble. If ratified, it was explained that the preamble would be tabled in the Australian Senate. The penultimate vote saw a resounding 70.9 per cent 'Yes' result. It was endorsed by an absolute majority and a majority from each individual State and Territory. Only the students from New South Wales were close to rejecting the proposal with a vote of 15 'Yes' and 13 'No'. The students' preamble was tabled in the Senate on 2 April 2019 and entered into Hansard.

Some of the themes from the student's preamble would have resonated with Australia's constitution drafters but many others would appear quite alien. Direct similarities include the reference to an 'indissoluble Commonwealth' and the appeal to the 'people'. In the latter case though, it must be

55 Benjamin Jones and John Warhurst, 'Young Australians Champion "Democracy" and "Freedom" in Designing Constitutional Change', *The Conversation* (online, 17 June 2019) <theconversation.com/young-australians-champion-democracy-and-freedom-in-designing-constitutional-change-118530>.

remembered that the students' conception of who is included in this often nebulous term 'the people' is likely broader than that of the constitution writers.[56] Soon after federation, women were included in the Australian polis through the *Commonwealth Franchise Act 1902*, but First Nations peoples were generally excluded. Similarly, the first significant legislation of the new federal Parliament was the *Immigration Restriction Act 1901*, part of the legislative architecture of the broader White Australia policy. The students' commitment to the 'principles of equality, democracy and freedom' would have been familiar to the constitution writers, and possibly approved by them, as they were proud of the democratic nature of their constitution. But the concept of equality would have had a different meaning. In 1901, in its narrowest form, it would have meant equality for white, adult, male British subjects; the broader conception would have included white, British women. However, for the students, it means equality for all adult Australian citizens 'regardless of heritage or identity'.

Other concepts from the students' preamble would have been completely foreign to the constitution writers. Although it did not make the final draft, the students debated if a commitment to protecting Australia's natural environment should be included—a notion that would not have occurred to many in 1901. The most controversial line in the students' preamble was the admission that 'sovereignty was never ceded'. There was much debate over the inclusion of this line and around a quarter of the students supported a motion to remove it. It is a line that would have made no sense to constitution writers who saw themselves as bringing the blessings of British civilisation and Christianity to Indigenous peoples. Today, the treatment of First Nations people, the negative impact of colonisation and the way Australian history is taught has been caught up in a culture war.[57]

A key message from the students' preamble is that values matter and that the constitutional preamble is a place to house and express national ideals. Just like Howard's preamble in the 1990s, the wording of the students' preamble sparked passionate debate about what Australian national values are and how they can best be articulated. In both cases, there was an implicit recognition that, unlike the current preamble, a new preamble, deliberately crafted to serve as an important civic document, would carry moral power. While there is a great diversity of opinions as to what should be included

56 See Elisa Arcioni, Chapter 2, this volume, for further reflection on the meaning of 'the people' in the Australian Constitution.

57 See Stuart Macintyre and Anna Clark, *The History Wars* (Melbourne University Press, 2003).

and excluded from a new constitutional preamble, there has been a general consensus since the 1990s that the current preamble does not accurately reflect the Australian polis and its democratic pillars.

V. Conclusion

In many nations, the constitutional preamble is well known. It is studied at school, recited regularly and exists as part of the nation's moral fabric. The Australian constitutional preamble, by contrast, is largely unknown. It is a legalistic document that primarily reflects Australia's place in the turn of the century imperial order. It does not attempt to establish national values or ideals. Despite broad agreement in the 1990s that the preamble should be changed (and no shortage of alternative preambles to consider), Howard's offering at the 1999 referendum lacked popular support.

The issue regained some momentum in 2012 when Prime Minister Julia Gillard launched the 'Recognise' campaign. She promised that: 'If re-elected, I will put to the Australian people within 18 months a referendum to formally recognise Indigenous Australians in our Constitution.'[58] However, Gillard would not face the 2013 election. She was replaced by former Prime Minster Kevin Rudd who would then lose the 2013 election to the Liberals, led by Tony Abbott. The Recognise campaign persisted but was criticised for its narrow scope and for appearing tokenistic. As Referendum Council member and law professor Megan Davis notes, even the word 'recognition' has been 'really problematic'.[59] On 6 July 2015, Aboriginal and Torres Strait Islander leaders met the prime minister to deliver the Kirribilli Statement on constitutional recognition. In it they stated:

> A minimalist approach, that provides preambular recognition, removes section 25 and moderates the races power [section 51(xxvi)], does not go far enough and would not be acceptable to Aboriginal and Torres Strait Islander peoples.[60]

58 Julia Gillard, 'Prime Ministerial Statement: "Closing the Gap"', *Department of the Prime Minister and Cabinet* (Web Page, 15 February 2012) <pmtranscripts.pmc.gov.au/release/transcript-18388>.
59 Bridget Brennan, 'Recognise Campaign Ends after Making "Significant Contribution"' (online, 11 August 2017) *ABC News* <www.abc.net.au/news/2017-08-11/recognise-campaign-wound-up/8797540>.
60 'Statement Presented by Aboriginal and Torres Strait Islander Attendees at a Meeting Held with the Prime Minister and Opposition Leader on Constitutional Recognition', *ANTaR* (Web Page, 6 July 2015) <www.austlii.edu.au/au/journals/ILB/2015/37.pdf>.

The Recognise movement has since been eclipsed by the 2017 Uluru Statement from the Heart that calls for structural change, including a Voice to Parliament, Treaty and a Makarrata (or truth-telling) Commission.[61] The message from supporters of the Uluru Statement is clear: recognition in the preamble, by itself, is inadequate. As Davis puts it: 'However important symbols are … Aboriginal and Torres Strait Islander peoples do not seek more symbols.'[62] There is an important nuance, however, between updating the preamble in an attempt to achieve reconciliation and doing so as part of a broader project of updating Australia's impartial symbols. John Pyke argues that 'if the consultation with Indigenous Australians shows that they do not want recognition by way of a "preamble", then we should not add a new preamble *as part of the recognition project*'.[63] A new constitutional preamble is not a substitute for structural change and should not distract from that mission. Nor should politicians be able to use a new preamble as a quick fix or excuse to stop listening to Indigenous voices. Nevertheless, updating the preamble remains a worthy goal and one that requires deep discussion and wide consultation. Further, any new preamble would have to acknowledge both the historic and continuing place of First Nations peoples in Australia.

As a multicultural and secular democracy, Australian values are contested and malleable. They spring from its citizens, not from any document, however revered. Of course, just writing something down in a preamble does not make it so, but neither is it meaningless to write it down. To this end, there is a symbiotic relationship between the lived values of a people and their stated values in a preamble or anywhere else. Each can reinforce and support the other. Although it would not be legally binding, a statement of values in the preamble to the Australian Constitution would lend it a moral authority to both guide and reflect national identity. The moral power of a preamble is what Max Weber called an 'ideal type'.[64] In other words, the values will not exist in reality, at least not in a pure form, but can be an aspiration. Hans Kohn makes the important distinction between ethnic and civic nationalism. The former is exclusive and race-based while the latter is

61 'Uluru Statement from the Heart', *Referendum Council* (Web Page) <www.referendumcouncil.org.au/sites/default/files/2017-05/Uluru_Statement_From_The_Heart_0.PDF>.

62 Megan Davis, *Constitutional Recognition for Indigenous Australians Must Involve Structural Change, Not Mere Symbolism* (online, 18 February 2020) *The Conversation* <theconversation.com/constitutional-recognition-for-indigenous-australians-must-involve-structural-change-not-mere-symbolism-131751>.

63 John Pyke, 'Reasons Not to be Scared of a New Constitutional Preamble', *AUSPUBLAW* (Blog Post, 18 May 2015) <auspublaw.org/2016/05/reasons-not-to-be-scared/> (original emphasis).

64 Max Weber, tr Edward A Shils and Henry A Finch, *Methodology of Social Sciences* (Routledge, 2011) 43.

inclusive and rights-based.[65] For much of the twentieth century, parts of the Australian Constitution, as well as many laws, were overtly racist and built on the presumed superiority of a white British monoculture. A new preamble, explicitly based on civic national ideals, clearly stating the equality of citizens and acknowledging the prior occupation of First Nations, would possess moral power and be a conscious act of decolonisation.

There will never be perfect agreement on the wording of a new preamble. To survive a referendum, Australians must be willing to compromise and cooperate. If a new preamble, doubtless still with critics, is put to a referendum, Australians will be called on to calmly consider if the proposed alternative serves the nation better than the present one. If the perfect becomes the enemy of the good, the States and Territories that make up the Australian Commonwealth will be known in perpetuity as a 'possession of the Queen'.

65 Hans Kohn, *The Age of Nationalism: The First Era of Global History* (Greenwood Press, 1962).

13

Can Citizen Assemblies Make a Difference to Constitutional Reform? Some Lessons from Ireland

Sarah Sorial

Citizen engagement with constitutional reform is important for the formation of national identity. However, any claim that the Australian Constitution reflects or shapes national identity encounters an immediate obstacle: most Australians do not know or care enough about the Constitution. It has also been over 20 years since we have had to vote on a constitutional amendment (the last referendum was in 1999, on the republic), so Australians are somewhat out of practice in deliberating about the Constitution. This chapter examines the use of citizens' assemblies (CAs) as a way of overcoming some of these challenges. CAs are small-scale groups of randomly selected citizens who come together to discuss and decide on an issue of public policy. This chapter suggests that CAs are an effective mechanism for improving citizens' democratic literacy about constitutional issues, and motivating informed public debate. Using the recent assemblies conducted in Ireland on marriage equality and abortion as case studies, I argue that CAs, when designed in the right way and connected to the wider public sphere, are effective at improving deliberation about constitutional reform in at least two significant ways. First, they are effective at developing the democratic literacy of both participants and the voting public. Second, they can help foster a constitutional culture by giving citizens ownership over constitutional issues, irrespective of a referendum outcome. For these reasons, the Irish experiments in deliberation are instructive in the Australian context, where lack of democratic literacy among the voting public, and disengagement with constitutional issues, have been identified as major impediments to constitutional reform.

In section one, I examine some of the well-documented challenges to achieving constitutional reform in Australia, namely, the lack of democratic literacy among Australian voters, citizens' lack of 'identification' with the Australian Constitution, and the nature of the Australian Constitution itself, famously described as a 'prosaic document'.[1] Section two examines two recent case studies of CAs in Ireland: the Constitutional Convention, which led to the referendum on marriage equality, and the Citizens' Assembly, which led to the referendum on repeal of the Eighth Amendment of the Constitution of Ireland restricting access to abortion. In section three, I examine some of the criticisms of the Irish CAs' focus on issues of representation, their connection to the wider public sphere and their legitimacy.[2] In section four, I argue that, despite some of the criticisms of the composition of the CAs, and some of the scepticism about whether they did, in fact, influence wider public debate about these issues, they were successful in two significant ways. First, with reference to empirical evidence, they were successful in building the deliberative literacy of assembly members and the deliberative capacity of voters more generally; and, second, in the way they gave 'ordinary' citizens ownership of constitutional issues, thereby circumventing voter distrust of political elites. Using the theoretical model of 'deliberative systems', I demonstrate the ways in which CAs not only bring citizens into law reform processes, but also act as conduits between political elites and voters to achieve meaningful debate about constitutional reform. In the final section, I explore some of the lessons of the Irish experiments in deliberative democracy for the Australian context, where CAs have been used, but with limited success, and suggest that CAs could be one strategy for addressing the aforementioned challenges to constitutional reform in Australia.

1 Sir Anthony F Mason, 'The Australian Constitution in Retrospect and Prospect' in Robert French, Geoffrey Lindell and Cheryl Saunders (eds), *Reflections on the Australian Constitution* (Federation Press, 2003) 8.

2 Eoin Carolan, 'Ireland's Constitutional Convention: Behind the Hype about Citizen-Led Constitutional Change' (2015) 13(3) *International Journal of Constitutional Law* 733, doi.org/10.1093/icon/mov044.

I. Impediments to constitutional reform in Australia

Many countries, including Australia, require referenda by law for constitutional reform.[3] Given the importance of constitutional change, deliberation is crucial to ensure the legitimacy of any constitutional amendment pursued via a referendum. However, informed debate and constitutional amendment have been limited in Australia. For example, there have been 44 attempted referenda to amend the Constitution since federation (1901), but only eight have succeeded. This has led some scholars to argue that Australia is constitutionally a 'frozen continent' and is in the grip of 'constitutional deadlock', by which they mean that formal constitutional reform no longer occurs.[4] This has been attributed to a variety of complex reasons, including lack of democratic literacy among voters,[5] lack of citizen identification with the Constitution, the nature of the Australian Constitution itself[6] and a politically conservative culture.

Democratic literacy refers to the knowledge citizens need to deliberate effectively and make informed voting decisions about constitutional issues, such as knowledge about lawmaking processes, and the content and function of the Constitution. It also includes having deliberative skills, such as being reflective, other-regarding and able to give reasons for one's views. There is growing scepticism about whether citizens have the relevant democratic literacy to participate in law reform, and whether they can, in fact, acquire it.[7] There have been some calls to weaken the requirement for citizen participation in constitutional reform via referenda, and leave technical constitutional reform to elites. For example, Canadian political scientists

3 Australian Constitution s 128.

4 Ron Levy, 'Breaking the Constitutional Deadlock: Lessons from Deliberative Experiments in Constitutional Change' (2010) 34 *Melbourne University Law Review* 805, 807.

5 Paul Kildea, 'Worth Talking About? Modest Constitutional Amendment and Citizen Deliberation in Australia' (2013) 12(4) *Election Law Journal* 524, 526, doi.org/10.1089/elj.2013.0206; S Sorial, 'Constitutional Reform and the Problem of Deliberation: Building a "Civics Infrastructure" for Meaningful Debate' in Ron Levy, Hoi Kong, Graeme Orr and Jeff King (eds), *The Cambridge Handbook of Deliberative Constitutionalism* (Cambridge University Press, 2018) 324, doi.org/10.1017/9781108289474.025.

6 Justice Ronald Sackville, 'The 2003 Term: The Inaccessible Constitution' (2004) 27(1) *University of New South Wales Law Journal* 66. See also George Williams and David Hume, *People Power: The History and Future of the Referendum in Australia* (UNSW Press, 2010).

7 Shawn Rosenberg, 'Citizen Competence and the Psychology of Deliberation' in Stephen Elstub and Peter McLaverty (eds), *Deliberative Democracy: Issues and Cases* (Edinburgh University Press, 2014) 98–117, doi.org/10.1515/9780748643509-008.

such as Janet Ajzenstat[8] and Michael Atkins[9] argue that public involvement in constitutional processes makes change impossible, and is best left to political elites. While this may be a viable option in other jurisdictions where constitutional reform can be achieved without referenda, the Australian Constitution can only be amended by a majority in a referendum in which voting is compulsory, as per s 128. The issue of how to develop democratic literacy for informed debate about constitutional reform is, then, of utmost importance in Australia and yet it has received very little attention. This lack of attention has been compounded by what Paul Kildea calls the 'conventional wisdom' that proposals for constitutional amendment must have bipartisan support if they are to succeed.[10] Unless this condition is met, there has been a reluctance to pursue amendments because of a perceived risk of failure. The focus on referendum outcomes rather than deliberative processes has functioned to stifle constitutional debate, making us risk-averse about pursing constitutional reform, and rendering us out of practice about how to deliberate about constitutional issues.[11]

While there have been concerted efforts to embed civics and citizenship within the primary and high school curriculum, the recently released results of the 2016 sample assessment of civics and citizenship within the National Assessment Program suggests poor uptake and results of the program.[12] The results suggest that, while there has been an increasing focus on civics in Australia's curriculum, this is not reflected in young people's civics and citizenship understandings. In their research with young Australians of school-leaving age, Ghazarian, Laughland-Booy and Skrbis have found

8 Janet Ajzenstat, 'Constitution Making and the Myth of the People' in Curtis Cook (ed), *Constitutional Predicament: Canada after the Referendum of 1992* (McGill-Queen's University Press, 1994) 112.

9 Michael Atkinson, 'What Kind of Democracy Do Canadians Want?' (1994) 27(4) *Canadian Journal of Political Science* 717, doi.org/10.1017/S0008423900022009.

10 Paul Kildea, 'Getting to "Yes": Why Our Approach to Winning Referendums Needs a Rethink' AUSPUBLAW (Web Page, 12 December 2018) <auspublaw.org/blog/2018/12/getting-to-yes-why-our-approach-to-winning-referendums-needs-a-rethink/>.

11 Ibid.

12 The Australian National Assessment Program is the Australian government's main initiative for measuring whether young Australians are meeting key educational outcomes. The program includes a triennial assessment of civics and citizenship. For example, the results for Year 10 students decreased from 49 per cent of those who reached the target in 2010 to 38 per cent in 2016, meaning that 62 per cent of Year 10 students failed to reach the standard understanding of civics expected of that age group. J Fraillon et al, *National Assessment Program: Sample Assessment: Civics and Citizenship Report: Years 6 and 10: 2016* (Australian Curriculum, Assessment and Reporting Authority, 2017) (Web Document) <research.acer.edu.au/civics/27/>.

that 'many young people still aren't sure about how Australia's system of government works by the time they leave school. And they may also not have the skills to confidently participate in the political process'.[13]

This lack of democratic literacy is seemingly widespread in Australia, with a 2004 study conducted by the Civics Experts Group finding that '18 per cent of Australians surveyed had some knowledge of the Constitution, only 41 per cent were aware that the Constitution could be altered by referendum and only 50 per cent understood that the High Court was the highest court in Australia'.[14] In relation to citizenship, 'only 33 per cent felt that they were reasonably informed about their rights and responsibilities as Australian citizens'.[15] This lack of democratic literacy is not unique to Australia, and similar levels of public disengagement and ignorance about national constitutions and political processes are widespread in both the United Kingdom[16] and the United States.[17] Arguably, there may be different causal factors for this lack of democratic literacy in each of these jurisdictions, although one advantage Australia has over these countries is compulsory voting. It might be expected that this feature would increase democratic literacy, but this has not translated into constitutional literacy. Once again, this could be related to the lack of opportunity to engage with referenda.

In Australia, another causal factor that potentially impedes constitutional reform and compounds the problem of democratic literacy is the Constitution itself. As Lael Weis argues, the Australian Constitution does not contain a central founding moment that defines Australian values.[18] As a result of its origins as a 'pragmatic exercise in nation building',[19] as well as its historical roots as an Act of British Parliament, Weis notes that 'the *Australian Constitution* failed to "constitute" the Australian people in

13 Zareh Ghazarian, Jacqueline Laughland-Booy and Zlatko Skrbis, 'Young Australians Are Engaged in Political Issues, but Unsure how Democracy Works' *The Conversation* (online, 28 September 2017) <theconversation.com/young-australians-are-engaged-in-political-issues-but-unsure-how-democracy-works-84360>.

14 Ibid 133.

15 Ibid.

16 Bernard Crick, 'Citizenship: The Political and the Democratic' (2007) 55(3) *British Journal of Education Studies* 235, 242, doi.org/10.1111/j.1467-8527.2007.00377.x.

17 W Galston, 'Civic Knowledge, Civic Education, and Civic Engagement: A Summary of Recent Research' (2007) 30(6–7) *International Journal of Public Administration* 623, 630, doi.org/10.1080/01900690701215888.

18 Lael K Weis, 'Does Australia Need a Popular Constitutional Culture?' in Ron Levy et al (eds), *New Directions For Law in Australia* (ANU Press, 2017) 379, doi.org/10.22459/NDLA.09.2017.35.

19 Lael K Weis, 'What Comparativism Tells Us about Originalism' (2013) 11(4) *International Journal of Constitutional Law* 842, 850, doi.org/10.1093/icon/mot049.

any meaningful sense'.[20] It does not, for example, reflect a shared narrative of the events leading to federation and national independence. Significantly, it also does not contain a 'Bill of Rights' with which the Australian people might identify. Nor is it written or interpreted in a way that is accessible to lay audiences.[21]

For these reasons, Justice Ronald Sackville argues that it should come as no surprise that, with the exception of some sporadic debates about becoming a republic or a new preamble, ongoing discussion of constitutional principles in Australia is conducted by specialists; nor should it come as a surprise that the Australian people are reluctant to approve proposed amendments. The principles underlying constitutional arrangements are too difficult to understand, and there is little attempt made by both governments and the High Court to engage the community in a sustained dialogue about constitutional development.[22]

This inaccessibility is compounded by the style of the judgments of the High Court, which are often legally technical, limiting the access of genuinely important constitutional cases to a non-specialist audience. Sackville concludes that:

> These characteristics limit the extent to which the Constitution is capable of reflecting and influencing the aspirations of the Australian people. They also impede the prospects of significant constitutional reform, since uncertainty and obscurity breed fear of change.[23]

He suggests that much more is needed to develop a genuine dialogue between the High Court and the Australian people.

The question about how to engage citizens in ongoing dialogue about constitutional development has become all the more urgent, because, for the first time in Australia's history, there is a national Indigenous position on constitutional recognition, as contained in the Uluru Statement from the Heart (Uluru Statement) and momentum for a referendum on the issue. The Uluru Statement is itself the product of a very successful citizens' assembly–like process among Indigenous groups, known as 'The Dialogues'.[24] There is also promising evidence to suggest that a majority of Australians

20 Weis (n 18) 379.
21 Sackville (n 6) 66.
22 Ibid 67.
23 Ibid 86.
24 See Shireen Morris, *Radical Heart* (Melbourne University Press, 2018).

would support an Indigenous constitutional Voice to Parliament at a referendum.[25] However, there remains strong opposition to this proposal, based largely on misinformation, including that it would constitute a third chamber of Parliament.[26] Investigating ways of building democratic literacy among the wider voting public will potentially better equip citizens to make informed decisions about constitutional reform at this critical juncture in Australia's history.

Citizens' assemblies and other mini-publics could be one way of developing a genuine dialogue between the government, the High Court and the Australian people about constitutional issues, including constitutional amendment. Citizens' assemblies might perform two different functions in the Australian context, including in relation to Indigenous constitutional recognition: first, they might help develop the democratic literacy of voters more generally, enabling them to make informed decisions about constitutional amendments, thereby addressing one of the impediments to reform;[27] second, they might also give Australian citizens ownership over their constitution, circumventing the growing distrust of political elites.[28]

II. Citizens' assemblies

In the last two decades, there has been a growing use of various democratic innovations, such as CAs in other jurisdictions as a way of institutionalising citizen deliberation and legitimising lawmaking. The Republic of Ireland is one jurisdiction that has used CAs to drive reform on controversial issues, including marriage equality, abortion, divorce and blasphemy. In 2011, the Irish coalition government referred the constitutional matter of marriage equality to a proposed Constitutional Convention, a one-off body consisting of 66 randomly selected citizens, selected to ensure representation on the basis of four demographic targets—sex, age, social

25 Ibid.

26 Ibid.

27 For instance, an expert panel on Indigenous recognition recommended in 2012 that 'before the referendum is held, there should be a properly resourced public education and awareness program': Expert Panel on Constitutional Recognition of Indigenous Australians, *Recognising Aboriginal and Torres Strait Islander Peoples in the Constitution* (Report, January 2012) 227.

28 See Paul Kildea and Rodney Smith, 'The Challenge of Informed Voting at Constitutional Referendums' (2016) 39(1) *UNSW Law Journal* 368, 374–6.

class and religion—and 33 politicians, and an independent chair.[29] The 100 members of the convention were tasked with deliberating on eight specific issues, including whether to reduce the voting age, a review of the electoral system, the representation of women in public and political life, and, most significantly, marriage equality.[30]

The convention discussed the issue of marriage equality in its third session held on the weekend of 13–14 April 2013. As with all the other topics for deliberation, the convention members were informed by expert briefing documents, presentations, advocacy groups and individuals. There were over 1,000 pieces of submission of varying lengths, and presentations by a number of advocates, including a Catholic bishop, the grown-up children of same-sex couples and a gay man opposed to marriage equality. Members were given time to read and reflect on the materials and to hear from and question the experts and advocates. The members then deliberated in groups, after which they were required to vote on whether to recommend the introduction of marriage equality. This was met with 79 per cent support. In its report on 2 July 2013, the convention recommended that the Irish Constitution be amended to introduce marriage equality.[31] Two years later, the referendum was called, and a 62.07 per cent majority voted 'Yes' to marriage equality.[32]

The second 'mini-public', the Citizens' Assembly, was established by the Irish government in October 2016 and it concluded in 2018. It closely followed the model of the 2012–14 Irish Constitutional Convention, with some modifications, including 99 citizen members randomly selected by a market research company and an independent chair. It was also given five issues to consider, including abortion, the challenges and opportunities of an ageing population, fixed-term parliaments, the manner in which referenda are held and how the State can make Ireland a leader in addressing climate change.[33]

29 Johan A Elkink et al, 'Understanding the 2015 Marriage Referendum in Ireland: Context, Campaign, and Conservative Ireland' (2017) 32(3) *Irish Political Studies* 361, doi.org/10.1080/07907184.2016.1197209.

30 Ibid.

31 Ibid 363.

32 'Thirty-Fourth Amendment of the Constitution (Marriage Equality) Bill 2015', *Referendum Ireland* (Web Page, 9 August 2015) <web.archive.org/web/20150809115721/http://www.referendum.ie/results.php?ref=10>.

33 David M Farrell, Jane Suiter and Clodagh Harris, '"Systematising" Constitutional Deliberation: The 2016–18 Citizens' Assembly in Ireland' (2019) 34(1) *Irish Political Studies* 113, doi.org/10.1080/07907184.2018.1534832.

The design of the Citizens' Assembly was characterised by two main features. First, the members were regular citizens selected from the wider population and, like the convention members, were selected on the basis of representation of four demographic targets: sex, age, social class and religion. The second feature was the assembly's design: the members were arranged in circular tables of seven to eight people, each with a facilitator. The role of the facilitator was to ensure that round table discussions stayed on point, were respectful and that every member had an opportunity to speak. Meetings took place once a month, lasting for most of the weekend.[34]

Sessions included presentations by legal, ethical and medical experts. Briefing papers were circulated days in advance, giving participants an opportunity to read them. The briefings and presentations aimed to be as objective as possible, although there is some scepticism about the extent to which they were.[35] Like the convention, there were presentations by advocacy groups and, on occasion, personal testimonials by a number of women. There were also question-and-answer sessions, followed by facilitated discussions in small groups in closed sessions. Post-assembly interviews with participants confirmed high levels of satisfaction with the process.[36] Like the convention deliberating on marriage equality, the Citizens' Assembly was followed by a referendum on abortion, in which 66.40 per cent voted to repeal the Eighth Amendment.[37]

There has been a great deal of interest among political theorists and some constitutional scholars about the Irish CAs. Much has been written about their success in motivating constitutional reform (the convention was the first time a referendum had been called at the behest of 'ordinary' citizens), and their success at motivating informed public debate.[38] But some questions remain: How did the CAs develop democratic literacy among voters more generally, and how were they connected to the debates occurring in the 'real world', among ordinary voters?[39] What other variables need to be in place other than CAs to develop the relevant democratic literacy and improve the quality of public debate about constitutional amendment?

34 Ibid.

35 See, eg, criticism about issues framing in Carolan (n 2).

36 Farrell, Suiter and Harris (n 33).

37 'Referendum of 25 May 2018', *Regulation of Termination of Pregnancy (Repeal of 8th Amendment)* (Web Page) <www.electionsireland.org/results/referendum/refresult.cfm?ref=201836R>.

38 Farrell, Suiter and Harris (n 33). See also Ron Levy, 'The Deliberative Case for Constitutional Referenda' (2017) 16(2) *Election Law Journal* 213, doi.org/10.1089/elj.2016.0412.

39 Simone Chambers, 'Rhetoric and the Public Sphere: Has Deliberative Democracy Abandoned Mass Democracy?' (2009) 37(3) *Political Theory* 323, doi.org/10.1177/0090591709332336.

There is no doubt that both mini-publics—the Constitutional Convention and the Citizens' Assembly—had a significant effect on the referendum process. The fact that members of both voted so overwhelmingly in favour of the recommendations to amend the Constitution to allow same-sex marriage and repeal the Eighth Amendment prohibiting abortion put increased pressure on the government to agree to a referendum.[40] Second, Constitutional Convention and Citizens' Assembly membership included representatives from all the political parties; this ensured that there was strong cross-party agreement on the issues.[41] Third, both fora allowed space and time for careful, measured and informed deliberation about controversial matters and this debate was connected to wider deliberative networks. For instance, there was extensive media coverage of the deliberations and all information available to participants was also made available to the general public.[42] All the public meetings were live streamed and then archived online, together with the papers presented to assembly members and any policy decisions that were made, including the reasons for the decisions.

In their empirical analysis of the impact the convention had on the marriage equality referendum and the subsequent campaign, Elkink et al found that voters who were familiar with the convention tended to vote differently to those who were not aware. Those who were more informed about the convention were more likely to vote and more likely to vote 'Yes', thereby significantly affecting the referendum outcome.[43] Elkink et al argue that less informed voters are more likely to be persuaded by misleading campaign messages.[44]

Also significant was the fact that the referenda were called at the behest of 'ordinary' citizens. According to the 'second-order' theory of voting behaviour, in elections or referenda that are of secondary importance to voters, voter behaviour typically reflects the voter's evaluation of other factors rather than the issue itself. For example, in European integration referenda where the issue at hand is complicated, there is a distance between the European Union and the voter, and the governments of individual States in the EU typically initiate the referendum. It is common for voters to use the referendum to express their evaluation of the governments, regardless of

40 Elkink et al (n 29) 364.
41 Ibid.
42 Ibid.
43 Ibid 372.
44 Ibid.

their view on the referendum question.[45] By contrast, the marriage equality referendum was based on the recommendation of the convention. This, coupled with the fact that all parties in Ireland supported the 'Yes' vote and that it was a 'values' issue, had an impact on voter mobilisation and the outcome.[46] Bipartisan support has long been considered a highly significant factor for success. There is some evidence that the assembly deliberations helped foster this by leading politicians to change their minds when they realised the extent of public support for the proposals, as reflected in the representative sample of deliberating citizens.

Despite the excitement in some academic and political commentary about the success of the Irish experiments in deliberative democracy, there is an equal amount of scepticism among Irish constitutional scholars about whether the mini-publics did, in fact, influence voter deliberations or improve democratic literacy. There are five main criticisms about the success of the Irish mini-publics in particular, and mini-publics more generally. First, it is unclear how the mini-publics were connected to the wider public sphere. Colm O'Cinneide, for example, has suggested that it is difficult to identify how the mini-publics heightened deliberate debate across society at large. He writes:

> At best, voters may be influenced by learning that a broadly representative cross-section of society reached certain conclusions after a suitably deliberative debate. However, beyond that hypothetical possibility, it is unclear how exactly the deliberations of an Assembly-style body might play a substantial role in shaping large-scale public debates—especially given the cacophony of voices usually engaged in such debates, which risk drowning out its particular take on the subject in hand.[47]

45 Ibid 373–4.

46 Ibid 374.

47 Colm O'Cinneide, 'Symposium: The Citizens' Assembly Viewed in External Perspective: Useful, but Not a Deliberative Deus Ex Machina' *IACL-AIDC Blog* (Blog Post, 12 December 2018) <blog-iacl-aidc.org/blog/2018/12/12/the-citizens-assembly-viewed-in-external-perspective-useful-but-not-a-deliberative-deus-ex-machina-j3tyl>.

Similarly, Eoin Carolan has argued that the extent to which the wider voting public paid attention to the nuances of the discussions is unclear. He cites as evidence the poor viewing figures for the material presented at the assembly, which was made available to the general public.[48]

Second, the careful and nuanced deliberation in mini-public contexts may not be reflective of the debates taking place in the wider public sphere. As O'Cinneide argues, popular democratic processes often involve agonistic conflict, while CAs encourage greater democratic deliberation. They attempt to shape the content of deliberation with reference to prudential considerations, expert opinion and embedded norms. As such, they take the 'agonistic sting' out of debate and, in doing so, may not be genuinely representative of the arguments and sentiments of the wider public sphere.[49]

Third, there are concerns about the extent to which the mini-publics were genuinely representative. While they did represent a broad demographic in relation to age, sex, social class and religion, mini-publics, especially when they are unpaid, are likely to consist of those with atypical levels of interest in political or constitutional issues and who, as a consequence, may already have a sufficient grasp of the legal matters under consideration. Consequently, it is unclear how effective mini-publics are at building the democratic literacy of participants and the wider voting public.[50]

Fourth, there have been criticisms about the operation of the convention in relation to issues of transparency. Carolan argues that there was no guidance about the principles and procedures applied to agenda setting, to the recruitment of experts, or to the identification of persons to advocate for and against the proposals being considered by the convention. This may have been by design or oversight, but either way:

> the absence of any clear rules or principles by which to regulate the Convention's procedures is normatively troubling. Such procedures are critical to the pursuit of a fair, representative and deliberative process, especially in light of the evidence from previous mini-publics about the potentially decisive influence of expert input.[51]

---

48 Eoin Carolan, 'Symposium: Ireland's Citizens' Assembly on Abortion as a Model for Democratic Change?: Reflections on Hope, Hype and the Practical Challenges of Sortition' *IACL-AIDC Blog* (Blog Post, 28 November 2018) <blog-iacl-aidc.org/blog/2018/11/28/irelands-citizens-assembly-on-abortion-as-a-model-for-democratic-change-reflections-on-hope-hype-and-the-practical-challenges-of-sortition-6j5rw>.

49 O'Cinneide (n 47).

50 Ibid.

51 Carolan (n 2) 743.

Finally, because it was clear from opinion polls in the years and months prior to the assembly that there was clear support for repeal of the Eighth Amendment, attributing the success of the referendum to the assembly risks underplaying the active work of repeal campaigners over many years prior to the assembly and the significant wider changes that had occurred in Irish society over the previous few decades.[52] If we examine mini-publics (for example, citizens' assemblies) as isolated sites of deliberation, disconnected from the wider public sphere, then they may be vulnerable to these criticisms. However, a successful citizens' assembly is one that is but part of a wider deliberative system, playing very specific kinds of functions within it.

III. Mini-publics and the 'deliberative system'

Variations on the systems approach in the theoretical literature are developed by Robert Goodin, John Parkinson and Jane Mansbridge. For Goodin, the virtues associated with deliberation do not need to be located in any one particular site, but can be dispersed between and across different institutions, including mini-publics. This approach is described as an:

> Alternative to the 'unitary' model of deliberation that presently dominates discussion among deliberative democrats. In this model of 'distributed deliberation', the component deliberative virtues are on display sequentially, over the course of this staged deliberation involving various component parts, rather than continuously and simultaneously present as they would be in the case of a unitary deliberative actor.[53]

With reference to the institutions of representative democracy, including caucus room, parliamentary debate, election campaigns and post-election bargaining, to name a few, Goodin argues that, although none of these institutions alone realise deliberative standards, as a system they express the relevant deliberative qualities.[54] Parkinson also offers an account of a sequence of institutions that define, discuss, decide and implement proposals. He argues that different actors, such as activist networks, experts,

52 Ibid.
53 Robert Goodin, *Innovating Democracy* (Oxford University Press, 2008) 186, doi.org/10.1093/acprof:oso/9780199547944.003.0009.
54 Ibid 201.

bureaucracy, media and elected assembly play different roles in each of these stages: 'each element in such a system may not be perfectly deliberative or democratic in its own right, but may still perform a useful function in the system as a whole'.[55] Mansbridge defines systematisation as such:

> A *system* here means a set of distinguishable, differentiated, but to some degree interdependent parts, often with distributed functions and a division of labour, connected in such a way as to form a complex whole. It requires both differentiation and integration among the parts. It requires some functional division of labour, so that some parts do work that others cannot do so well. And it requires some relational interdependence, so that a change in one component will bring about change in others.[56]

Rather than focusing on CAs as an independent or individual site of deliberation, a systems approach focuses on the interdependence of different sites, including mini-publics, within a larger system. This includes the wide variety of institutions and associations, including informal networks, the media, organised advocacy groups, schools, universities, foundations, private and non-profit institutions, legislatures, executive agencies and the courts.[57] Not all of these deliberative sites will exhibit the ideal features of deliberation; some of the discussion might be low quality, uninformed or vitriolic, but the ways in which these sites interact with one another could potentially improve the quality of deliberation overall.

For instance, if the information presented to participants in CAs is distilled in a clear and accessible form, and sent to various media outlets, including social media, it could potentially reduce the level of misinformation in the public sphere. Misinformation can arise in adversarial contexts, either because of an intention to deliberately deceive or because a distortion of information enables a side to 'win' an argument. Debates over polarised issues typically use these tactics. In the Australian context, the 'official pamphlet' used to inform voters has contained misinformation. Kildea and Smith offer examples:

55 John Parkinson, *Deliberating in the Real World: Problems of Legitimacy in Deliberative Democracy* (Oxford University Press, 2006) 7, doi.org/10.1093/019929111X.001.0001.

56 John Parkinson and Jane Mansbridge (eds), *Deliberative Systems: Theories of Institutional Design* (Cambridge University Press, 2012) 4–5.

57 Ibid 1–2.

> In 1974, the 'No' case suggested that '[d]emocracy could not survive' under a 'deceitful' proposal to determine the average size of electorates by population, rather than the number of electors. In 1988, the 'No' case claimed that a proposal to extend freedom of religion would threaten 'the future of State Aid for independent schools' and 'open the way to extreme sects and practices.'[58]

Distributing objective and more nuanced arguments from CAs into the public sphere via the media may help to reduce the level of misinformation, giving voters access to more informed and reliable sources than they would otherwise get. While not all media will adopt the principles of sincerity, truthfulness, accuracy and so on in how they report the information, even if some do, it at least helps build the democratic literacy of the voting public in *general*. If the deliberations and opinion formation occurring in mini-publics are adequately tracked and reported, it could signal to others that shifts in perspective are possible, and encourage people to rethink their ideological commitments in light of new evidence. The Irish education campaigns also used social media in a strategic way to deliver objective and impartial information. The extensive use of social media for these purposes may be a good way of circumventing traditional and, sometimes, partisan media, and could reach more diverse groups of people, especially young people.

In recent work, Curato and Boker have argued that, while there is a general consensus in the literature that mini-publics have the potential to play a role in relation to legitimacy and in relation to deliberation more generally, there must be clear evaluative criteria identified against which the success or otherwise of a mini-public might be measured.[59] They propose that the external deliberative quality of successful mini-publics must be comprised of the following three features: the deliberative virtue of (further) deliberation-making, (further) fostering legitimacy and building (further) capacity.[60]

Successful mini-publics need to meet the criteria of deliberation-making. This refers to the ways in which they distil and synthesise relevant information and discourses to wider publics, rather than simply engaging in direct decision-making. In this respect, mini-publics play a role as 'brokers of

58 Kildea and Smith (n 28) 379.

59 Nicole Curato and Marit Böker, 'Linking Mini-Publics to the Deliberative System: A Research Agenda' (2016) 49 *Policy Sciences* 173, doi.org/10.1007/s11077-015-9238-5.

60 Ibid 176.

knowledge'.[61] Participants in these fora are given time and resources to work out and discuss complex issues, which non-participants do not have access to. As such, they are able to perform a number of important deliberative functions: they could synthesise cases both for and against a referendum proposal in an accurate way; they could take polarised issues out of the public sphere and subject them to more careful analysis, enabling citizens to see the issues in a more nuanced way; or they could encourage the wider public to reconsider unpopular proposals that have been considered to be just or appropriate after careful consideration. However, as they caution, such distilled information will only constitute deliberation-making if it enriches, rather than puts an end to, public deliberation. At best, mini-publics can contribute to the formation of a meta-consensus or public understanding on the range of legitimate positions; at worst, they can shut down debate by claiming epistemic authority instead of engaging mass publics.[62]

A successful mini-public will thus need to strike the right balance between prompting deliberation and reflection among non-participants, rather than claiming the final word on a particular issue and being sufficiently authoritative to make an impact:

> [I]f mini-publics are perceived as authoritative in their ability to claim epistemic superiority, they potentially distort the inclusiveness of public debate and render it less rather than more democratic. Equally, however, if their status is insufficiently prominent, mini-publics' recommendations might be undermined by partisan campaigners manipulating public debate.[63]

The second and related criterion is that successful mini-publics have an obligation to seek legitimacy. In systemic terms, the epistemic quality of mini-publics' outcomes is only as good as the process that feeds it back to 'public authorisation and accountability'.[64] This legitimacy does not result from the mini-publics' internal features alone, nor with its formal links to authoritative institutions. Rather, it depends on the nature of its relationships with the wider mass public, comprising of non-participant citizens. Mini-

61 Ibid 177.
62 Ibid.
63 Ibid.
64 Espen DH Olsen and Hans-Jörg Trenz, 'From Citizens' Deliberation to Popular Will Formation? Generating Democratic Legitimacy in Transnational Deliberative Polling' (2014) 62(1) *Political Studies* 117, doi.org/10.1111/1467-9248.12021. For statistics regarding the Europolis deliberative poll see 118.

publics have an 'external' obligation to persuade, a duty to justify, clarify, respond, and change recommendations or collective decisions. This ensures that mini-publics do not perpetuate 'participatory elitism'.[65]

Finally, a successful mini-public must contribute to building the capacity of a political community to engage in inclusive and authentic deliberation. Niemeyer has argued that mini-publics can play a role not only in improving the civic skill of participants but also in fostering truth-seeking behaviour and the deliberative abilities of non-participants by acting as 'exemplars' of deliberation.[66] A deliberative system that has institutionalised mini-publics in policy formation can play an important educative role in socialising citizens to civic virtues. They can also promote further citizen engagement by reaching out to broader publics and setting deliberative rather than confrontational terms of public discourse.[67] Arguably, the Irish mini-publics were successful according to Curato and Boker's evaluative criteria: they fostered further deliberation-making, sought legitimacy and contributed to capacity building.

A. Deliberation-making

The Irish mini-publics fostered deliberation in at least two ways: first, because of the ways in which they influenced wider public deliberation, which affected how the voting public understood the issues; and, second, because of the way they acted as intermediaries between the political class and ordinary voters. Historically, Ireland is a deeply religious country, and the issue of abortion had long been considered politically toxic.[68] Public debate about the issue tended to be extreme and intractable. Public sentiment when the assembly was first proposed was sceptical. Many citizens considered the assembly a 'cop-out' by politicians, or an attempt to 'kick the can down the road', because politicians were too fearful the issue would end political careers.[69]

65 Curato and Boker (n 59).

66 Simon Niemeyer, 'Scaling up Deliberation to Mass Publics: Harnessing Mini-Publics in a Deliberative System' in K Gronlund, A Bachtiger and M Setala (eds), *Deliberative Mini-Publics: Involving Citizens in the Democratic Process* (ECPR Press, 2014) 177.

67 Curato and Boker (n 59) 178.

68 Guardian Readers and Caroline Bannock, '"Transparency and Fairness": Irish Readers on Why the Citizens' Assembly worked' *The Guardian* (Web Page, 22 January 2019) <www.theguardian.com/commentisfree/2019/jan/22/irish-readers-citizens-assembly-worked-brexit>.

69 Ibid.

Instead, as many ordinary citizens noted, the assembly on the Eighth Amendment took the debate out of the heightened tensions of the public sphere and into a forum where 'evidence and experience' could take centre stage.[70] The media reporting of the event meant that the public were better informed. As one voter put it:

> [T]here was no trouble accessing the assembly findings as every time they met, the national TV channel, the newspapers and online-only news forums comprehensively reported the assembly's activities. Unless you chose to stick your head in the clouds, you could not avoid hearing or reading about the assembly.[71]

Others reported that the media coverage of presentations triggered a lot of discussion, and this discussion was more informed than it otherwise would have been: 'expert input at the forum informed public opinion and thus facilitated greater understanding of the issues at play in crisis pregnancies'.[72] Insofar as the assembly promoted further deliberation within the wider public sphere, the Irish mini-publics were extremely successful at 'brokering knowledge' within the wider public sphere.

But the CAs were only one part of a much larger and concerted campaign occurring in civil society, including a door knocking and grass roots campaign. For example, there were multiple and intersecting civil society groups who played critical roles in bringing the issue of abortion to the forefront of public consciousness, moving it from a peripheral issue into a human rights one. This put pressure on the government to act, motivating it to set up the assembly. For example, the Coalition to Repeal the Eighth brought together more than 80 organisations, including Doctors for Choice, who supported physicians who wanted to become providers, and Lawyers for Choice, who produced legal analysis. Members of Terminations for Medical Reasons who told their stories played a crucial role in generating compassion among voters. Submissions by these groups to the CA demonstrate the ways in which the 'deliberative system' functions, with each group sharing the 'deliberative labour' based on expertise, experience and personal/religious beliefs.[73] The CAs sit in this context, rather than above it. The need for the CA grew out of these networks of civil society, and provided further

70 Ibid.
71 Ibid.
72 Ibid.
73 Anna Carnegie and Rachel Roth, 'From the Grassroots to the Oireachtas: Abortion Law Reform in the Republic of Ireland' (2019) 21(2) *Health and Human Rights Journal* 109, 110.

impetus for a referendum on the issue. While it was the government that called the referendum, it was in response to the recommendations made by the CA. This has the effect of increasing the legitimacy of the process and also attracting media attention, as CAs are able to circumvent voter distrust of government and political elites.

The CAs represented 'sustained and focused deliberative moments'. They promoted the deliberative ideals of exposure to differing values, and mutual respect and concern for the views of others. Significantly, they brought opposing sides closer to common ground.[74] While they did take the 'sting' out of agonistic democratic politics, they also modelled what ideal and respectful deliberation looks like. Moreover, in relation to 'values issues'—defined as deliberation 'over the foundational interests, commitments, principles, ideologies, and worldviews that citizens hold, either individually or collectively, and that inform their policy preferences in a given context'[75] where the stakes are high, especially if they concern the rights of individuals, as both marriage equality and abortion do—it is important to model good deliberative practices, and not leave it to the unregulated public sphere to manage the deliberative labour on its own.

In Australia, civil society groups, academics and concerned parties were reticent to have a plebiscite on marriage equality because of concerns that the voting public would not be able to deliberate respectfully about the issue, and that unregulated, 'agonistic' debate would have significant harmful effects on those affected, especially the children of same-sex parents. This reservation was confirmed in subsequent post-analysis findings that the discriminatory public debate in the lead-up to the plebiscite had an adverse impact on the mental health of LGBTQIA+ people.[76] In these respects, the Irish mini-publics contributed to the formation of a meta-consensus or public understanding on the range of legitimate positions, affecting the framing and tone of the national debate. Significantly, they did not shut down deliberation about the issues of marriage equality and abortion, or have the final say, but facilitated further deliberation-making among ordinary voters.

74 Levy (n 38) 213, 220.

75 Ibid.

76 Stefano Verrelli, 'New Research Reveals how the Marriage Equality Debate Damaged LGBT Australians' Mental Health' *The Conversation* (Web Page, 24 January 2019) <theconversation.com/new-research-reveals-how-the-marriage-equality-debate-damaged-lgbt-australians-mental-health-110277>.

The mini-publics affected the wider public sphere in less direct ways by acting as intermediaries between the voting public and the political class. The Constitutional Convention gave politicians and the media insight into the level of majority support for marriage equality and the Citizens' Assembly gave them a better understanding of voters' preferences in relation to repeal of the Eighth Amendment, support that had long been underestimated by the political classes.[77] The mini-public deliberations also succeeded in shifting the views of some politicians, or, at the very least, forcing them to take action on issues they otherwise would have ignored for longer. In this respect, the mini-publics were successful at 'brokering' knowledge between voters and the political class, giving political elites better insights into voter preferences. They were successful also in modelling what informed deliberation about a set of issues would look like and the kinds of recommendations such deliberation could achieve.

Adopting a systems approach to mini-publics enables us to assess or determine the role they played within the wider *deliberative system.* The Irish mini-publics demonstrate that when designed in the right way and connected appropriately to the wider public sphere by way of a rigorous media campaign, they have the capacity to foster further, more informed and more reasoned deliberation not only within the closed and highly regulated mini-public forum itself, but also with the wider public sphere. They can act as powerful intermediaries between an, at times, out of touch political class and the voting public.

B. Legitimacy

The empirical evidence seems to suggest that the Irish mini-publics *increased* the legitimacy of the amendments. While, theoretically, the recommendations and decisions made by elected representatives are more legitimate than those made by an unelected, supposedly representative sample of citizens, this is based on the ideal that elected representatives will *in fact* represent the interests of the constituencies they represent. However, as Philip Pettit has pointed out, even if elected officials consider the best interests of the community as a whole, they are ultimately responsive to their own interests or their party's interest in being re-elected.[78] If these interests play a significant role in determining outcomes, then elected representatives

77 IACL-AIDC Blog, '2018 Posts' (Web Page) <blog-iacl-aidc.org/blog>.
78 Philip Pettit, 'Depoliticizing Democracy' in Samantha Besson and Jose Luis Marti (eds), *Deliberative Democracy and its Discontents* (Ashgate, 2006) 94.

cannot reliably be expected to decide issues with reference to the common good. In these cases, there may be good reasons for an independent and depoliticised body to deliberate and decide these issues.[79] Its deliberations, while not necessarily inclusive in the wider sense of the term, and while not made by elected representatives, are in fact more legitimate than if the decision had been made according to partisan political interests.[80]

Moreover, the growing voter distrust of the political elite, and disaffection with political processes, suggests that voters no longer feel they are able to participate or have ownership over the issues that affect them. Mini-publics potentially increase legitimacy rather than undermine it because they give voters ownership over the issues, and bring them more directly into decision-making processes. In giving citizens ownership over these complex legal and moral issues, the mini-publics signalled to the wider public sphere that the recommendations were driven by ordinary citizens, thereby circumventing the cynicism and distrust voters may have felt if they were driven by political elites and ensuring the legitimacy of the process.

The empirical evidence bears this out. Ordinary voters stated that 'the fact that it was citizens who recommended the terms of the referendum and informed the proposed legislation introduced greater clarity, and meant voters did not just have to trust politicians';[81] '[t]he Citizens' Assembly meant the discussion about our abortion laws was led by the people rather than politicians';[82] and:

> crucially, a citizens' assembly is non-partisan and so it creates a people-led discussion and understanding of an issue. I think this also helps create a debate that isn't dominated by black and white mantras from political parties but a more nuanced discussion of the issue in question.[83]

C. Capacity building

The Irish mini-publics were also successful at building the capacity of both participants and the political community to engage in inclusive and respectful deliberation. While citizens who voluntarily choose to give up

79 Ibid.
80 Ibid.
81 Dee, works in education, County Louth, quoted in Readers and Bannock (n 68).
82 Eve, data analyst, Dublin, quoted in ibid.
83 Ibid.

their time to participate in mini-publics may already be well informed, they, nevertheless, learn new knowledge and deliberative skills from the mini-public. For example, there has been considerable debate among Irish constitutional law scholars about the legalistic and lawyerly approach to the Citizens' Assembly and whether it should have been tasked with providing answers to specific and complex legal questions. David Kenny argues that such complex legal issues are unavoidable, and that the assembly was suitably designed in a way that 'up-skilled' participants to make informed decisions based on expert legal advice.[84] In this respect, the mini-publics seem to have developed the democratic literacy of participants, increasing their knowledge and understanding of complex constitutional reform.

The mini-publics also developed participants' deliberative capacities, including the ability to give reasons for one's views, assess and weigh up evidence, demonstrate sincerity and listen to the views of others. Empirical evidence conducted by Jane Suiter and David Farrell tracking the deliberation of participants during the assembly demonstrates the quality of deliberation over the course of the assembly. The majority of participants felt they were free to raise their views, that they had ample speaking opportunities and that other members respected what they had to say.[85]

At a more general level, mini-publics demonstrate that when the right kind of information is presented to citizens, and when they develop deliberative capacities, they are in fact able to deliberate over complex legal issues in general and constitutional reform in particular. Mini-publics provide concrete empirical evidence of how to build democratic literacy, thereby addressing the growing scepticism about citizen capacities to deliberate. Provided that citizens are presented with the appropriate information, and are able develop the relevant deliberative skills, there is no reason why lay persons cannot build the relevant democratic literacy to deliberate and make informed decisions about constitutional reform.

The Irish mini-publics not only built the capacity of participants but also played an important *capacity-building* function within the broader political community. Because of the ways in which they were connected to the

84 David Kenny, 'Symposium: Repeal or Replace? The Challenge of Debating Complex Legal/ Constitutional Questions in the Citizens' Assembly', *IACL-AIDC Blog* (Blog Post, 10 December 2018) <blog-iacl-aidc.org/blog/2018/12/10/repeal-or-replace-the-challenge-of-debating-complex-legal constitutional-questions-in-the-citizens-assembly-kyp59>.

85 Farrell, Suiter and Harris (n 33).

wider public sphere through social and traditional media, the mini-publics educated the wider public and modelled ideal deliberation. As one voter put it:

> It very much helped me—not to decide as I already knew how I was voting, but to listen, understand and develop empathy for those who planned to vote the other way. The issue was a very complex and divisive one, and the Citizens' Assembly helped the issue be seen from all sides ... the Citizens' Assembly kept information flowing whether we liked to hear it or not.[86]

The more they are used for the purposes of deliberation about constitutional reform, the more capacity they will build among ordinary citizens.

IV. Managing constitutional reform in Australia: Could mini-publics be effective?

In section one, I identified at least three significant impediments to constitutional reform in Australia: civics deficiency among voters, a lack of identification with the Constitution and insufficient ownership of constitutional issues. My claim is that mini-publics, like CAs, if designed in the right way and connected to the wider sphere, could improve the democratic literacy of Australian voters, improve the quality of public debate and give citizens ownership of constitutional issues, increasing their identification with the Constitution.

Section 128 of the Constitution sets out two steps for constitutional amendment. First, the federal Parliament must pass a 'proposed law' for changing the text of the Constitution, which ideally wins the support of an absolute majority of both Houses. In the event that it does not, a special procedure may be invoked where the proposal can instead be passed twice by an absolute majority of the members of a single House.[87] Second, between two and six months after the proposal has been approved by Parliament, it must be submitted to the people at a referendum, in which voting is compulsory. The proposal must achieve a double majority, meaning that a majority of people across the nation must vote 'Yes', and a majority of the people in a majority of the States (not Territories) must vote 'Yes'.

86 Claire Farnon, academic, Dublin, quoted in Readers and Bannock (n 68).

87 Megan Davis and George Williams, *Everything You Need to Know about the Referendum to Recognise Indigenous Australians* (NewSouth, 2015) 127–8.

The Referendum (Machinery Provisions) Act 1984 (Cth) sets out the process for conducting a referendum. Under s 11, the electoral commissioner must send each household a 2,000-word pamphlet at least two weeks before voting day with the proposed amendment, and arguments for and against it. These arguments are authorised by Parliament on each side of the debate. If no parliamentarians vote against the proposal, as occurred in the 1967 referendum, a 'No' case is not prepared.[88]

The last referendum to be passed was in 1977, when Australians voted to set the retirement age for High Court judges at 70. There have been no other successful amendments in the last 43 years, although there have been three more referenda since then: in 1984 (terms of senators and interchange of powers), 1988 (parliamentary terms, fair elections, local government and rights and freedoms) and 1999 (establishment of a republic and the preamble). This could, in part, be attributable to the broad national consensus required by the double majority, as per s 128; it could be partly attributable to the nature of the proposal put to the people, with many proposals seeking to expand the powers of the Commonwealth being (unsurprisingly) rejected;[89] or it could be that Australian voters do not have ownership over constitutional issues. A recent study by Kildea, Brown and Deem on direct democracy in Australia and the factors driving support for it found that people want a say over fundamental and potentially long-lasting reforms to Australia's system of government.[90]

As Scott Stephenson puts it, a major amendment is a different form of constitutional change than a minor or technical amendment, because it requires public ownership of the amendment process. That is, it concerns a change between the bargain that is struck between the government and the people: 'if the people do not understand the new bargain to be one that they have authored, there is ample reason for them to use the power given to them by the referendum requirement in s128 to reject it'.[91] Stephenson rightly argues that the referendum process is different to public ownership of the amendment process; a referendum gives people the opportunity to ratify

88 *Referendum (Machinery Provisions) Act 1984* (Cth).

89 Davis and Williams (n 87) 131–2.

90 Paul Kildea, AJ Brown and Jacob Deem, 'When Should the People Decide? Public Support for Direct Democracy in Australia' (2021) 74(4) *Parliamentary Affairs* 14, doi.org/10.1093/pa/gsaa019.

91 Scott Stephenson, 'Reforming Constitutional Reform' in Ron Levy et al (eds), *New Directions For Law in Australia* (ANU Press, 2017) 373, doi.org/10.22459/NDLA.09.2017.34; Weis (n 18).

a proposal, but does not ensure that they have any say over the identity or content of the proposal. The amendment process is a 'top-down' one rather than a 'bottom-up' one.[92]

For example, the Australian Constitutional Convention convened between 1973 and 1985 demonstrates a historical tendency to adopt an exclusive rather than inclusive process, mostly consisting of representatives of Parliament and other political elites. While the Constitutional Commission, established in 1985, did try to include citizens in the process, conducting public hearings and inviting written submissions, citizens did not have any direct role in contributing to the proposals made by the commission.[93] The Constitutional Convention commissioned in 1998 to consider whether Australia should become a republic made a better attempt to include members of the public, with half the delegates elected by a voluntary postal vote and the other half appointed by government in consultation with other groups. However, it was not genuinely representative because most of the elected volunteers were public figures with strong views on the issue.[94]

Moreover, the referendum campaign was marred by shallow and superficial statements that did little to inform voters of the consequences of the reform proposal. The 'No' case, for example, consisted primarily of empty slogans, including: 'Don't Know? – Vote "No"'; 'No gain, only pain – Vote "No"'; 'No Prime Ministerial puppet for President'; and 'When in doubt, throw it out. Vote "No" to this republic'.[95] The 1999 pamphlet assumed that voters understood what the current powers of the Australian Governor-General were, and the implications of replacing this position with a president. It did not make clear all the consequential changes to the Constitution; nor did it adequately explain the way in which the president would be elected, and what the powers attached to the position would be.

The combination of poor democratic literacy among voters, lack of informed public debate and lack of ownership over constitutional issues are all contributing factors as to why constitutional reform is so difficult to achieve in Australia. Of course, it is possible that a more informed public debate and better awareness of the issues could have led to the same referendum

92 Stephenson (n 91).
93 Ibid 373.
94 Ibid.
95 Australian Electoral Commission, 'Yes/No Referendum '99: Your Official Referendum Pamphlet' (Web Page, 20 January 2011) <www.aec.gov.au/Elections/referendums/1999_Referendum_Reports_Statistics/yes_no_pamphlet.pdf>.

outcome on the republic: voters may still have rejected the amendment. There is a difference, however, between deciding to reject an amendment based on informed reasons, and rejecting it based on lack of understanding of the issues. While the former is a genuine choice, the latter is not.

The use of CAs might be one way of addressing some of these issues. If CAs are designed in the right way, if they are genuinely representative of a diverse range of social groups and properly connected to the wider public sphere and other civil society networks, they might contribute to a more effective and informed education campaign, and might give people ownership over the issues, enabling them to better identify with their constitution.

Australia has already experimented with mini-publics in various forms. In 2015, a Referendum Council was established by the then Turnbull government to address the issue of Indigenous 'constitutional recognition'. As part of the council's work, the Aboriginal and Torres Strait Islander members conducted a deliberative dialogue process with Indigenous communities in order to understand the form that recognition would take. 'The Dialogues', as they have come to be known, culminated in the First Nations Constitutional Convention at Uluru, where participants called for a 'Voice to Parliament' to be enshrined in the Constitution.[96] The Dialogues were enormously successful in building the democratic literacy of participants and their deliberative capacities. They led to the first ever Indigenous position on constitutional recognition, as contained in the Uluru Statement and gave Indigenous people ownership over the debate. Significantly, the process is an example of a 'bottom-up' proposal, in which it is those who are most affected who initiate and draft the proposal. However, what is missing here is a subsequent process like a CA, in which a cross-section of the community come together to learn about the proposal and discuss its implications. This CA could then be used to inform the wider voting public and begin a broad national debate.

In 2009, the Australian Citizens' Parliament was convened to deliberate on '[h]ow we can strengthen our political system to better serve the people'. The subject matter was deliberately broad to give participants the opportunity to 'set the agenda' and to focus on issues that they were interested in or

96 Sean Brennan and Megan Davis, 'First Peoples' in Cheryl Saunders and Adrienne Stone (eds), *The Oxford Handbook of the Australian Constitution* (Oxford University Press, 2018) 45.

concerned about.[97] Participants were randomly selected to ensure diverse representation of the Australian people. They initially met in smaller regional meetings, were briefed about the process, experienced several different methods of deliberation and then began developing proposals in preparation for the online deliberation.

There is strong evidence that both The Dialogues and the Citizens' Parliament improved the democratic literacy of participants. Feedback from participants indicates that they learnt a great deal about the Australian Constitution and political processes and were more confident and interested in discussing political issues. However, against the proposed evaluative criteria, it is questionable whether the mini-publics succeeded in having an impact on the wider public sphere. The lack of concrete proposal for constitutional change may have rendered the discussion too abstract to capture the popular imagination; nor was there much at stake for ordinary voters, given that the CA did not lead to any referendum that voters would be called upon to decide. For these reasons, there was minimal media coverage and little information flow about the progress of deliberation was communicated to the public sphere.[98] This connection between mini-publics and the wider voting public is crucial in the Australian context, given the stringent requirements of s 128. CAs can function as mechanisms for increasing civic knowledge and can set the parameters for a more informed public debate about constitutional issues. In this respect, there is much to learn from other jurisdictions, such as the Irish Constitutional Convention and Citizens' Assembly, about how mini-publics can foster further deliberation-making and legitimacy, and build deliberative capacity more generally. What we could also learn from the Irish experiments in deliberation is that we should not fear ambitious proposals for constitutional change. As Kildea has argued, we have lost the appetite to hold referenda because the focus is on the outcome rather than the process. Fear of unsuccessful reform proposals, coupled with the costs associated with running them, have made governments too timid to hold them unless success is guaranteed. Consequently, we are out of practice in deliberating about the Constitution and how it might shape our national identity. CAs might be one way of overcoming the risk-averse approach to constitutional change in Australia.

97 A Felicetti, S Niemeyer and N Curato, 'Improving Deliberative Participation: Connecting Mini-Publics to Deliberative Systems' *European Political Science Review* (2016) 8(3) 427–48, doi.org/10.1017/S1755773915000119.
98 Ibid.

Despite living in a stable and mature democracy, Australian voters are disaffected and alienated from political processes. This is reflected in high levels of cynicism towards politics, declining membership and support of political parties, increasing numbers of young people seeking to avoid mandatory voting, increased polarisation of issues by political partisans, over-simplification of issues in the media and short time frames for policymaking.[99] The increased use of CAs for the purposes of constitutional reform could circumvent voter distrust of political elites, enable more nuanced deliberation over controversial issues by taking them out of partisan hands and give people ownership over their constitution.

99 Nicole Curato and Lucy Parry, 'Deliberation in Democracy's Dark Times' (2018) 14(2) *Journal of Public Deliberation* 1.

Author Biographies

Elisa Arcioni is an associate professor at the University of Sydney. Prior to joining Sydney Law School in 2012, Elisa was a lecturer in law at the University of Wollongong and associate to the Honourable Justice Michael Kirby, High Court of Australia. Elisa works in the field of public law, particularly constitutional identity and constitutional membership. Elisa has completed the first major study of the identity of 'the people' under the Australian Constitution and is currently undertaking Australian Research Council (ARC)–funded research on claims of belonging in Australian constitutional law.

Peter D Burdon is an associate professor at the University of Adelaide. Peter is the director of the Australasia chapter of the Global Network for the Study of Human Rights and the Environment. Peter also sits on the steering committee of the International Union for the Conservation of Nature, Ethics Specialist Group and the Ecological Law and Governance Association. Peter is an expert in environmental theory and has written and edited books on Earth jurisprudence and Earth democracy. In 2017 he published a book on Hannah Arendt and the trial of Nazi war criminal Adolf Eichmann.

Robyn Hollander was, prior to her retirement, an associate professor at Griffith University. Robyn has longstanding interests in federalism and regulation, focusing on relationships—between the Commonwealth and the States, and between governments and markets—in policy areas including the environment, competition and higher education. She has published in numerous highly regarded journals including *Publius*, the *Australian Journal of Political Science*, the *Australian Journal of Public Administration* and the *Australian Journal of Politics and History*.

Benjamin T Jones is a senior lecturer in history at Central Queensland University. He is a Fellow of the Royal Historical Society and a Foundation Fellow of the Australian Studies Institute. His most recent books include *Australia on the World Stage: History, Politics, and International Relations*

(Routledge, 2022), *History in a Post-Truth World: Theory and Praxis* (Routledge, 2020), *This Time: Australia's Republican Past and Future* (Redback, 2018), and *Elections Matter: Ten Federal Elections That Shaped Australia* (Monash University Publishing, 2018).

Lydia McGrady is a Kamilaroi woman and a PhD candidate at the University of Technology Sydney. Her work focuses on self-determination, governance and treaty. She holds a Juris Doctor and a Master of Laws. Her PhD is on the concept of Indigenous legal rights and its interaction with the State. She has also done research on democracy, jurisprudence and comparative law. She has contributed to research projects on Indigenous policymaking and health.

Joe McIntyre is an associate professor in law at the University of South Australia. He has held teaching positions in Australia, Canada and the UK, and has practice experience in both Australia and the UK. He was awarded his PhD in 2013 from the University of Cambridge. His thesis, entitled 'The Nature of the Judicial Function', is now published as a monograph for Springer. Prior to commencing his doctoral studies, he worked at the South Australia Crown Solicitor's Office for a period of two years. When in the UK, he was a member of the elite Academic Research Panel at the prestigious Blackstone Chambers, providing academic opinions on a broad range of civil and criminal matters.

Lorne Neudorf is a professor of law at La Trobe University. He holds a Doctor of Philosophy in the field of comparative law from the University of Cambridge. He is author of *The Dynamics of Judicial Independence: A Comparative Study of Courts in Malaysia and Pakistan* (Springer, 2017). Lorne is the co-founder and editor in chief of the *Canadian Journal of Comparative and Contemporary Law*, was formerly managing editor of the *Cambridge Journal of International and Comparative Law*, and is the general editor of a new global book series examining the rule of law in context for Hart/Bloomsbury. Lorne's research takes a comparative perspective and focuses on public law, including judicial review, legislation, delegation, the lawmaking process, statutory interpretation, legal institutions, institutional design and government and politics.

Anna Olijnyk is a senior lecturer in law at the University of Adelaide. She is director of the Public Law and Policy Research Unit. She is author of *Justice and Efficiency in Mega-Litigation* (Hart, 2019) and co-author of *Government Accountability: Australian Administrative Law* (Cambridge University Press, 2nd ed, 2018) and *Judicial Federalism in Australia* (Federation Press, 2021).

Her work has been published in leading journals including the *International Journal of Constitutional Law*, *Public Law Review*, *University of New South Wales Law Journal* and *Sydney Law Review*.

Alexander Reilly is an adjunct professor of law at the University of Adelaide and a tribunal member at the South Australian Civil and Administrative Tribunal. He is co-author of *Australian Public Law* (Oxford University Press, 3rd ed, 2018) and *Rights and Redemption: History, Law and Indigenous Peoples* (UNSW Press, 2008), and co-editor of *Sovereignty: Frontiers of Possibility* (University of Hawai'i Press, 2013). Alex has written extensively on a wide range of public law issues in Australian and international journals focusing on refugee law and policy, citizenship and constitutional law.

Kim Rubenstein is a professor in the Faculty of Business Government and Law at the University of Canberra and an honorary professor at ANU College of Law. Professor Rubenstein is one of Australia's leading experts on citizenship law, through her book *Australian Citizenship Law* (Thomson Reuters, 2nd ed, 2016), scholarly articles and book chapters. Kim was appointed a consultant to the Commonwealth in its redrafting of Australian citizenship legislation, resulting in the 2007 Act, and later was a member of the Independent Expert Committee set up to review the Australian Citizenship Test that reported in 2008. In October 2013, she was awarded the inaugural Edna Ryan award for 'leading feminist changes in the public sphere'. She has completed two ARC grants on 'Trailblazing Women and the Law' and 'The Court as Archive'. She is a Fellow of the Australian Academy of Law and the Australian Academy of Social Sciences.

Sarah Sorial is a professor of law at the Macquarie Law School. Her research specialisation is primarily in jurisprudence and related areas at the intersection of philosophy and law. She has published extensively on speech regulation, ethical theory, democratic deliberation and legal legitimacy, the place of rights in liberal democracies, punishment for collective crimes and the management of emotion in criminal trials. More recent work investigates the ways in which we can improve public deliberation about law and policy reform, through mechanisms such as citizens' assemblies and civics education, including in schools.

Tiziana Torresi is a lecturer at the University of Adelaide. Tiziana received her BA Hons (first class and University Medal) from the University of New South Wales, Sydney, and her D. Phil in politics and international relations from the University of Oxford, where she also held a lectureship in politics at Worcester College.

Printed in the USA
CPSIA information can be obtained
at www.ICGtesting.com
LVHW070825170923
756873LV00060BA/585